ghosts
Journeys To Post-Pop

How David Sylvian, Mark Hollis and Kate Bush
reinvented pop music

Matthew Restall

SONIC**BOND**

sonicbondpublishing.com

Sonicbond Publishing Limited
www.sonicbondpublishing.co.uk
Email: info@sonicbondpublishing.co.uk

First Published in the United Kingdom 2024
First Published in the United States 2024

British Library Cataloguing in Publication Data:
A Catalogue record for this book is available from the British Library

Copyright Matthew Restall 2024

ISBN 978-1-78952-334-8

The right of Matthew Restall to be identified as the author of this work
has been asserted by him in accordance with the
Copyright, Designs and Patents Act 1988.

All rights reserved. No part of this publication may be reproduced, stored
in a retrieval system or transmitted in any form or by any means, electronic,
mechanical, photocopying, recording or otherwise, without prior permission
in writing from Sonicbond Publishing Limited

Typeset in ITC Garamond Std & ITC Avant Garde Gothic Pro
Printed and bound in England

Graphic design and typesetting: Full Moon Media

Cover image of David Sylvian by Fin Costello,
taken from Japan's *Quiet Life* album cover.

Follow us on social media:
Twitter: https://twitter.com/SonicbondP
Instagram: www.instagram.com/sonicbondpublishing_/
Facebook: www.facebook.com/SonicbondPublishing/

Linktree QR code:

ghosts
Journeys To Post-Pop

How David Sylvian, Mark Hollis and Kate Bush
reinvented pop music

Matthew Restall

SONIC**BOND**

sonicbondpublishing.com

Acknowledgments

I was clearly not the only pop music fan born in the 1960s to listen to a lot of Talk Talk after Hollis died. But not everyone was inspired to go off and write a book. For that, I owe a debt of gratitude to many friends and family, musicians and music writers. In 2019, I wrote a book for the wonderful 33 1/3 series – *Blue Moves*, on the Elton John album of that name (Bloomsbury, 2020) – thanks to the encouragement of Amara Solari, my spouse and my co-author of books on Maya history. *Blue Moves* proved that Amara was right (as if that was ever in doubt): I could write about Aztecs and Mayas, Spanish *conquistadors* and Africans in the Americas *and* write about pop music. *Blue Moves* also resulted in my friendship with artist and music writer Hope Silverman, whose encouragement fertilised this book countless times.

Meanwhile, I found inspiration in Dylan Jones's *The Wichita Lineman*, a book as brilliant as the song it is about. I toyed with writing a book entirely about 'Ghosts', diving into other one-song books (most notably those cited below on 'I Feel Love', 'Hallelujah' and 'Strange Fruit'). But then I realised that I could not ignore the fact that 'Ghosts' had acted as the book's starting point in 1982, patiently waiting for me to understand that I needed to begin the story with 'Ghosts' and discover where it led – 'Ghosts' was the story's alpha, but not its omega, too. I was also halfway through writing this book when I began to wonder if it made sense to pair Sylvian with Hollis and Bush, too. However, a deeper dig into the secondary literature revealed very similar groupings made by other scholars of popular music: Jeanette Leech's short chapter in *Fearless* on Sylvian, Talk Talk and Scott Walker made much sense, as did Jack Chuter's connecting of the same three artists in *Storm, Static, Sleep*; while Rob Young discussed Sylvian, Talk Talk and Bush with Julian Cope in his brilliant *Electric Eden*; and Hegarty and Halliwell positioned Sylvian and Talk Talk as the precursors to Radiohead, with Bush given 'post' treatment, too, in a chapter in *Beyond And Before* on 'Post-Progressive'. When this book was still an unpublished manuscript, Gary Steel's *On Track* book on Talk Talk came out, and there at the start was his assertion that no artist had a comparable trajectory – save perhaps for Sylvian and Bush. What I lost in the originality of my triple-protagonist vision, I gained in the reassurance of smart company. Meanwhile, Chuter's choice of subtitle, *A Pathway Through Post-Rock*, seemed to affirm the efficacy of seeing the development of 'post' music as a collective journey. And the work of the late, brilliant Mark Fisher helped me see the hauntological nature of post-pop. So, I thank those writers for their inadvertent encouragement, as I do the authors in the class-leading Sonicbond series, *On Track* (especially Steel and Bill Thomas); the authors in the endlessly inspiring 33 1/3 series; the authors of the Sylvian biographies (Martin Power and Christopher Young) and fan websites; and the authors of the exhaustive and ever-insightful Japan chronicles (Anthony Reynolds) and of the book that did what seemed impossible – reconstruct Hollis's life (Ben Wardle). I also salute two wonderfully frank memoirists: Talk Talk engineer Phill Brown and veteran pop manager Simon Napier-Bell.

Last in this category, but most important, for otherwise you'd not be reading these words, is Sonicbond publisher Stephen Lambe. After enduring the prevarications of other editors, I found his clear and decisive support to be extraordinarily encouraging. He is a true visionary, and I feel most fortunate and grateful to him for accommodating my labour of love within that vision. I am likewise indebted to Sonicbond's Dominic Sanderson, whose editing insights and sharp suggestions made this a much better book. Thank you, Dom.

Finally, I am grateful to those who regularly play music with me (tolerating my stunning lack of virtuosity), go to see live music with me, talk about music with me or just listen to my ramblings. You all unwittingly contributed to this book in myriad ways: Patrick Alexander, Jessica Ambler, Susan and Nate Allerheiligen, Bob Aronson, Dan Beaver, Laurent Cases, Chris Castaglia, Steve and Sam Christensen, James Collins, Richard Conway, Julitza Cordero, Robert Denby, Liz Grove, Mark Guiltinan, Chris Heaney, Carter Hunt, Evan Jones, Olivia Jones, Alex Killough, Michael Kulikowski, Dan Letwin, Jonathan Mathews, Bryan Mesenbourg, On-cho Ng, Bianca Nottoli, David Orr, Naomi Pitamber, Emma Restall Orr, Isabel Restall, Lucy Restall, Robin Restall, Sophie Restall, Tatiana Seijas, Steve Sherrill, Stephen Shoemaker, Hope Silverman, Eric Spielvogel, Ian Spradlin, Dan Zolli – and Al Stewart (to whom I apologise, again, for being a historian of Mexico, not Russia). I am particularly grateful to the above-listed Laurent, Richard, David, Sophie and Hope for feedback on the first draft. I also thank Micaela Wiehe for her research assistance.

This was the last book of mine that my father Robin read; he died between its writing and its publication. His response that surely *all* music is 'post something' was both intriguingly helpful and wonderfully unhelpful. Knowing his time was running out, he still read the whole manuscript. One could hardly ask for anything more. Cheers, Dad.

Above all, I thank the incomparable Amara Solari, who, with unfailing generosity, never questioned whether this book was a good idea or not.

ghosts
Journeys To Post-Pop

Contents

Preface 11
Side A (1955-2019)
   1: Ghosts/Sat In Your Lap 17
   2: It's My Life/A Life 25
   3: Suburban Love 33
   4: Life In Tokyo 48
Side B (1980-84)
   5: The Other Side Of Life 56
   6: Swing 64
   7: Visions Of China/The Dreaming 76
   8: Talk Talk 93
   9: Tomorrow Started/Brilliant Trees 106
Side C (1985-91)
   10: Happiness Is Easy/Let The Happiness In 122
   11: April 5th/September 137
   12: Desire 150
   13: Pop Song/The Ninth Wave 160
   14: Cries And Whispers/After The Flood 177
Side D (1992-2024)
   15: Heartbeat 184
   16: A New Jerusalem/I Surrender 193
   17: A Fire In The Forest 200
   18: A Sky Of Honey/Among Angels 207
   19: Playground Martyrs 217
   20: Approaching Silence/Do You Know Me Now? 229
Discography 234
Bibliography 239
Endnotes 251

Preface

Little did I know on my 18th birthday, as I stood transfixed in front of *Top Of The Pops*, that David Sylvian had just planted the seed for this book. 'Just when I think I'm winning,' he crooned on the chorus to 'Ghosts', a 1982 hit by his band Japan, 'when my chance came to be king, the ghosts of my life grew wilder than the wind'.

Spooked by spectral doubt, at the peak of Japan's success, Sylvian broke up the band. Retreating into a long and varied solo career, he then spent four decades experimenting with pop music. Through his creative arc from neo-glam rock to ambient compositions accompanying art installations, through his evolution from new romantic pop idol to reclusive cult-pop icon, Sylvian changed how we see and understand pop music and the role of its creators in modern society.

Through those decades, the seed planted in my mind by Japan's miming of 'Ghosts' on that legendary British TV program lay dormant. Six years younger than Sylvian, I continued to listen to his records, following him into middle age, my musical tastes just about managing to keep up with his creative evolution. However, despite my youthful daydreams of a life in the music business – a few fleeting, failed forays into writing gig reviews, DJ'ing and assembling rock soundtracks for Hollywood movies that were never made – I ended up as a professor of history, teaching in the United States, writing books about Mexico's past. The only ghosts in my work were those acknowledged during the Día de los Muertos.

Then, 37 years after Sylvian unwittingly planted that seed, a seemingly unrelated event caused it to start sprouting: I read an obituary of Mark Hollis. The connection to Sylvian was not obvious at first. Hollis's band, Talk Talk, had stormed the charts in the wake of Japan's demise, their careers seemingly unrelated. Yet, both bands had perfected variants of a kind of catchy art pop rooted in the new wave of the late 1970s and early 1980s. Furthermore, Hollis had been as uncomfortable as Sylvian with fame and the creative limitations of the music industry. He, too, turned his back on conventional success, retreating into experimental pop, stunning fans and label executives alike with records that defied categorisation and shunned the charts. Despite being hailed as the architect of post-rock, Hollis took minimalism to its logical end, completely withdrawing from music-making and from the public eye 20 years before his death in 2019.

For decades, Hollis's music had periodically rotated through my turntable, CD player, iPod and smartphone, along with Sylvian's. In 2019, in the wake of his sudden passing, I listened with new ears to everything Hollis had ever recorded. I read with curiosity the repeated claim that Hollis had – unintentionally – founded something called post-rock. Then I side-stepped into Sylvian's far more extensive catalogue and something clicked: I sensed a story begging to be told, a seed yearning to sprout.

As I dived in deeper, dusting off old cassette tapes and mix CDs to emulate how I had enjoyed the albums in the 1980s and 1990s, I read all I could on Hollis and Sylvian. That led me to the cast of other musicians who appear in the pages below – from their brothers to their old band mates; from the artist who inspired an entire generation of musicians, David Bowie, to influences like ambient inventor Brian Eno; from prog rock veterans and mentors like Robert Fripp and Holger Czukay to potential fellow travellers like John Foxx and Scott Walker. Amidst all the men, Kate Bush kept cropping up, her significance to the story becoming steadily more apparent. Before long, I realised that Bush needed to be made the third main protagonist of the story, completing its triangulation. She, too, had created a career arc into pop stardom and then beyond it to a place that confounded the press, who could do no better than call her eccentric and reclusive. In fact, Bush had pioneered something new – post-pop stardom. With Hollis gone and Sylvian genuinely reclusive, Bush is arguably the quintessential post-pop star. That fact, combined with her enduring fame, her gender (offering an illuminating and contrasting parallel to Sylvian and Hollis) and her creation of 21st-century post-pop masterpieces, all make her crucial to the story.

This is the story, then, of three ambitious teenagers from suburban London. Inspired by the dynamic genres of 1970s pop and rock, they started bands and reached for the stars. But as soon as they achieved international fame, they fled from it. Repulsed by celebrity life, they sought normalcy, forced to become apparent recluses. Yet, their journeys were also musical ones, resulting in something remarkably and compellingly new: a loosely defined, ever-evolving, experimental genre of music, yet one that was never completely severed from its pop roots. Although their journeys were separate and distinct, they connected in multiple ways to collectively arrive at a place I began to think of as post-pop. The results were compositions and creations so captivating and vital that it is hard to imagine popular music in the 21st century without them.

I, too, had taken such a journey over the decades, but as a mere listener. I had followed the likes of Sylvian, Hollis and Bush without giving the act of following much thought. Without much pondering on their connections of collaboration and influence, I had thereby been led to artists ranging from Porcupine Tree to Florence Welch, from Harold Budd to Radiohead. I discovered Slint, revisited Fripp and Eno and Ryuichi Sakamoto, and came to appreciate the likes of Delius and Bartok in new ways. I am hardly alone in that half-thinking, half-following; some of my stopping points on that journey likely resonate with some of yours.

If *our* journeys were made so fruitful by musical pioneers like Sylvian, Hollis and Bush, why had *they* taken *their* journeys? Did answers lie in their personal lives, in their family relationships and in their inner psychological struggles – in the ghosts of their lives? Or was the more revealing context that of London, with its dynamic tension between the city's centre and its suburbs, a tension that contributed to a sequence of vibrant cultural scenes – from the swinging 60s to the new romantic 80s? Or have Sylvian, Hollis and Bush been mere exemplars of a larger cultural process, the cross-fertilising evolution of modern musical genres, leading inevitably to the studio productions that are neither pop nor rock, neither classical nor jazz, but all of the above? Are all these artists better understood not for their individual genius but for their contributions to a collective creative phenomenon or 'scenius' (as Eno has put it)?[1] In the end, does all of the musical experimentation of the last 100 years, fuelled by the digital revolution's granting of access to every song ever recorded, simply bring us back to innumerable forms of modern classical music?[2] Or were Sylvian, Hollis and Bush freedom fighters defying class prejudice or gender barriers to take on 'the machine' of the music industry? Are their parallel tales about a parallel cultural phenomenon – the clash of creativity and celebrity – the fight to escape fame's perilous paradox?

In pursuing these questions, I gained a deeper appreciation for pop music, even as I simultaneously discovered its misunderstood lovechild, post-pop. 'Pop is encompassing and capacious', in the words of one music scholar. 'Inclusive, multiracial and global in its appeal', pop reaches across genres, inviting rather than excluding, yet still permitting 'insurgency and opposition'. Pop music must also withstand repetitive listening; more than that, it requires repetition to realise its potential as a social balm soothingly elemental to daily life. We personally invest 'private associations and existential symbolism' in pop songs (to quote another cultural critic), music that becomes, through repeated listening, 'part of the existential fabric of our own lives, so that what we listen to is ourselves.'[3] More often heard than listened to, pop songs soundtrack our quotidian life; they become part of us while we drive and run, cook and eat, work and play. We listen; therefore, we are.

As such, pop music emerges from popular culture, mass culture and 'low' culture – as opposed to the more challenging expressions of 'high' culture, which may demand listening, not hearing, and which may be less conducive to repeated or background playing. In trying to understand what post-pop is and where it came from, I came to the crucial realisation that its roots lie in both 'low' *and* 'high' culture and, even more importantly, in that place where the barrier between the two breaks down. In such a place, post-pop germinated and developed. The 20th century produced numerous artistic expressions of that dynamic cultural breakdown – in the visual arts, in literature, in music and so on. But seeing post-pop as one such expression was a revelation to me, an insight that serves as necessary grounding before exploring the pop/post-pop relationship.[4]

We shall see in some detail what that means in terms of media and genres of artistic expression. So, suffice to note here that numerous influences from so-called high and low cultures fuel the journey from being in a rock band making pop songs about love and lust to being part of a scenius of artists crafting compositions of musical and lyrical complexity. Those influences might be in the visual arts, literature and cinema, as well as in musical genres ranging from modern and minimalist classical, chamber music and modal jazz to *kosmische* or krautrock, folk, prog (progressive rock), ambient and experimental electronic music. Above all, the studio plays a crucial role in such journeys, both in conceptual terms as a new kind of overarching instrument, and as the place – literally – where barriers between genre cultures could be explored and dismantled. As recording technology rapidly evolved, so did all genres of music, opening up paths into that 'post' world.[5]

Another necessary grounding is the history of the term 'post-rock'. Its occasional use before 1994 was of no lasting significance, but in that year, the English music journalist Simon Reynolds published a short essay titled 'Post-Rock' in *The Wire*. He intended the label as an open-ended way to group contemporaneous British bands such as Bark Psychosis, Stereolab, Disco Inferno and Pram – whose experiments in ambient instrumentation, art rock and avant-garde rock were 'financially precarious, but aesthetically vital.' In other words, they weren't going to sell many records, but they might influence the evolution of popular music. The label stuck, eventually settling into use on two levels. One was fairly narrow and formal, used as a section heading in record stores to tag 1990s bands, mostly British, like those initially identified by Reynolds.[6]

The other usage of 'post-rock' developed more slowly and expansively, embracing the spirit of Reynolds' open-endedness and of Eno's view of 'rock' as part of music's boundless 'soundscape'. This contrasted with the narrow definitions of rock that insist on the indispensability of live performance, of the anchors of drums, bass and rhythm guitar and signature elements, such as choruses and guitar solos. Such definitions have been critiqued as static and 'rockist' (as we shall see). But they have also served as a basis for seeing music that deconstructs those elements – that dismantles the rituals governing the usage of guitars and drums and blithely ignores 'rock's principles of machismo and muscle' in favour of 'innovation and progression' – as post-rock.[7]

Similarly, when pop artists disassemble pop music and abandon or rework its elements in unconventional and creative ways, they journey into post-pop. The rock/post-rock relationship is, therefore, paralleled in the pop/post-pop dynamic. Just as pop and rock dovetail, so do post-rock and post-pop, and indeed, my discussions below of genre emphasise its overlapping, organic and expansively inclusive nature. Issues of rockism and authenticity policing aside, there is no right and wrong to genre labelling: my post-pop classic might be a post-rock essential to you, or vice versa; or to your ears and mind, it may not be 'post' anything.

In the 20 chapters that follow, I narrate a trio of interwoven journeys that unfold on multiple levels: from the macro-level of the human creative process to the historical levels of the changes in popular culture and music across the past half-century, from the biographical level of the lives of Sylvian, Hollis and Bush to the micro-level of the lives of listeners like you and me. The post-pop story is one of music and fame, ambition and fear, happiness and melancholy. It is about creating and listening, engaging and retreating, noise and silence, culture and life. It is about feeling haunted, craving exorcism and finding solitude.

Moments of personal memoir are a minor feature of this book. If they seem self-indulgent, be reassured that they fade as the book progresses. Their inclusion is not because I have the insight of an industry insider or a writer with rare access to my subjects – I have neither. On the contrary, I am just a lifetime listener like you, and you surely have your own equivalent of those moments.

The contrivance of this book's structure is that of a playlist or a four-sided double album. Each of the 20 chapters carries the title of a track or two discussed in the chapter from either a Japan/Sylvian/Jansen (17),

Talk Talk/Hollis (9) or Kate Bush album (5). That balance roughly reflects the book's attention devoted to those artists, a hierarchy determined not by their relative importance but by their catalogues and relevance to the narrative. The table of contents thus serves as a playlist for the book, but with tracks selected for their contribution to my narrative and argument, not as a 'best of' or 'favourites' mix (although I do heap praise on many of those chapter-title tracks). The discography at the end will help you to place songs and albums discussed in the chapters within the full album catalogues of Sylvian, Hollis and Bush, as well as ex-Japan and ex-Talk Talk artists. I listened as I wrote, imagining you might listen as you read.

Side A (1955-2019)

1: Ghosts/Sat In Your Lap

'Ghosts' Japan (1982, 7', 3:55)
'Sat In Your Lap' Kate Bush (1981, 7', 3:29)

My memory of that 'Ghosts' performance on *Top Of The Pops* is very clear: it was my 18th birthday, 17 March 1982. The historical record is equally clear: Thursday that week was, in fact, 18 March, and as *TOTP* only ran on Thursday nights, it must have been the day after my birthday, despite my memory's insistence. That's what 'Ghosts' does; it gets into your head and changes your perception of reality. It's a spectral brain worm.

I was in an English boarding school where access to television was highly restricted. The school was divided into dormitories and houses. In the house where I lived with 60 other boys, there was a downstairs room with an open fireplace and a few shelves of old books (it was called the library, but books there were used as projectiles or fire-starters more than sources of edification). In a corner sat an old television set in a wooden cabinet. On weekend nights, we all squeezed in, older boys closest to the screen, younger boys sharing chairs and crammed into the back of the room. It was forbidden to turn the thing on during the week. But most of the policing was done by the oldest boys, and that year, I was one of them – a prefect. That meant a few of us slipped in at 7:30 every Thursday, assigning a pair of younger boys to keep watch at the door to stop others coming in and to warn us if the housemaster was striding down the long corridor from his end of the building.

The half-hour show that March evening was the usual mix of genres, reflecting the wonderful yet often ghastly eclecticism of the UK singles charts in the pre-internet age, the great Album/Singles Era. I can't claim to have remembered any of the other band appearances, but I know that ABC, Visage and Gary Numan were on that night (all artists that I was into), that the Goombay Dance Band performed (we would have booed and hurled books at the screen) and that it was one of several weeks when Tight Fit were number one. Their dire cover of 'The Lion Sleeps Tonight' was a song we loved to hate, and we would gleefully sing along to it at the top of our voices – no longer concerned with getting caught – as each week's number one was always played at the show's end.[8]

The one performance I do remember came somewhere in the middle of the episode, introduced by Radio DJ Richard Skinner with the words, 'Here's a brave new record!' It began with the camera zoomed in on David Sylvian's face. He looked impossibly beautiful, his face delicate, vulnerable, yet self-possessed. He wore a pale shirt buttoned to the neck. As he began to sing, he looked up and right into the lens, his Bryan Ferry baritone crooning, 'When the room is quiet...' And quiet the room was – we were mesmerised. At the first chorus, the camera pulled back to reveal two other band members, one on a synthesizer and the other playing a marimba. There were no guitars in sight, no drum kit. There were no microphones (this was still the time when all performances on *Top Of The Pops* were mimed). It was as if they were right there in *our* quiet room.

At the end of the first chorus, the producers cut to the camera suspended overhead, giving home viewers a glimpse of the studio audience. They seemed perplexed, throwing nervous glances at each other. As *Classic Pop* later put it, they were 'stunned into bovine silence. There can't ever have been a more subversively funereal performance on the show.'[9] As Sylvian dug deeper into his despairing lyrics, Richard Barbieri picked out an ominous melody on his polyphonic Prophet-5 synthesizer. After the second chorus, Sylvian's brother, Steve, mimed his marimba solo – a *marimba*, of all instruments, on *TOTP*, played in deadly earnest. In the final chorus, Sylvian raised his voice for the only time – at the 'not' in 'just when I thought I could *not* be stopped'. It was a moment of restrained anguish, rendered all the more poignant by Sylvian lowering his head at the next line, at the point when he thought his chance had come to be king. But that chance was lost, swept away by the ghosts of his life, by self-doubt, by himself. As the audience applauded, instructed to do so over the final notes, Sylvian again looked down. His head stayed bowed through the camera cut.

Although that end now seems an understated theatrical moment to an obviously mimed performance, at the time, it struck me as stunningly lacking in artifice. In fact, it didn't seem like a performance at all but more like Sylvian sharing his angst and his feelings and baring himself on television in front of everyone. This was not pop frivolity. It was something serious, something new, something beyond new wave and new romanticism and all the other pop genres that had emerged from the creative Big Bang of the late 1970s. It anticipated where pop music might go.

The four-decade run of *Top Of The Pops* that began in 1964 had many peaks and valleys, but 1982 was arguably right within its highest peak era, that of Michael Hurll's 1980-87 stint as producer. The show had become stodgy and stale by the late 1970s (even as its ratings reached new heights). The occasionally panning cameras were far more likely to catch kids on the floor looking bored or waving at Mum watching at home than to capture a moment of audience rapture. But under Hurll, the studio received a full face-lift. The new style of presentation exuded 'a sense of perpetual motion', with everything 'shiny and new, and very, very '80s.' The audience were encouraged – ordered, if need be, on threat of expulsion – to respond enthusiastically to the bands miming on stage. A song like 'Ghosts', however, was hard to reconcile with the enforced 'frantic party atmosphere.'[10] The audience must have wondered, *how* can we respond enthusiastically to *this* – something so sombre and strange?

In the week of its *Top Of The Pops* performance, 'Ghosts' entered the UK singles chart at number 42 (the highest-ranking new entry that week, hence their invitation to appear on the show). *TOTP* appearances were famous – and treasured – for their positive impact on sales. Like radio play, they were a reinforcement loop, stimulating sales that, in turn, prompted more radio play and more *TOTP* appearances. Sure enough, 'Ghosts' leapt the following week to number 16, then to number nine, and in April, it peaked at number five. It would later be called 'one of the most remarkable and unlikely entries in British chart history' by one music writer and, by another, 'quite possibly the least commercial song ever to grace the top five.' Sylvian himself admitted years later that he was 'amazed it did as well as it did. It's a little oblique, to say the least.' *Classic Pop* noted that 'Steve Nye's spare, minimalist production, married to David Sylvian's idiosyncratic songwriting and anguished vocals, made for a pop song unlike any other.'[11] When compared to the other songs clustered near the top of the charts that month, it is astonishing that 'Ghosts' climbed so high, and no wonder that it failed to climb higher. In the week it dropped to number seven, the nation's top five comprised an unsophisticated grab-bag of preposterous pop: the wretched Goombay Dance Band (number four) knocked off the top by Bucks Fizz (number one), of the same forgettable ilk as Dollar (number five), with pub singalong 'rockney' duo Chas & Dave (number two) and the ever-awkward Paul McCartney and Stevie Wonder duet, 'Ebony And Ivory' (number three), still moving up.[12] Such maladroit company made Japan's surprise hit seem even more ethereal, sublime, subtle and – yes – haunting.

To call 'Ghosts' haunting and spooky may seem like lazy music journalism, and those adjectives have certainly become tired clichés of writing about the band Japan. But they are inspired not only by the title but by the music itself, which is deliberately composed and produced to hauntingly raise the lyrics aloft so that, long after the song has ended, they float and follow you – and never quite leave you. Like all pop masterpieces, it clearly reflects its genesis point in the history of modern music, but it is not tethered to it. It is transcendental and as distinct and poignant and unnerving now as it was then.

It was also prophetic. Catalyzed by 'Ghosts', parent album *Tin Drum* climbed the charts and settled in there for a year. Japan started selling records in quantities that had thus far eluded them. Their back catalogue was re-released, turning old flops into new hits. Media attention was intense. Sylvian was on the cover of *New Musical Express, Smash Hits, Noise!* and music magazines in Europe and Japan. The band's concerts filled quickly. Recordings from a sold-out six-night run at London's Hammersmith Odeon in the autumn, released as a double album six months later, became the band's highest charting record yet. Their imperial phase was finally upon them; the moment when Japan had 'broken every door', when Sylvian had his chance 'to be king'.

And so, as if the lyrics to 'Ghosts' were his playbook, Sylvian broke up the band. He even blamed the song: 'It was the only time I let something of a personal nature come through, and that set me on a path in terms of where I wanted to proceed in going solo.' He also blamed the success that 'Ghosts' had ushered in and the fame it brought him: 'It wasn't what I wanted, and that was a revelation. So, I had to re-evaluate.'[13]

I was, to say the least, disappointed by the death of Japan. It felt like a loss and a betrayal, as if David and his brother Steve and their schoolmates Mick and Richard had lured me in and left me with nothing. Or, at least, with no hope of more, as I still had their catalogue of great records. But when I listened to the 130 minutes that make up their final trio of albums – *Quiet Life, Gentlemen Take Polaroids* and *Tin Drum* – I'd only get more peeved. Sylvian's explanation – that he had decided he didn't want to be famous after all – struck me as petulant in the extreme. It was also unconvincing to my teenage mind. I had read that he, Steve and Mick had started the band when they were 15, working incessantly since then to succeed. Now, aged 24, about to be crowned, he wanted to throw it all away. It made no sense to me. Why had Sylvian *really* done it?

I stopped being annoyed with Sylvian decades ago (his first solo album dissolved any remaining residue of resentment). But curiosity over his

ghosts – Journeys To Post-Pop

decision lingered, and rather than fade with time, my curiosity grew with each album that Sylvian created, nourishing the seed planted by seeing 'Ghosts' on *Top Of The Pops* until it bloomed and took the form of this book. What exactly were – *are* – the ghosts that Sylvian was banging on about? And did his lifelong attempt to exorcise them result in the creation of a new kind of pop music – something that was still pop, yet also not pop?

As critical theorist Mark Fisher observed of the song, it 'derives much of its potency from declining to answer, from its own lack of specificity: we can fill in the blanks with our own spectres.'[14] Fisher brilliantly did just that, weaving cultural criticism into commentary on the depression that haunted Fisher (most notably in an essay collection titled *Ghosts Of My Life*) until he took his own life in 2017. Sylvian does not use 'Ghosts' to take us to dark places; he merely shows us a door that leads to them. That door was one with which Fisher was tragically all too familiar and one that he allowed drum-&-bass pioneer Goldie to take him through with his own 'Ghosts Of My Life'. Released under Goldie's pseudonym Rufige Kru, the 1993 single places samples from the Japan song within 'the sonic signatures of darkside Jungle' to create a menacing rumination on the crush of personal spectres. Left behind, of course, is the self-doubting angst of David Sylvian as he faced the fulfilment of his ambitions at the tender age of 23.

As a song about self-defeat and self-denial, about finding the race more thrilling than the win, about fearing that the chase is misguided and the crown made of fool's gold, the timeless appeal of 'Ghosts' is clear. But as a song specifically about Japan's success and Sylvian's response to that, the song is deeply ironic. 'Not just one of Japan's best songs, but one of the best songs of the 1980s' (as one critic put it four decades later), 'Ghosts' was both the fuel that rocketed the band into the stratosphere of success and the artfully designed program that brought the rocket crashing back to earth – all made perfectly transparent in its 'defiantly uncommercial' music and end-prophesying lyrics. Singing about the band's end made him want the end more. The rapturous response by critics and fans, which intensified the pressure to postpone that end, only made Sylvian want it *even* more.

In pondering 'Ghosts' at the time of its ironic triumph, I soon noticed what struck me as an echo of Kate Bush's summer 1981 hit, 'Sat In Your Lap'. Not a musical echo, as the song's Burundi beat and frantic energy is more Adam Ant than Japan, but a lyrical echo in her chorus: 'Just when I think I'm king'. At the time, and for many years, I thought the phrase that followed was 'I masturbate' (it is, in fact, 'I must admit'). It did not occur to me back then that Bush had influenced Sylvian, although 'Sat In Your Lap' was released five months before 'Ghosts' hit shops as part of *Tin Drum*. Rather, I imagined that the phrase, 'just when I think I have a chance to be king' – and variations thereof – was a common metaphor for existential angst. Both songs were certainly about facing an existential crisis and both signalled that crisis musically by sounding unlike other chart hits ('Sat In Your Lap' reached number 11). But while Bush's solution was apparently self-pleasure – most thrillingly, as she was, to my 17-year-old self, a mind-blowing bomb of subtle sex and strange sound – Sylvian's response seemed to be that there was 'no particular place to go'. Perhaps he was suggesting that, without a solution or a destination, we are left merely with the journey and its struggle. Perhaps Bush was suggesting that, too. After all, her meteoric rise to stardom in 1978 had culminated in her third album *entering* the UK charts at number one, the first time a solo female artist had achieved that or, indeed, even hit that top spot. She was arguably already queen and king, and now the months were slipping by with no new album, no new tour and only this strange single – for 'Sat In Your Lap' was as peculiar a choice for a single as was 'Ghosts'. Fans were nervous and, as we shall see later, they were right to be.[15]

'Sylvian is a samurai, and he fights against both the world and himself', Italian philosopher and superfan Leonardo Arena has written of the song, whose creator is 'a *ronin*, the wave-man who has got no masters.'[16] That much was already clear to Sylvian's bandmates by the time of that *Top Of The Pops* appearance. Indeed, two weeks earlier, the band had performed 'Ghosts' for another BBC TV program, *The Old Grey Whistle Test* – not a mimed appearance but a live rendering of the song, one that revealed the cracks in Japan's façade. The band had not 'appeared together since their British tour of last year', noted BBC DJ Annie Nightingale as she introduced them, having 'for the time being split up, to produce what they call in music circle parlance 'solo projects'.' 'Well,' continued Nightingale, 'this would appear to be somewhat of a kamikaze mission, bearing in mind that after being denigrated for years, Japan has now gained the sort of respect that had eluded them for so long.'[17]

Nightingale then went on to introduce Ryuichi Sakamoto – who materialised behind the Prophet-5 synthesizer where one would normally expect to see Richard Barbieri – and suggested ambiguously that Japan's future 'individual endeavours' would prove to be 'very interesting.' Sakamoto – then a member of the Japanese electronic pop band Yellow

Magic Orchestra and yet to embark on an award-winning career as a solo artist and film score composer – was very much Sylvian's collaborator rather than a guest of the whole band. Immediately after this appearance, the two went into the studio to record a single to be released under their names only.[18] Also on stage was guitarist David Rhodes, another non-band member who had toured with Japan in 1981; this would be the last time he would ever play with them.

But oddest of all was Japan bassist Mick Karn's presence. Having initially refused to come, thus forcing Japan's appearance on the show to be postponed from earlier in the year, he now sat on the stage, cross-legged, cradling his bass, behind dark glasses, playing not a note throughout 'Ghosts'. Karn later stated that he showed up out of 'my allegiance to Steve [Jansen] and Rich [Barbieri]', bandmates who 'were caught in the middle of all this nonsense.' As Barbieri recalled, 'I think he made a point of being on stage but not playing to annoy David probably.'[19] The 'nonsense' to which Karn referred was the breakdown of his friendship with Sylvian, itself exacerbated by Sylvian's imperious and impervious piloting of the band into oblivion (as Karn and, to some extent, the others saw it). Japan stayed together long enough to meet their commitment to a two-month tour in the autumn of that year. But, according to Sylvian, the tour succeeded in 'a spirit of cooperation' only because there was 'already some sense of nostalgia that whatever we had is now finished, it's over.'[20]

The immediate context of 'Ghosts', therefore, tempts us to see its meaning as fleeting, as a reflection of the old rock band cliché of success poisoning friendships within the band and thereby quickly killing it. But, of course, the story doesn't end with the band's demise at the end of 1982. For now, let us briefly jump forward 32 years, when Sylvian, aged 56, released what is – at the time of writing – his final solo album. Titled *There's A Light That Enters Houses With No Other House In Sight*, the album consists of a single track that runs an hour and four minutes. The music is minimal, comprising an experimental electronic backdrop to the prose poetry of Franz Wright. Less than two minutes into the track, the Austrian-born American poet starts reading from his own poetry collection *Kindertotenwald*, and he continues, on and off, until the closing minute. The Austrian electronic music composer and producer Christian Fennesz is also credited as playing guitar and 'laptop'. There is nothing remotely pop or rock about the album. It isn't even post-pop – just non-pop.

So, is this the destination that Sylvian refused to articulate in 'Ghosts' that he himself could not yet envisage? Is this what would lie beyond post-pop? And if so, what happened in between 'Ghosts' and *There's A Light That Enters Houses With No Other House In Sight?* Who else made such a journey, and why? And, above all, what did that journey sound like?

2: It's My Life/A Life

'It's My Life' Talk Talk (1984, 3:51; 2003, 3:46)
'A Life (1895-1915)' Mark Hollis (1998, 8:10)

By 2019, we were all living in a world of endless notifications on devices in our pockets. The days of waiting a week to see if your favourite band would appear on a half-hour television show were long gone. I, therefore, heard of Mark Hollis's death just a few days after it happened in February of that year. I took notice because I had never stopped listening to the six albums he had made in the 1980s and 1990s, five with his band Talk Talk and the last as a solo album. So, Hollis's music and his premature passing – he was only 64 – mattered to me. But for decades, he had seldom been a topic of conversation among my friends or of commentary in music magazines and books. Perhaps I was talking to the wrong people and reading the wrong things. Nonetheless, I was surprised by the flurry of obituaries and the effusive way in which Hollis was described as a visionary artist and a crucial influence on generations of musicians.

I had marvelled for years at the contrast between 1982's *Talk Talk* and 1998's *Mark Hollis*, a creative evolution of rare extremes in pop music history. The two albums are dramatically different but, paradoxically, also closely connected. Beyond the superficial similarities (both eponymous, both featuring Hollis's distinctive voice), there is a thread linking them together, marked by the musical and lyrical elements audible on all six Talk Talk/Hollis albums. But did that thread take pop music forward into brave new territory, or did it trace what Depeche Mode's Alan Wilder once called, in specific reference to Talk Talk, 'a career in reverse'?[21]

That evolutionary linking thread had long intrigued me, yet I had no sense of how important it had been to the professionals who thought and wrote about music and to those who composed and recorded it. I was thus struck by the emphasis in all the Hollis obituaries on his later work. One obit after the other glossed over Talk Talk's international, commercial and critical heyday – their mid-80s imperial phase – in order to focus on the commercially catastrophic later albums. The derisive reviews of those later albums, the low sales and a record company lawsuit – all were dismissed or hailed as signs of Hollis being ahead of his time. They were now used as evidence that he had anticipated the time when 'rock became post-rock', that he was 'a chief influence on the post-rock genre' and that he had 'provided a brave and uncompromising lesson in elevating pop music to the realms of true art' – inspiring '21st-century post-pop' and crafting 'what you could even call post-music.'[22]

Post-music? Pondering that phrase (was it brilliant or was it nonsense?) took me back to the last couple of times that I had bought new recordings written by Hollis. Two recordings, two stories, two points on a line asking to be traced and given meaning.

Two decades after 'Ghosts' was on *Top Of The Pops*, almost to the day, I was on a flight to Caracas, bringing one of my children to visit some of her grandparents for Spring Break. As I stood outside the restroom at the front of the plane, waiting for my daughter – she was only five at the time – a man almost my age ambled up and stood in the galley. He looked vaguely familiar (perhaps I had seen him at check-in), so I said hello, and we made small talk. I explained my Venezuela connection, and he told me he played guitar in a band that was appearing at the Caracas Pop Festival that weekend. When my daughter emerged, he didn't take the empty restroom, saying he was only there to stretch his legs – and so, we kept chatting. Only when I noticed my daughter staring at a glamorous figure in dark glasses – sitting in the window seat of the first row a few feet away – a woman whom I realised was unmistakably Gwen Stefani, did the penny drop: I was chatting with No Doubt's Tom Dumont.

There are two kinds of celebrity encounters: the most common kind, where the fan gushes and wants a signature or a selfie, and the more accidental kind, where the fan attempts to stay cool and pretends to have a normal conversation. My slowness to realise whom I was chatting with (considering that I owned all the band's albums and had recently seen them in concert) made the latter possible, allowing our conversation to drift on for 15 or 20 minutes until my daughter became bored of staring at a stone-faced Stefani and dragged us back to our seats. We talked about Venezuelan politics and about early 1980s pop music. Blondie came up – No Doubt would cover 'Call Me' as their encore in Caracas – as did Talk Talk. What stuck in my mind was our conclusion that Talk Talk were a relatively obscure band in the US, perhaps even a cult band, appreciated only by a small group of fanatics, professional musicians (like him) and ex-pat Brits of a certain age (like me). I don't remember Dumont mentioning 'It's My Life'.

The following year, however, No Doubt recorded a cover of Talk Talk's 'It's My Life'. The band chose it over other songs they had covered live, instead of writing a new song, to be the sole new recording and single for a compilation album, *The Singles 1992-2003*. The new single was a smash, hitting the top ten in 15 countries, including the US, and the top 20 in half a dozen more – the UK included. It was nominated for a Grammy, and a remix of the single actually won a Grammy. I was not the only person to buy *The Singles* because of the single; the cover song helped make the hits collection a hit album, top five in the US and UK, a steady seller while Stefani pursued a solo career for the rest of the decade. No Doubt went on a studio hiatus, but not a touring one; in 2003, they started playing 'It's My Life' live, and over the next dozen years, they played it over 100 times.[23]

It is not surprising that No Doubt's 'It's My Life' was a big hit. It's a great cover. It somehow manages to be faithful both to the original and to No Doubt's own style at the century's turn (sitting even better with 2001's *Rock Steady* than with the full catalogue of their hits on *The Singles*). The band's beefy rhythm section gives their version a club-friendly muscularity, Stefani's slightly nasal but agile high tones drawing out the song's upbeat, singalong potential. As Stefani said at the time of its release, the band picked it because it was a 'feel good' song.[24]

But therein lies the rub: Hollis's vocal does the opposite; his plaintive tone has a melancholic, strident edge to it. When Stefani sings the title phrase – followed by 'don't you forget!' – it seems celebratory; when Hollis sings it, it seems threatening. The lyrics are a brief lament over unrequited love, which Hollis delivers with conviction (he wrote them, after all), but when Stefani sings the same words, their disquiet is easily forgotten.[25] The Talk Talk video that accompanied the single in 1984 likewise highlights Hollis's angst, but oddly. The video was frankly bizarre, especially considering this was the height of the MTV era. It consisted of a collage of nature footage with a few scenes of Hollis standing in a zoo with his mouth firmly and stubbornly closed – and with animated tadpoles over his lips, which turn into black censorship blocks.

Talk Talk's 'It's My Life' is both a song of its moment and a slice of timeless pop. It conveys a kind of restrained and compromised joy, like other European electronic pop hits of the mid-1980s – 'Big In Japan' by Germany's Alphaville, 'West End Girls' by England's Pet Shop Boys, 'Take On Me' by Norway's a-ha. The mood of all these hits is upbeat and affirming; they are singalong songs. But at heart, they are also yearning and anxious. The lads in Alphaville aren't really big in Japan; the title phrase is a metaphor for imagined success, for a future in which – unlike the present – 'things are easy.'[26] The boys in a-ha don't have the girl yet; they are trying to seduce her, but in a tone that is just a tad demanding, almost desperate ('take on me, take me on' and on and on). And what really happens if the West End girls and East End boys get together? 'Just you wait 'til I get you home' has a menacing edge to it, paralleling that 'don't you forget' suffix to the title phrase of 'It's My Life'. That contradiction, therefore, between lyrics and music – a paradox as old as pop music itself – made Talk Talk's 1984 single part of a moment when male romantic angst was offset by a radio-friendly, even dance-floor-friendly, pop. At the same time, it gave the song a timelessness that helps explain its success in 2003.

In fact, 'It's My Life' was a hit in three successive decades, with its success increasing each time – ironically coinciding with the dramatic shift by Hollis and Talk Talk away from pop hits. Following its initial release in January 1984 as the lead single from their second album, also titled *It's My Life*, the song was a minor hit, peaking at number 31 in the US and number 46 in the UK. That odd video, a protest by Hollis and the director, Tim Pope, against the banality of lip-syncing and music-video culture, didn't help. When their label, EMI, insisted on a replacement video, in which the band mimed the song in front of a projection of the original video, Hollis and his bandmates fake-performed with deliberately comic incompetence – further parodying the promotion of their own single.[27]

'It's My Life' did a tad better in continental Europe, where the single that followed it ('Such A Shame') was a huge hit, inspiring EMI to re-release 'It's My Life' in the UK. That strategy failed (it reached number 93), but in 1990, the label tried yet again, releasing it as the lead single to promote *Natural History: The Very Best Of Talk Talk*. This time, it reached number 13 in Britain, the highest spot of any Talk Talk single in the band's home country. And that helped *Natural History* sell better than any of the band's other albums.

The song thus did for Talk Talk the same thing that it would do for No Doubt. That was something of an odd twist in both cases. After all, the rest of the No Doubt hits compilation comprised their own songs. *Natural History* was EMI's attempt to offset the commercial damage of Talk Talk's fourth album, whose experimentalism had contributed to legal action between EMI and the band. With *Natural History* heading towards a million sales worldwide, having reached number three in the UK, the following year, EMI put out a compilation of remixes titled *History Revisited*. The band, who had not approved the album, sued the label in return, forcing them to withdraw it. That same year, 1991, Talk Talk – now on Polydor's jazz imprint, Verve – released their final album, yet more experimental than the previous one. They then disbanded.

There was thus not only a complex story to 'It's My Life' but a contradictory history behind the song, one that suggested multiple layers of conflict and success. 'It's My Life', as Talk Talk's best-known and best-selling song, might seem like an obvious way to access the band's history – that, after all, was EMI's idea in 1990 – and it was certainly one that made money. But to dig behind that song and its story is to open a Pandora's Box.

While No Doubt's cover of 'It's My Life' was still in heavy radio rotation throughout the world, I found myself at loose ends for a few hours in Manchester. As it was a little early in the day to hit that pub with all the Smiths posters (or was there more than one?), I headed for the Vinyl Exchange. There, I stumbled across a gently used CD of *Mark Hollis*. I half expected it to be attributed to Talk Talk, as I had read somewhere that, up until the last minute, it was titled *Mountains Of The Moon* and labelled under the band's name.[28] My confusion, combined with my failure to hunt hard enough for the album, explains why it took me five years to buy it. But its patchy release history was also a factor: I was living in the US at the time, and its 1998 release was only on CD and only in the UK and Europe. It was not put out on vinyl until 2003 in Europe and not until 2011 in the US.[29] In other words, this was not an album that the label, Polydor, expected to sell well anywhere – or at all in the US. The album was the second of a two-record deal, the first of which was that final experimental Talk Talk album – 1991's *Laughing Stock* – which had apparently 'gutted' label executives upon first listen. I, therefore, expected *Mark Hollis* to be uncommercial in the extreme, perhaps deeply odd, a far cry from 'It's My Life'.

When the man who rang up my purchases at the cash register in Vinyl Exchange picked up *Mark Hollis*, he held it for a few seconds, nodding his head. 'A life,' he said. 'Yeah. A life. Wow.' Perplexed, I said nothing.

I found a pub (no Smiths posters), grabbed a pint, sat in a quiet corner, slipped on my headphones and popped the CD into my Discman (this was 2003). I slowly worked my way through a liquid lunch, getting tipsier with each track, transfixed by the spare beauty of the album. I had expected experimental oddness. Instead, I was treated to songs that were intimate, minimalist, sometimes halting and often gorgeous. When I reached the fifth track, I realised what the Vinyl Exchange cashier meant. Titled 'A Life (1895-1915)', at over eight minutes, it is the longest song on the album and, arguably, its centrepiece. From the opening, tentative notes on a clarinet, the track seems both assembled and disassembled, carefully crafted and, at the same time, an incomplete collection of found sounds. It is as if Hollis had invited us for tea, and sitting in his kitchen, we hear one of his kids practising on the clarinet next door (or, as an *NME* review put it, the sound of 'the apes from *2001: A Space Odyssey* having their first clarinet lessons').[30] But then we hear some piano, a bass, murmured lyrics, Hollis's fingers squeaking as they move on the frets of an acoustic guitar, and eventually, a drum beat. The effect is hypnotic; it combines but never fully reconciles the elements of a song that consequently defies classification, that demands to be played over and over, its mood and meaning slowly settling in.

Upon first listening, I had no idea whose life was referenced in the title. I later discovered that the life in question was that of Roland Leighton, an English poet who, aged 19, was sent to fight in France soon after the outbreak of the First World War. He died within a year, mourned by his fiancée, Vera Brittain, who also lost her brother and all their male friends to trench warfare. Brittain survived the war as a nurse in England, France and Malta, later publishing a memoir that became a best-seller. Only thus did Leighton achieve some immortality, thereby coming to Hollis's attention. He was fascinated by what he called 'the very severe mood swings' that afflicted the protagonists of the story, the contrast between 'the expectation that must have been in existence at the turn of the century, the patriotism that must have existed at the start of the war and the disillusionment that must've come immediately afterwards.'[31]

Expectation was followed immediately by disillusionment: Hollis did not overtly connect those dots to his own experience as a pop star, perhaps rightly unwilling to compare the success of Talk Talk to the First World War. But the source of his fascination is clear. As Mark Beaumont put it in the *NME*, in the 1980s, Hollis had 'grabbed all the tinsel trappings of The Pop Star Life' and then 'flushed them gleefully down the nearest bog.' The discovery that pop stardom is not all it is cracked up to be is a tired cliché of the modern world. But Hollis did not respond to that disappointment by whining about it or by hitting the heroin (although lazy journalists assumed he must have, and they were still repeating the rumour when *Mark Hollis* was released, much to his fury). Instead, he let the band quietly fade away ('It just sort of ended, I suppose') while he slipped out of the limelight and back into the London suburbs, 'cultivating the general demeanour of a startled tumble dryer mechanic.' That is Beaumont, who ended his interview with Hollis about the solo album with: 'There will be no single from this album, and no tour ever. Just the soft shuffle of a maverick and visionary melting back into the shadows. And elegantly licking his scars.'[32]

It's my life, indeed. 'Maybe others are capable of doing it, but I can't go on tour and be a good dad at the same time,' Hollis once remarked. 'I choose for my family.'[33] And therein, perhaps, lies the solution to the mystery of post-pop. Hollis, like Sylvian and Bush, made a simple, prosaic choice: each picked themselves over the band, domestic life over The Life. Might a closer look at their personal arcs of expectation and disillusionment confirm such a solution?

Perhaps. But there's a catch. That choice was not so simple and prosaic because it involved a decision to keep making music. And not just any music, but the music those three wanted to make, music 'that could exist outside of the period in which it's written or recorded' (as Hollis put it in 1998) and music that was deliberately 'not commercially satisfactory' (in the oft-quoted phrase from Talk Talk's 1989 court battle with EMI).[34] Just days before news of Hollis's death emerged, *Classic Pop* ranked Talk Talk as one of the top 20 pop artists of the 1980s, asking, 'Were Talk Talk ever actually real? No, honestly, their fourth album, *Spirit Of Eden*, is such an out-there masterpiece that it couldn't have been made by regular people. Mark Hollis retired 20 years ago and has shown no signs whatsoever of returning. The myth of Talk Talk is the most enigmatic in pop, primarily because their music lives up to the mystery.'[35]

So, while the personal lives and individual creative journeys of musicians like Hollis, Sylvian and Bush are clearly part of the solution to post-pop's mystery, that cannot explain everything. By making music that is then made available to the world, the internal struggle of its creators becomes – in awkward and contradictory ways – a public one; it becomes ours. 'If the territory of pop music is everywhere, how and where does a piece of art pop – something challenging and engaging in equal parts – make its home?' asked the fiction writer Alexandra Kleeman (in a non-fiction essay on Julia Holter). Searching for genre categories to describe Holter's music, Kleeman pondered 'cerebral pop' as 'an uneasy category.' What is such music asking us to do with our bodies? Where to go in our minds? Tags like art pop and cerebral pop might also be given to albums that Hollis, Sylvian and Bush made on their journeys into post-pop. Kleeman concludes that music like Holter's is 'a trap door leading someplace that's not your own.'[36]

Perhaps that is post-pop: a trap door between pop and the place beyond it, a place that is not our own but which is made for us to visit. Perhaps post-pop is simply a home away from home. After all, post-pop is not non-pop; it is music whose ambiguity of intention and form makes it both against pop (contra-pop, perhaps) – a reaction to pop and all its conventions, its commercial constrictions, its attached Pop Star Life – and at the same time, something linked to pop, defined in relation to it. As with post-pop's sibling and overlapping genre, post-rock, 'grounding elements' like 'a steady beat, verses, choruses and clear distinction between instruments' may be absent or reconfigured in post-pop.[37] But the listener is still conscious of them as missing or altered in unexpected ways, and that thereby allows them to remain present in some sense – the pop or rock to which post is attached.

There is, therefore, a linear progression to the journey into post-pop. It must come from pop, as (arguably) must its creators. But there is also a circularity to that journey, whereby the composer travels from the margin into the centre and then, very deliberately, back out to the edge. And that fact prompts us to consider a larger context, one that adds a further explanatory element to post-pop. In the decades between and including the 1960s, when Sylvian, Hollis and Bush were children, to the 1990s, when they passed into middle age, music of all kinds experienced a rapid turnover of styles.[38] Although there was always an obsessive musical recycling – Fisher called it 'a recombinatorial delirium' – there were also feeding frenzies around the latest, newest sound, rendering yesterday's new sound so, well, yesterday. But at the turn of the new century, all the sounds and styles of the past became accessible with such rapidity and totality that the machine of cultural time ground to a halt. Our sense of 'linear development' was – and remains – swamped by 'a strange simultaneity' as cultural time 'folded back on itself.'[39]

The 1960s seem closer to us now than they did to those who laboured to create, embrace and then discard the new sounds of the late 1970s and 1980s – as did Bush, Sylvian, Hollis, their bandmates, their collaborators and their fellow travellers. In rejecting the intense fixity of the present, these artists were merely anticipating 'the slow cancellation of the future.' In seeking to make music that was outside of the present period (to paraphrase Hollis), they were helping to create the soundtrack to that cultural transition into this century of exhausting everything-ness. If the future has been cancelled, and the present so deeply accommodates the past that 'there is no present to grasp and articulate anymore', then what are we living in? The post-present?

Now, that sounds like a home for post-pop.

3: Suburban Love

'Suburban Love' Japan (1978, 7:27)

'There's a lot of talent in the green belt and there is a load of tripe in Drury Lane.' So declared an aspiring young musician and performer from Beckenham named David Jones – who had recently changed his surname to Bowie – in a 1969 *Melody Maker* interview.[40] Originating in the 1930s, the Metropolitan Green Belt was designed to create a ring of protected, undeveloped space around outer London. But long before Bowie made his oft-quoted quip, the phrase had become shorthand for the fat doughnut that ringed the capital city – filled less with green and more with hundreds of towns that were awkwardly both urban and suburban, both part of London and yet outside it. By contrast, Drury Lane, famous for its theatres, is in the heart of London. It was Bowie's shorthand for the cultural mainstream, for those artists who were on the inside and at the centre.

As it turns out, Bowie was on to something in 1969, something of which he was already a part – perhaps unwittingly, despite his characteristic bravado. Imagine a map of greater London dotted with the birth and growing-up places of the musicians who were born in the baby boom years and who went on to transform rock and pop music in the great Album/Singles Era that began in the mid-1960s (lasting about four decades). The resulting ring of dots coincides remarkably with that Green Belt doughnut of villages, towns and suburbs. If we follow Bowie's lead and, for simplicity's sake, take Drury Lane as London's centre, those dots are between nine and 15 miles away. To the northwest lies Pinner (where Elton John was born and raised as Reginald Dwight); to the west, Heston and Hillingdon (which produced Jimmy Page and Ronnie Wood, respectively) and Feltham (where Farrokh Bulsara moved as a teenager and became Freddie Mercury); to the southwest, Twickenham (Brian May's birthplace) and Surbiton (where Eric Clapton grew up); due south is Wallington (where Jeff Beck was born) and Sutton (where he grew up); and to the southeast, Beckenham (where Peter Frampton was born, and where we just found Bowie) and Bromley (where both of them went to school); and more east than south, Dartford, then just outside the Green Belt but now within it (the home town of Keith Richards and Mick Jagger). To the north, slightly closer to Drury Lane but still not in the centre of things, is Muswell Hill (where Rod Stewart grew up) and Upper Clapton (where Marc Bolan grew up as Mark Feld).

All those musicians were born between 1943 and 1950. They are merely a small representative sample of the many who comprise the pattern of future culture-changers raised 'in the growing shadow of London', tantalisingly close yet outside it. This was a new generation of young men from modest backgrounds who were English 'at the exact moment when the invocation of the word no longer instilled confidence.' They were rebels without a cause, becoming devoted to the new music 'because there wasn't anything to rebel or fight against', according to (King Crimson drummer) Michael Giles: 'If we were seeking to escape, then it would have been from a kingdom of nothingness.'[41]

Giles grew up in Portsmouth, south of London and well outside the Green Belt, and indeed, there was an outer ring of towns and villages – the fringes of that kingdom of nothingness – that were touched by the capital's shadow. With the influence of English pastoralism stronger, those places produced the future members of bands like King Crimson, Genesis, ELP and the many others that would invent progressive rock in the late 1960s and 1970s.[42]

Meanwhile, within the Green Belt, the pattern persisted with the next half-generation of boys (yes, the pattern is dominated by boys) born between 1952 and 1964, impacting music culture further in the late 1970s and early 1980s. For example, The Clash's Joe Strummer and Mick Jones both grew up in Greater London towns that were six to 18 miles southwest of Drury Lane. The future members of The Sex Pistols mostly grew up in neighbourhoods closer in – all about four miles from Drury Lane – but many other budding musical talents were raised in that nine-to-15-miles ring, such as Elvis Costello (as Declan MacManus in Twickenham), and five miles further west, Gary Numan (né Webb). Within that same doughnut of distance from the centre, George Michael grew up to the northwest (in Kingsbury, as Georgios Panayiotou) and Boy George to the southeast (born in Bexley as George O'Dowd, raised in Woolwich).

Amidst the boys, there were some girls born in the Green Belt during those same years who would make an impact on an overwhelmingly male-dominated industry. Most notably, Kate Bush was born in Bexleyheath (a mile away, but a few years before O'Dowd), and she grew up in neighbouring Welling (both within that nine-to-15-mile ring). Siouxsie Sioux grew up as Susan Ballion in Chislehurst (just a few miles east of the above-mentioned Bromley). Alison Moyet, like the future members of Depeche Mode, was born and raised in Basildon, a postwar New Town built 20 miles east of the outer edge of London's East End (and now, although not originally, in the Metropolitan Green Belt). The parents and grandparents of the first working-class generation born in Basildon had typically grown up in the East End or in adjacent parts of London, lending an additional dimension to that tantalising sense of being both inside and yet ultimately outside the centre's cultural scene.[43]

Five miles east of Basildon lies the smaller and far older Essex town of Thundersleigh, where Lee Harris and Paul Webb – both born in 1962 – went to school together. Their future Talk Talk bandmate Mark Hollis, although born in Tottenham (in London, seven miles north of Drury Lane), grew up from the age of seven in the cluster of small Essex towns that includes Thundersleigh. The southernmost districts of the county of Essex were becoming virtual suburbs of London's East End, connected to it directly by road and rail and, from there, into the whole metropolis. That distance fuelled the ambitions of those outside a centre that was just about reachable, even if Essex lads might rightly feel that they would never be fully accepted in that centre; like the future Mode boys, the three future Talk Talkers spoke the dialect broadly associated with the East End and Essex, an accent that in class-conscious Britain marked the trio as beyond the pale of privilege.[44]

We shall return to Talk Talk's origins in a later chapter. For now, we leave them in the 1970s, with Harris and Webb as Essex schoolboys who have yet to meet Hollis, and he, seven years their elder, caught in an uneasy post-school pre-career limbo of temporary jobs and unfinished college courses. We likewise leave Kate Bush at East Wickham Farm, the Outer London suburban family home, where teenage Cathy was obsessively writing songs on her piano – by age 14, 'writing a song, maybe two songs, every day. I must have had a couple of hundred.'[45] Meanwhile, some six miles west of the Bush family home, the Batt brothers had begun a musical journey that likewise began in the Green Belt.

David Batt was born in 1958 in Beckenham, Stephen 21 months later in Sydenham, and a year later, the family moved to Lewisham. At the decade's end, David began school in Catford, with Stephen soon following. All four adjacent suburbs sit seven to ten miles from Drury Lane. By train and Tube (London's subway system), it would have taken the Batt boys, as teenagers in the 1970s, an hour to get from Catford Bridge to the music venues around Covent Garden (as it does today). Those clubs were thus so close and yet so far. The four suburbs of the Batts' childhood are only a few miles from each other, all connected in a swathe of then-working-class neighbourhoods, just beginning to receive immigrants from the colonies and former colonies, and still a long way from the price increases (or 'gentrification') that would later have excluded the family of a man like Bernard Batt, who toiled as a plasterer and labourer on building sites.[46]

'As a family, we never ventured far on our infrequent travels. My family never had money to burn', David later said. The older Batt was sufficiently introverted, disinterested in sport and finely featured to be a misfit, inspiring him, even as a boy, to seek an identity – and an escape – in music. He pulled his younger brother into his orbit, along with a boy his age who sought escape for similar reasons: Andonis Michaelides's family were immigrants from Cyprus, settling in Catford when he was three. A sensitive child whose parents, he later claimed, were cold and unaffectionate, Mick (as he was soon nicknamed) was bullied for being brown (called, following the ignorant logic of racism, a 'Paki'). Lacking any musical training or access to instruments, the trio found ways to teach themselves how to play music, becoming an unnamed band by 1973 (the year the older two turned 15 and Stephen 13).[47]

That band would soon become Japan. Little did they know it – although the Batts believed in their future with that confident conviction with which teenage boys can be blessed – that forming the trio was the first step on a five-year, six-step journey to becoming international recording artists. The second step was to find and commit to an image: in their early teens, David and Mick adopted the 'trashy, androgynous look' of glam, complete with costumes, full makeup and long, brightly coloured hair. Living in working-class suburban London, they endured 'beatings and lots of running away from people' (David); 'it was hell' (Mick). At the insurance company where David and Mick briefly worked after dropping out of school aged 16, 'they called us Anthony and Cleopatra.' Even as they slowly struggled towards local success as a band, the abuse persisted. 'It was worse in Catford', but anywhere in Greater London, they might be spat at, threatened, or spark 'the 'you wanker/poof/queer!' reaction.' David was the most dogmatically committed to the look. As his manager mused years later, 'he simply couldn't wait any longer to be a star'; 'looking like a star' meant he would *feel* like a star' and that was elemental to being one as soon as possible.[48]

Leaving school was the third step, permitting a full commitment to writing songs, practising instruments and being a band. The fourth was to perform before an audience. The first gig by the trio was at Mick's older brother's wedding in 1974, but it was two years before the full band (with Barbieri on keyboards and Rob Dean, an East Ender a few years older, on guitar) would start playing London's social clubs and college bars. By

1977, they were playing punishing gigs up and down England. This was also the year that Kate Bush, still only 18, performed in public for the first time: she played the pub circuit, beginning with a regular Tuesday night gig at the Rose of Lee in Lewisham. This was the home territory of Mick and the Batt brothers, and indeed, in 1977, Bush also performed at the Black Cat pub in Catford. It is tempting to imagine the boys catching one of her shows in between their own gruelling treks up and down the country. The difference between the two was that Bush flouted no gender norms (not yet); looking very feminine, she fronted the KT Bush Band, whose musicians were very male-looking men. Their set was heavy on popular covers, and they opened for nobody. By contrast, Japan comprised men deliberately looking un-male, according to the norms of the time, and they mostly performed their own material. The abuse they suffered grew worse in 1978 when they toured as support for The Damned and then the Blue Öyster Cult. In addition to projectiles and spit, they endured a hail of 'Go home, you bent cunts!' and similar vitriol.[49]

The fifth step for Japan was potentially a leap, more than a step, out of the Green Belt and into the music industry by signing contracts – most notably with a manager and a record label. When David auditioned for Simon Napier-Bell – an industry veteran who had managed The Yardbirds and, briefly, Marc Bolan, and who was from the other side of London's tracks – the 18-year-old was offered a contract on the spot. 'He was a natural,' said Napier-Bell, 'irresistibly stamped with instant success.' David persuaded Napier-Bell to take on the whole band, and after a frustrating year of dead-ends, the manager secured a contract with German label Ariola-Hansa.[50] That made possible the final step: to record, release and promote an album.

These 1970s years have been detailed by biographers of Sylvian and the band and in Mick's autobiography. Running through those accounts is a thread that is visible but not highlighted by their authors. To my mind, however, that thread – the multifaceted influence of a man born a decade before them in the very same stretch of the Green Belt – ties the story together, both in the 1970s and beyond. As Mick noted, explaining what drew him and the Batts together in their early teens: 'Music was our common interest, namely David Bowie.'[51]

In 1972, as Mick and David entered their teens, with Stephen two years behind them, their idol was Marc Bolan of T. Rex, both his music (the pop-rock sound of glam) and image (glam's androgynous costume-and-makeup look). But for the three of them, as for so many British teenagers,

Bolan would prove to be merely a John the Baptist to the Messiah that Bowie became when he invented Ziggy Stardust. Ziggy was being birthed while T. Rex released 'Telegram Sam' and 'Metal Guru' – winter and spring teaser singles for the summer's new album. But a month before that album (*The Slider*) was released, *Ziggy Stardust And The Spiders From Mars* came out – on the same day as Roxy Music's self-titled debut. Witnessing the parallel arrival of Stardust and Roxy in real time, the three boys were swept away. Days later, Roxy opened for Bowie in Croydon (another London suburb, just a few miles from Beckenham); Bowie and Brian Eno 'hit it off immediately', sowing the seeds of a relationship to which we shall return. The Batt boys did not see that concert, but – again, just days later – they did witness what would become one of the most influential and celebrated appearances in the four-decade history of *Top Of The Pops*: Bowie miming 'Starman', the lead *Ziggy* single. Mick and David immediately bought the album and flogged it, as Bolan 'slid down the pecking order' and Bowie rose rapidly to the top of their list of musical 'heroes'.[52]

Meanwhile, that 'Starman' appearance on *Top Of The Pops* had a similar impact on 13-year-old Kate Bush, who was so entranced that she added Bowie's picture to 'my bedroom wall next to the sacred space reserved solely for my greatest love, Elton John.' The summer that Bowie's 'Starman' performance on *Top Of The Pops* made him a star in Britain, John's latest hit was 'Rocket Man'. Young Cathy could surely not have imagined that, two decades later, her own version of 'Rocket Man' would be almost as big an international hit as the original, or that another two decades after that, John would sing on what so far seems to be her final album. Back in 1973, she was at the Hammersmith Odeon when Ziggy Stardust shocked the audience with his sudden declaration of retirement: 'I remember that Bowie gig quite clearly,' she reminisced 40 years later, 'I cried.' The connections are myriad. The notorious 'frenemies', the Starman and the Rocketman, were to inspire Bush throughout her career.[53]

The next month (after the *Top Of The Pops* 'Starman'), Bowie and Roxy sold out shows in Finsbury Park (in north London), and days after that, Roxy Music appeared for the first time on *Top Of The Pops*. Miming their debut single, 'Virginia Plain', they looked like fashionista guests causing a stir at the Ziggy party.[54] Inspired to the point of obsession, the Catford boys wanted in on the party, too. Mick later recalled how, one day, the three of them played hooky from school, 'roaming the streets of Lewisham borough, with a picture of David Bowie, searching for a barber that would attempt to cut our hair in the same style.'[55] The following spring, Roxy and Bowie-as-Ziggy released sequel albums just three weeks apart – *For Your Pleasure* and *Aladdin Sane*. They were quickly bought at the Catford record shop by Mick; in his bedroom, the boys then listened to the records – especially *Aladdin Sane* – over and over. The following month, they finally saw Bowie play live, catching his biggest gig yet, joining a crowd of 18,000 at London's Earl's Court. Having abandoned their seats for the crush of fans at the foot of the stage, at the interval, the boys found their seats taken by Bowie's wife Angie and her friends. 'Angie autographed our badges,' one of the boys later recalled, 'she looked stunning and was so kind and gentle to us.' Serendipity – or the ambition of the boys – would ensure that it would not be the last time they would see her.[56]

It was around this time that the trio made the decision to form a band. With David as guitarist and songwriter, Stephen acquired his first drum kit, and Mick – whose school instrument, the bassoon, failed to fit their ambition – agreed to learn bass and be the singer. Only minutes before their first public performance, Mick lost his nerve and asked David to step in.[57] After all, David knew all the words. The first song he sang was 'Aladdin Sane'.

Why did Bowie and his Stardust alter ego matter so much to Mick and the Batts? The music and the look were strikingly, viscerally new enough to answer the question. But there was another factor, one that allowed Bowie to resonate with these boys more than Roxy Music, the New York Dolls or any other artist. He was their neighbour. His origins were their origins. And yet, he had transformed himself from Jones to Bowie to Stardust, existing as all three in humble Beckenham – David Batt's birthplace, just a few miles south of Catford – while at the same time, escaping onto the world stage. More than simply their inspiration, he was *theirs*.

A week or two after that May 1973 Earl's Court concert, Bowie played the Lewisham Odeon, just a mile from the Batt home. David and Mick tried in vain to get in, but their old school friend Richard Barbieri saw the show (he would become Japan's fourth member two years later). 'It's weird to think,' he would later muse, 'that when I was about 14, David Bowie was making *Hunky Dory* and was living up the road from my house in the same drab suburbia.' Indeed, that same spring of 1973, the Batt boys 'somehow found out where David Bowie's house was in Beckenham, and just hung around outside all day until it was dark' (Mick recalled). Eventually, David Batt, sporting his new Ziggy haircut, persuaded Stephen to ring the doorbell. A young girl 'politely told him Mr Bowie was busy.' Later seeing 'Dave's increasing anger at [Japan] fans waiting outside his apartment', Mick would wonder if the former Dave Batt 'ever recalled his own fanatical, lookalike behaviour when he was their age.'[58]

Meeting Bowie himself was not on the cards, but four years later, David and Mick would again encounter Angie – by then estranged from her husband, who was busy making *Low* and *'Heroes'* in Berlin. After one of the many poorly attended gigs Japan played that year in London, their manager's assistant introduced David to a friend of hers, a Swiss model named Charlie – whose flatmate was Angie Bowie. For a few months, Mick and David played the role of toy boys to these glamorous older women, who – among other things – taught the 19-year-olds how better to apply makeup. Mick said, 'It reminded them of doing the same for David Bowie and his band.'[59]

Around this time, the original trio of David, Stephen and Mick finally did what they had considered for a while: formally changing their names, just their surnames, the way that David Jones had done. Mick's nickname was already well established, and so he toyed with adopting Ronson as his surname – Mick Ronson being Bowie's guitarist in the Spiders from Mars. But realising that would have taken mimicry to a confusing level, he instead picked 'Kahn' out of the phone book, spelling it 'Karn'. Stephen Batt, flipping the same pages, chose Jansen. He later admitted that he liked its similarity to Johansen, as 'I was into the New York Dolls at the time' (David Johansen being their lead singer). The Dolls homage seemed to be confirmed by Steve's brother, who picked Sylvian in an apparent nod to Dolls' guitarist Sylvain Sylvain. As early Japan's hair-and-makeup look was reminiscent of the New York Dolls, the press – once the band started to attract some – accepted the connection without question. However, Sylvian denied it. He claimed he simply chose 'a boy's name' he liked, the change resulting from 'a very private need', not a homage to anyone.

But with Bowie as the divine and omnipresent muse, it is impossible not to see the name's origin in this line from 'Drive-In Saturday', a top three hit from the Batt-revered *Aladdin Sane*: 'He's crashing out with Sylvian/ The bureau supply for ageing men.'[60]

Japan recorded two albums in 1978, released a mere six months apart. *Adolescent Sex* and *Obscure Alternatives* are best understood as two parts of a single musical project: a permanent record of teenage years of creativity and hard practice, an intriguing statement of arrival. A decade later, Sylvian had a different verdict, dismissing the pair as *'massive mistakes.'*[61]

He has never wavered from that position, acting for the last 40 years – in interviews, live performances and track selections for compilations – as if the first two Japan albums never existed.[62] The contrast with the band's final three albums is certainly striking. The 1979-81 trio are a study in inventive brilliance, whereas the 1978 pair are a display of many of the same brilliant ingredients but insufficiently developed and clumsily assembled. In retrospect, that weakness – the embryonic nature of the band's creativity – is what validates the albums. They fascinate because of the transparency with which they explore ways to turn the boys' influences into something new.

The conclusion by band biographer Reynolds that *Adolescent Sex* was 'merely the best songs of the last few years from a band barely out of their own adolescence', with a blatant 'lack of unifying concept', applies loosely to both records.[63] If the albums are about anything, they are about sex; they are, after all, the creative product of teenage boys. But even then, what makes an otherwise predictably dull theme interesting is, paradoxically, Sylvian's apparent *disinterest* in it. The purpose of music, for these boys, is not to get laid but to get out. The goal is to escape to the centre of things, not sex *per se*, and certainly not the sex of the suburbs. That is why 'Suburban Love', which opens side two of the debut album, *Adolescent Sex*, is so revealing. The song's first half is a distinctly unsexy ode to the orgasm. I confess that, for many years, I assumed the chorus – 'Earth, wind, earth, wind and fire/Cannot take me, take me much higher' – was a tribute to the band of that name. It never occurred to me that sex was the subject. If you wanted eroticism in a pop song in 1978, you'd have done better with Sylvester's 'You Make Me Feel (Mighty Real)', probably not Exile's 'Kiss You All Over', perhaps the adolescent-lust trilogy on side two of Kate Bush's debut album, kicked off by 'Feel It'. But 'Suburban Love', after about three minutes, seems spent. Then it shifts into an instrumental jam that lasts over four minutes: spacey disco-rock that mercifully takes us far from the grunts of suburban love and onto an urban dancefloor. The song goes from being a drag to a trip.

Even on the title track, which immediately follows, the act that 'gets you through the night' isn't the carnal one; it's the one that was all the rage in 1978: the main refrain of the chorus is 'Just keep on dancing'. That mirrors the use of the same verb in the best song on side one, 'The Unconventional', whose chorus declares repeatedly that 'I'm dancing to your heart'. One might imagine that Sylvian has borrowed disco's use of dancing as a metaphor for fucking. But these albums are punk-disco, not funk-disco.

'Adolescent Sex' and 'The Unconventional' are songs for sexually frustrated dancers (feigning disinterest), not dancers indulging in foreplay.

In addition to nine Sylvian originals, *Adolescent Sex* featured a cover of Barbara Streisand's 'Don't Rain On My Parade', which *Sounds* rightly dismissed as 'a nice joke.' The band had played it live when supporting The Damned on their UK tour earlier in the year, in a witty response to the furious efforts by Damned fans to cover Japan in spit and phlegm. Deliberately recording a rough version with out-of-tune backing vocals, they imagined it serving as an amusing B-side; Hansa, who struggled from the start to pigeonhole and promote the band, 'went overboard about it' and released it as the first single.[64] It was met with 'a monsoon of indifference.' Like its parent album – indeed, like both 1978 albums – it was 'too musical to be punk and too weird to be pop.' As an 'art-punk (!) outfit', Japan were surely destined for the cult category.[65]

Kate Bush's first two albums were likewise both released in 1978, just weeks apart from Japan's first two. However, hers launched her into the stardom that Japan craved, while theirs left them in the alternative of obscurity. *Adolescent Sex* was a very minor hit in Japan, Belgium and the Netherlands; its title track also briefly visited the Dutch top 20. *Obscure Alternatives* similarly bombed, save in Japan (should they have named the band England?).[66] A critic for the *NME* condemned the first as 'stillborn' and letting off 'a grotesque stench of musical decay' ('the cunt can't have listened to the LP', complained Sylvian), and the second as 'exquisitely awful.' In rare moments when Sylvian later talked about these albums, he was most dismissive of the first, conceding that *Obscure Alternatives* was slightly better, especially where it pointed towards Japan's future. The 'European angst and post-punk reggae' of *Obscure Alternatives* showed the band digging into 'a weirder groove' concluded *Uncut* magazine, four decades after the album's release, its 'uniquely enigmatic poise' making the long-forgotten record now worth collecting. Yet the smear of old accusations that Japan's first two albums were failed attempts to blend Roxy Music with the New York Dolls have never faded; that favourable *Uncut* verdict was undercut by the phrase 'too late for the Dolls/Roxy party.'[67]

In fact, the two albums sound almost nothing like the New York Dolls.[68] They *do* sound a little like early Roxy, but Sylvian's voice is mostly a Bolan imitation, with some Bowie thrown in; the Ferry-like croon came later. Above all, the albums are an attempt to reconcile Bowie's various alter egos and musical styles to date. That meant, in effect, updating glam by

ghosts – Journeys To Post-Pop

trying to merge the two genres that dominated the day – disco and punk. That they largely failed at it should not detract from the fact that the idea was a brilliant one. After all, many others would soon try (from The Rolling Stones to Duran Duran, from Blondie to Bowie himself), with the notion underpinning the new waves that would soon dominate popular music – of which Japan would, finally, be a part.

'The trajectory of Sylvian's career,' mused London's *Sunday Times* in 1989, 'from heavily mannered glam rocker to introspective balladeer and composer of delicately textured instrumental mood pieces, is one of the strangest in recent pop history.'[69] That trajectory, as we shall see, would become far stranger. But to understand its dynamics – to grasp why it is one of pop history's 'strangest' – its simple starting points are as important as its later twists and turns. In other words, to define post-pop, we need to tell some pop stories. For 'post' only has meaning in relation to the 'pop' that preceded it.

The time loop upon which this use of 'post' depends has been explored in countless works of scholarship in such fields as intellectual history and cultural criticism. Take this statement, for example: 'The 'post' of postcolonialism turns out to be an anti-colonialist 'post' at the service of decolonizing decolonization.'[70] How does this help us here? It reminds us that the 'post' in post-pop is an anti-pop lunge that deliberately fails to meet its mark, threatening pop while at the same time reifying it and reassuring itself that pop is still there. Post-pop cannot exist in a pop-less void; it still needs pop, however far it may roam from it.

The same is true of how modernism and postmodernism were conceived (an 'ism' pair close to our topic). The rallying cry for modernism – which first emerged as a grab bag of other 'isms' that defined artistic trends on both sides of the Atlantic between the world wars – was the ancient Confucian motto, 'make it new', made famous by Ezra Pound. Modernism's problem, however, was the challenge of reconciling destruction and invention, renovation and innovation; does renewal really make it new? Postmodernism, on the other hand, was spared that problem because, by definition, it was both old *and* new. Postmodernism was free to be expansive (anything can be art!) because, paradoxically, it was tied to the anchor of modernism.

Music historian Simon Morrison has written of Bryan Ferry as 'a latter-day modernist' and of *Avalon* ('Roxy Music's 1982 apotheosis') as 'nostalgic modernism.'[71] But Morrison also recognises the incipient postmodernism of Ferry's attitude towards aesthetics, style and cultural chronology – quoting this response by Ferry, when asked how he can look and act conservative while 'doing such radical work': 'Yeah, but you look through the history of art and you'll see that people who did even revolutionary work were often quite bourgeois in their life and in their tastes. They needed that anchor to get the work done.'[72]

Pop, then, is the anchor that gets the work of post-pop done. And even if the Roxy Music and solo Ferry catalogues never veered into post-pop (that was left to ex-Roxy Eno), it is surely true that their output in the 1970s (especially those first two albums made before Eno left) laid claim to 'a postmodern celebration of artifice and decadence, rearranging pop culture to suit their own needs.'[73] In that sense, Sylvian (and, as we shall see, Hollis, too) became a mimic modernist who sought paths into postmodernism. And, not coincidentally, the half-decade that took the Catford boys from teenage dreamers to incipient rock stars was precisely when the artists whom they idolised most were exploring ways to disassemble pop, to 'make it new' and then to see where the 'post' of things took them.

More specifically, during 1977 – while Japan struggled to escape the Green Belt, enduring rejection from audiences and record labels, and Sylvian continued to process the influences of Bolan, Roxy and Bowie into new compositions – Bowie released *Low*, then made and released *'Heroes'*. At the time, his diptych confounded and divided critics and fans (*Low* 'doesn't make sense,' one favourable review explained, 'nothing follows the formal or practical rules of the game').[74] But before long, the two albums would begin to make their ascent into the pantheon (of Bowie records and then of rock music), hailed as yet another triumphant reinvention of sound and vision, another Bowie 'blast from the future.'[75] Sylvian and his bandmates were paying rapt attention, and in time, they, too, would figure out how to separate influence from imitation, modern from postmodern, pop from post.

The previous autumn, Bowie had moved to Berlin to finish *Low*. Most of the album had already been recorded in Chopin's old French mansion, the Château d'Hérouville, with Brian Eno as a collaborator and Tony Visconti as producer. Bowie then rented a Berlin flat with Iggy Pop, with whom he co-wrote and recorded two Iggy albums, as well as making *'Heroes'* with Eno and Visconti, all in 1977, at Hansa (the home studio of the label that would, at the end of 1977, sign Japan). *Low* and *'Heroes'* remain a pair of astonishing creations. The latter is usually seen as the stronger album, a more visceral and coherent 're-evaluation of the groundwork laid out on its predecessor.' But *Low* must take credit for coming first, for its 'overall canonical importance and sheer artistic bravery.'[76]

Low is also particularly significant to our story here, for the way its 11 tracks separate out, display and contrast the elements of pop. Superficially, the two albums are very similar, both with pop-rock songs written by Bowie on side one and instrumental compositions by Bowie and Eno on side two. But that characterisation isn't quite accurate. Upon closer look, the contrasts between their vinyl sides and each other are less stark. *'Heroes'* is more of a rock album, its unity of anguished mood making it a step towards its sequel, *Lodger*, itself a more conventional rock album that took Bowie towards his early 1980s pop imperial phase.[77] As thrilling as it was to witness that journey – from *'Heroes'* to *Let's Dance* – in real time and as unpredictable as it then seemed, that path now appears straight and clear. By contrast, *Low* offers us a moment when the pieces have been disassembled and it is not clear how – or even if – they will be put back together. Side one packs seven tracks into 19 minutes, but the impression is more of something deliberately unfinished than a nod to punk's minimalist aesthetic. Side one fades in and out as if we have 'just arrived within earshot of something that's already started.' Its songs are fragmentary, their singing low-key, and the first and last are backing tracks to which Bowie never added words. Just as the 'song' side is not all songs, so is the 'instrumental' side partly vocal: Bowie sings on three of side two's four tracks but without discernable words ('in a made-up language of fractured syllables').[78]

This unexpected mix of styles and genres – the album as a collection of excerpts from other albums – had already been tried by Eno. His role in these albums has often been exaggerated (he only co-wrote one track on *Low* and four on *'Heroes'*, and, unlike the omnipresent Visconti, he was absent for much of the recording sessions). But his influence is inescapable, particularly in light of the two solo albums he released in 1975, *Discrete Music* (one of ambient music's foundational works) and *Another Green World*, as well as the one he worked on from 1975 until its release at the end of 1977, *Before And After Science*. *Another Green World* featured five songs and 11 instrumentals interspersed throughout. But after seeing how *Low* and *'Heroes'* were assembled and structured, with tracks clustered by genre, Eno gave *Before And After Science* two contrasting sides, one rock and the other atmospheric pop. With Eno part of the creative process in Berlin, especially on *'Heroes'*, the flow of influence went in both directions.[79]

Another Green World cannot compare to *Low* and *'Heroes'* in terms of the strength of its songs or the ineffable star presence of its prime creator. But, like *Low* in relation to *'Heroes'*, *Another Green World* has the advantage of having come first. Eno showed that instrumental fragments and odd pop songs could sit side by side in a way that should not have worked – and yet it did. Pop, it turned out, was not limited and simple; it was a world of possibilities. It was not music's lightweight and inferior genre, unworthy of being taken as seriously as prog rock and jazz, classical and avant-garde; it was unbounded, open to interaction with those other genres. Eno pointed the way to a set of paths or journeys to which Sylvian, Hollis and Bush would, in various ways, commit. But Eno's contribution was to emphasise the plurality of those paths without specifying a destination. Few artists willing to walk down such paths were game to venture into post-pop. Like Bowie, they usually stepped back into the more comfortable zones of rock and pop.

In the *'Heroes'* sessions in Hansa, Eno introduced his trademark recording gimmick of giving the musicians cards from his 'Oblique Strategies' deck, a set of roughly 100 first created in 1975. He met some resistance, most notably from guitarist Carlos Alomar, but he and Bowie spent hours experimenting with the cards 'like a couple of eccentric professors.'[80] Sylvian and Hollis were fascinated by such innovations and the ways they were reflected in the resulting albums. Both them and Bush would later experiment with Bowie's and Eno's in-studio strategy of not giving musicians clear instructions.

During the *Low* sessions, Bowie and Iggy 'pleasantly stunned Eno' by humming parts of *No Pussyfooting*, the proto-ambient album Eno had made with King Crimson founder Robert Fripp. Fripp was later flown to Berlin to play what became a legendary guitar part on "Heroes". Having already embarked on what would prove to be a long career of avant-garde music-making, Fripp's albums with Eno and his work on *'Heroes'* (he plays on half the album's tracks) caught Sylvian's attention. Reportedly, 'Dave had wanted Robert Fripp to produce *Obscure Alternatives*', but Napier-Bell 'reported back that Fripp was too busy.'[81]

Eventually, Sylvian and Fripp would connect and collaborate. But meanwhile, Sylvian and his bandmates slipped onto the end of *Obscure Alternatives* an irresistible homage to what Bowie, Eno and Fripp had created the previous year in Berlin. Eno has said that in his 1970s work, he was keen to explore what he called 'the background': 'I wanted to get rid of the element that, up to then, had been considered as essential in pop music:

the voice.'[82] At 7:14, 'The Tenant' was the longest and only instrumental track on *Obscure Alternatives*. The lilting piano riff composed by Sylvian but programmed by Barbieri on his Polymoog, combined with a synth-treated saxophone wail from Karn and an impressive Fripp impersonation by Dean, make 'The Tenant' sound like an unused track from the *'Heroes'* sessions.

Named after a Roman Polanski film (Sylvian's cinematic, literary and philosophical references would proliferate as he moved towards post-pop), 'The Tenant' was 'a time capsule from the band's future, marking exactly where they were headed' (as band biographer Reynolds put it). Sylvian insisted that Japan were not headed directly into Eno territory. Eno, he said, 'creates an atmosphere. It's just background music. It's a backdrop for something.' But 'The Tenant' was not 'a backdrop for anything.' A track that 'creates a lot of emotion; it connects to me more than anything else on the album.'[83]

Post-pop is its own walking ghost. That is surely why Bowie, perceiving this, would not again stray as far from pop and rock until the post-pop flirtation of his swansong album, created as he saw his own ghost approach.[84] For Bowie, the end of every creative stage contained the beginning of the next one. But for Sylvian, it was the opposite: with every start, he had his eye on the end, always seeing death embedded in birth.

At the request of the boys in the band, Napier-Bell arranged for Bowie to attend Japan's final Hammersmith Odeon gig – what would be their final concert in their home country. Bowie's presence was symbolically appropriate, considering his crucial influence on Japan's development, as well as the Batt brothers' reciprocal influence on Bowie's own early-1980s look. But it didn't happen due to an ironic twist.

The date was 22 November 1982, and Bowie was already sporting a top-heavy shock of ice-blond hair – a slightly more conservative version of Sylvian's hairstyle that, to the casual observer, must have made him look more like a Sylvian fan than like himself. In Napier-Bell's telling:

> When Bowie turned up in the back of a stretch limo and lowered the window, he was confronted with a snarling security guard.
> 'Who d'you think *you* are?'
> 'I'm David Bowie', said David Bowie.
> 'Well, I'm President Reagan', the guard sneered scornfully. 'So, you can piss off.'
> And he did. Which left Japan quite upset.[85]

4: Life In Tokyo

'Life In Tokyo' Japan (1979, 3:30)

Like the boys in Japan, I was born in southern London's Green Belt. Like them, I was an English schoolboy in the 1970s, obsessed with pop music, and my obsession intensified right as the band were making their first two albums. But at the time of their release in 1978, both records completely escaped my attention. Instead, in a peculiar, personal twist of irony, I was introduced to Japan *in* Japan by a Tokyo teenager through Japan's single 'Life In Tokyo'.

The band's first two albums passed me by because they failed to chart or birth hit singles in the UK, and as a boarding schoolboy, I had limited access to record shops (my privileged education was a far cry from the Batt brothers' Catford school, but we were seldom allowed to leave the school grounds during term time). I was vaguely familiar with 'Adolescent Sex', as it was on a mixtape I had copied from another boy. But I paid no attention to who the band were.

However, as the 1970s drew to a close, my father took a job in Tokyo, moving there with my stepmother and half my siblings. I joined them there that summer, falling in with some of the friends my sisters had started to make. One of them was called Shoe. It was really Xu, but it sounded like 'shoe' to us, and he liked to write his name in kanji, paired with a cartoonish drawing of a shoe. Shoe was obsessed with two foreign things – three, if you counted one of my sisters. The first was a mythical view of California culture, all Beach Boys tunes and surfing parties and grinning bikini-clad blondes (he owned a surfboard, which sat unused in his bedroom, quietly fuelling his dreams). The second was the London new wave music scene.

For Shoe, those two scenes were antidotes to each other, offering soundtracks tailor-made to his moods. Like me, he was in his mid-teens, and I instantly understood why one moment, he wanted the upbeat sounds of half-dressed Californians giddy with horny happiness, but the next moment, he needed the sulky cool and neurotic whine of overdressed London boys. My efforts to be one of the latter were half-hearted and pathetic but good enough for Shoe, who insisted I looked exactly like half of the members of Ultravox (when John Foxx was in it), Sniff 'n the Tears and pretty much any British band whose photos had appeared in Japanese magazines.

That included the band Japan; Shoe insisted I was a dead ringer for Sylvian's brother Steve. He was convinced that it was not coincidental that the brothers were named Batt and had grown up in Catford – which, half the time, he called Batford. A family named after a bat, in a town named after a cat – what could be the meaning of this? Shoe demanded. When I told him that the London neighbourhood where I was born was about 13 miles from 'Batford' – in a city of some six hundred square miles – he excitedly imagined a deeper connection; perhaps I looked like Steve because I was related to him?

This personal irony of me, a south Londoner by birth, being introduced to the south London band Japan in the country Japan was paralleled by a larger, more significant irony – one that determined the fate of the band and the musical directions that its members subsequently took. As much as we like to imagine meaning and purpose in all tales of human creativity, sometimes the impetus is accidental, the result of a random twist or turn in the road. The Batt brothers did not choose the name 'Japan' because the country or its culture informed the band's musical direction. On the contrary, they picked it on a whim, precisely because it seemed exotic and unknown. Or its choice reflected their influences, despite that connection being later forgotten or denied. It wasn't even intended as a permanent name, chosen on the eve of that first gig at Karn's brother's wedding in May of 1974 when the band were still only the trio of Karn and the Batt brothers.

'The name? No reason whatsoever,' Sylvian later said. 'We just needed a name because we were about to do our first show, and I came up with the name. I didn't know anything about the East. It was a temporary name because no one particularly liked it, and it stayed. You just get attached to things and think, why bother changing it? So, it stayed.' Karn claimed that the choice for his family wedding gig – which he couldn't recall but imagined the performance 'must have been awful' – was inspired by 'a fascination with the country itself, [but] we planned to use the name only once.'[86]

Jansen would much later remember a connection that rings true: yet again, David Bowie. 'The name was chosen out of innocence. We had no knowledge of Japan at all.' But the name's origin or 'influence might have all come from one of Bowie's lyrics, maybe even Ziggy Stardust': Ziggy was, Bowie sings a minute into that song, 'like some cat from Japan.' Continued Jansen, 'In those days, we listened to Bowie and Roxy Music and things like that, and I think that might have triggered some imagery; I think Bowie had some costumes and things like that and it all just filtered through.' But the brothers' 'actual knowledge' of the country of Japan 'was very little.'[87]

Sylvian and Bowie – both Davids from the same part of South London who changed their surnames as they reached for fame – were equally fascinated with Far East aesthetics. But, likewise, their access to places like Japan was only made possible by their later worldwide stardom – or, in Sylvian's case, his Japanese stardom. For Bowie, 'costumes and things like that' constituted an entire look that was inspired by Japanese fashion and theatre. That look took shape at the dawn of the 1970s as Jones evolved into Bowie-as-Stardust, and it was crucial to his success and to his consequent impact on aspiring musicians like the Batt brothers and their bandmates.

Having studied dance and mime with choreographer Lindsay Kemp (1938-2018), Bowie was soon drawn to Kemp's sources – especially Japan's traditional *kabuki* theatre, with its heavy makeup, dramatic gestures, striking costumes and the cross-gender role-playing of the *onnagata*. The struggle in the West to understand Bowie's Ziggy image and its projection of gender and sexuality – to which he responded with periodic semi-faux confessions of being gay (1972), bisexual (1974) or sort of neither (1976) – was arguably just a failure to understand that Bowie was an *onnagata*. That gender-bending ambiguity and androgyny of costume and makeup was just what Bowie wanted for Ziggy. As fashion historian Helene Thian has noted, it perfectly 'suited Kansai Yamamoto's unisex style' – Yamamoto being the Japanese fashion designer who would design much of the Stardust/Sane stage wardrobe. The facial lightning bolt, to this day the most enduring of Bowie's iconic looks, emerged after *kabuki* actor Bando Tamasaburo shared his makeup skills with Bowie in Tokyo.[88]

If the *kabuki* roots of Ziggy Stardust now seem strikingly obvious, they were largely missed at the time; as one might expect of the 1970s, the image prompted homophobic slurs rather than accusations of Orientalist appropriation. So did the full make-up and brightly coloured hairstyles that Sylvian and his bandmates adopted in homage to Ziggy (as argued above, less to the New York Dolls). By the early 1980s, the Orientalist leanings of Japan the band were too stark to miss, being central to their final album, while new romanticism made bright hair and striking makeup mainstream. But mere years before, as Japan struggled to succeed, their look and their name seemed strange and confusing.

That band name would be dropped and picked up again several times. But four years after the wedding gig, it had become permanent, printed on the cover of their debut album. Amidst the performance and promotion flurry of 1978, the Batt brothers, along with Karn and Barbieri, managed to crash a launch party for Kate Bush's debut, *The Kick Inside*. (Bush, incidentally, had also studied with Lindsay Kemp, dedicating and writing two *Kick Inside* songs about him). A photographer for the Japanese music magazine *Ongaku Senka* happened to be at the party. His editor, captivated by the shots of the dazzlingly dressed and hair-dyed photogenic foursome with the arresting band name, ran them in the next issue – causing 'a frisson of arousal back in Japan' that helped to nudge *Adolescent Sex* into the top 20.[89]

There was more: Simon Napier-Bell, before becoming their manager, had fallen in love with the Far East – a one-week trip to Tokyo in 1972 had turned into a year of travels throughout Japan and Southeast Asia. Napier-Bell was torn between the business that paid his bills and his new love. 'Was it to be the music industry or the Far East?' he mused. 'I was like a happily married man falling for an unsuitable mistress and I did what most men do in that situation – cheated on both.'[90]

Napier-Bell had thus been shuttling between Asia and London for years when he took on the management of Japan. His decision had nothing to do with the band's name and all to do with his conviction that Sylvian was world-star material. Inspired by the originality of the band's look – 'full make-up and pretty clothes' at a time when Londoners were clad 'in black leather and safety pins' – Napier-Bell signed Japan on the assumption that Sylvian had 'received advance warning of a new fashion trend.' He had not, of course (although, arguably, he helped to fulfil the prophecy that his look represented). When Napier-Bell (in his own words) 'launched the group Japan in the UK, they flopped miserably. However, when their records were released in the country whose name they'd adopted, Japan became huge.' This was due to the serendipity of their name and look, but also the fact that Napier-Bell understood Japanese culture and was personally motivated to wed his working life to his passion for 'the Far East' as much as possible. As he later explained: 'Japanese teenagers liked the idea of a group named after their country, and unlike their British counterparts, they didn't like pop stars in grubby punk fashions; they wanted their young men clean and neatly dressed. And if a little makeup was added, well, why not? Like Kabuki theatre, it was part of Japanese culture.'[91]

As much as Napier-Bell grasped the serendipitous irony of glam-looking Japan being a hit in the land of Kabuki, he later tired of Sylvian's commitment to the look, frustrated that the artist did not share his manager's practical view of it as no longer exigent. 'David, as always, was plastered with make-up', recalled Napier-Bell of their 1983 months in Berlin during the recording of his first solo album. 'I could never understand why. He wasn't gay; he wasn't even effeminate. 'Why do you have to wear that bloody stuff?' I asked him. 'It's important', he said, which wasn't much of an answer.'[92]

The two would soon part ways, and Sylvian would soon ease up on the makeup. And despite his insistence five years later that it was 'important', there were signs as early as 1978 of his self-defeating tendency to withdraw just when his chance came to be king. During the band's first trip to the United States, after one of their five gigs there, a local journalist noted that Sylvian's taciturn response to the press seemed more than just tiredness: 'He just looked like he wished he wasn't there.' Band biographer Reynolds later concluded that Sylvian was already bored playing songs from that year's albums, and he was 'beginning to feel trapped in a caricature he had strived to create.' It may have 'gotten him out of Catford and all the way to Hollywood', but Sylvian wanted something more and something different.[93]

If chronic disinterest was indeed Sylvian's state of mind that November in 1978, its context was the publicity circus that was already alienating him from his own youthful ambitions. It was not the location, which happened to be Los Angeles, for LA would prove to be one of three puzzle pieces that, once put together, promised a new way forward. The second was Tokyo, specifically the experience of the Japanese tour of seven shows in March 1979, three of them in that capital city.

Japanese audiences were well-primed. They welcomed English pop acts with notable warmth, if not unbridled enthusiasm; just nine months earlier, Kate Bush had performed on a pair of Japanese TV shows and at the Tokyo Music Festival in the Budokan, helping to boost her first single in Japan, 'Moving', to number one. Meanwhile, Napier-Bell (who had been learning Japanese) had flown out to meet with local A&R men for Victor Records, who licensed the band from Hansa for the Japanese market. He discovered a fan club already flourishing, based solely on photographs of the band. Furthermore, teenage girls were apparently taken by Sylvian's uncanny resemblance to the hero(ine) of a top-selling graphic novel, a beautiful teenage French noblewoman dressed as a man.[94] When *Adolescent Sex* finally saw its Japanese release in the autumn, it charted immediately. Arriving six months later, the band were mobbed everywhere they went by young fans, overwhelmingly female ('massive groupie situation', Barbieri would coyly remember). It was one thing to play the legendary Budokan two nights in a row, quite another to play 13 songs to a 'deafening waterfall of screams' (as Dean remembered) after only ever performing to hostile crowds. Unlike in the UK, the band were wanted in Japan – with a passion. Although Sylvian lamented that their fame prevented them from exploring 'the many faces' of the country, he confessed that the trip was 'a real high' and was imbued with 'a sense of homecoming. I believe I wasn't the only member of the band to feel this sense of belonging.'[95]

In the wake of the Japanese tour, Sylvian composed lyrics to a song that channelled the experience. But being Sylvian, his words to 'Life In Tokyo' perversely reversed that 'sense of belonging' and instead emphasised the band's alienation from the 'sound of distant living' in Tokyo, where 'life can be cruel'. Karn would have penned words of joy, for he loved Tokyo so much that he wept all the way back to London ('Why was I leaving a place where I was so wanted?'). The lyrics might have ended up on a track on their next album, but either Napier-Bell or someone at Hansa had a bright idea: Japan could be big somewhere other than Japan if they recorded with Giorgio Moroder.

Moroder was thus 1979's third puzzle piece. Hansa had a close relationship with the Italian-born German songwriter and producer, whose work with Donna Summer had brought him worldwide fame – most notably with the enormous success of 'I Feel Love'. The impact of that dance hit was immediate, and still today, it is frequently credited with having 'reinvented music.'[96] Bowie and Eno were making *'Heroes'* in Berlin when the song (recorded in Munich) flew up the German charts: 'I have heard the sound of the future', Eno yelled, according to Bowie, running into the studio with the record in hand. Mused Bowie, 'Eno had gone bonkers over it, absolutely bonkers. He said, 'This is it, look no further. This single is going to change the sound of club music for the next 15 years.' Which was more or less right.'[97]

This was also a watershed moment in the development of electronic music, with basic synthesizers suddenly becoming affordable. 'The technological revolution that happened in 1978 was astonishing', Midge Ure later reminisced. Whereas before, 'you had to be a boffin and a billionaire to buy one', now you could 'start recording in your bedroom' even if 'you didn't have a clue.'[98] Within a few years, there were digital samplers available, not just the hefty and costly Fairlight but also more affordable ones like the Synclavier and the E-mu Emulator – which took time to truly master ('the manual's very thick', deadpanned Depeche Mode's Martin Gore in an interview) but could, nonetheless, be of significant use right out of the box. The timing was perfect because punk was at its peak and the punk aesthetic promoted the notion of non-musicians recording and performing. As a result, new bands were being conceived and birthed – Depeche Mode, The Human League, Orchestral Manoeuvres in the Dark, Soft Cell, the reborn Ultravox and scores more – that would transform pop music in the early 1980s.[99]

For Japan, already with a foot in the door, eager to evolve and find a way to burst through, and with a naturally talented synth master in Barbieri, the moment was ideal. The Batts and their bandmates were as struck as anyone by the power of the completely synthesized track behind Summer's voice on 'I Feel Love', just as they were intrigued by Moroder's production on recent albums by bands like Sparks. So, they agreed to fly to LA, where Moroder was working at the time, with Harold Faltermeyer as engineer. The first day, remembered Sylvian, Moroder 'dishes out some old demo from his stack and says, 'Try working with this', and it's like, 'Okay.' It was odd but not unpleasant.' Sylvian replaced the melody and inserted his 'Life In Tokyo' lyrics ('he reinvented the song he was given', noted Barbieri). Karn's basslines were rejected, which left him feeling 'betrayed by the others' and 'very unhappy' with the song (his words). Faltermeyer played the keyboard parts (rather than sequencing them, to the band's surprise). Moroder's 'trademark arpeggiated synthesizer' remained the track's foundation.[100]

'Life In Tokyo' was released a few weeks later, in April 1979, on both sides of the Atlantic, in 7' and 12' formats. Among the 112 singles that *Billboard* reviewed in the third week of June, the magazine highlighted a dozen of them in the 'Pop' category as 'recommended', including 'Life In Tokyo'. But while the song was, not surprisingly, an instant hit in Japan, it failed to chart anywhere else in the world (it would eventually be a minor hit three years later).[101] 'When is David going to write a hit?' moaned the head of Hansa to Napier-Bell, adding that 'we give them £20 a week – that's the problem! Cut off the money, then he'll write a hit!'[102] Within a year, Hansa would drop Japan completely. Meanwhile, the failure of 'Life In Tokyo' in the US lost the band their label there, and it would be several years before any of their records were given American releases.

But the song, something of an under-appreciated gem, was a crucial evolutionary step. Sylvian's vocals still channelled Bowie, Bolan and Ferry, but far less obviously, finding a unique style for the first time. The 'existentialist disaffection' of the lyrics ('Why should I care?') anticipated much of Sylvian's future work. 'It set the ground for *Quiet Life*' – the next Japan album – Sylvian later said. But it arguably set the ground for more than that. It accelerated Japan's success in Japan, while also pointing Sylvian down a path that would draw upon the country's culture but also end the band. Its combination of Germanic synth sounds with Japan's neo-glam theatricality anticipated the new romantic movement, making the band 'a vital piece of the puzzle, whether they liked it or not.' The song suggested that if their previous attempt to use disco and punk to forge a kind of neo-glam art-pop was a problem, then its solution was synth-pop – if they could find the right producer, one who understood their vision and was willing to let them pursue it.[103]

Meanwhile, one spring night in Birmingham, shortly after the release of 'Life In Tokyo', a fledgling Duran Duran were backstage at Barbarella's. They had just played what would be the band's last gig with founding member Stephen Duffy, who would later recall that 'John Taylor was holding a 12' of 'Life In Tokyo' by Japan, and he said to me, 'We've got to sound like this.' I was like, 'Are you crazy? We just went on stage and danced to a drum machine in front of a bunch of punks and didn't get killed. Obviously, this is the way forward.' But that's what John and Nick [Rhodes] wanted at that point, to sound like Japan. I didn't want to make records that sounded like that. I left and went on to make records that sounded a lot worse than 'Life In Tokyo'.'[104]

That autumn of 1979, I returned to school in England and forgot all about Japan – both the band and, to a large extent, the country; I wouldn't be returning there until the next year. Around the New Year, I received a letter from Shoe. He rambled on mostly about my sister. But he also mentioned music, particularly the sophomore album by Yellow Magic Orchestra. That album, he wrote, made him 'proud' (although he thought the cover of 'Day Tripper' was an embarrassment). What did I think? (I had no idea that YMO had put out an album that autumn, and, in fact, it would not be released in the UK for a couple of years.) More exciting was a new album by Japan. On *Quiet Life*, said Shoe, Sylvian had become Bowie, and the band had become Roxy Music – but better. I must have heard it, insisted Shoe. Maybe I even saw 'the Cat brothers' walking around 'Batford'?

ghosts – Journeys To Post-Pop

Side B (1980-84)

5: The Other Side Of Life

'The Other Side Of Life' Japan (1979, 7:26)

As 1980 dawned, I had not, in fact, heard *Quiet Life*. The album was released in Japan, continental Europe and Canada shortly before Christmas but had failed to materialise in British record shops until January. Not that it was in my hands that early. As winter rolled slowly into spring, Japan continued to remain absent from the UK charts. The album was invisible (it had peaked at number 72, unbeknownst to me). Nobody I knew in school had it. The only single at the time, bizarrely, was a cover of Smokey Robinson's 'I Second That Emotion', which was not even on *Quiet Life*, while the album's brilliant title track (a 1979 single in Japan) was relegated to the B-side. The single flopped. The *NME* dismissed the album in a review with the astonishingly offensive title of 'There's A Nasty Nip In The Air.'[105] Despite growing fan bases and critical acclaim in continental Europe and Japan, and even interest in Canada (where *Quiet Life* appeared first), Britain was still catching up and the US was even further behind.

Hansa, in retrospect, failed the band, their efforts at distribution and promotion equally lamentable. They released not one song from the album as a single. In a cruel twist typical of the industry in its toxic heyday, the label used the weak sales of the album as an excuse to drop the band. Then, when the band took off with the help of their next label, Virgin, Hansa cashed in on *Quiet Life* by releasing the singles they should have put out earlier. Piggybacking off Virgin's efforts, Hansa finally squeezed some modest hits from the album.[106]

That was all in the future, but a future that loomed ominously over the band. As 1980 progressed, the third track on *Quiet Life*, 'Despair', must have struck them as a prescient evocation of their situation. Indeed, the whole album seemed apprehensive in mood, as if Japan anticipated that their hard work and vastly improved chops would fall on deaf ears. The band's leap forward in musicianship was stunning, with Karn's 'off-kilter, almost deranged basslines and stabbing saxophone breaks' announcing 'his arrival as a world-class musician.'[107] Jansen's drumming became distinctive and, in the verdict of Martyn Ford (the veteran conductor who worked on the album), 'excellent. He was 19? Good God!'[108] As for

Barbieri, he couldn't play a single instrument when he joined in 1976 – recruited because he was an old friend who had a job (and thus a modest income) and a cheap Woolworth's organ. 'Richard was to be the musical success story in Japan', mused Napier-Bell. The band's manager recalled that he used to have Barbieri round to his flat to try 'to teach him to play the piano. And he struggled and struggled until we got a synth. Then *everything* changed.'[109] That change – Barbieri's new-found skill, confidence, toolkit (he first used sequencers on *Quiet Life*) and even musical philosophy – hugely impacted the album and its sequels. As he himself later reflected: 'It's as if we discovered sophistication, subtlety and nuance overnight.'[110]

Meanwhile, I, a teenage fan-to-be, did not hear *Quiet Life* until the summer of 1980. I still have the cassette tape of the album, a pre-recorded Japanese issue, that I shop-lifted in Tokyo that summer. I confess with shame that, for a couple of Tokyo summers, I took advantage of the fact that it was incredibly easy to lift tapes from record stores there. In a manner typical of criminal behaviour (not that I'm an expert), I started small and then got greedy. At the end of one summer, my stepmother noticed my suitcase – packed in preparation for my return to boarding school – was stuffed with tapes. She stood staring, stunned. To her credit, she said nothing, but the look of confusion and then disappointment on her face spoke volumes. After that, I never lifted another tape. I even took a few of them back to the shops, stealthily reshelving them (but – another embarrassing confession – only the ones I didn't really like and *Quiet Life* I liked).

At the time, I only had the vaguest sense of what the title track of my stolen album was about. Listening to 'Quiet Life' during its first couple of years in the world, when I was still in school, my friend Elvis (he wore glasses like Elvis Costello's; we never called him James) and I concluded the title track was about death – the ultimate anti-climax, the quietest 'life' of all. Our education trained us to over-think every piece of literature we were assigned to read, so we gave Sylvian the courtesy of the same treatment. A few years later, however, when I was at university, I had a breakthrough moment of insight. Sitting in the back of an old Mini Cooper, with Japan playing on the jerry-rigged cassette deck, four of us headed to Stonehenge in the middle of the night. Delirious on cider and LSD, I suddenly saw that 'Quiet Life' was about travelling from the city to the countryside. (It is just as well that visitors can no longer just walk up to the ancient stones; later generations of young men have been spared the hangover we experienced the following dawn, brained-addled and nauseous after three hours of sleep, faces crammed against cold rock, the damp ground and morning dew seeping through to our bones. A quiet life, indeed.)

'Quiet Life', it turns out, is neither about death nor a trip to the country. It is a memo from Sylvian to his bandmates, warning them that the band seem to be 'stranded', that 'the going could get rough' and that he can see coming 'the quiet life again'. Do they not see the signs? he asks them. And after they have moved on, will they think of him? This is the theme of doubt that will blossom in 'Ghosts'. But the catch – where the song is so effective – is that its music offsets the lyrics, seeming to anticipate the end with a certain buoyancy. It is as if Sylvian is saying, be prepared, boys, for *me* ending all this in pursuit of a quieter life – because it is what *I* want.

In fact, the whole of *Quiet Life* could be read as a concept album about failing to find fame – and being relieved by that failure. The sole lyric on 'Despair', sung in French by Sylvian in his newly found quietly crooning baritone, is a plea that 'the artists of the future [*les artistes de demain*]' not be disturbed in their life of 'pleasant despair [*desespoir agréable*]'.[111] The morning-after breakup of 'In Vogue' ('how bitter the morning feels') is a metaphor for the band's potential dissolution (again, 'did nobody warn you, boy?'). In 'Halloween', a divided Cold War-era Berlin evokes possible band divisions ('you're detached and broken'). Originally tagged as the album's title track (until Ridley Scott's movie of the same name came out), 'Alien' questions the inseparability of the band. Singing again to the rest of them, Sylvian asks if being 'one of the boys' is 'all you want to be?' Despite being the embodiment of what was already an industry cliché, *big in Japan* (but there only), Sylvian is already wondering if it was 'all in vain?' After all, 'now that we're all together, we seem so alien'.

The title track and the long, moody closer 'The Other Side Of Life' bracket the album. Sylvian is only 21, yet he is already embracing the theme of nostalgia that will permeate his solo work. Gently reflecting on how 'we've travelled so far now' from the time when 'we were young', he anticipates the band's after-life as 'the other side of life'. Unwittingly or not, he thus foresees his post-pop future, for nostalgia is elemental to post-pop. Post-pop is nostalgic for its pop past, just as Sylvian is here anticipating his future nostalgia for a long-dead Japan.

A minuscule musical moment in 'The Other Side Of Life' also anticipates where Japan and Sylvian are headed. Just before the two-minute mark, the song ends – or at least, it almost does. What seems like the final chord resonates and echoes for a few seconds, with the last note fading, like the distant sound of howling wind, towards silence. That hint of silence remains unrealised as the song then resumes for another five and a half minutes. But this use of space – the tantalising offer of a tiny quiet moment within a composition – is significant. It is not the same as the silence between tracks. As a silence or a hint of one *within* a song, it is thus integral to the song – a moment of nothing that is something. It is an intake of breath, a pause of anticipation.

Pauses within songs are not uncommon in popular music, but in the context of this story, the use of silence is elemental to how pop evolved into post-pop. That is, once silence becomes part of the journey, the destination ahead starts to look more and more like post-pop. Beyond post-pop lies the quiet life.

The understanding of silence as an element in the soundscape, rather than an absence of sound, emerged in the 1960s, as prog rock emerged from psychedelic pop, jazz and classical music – the 'magical confluence of energies' that 'all the cross-influences' produced. One of those influences was John Cage, who 'used silence as much as he used sound.'[112] Indeed, Cage's best-known composition is *4'33'*, a piece of that length comprising nothing but rests. When, in 1952, pianist and experimental composer David Tudor gave the piece its first public performance in a small Woodstock theatre, he closed the keyboard cover and started a stopwatch, quietly lifting the cover after four minutes and 33 seconds. The audience were as unimpressed – as indignant, in fact, and even angry – as subsequent audiences would be. Just as someone at the 1952 Woodstock concert suggested the locals 'run these people out of town', so did members of a 2004 BBC Symphony Orchestra audience feel insulted by musicians who apparently thought the audience were 'stupid' enough 'to fall for' such a 'hoax'. Cage had mixed feelings about the regularity with which people missed the point of the piece. But miss it, they did. The point is not that there was no music to which the concert hall audience could listen (a book on the piece is aptly titled *No Such Thing As Silence*); Cage himself stressed that *4'33'* framed incidental noises, making it 'simply an act of listening.'[113] The point is that silence is a relative quality. Consequently, silence enhances the experience of listening to the sounds that are present, before, after or incidental to the pause in music – be it Cage's song-length pause or the micro-pause in 'The Other Side Of Life'.

Scientists have recently researched how the brain processes music so as to study impaired processing and thus better understand conditions like dementia. Their studies reveal that electrical neural signals of prediction and anticipation are activated during the pauses in music. Our brains don't rest when the music stops. On the contrary, our imaginations are stimulated and our cognitive predicting capabilities are activated, along with the auditory processing parts of our brains. 'Musicians have passed down the importance of rests from generation to generation', remarked Pacific Symphony concertmaster Dennis Kim, in response to these EEG (electroencephalogram) studies. In other words, musicians have always known that 'at times, the silences in the piece are more powerful than the actual music.'[114]

Paul Simon, for example, remarked not long ago that he tries 'to leave a space after a difficult line – either silence or a lyrical cliché that gives the ear a chance to 'catch up' with the song.'[115] Another musician who has pondered and explored the quiet life within compositions – and one who brings us closer, as a direct influence, to Sylvian and his bandmates – is Eno. Like Simon, Eno has the listener in mind, having learned that 'the listener wants much less than the creator. When you're creating something, it's very easy to get into a nervous state and think, 'Oh God, here's a whole bar where nothing happens', and try to get more stuff in. But as a listener, you're quite happy with these open spaces.'[116]

Listening to the first two Japan albums, it is hard to imagine their creators grasping why listeners might have wanted spaces within songs or what was meant by a comment such as 'Every record should be compared to silence.' The Blue Nile's Paul Buchanan once said that, adding, 'Silence is perfect, what are you going to put on it?'[117] An appreciation for such a perspective was, for the boys in Japan, just around the corner, as hinted at in 'The Other Side Of Life'. One could hardly have predicted in 1980 that Barbieri was destined to earn a sterling reputation as 'a pioneering synth-wizard', with a rich post-Japan catalogue ranging from classic Porcupine Tree albums to experimental, ambient solo projects. And yet, the signs were there by the time of *Quiet Life*. By then, Barbieri had realised that rather than squeezing a hundred notes into ten seconds, as he put it decades later, he would 'prefer to play one note that lasts ten seconds ... that does something interesting in context with the track or in isolation. It's just my instinct and not dissimilar in approach to artists like Eno, Harold Budd, Talk Talk, etc., who play with space and let the sounds 'breathe'.'[118]

Shoe had been right: Bowie and Roxy were all over *Quiet Life*. Japan had wanted the album's producer to be Ken Scott (who had produced Bowie's

Ziggy-era albums), Chris Thomas (who had produced several Roxy Music albums) or John Punter (who had co-produced Roxy's *Country Life* and worked on one of Ferry's solo albums). They landed Punter, who would produce both *Quiet Life* and its sequel and tour with the band – to ensure their live sound came as close as possible to what he helped them achieve in the studio. Punter brought in another Ferry veteran, Ann O'Dell, to arrange the strings on 'In Vogue' and 'The Other Side Of Life' (she had done the same work for the Punter-produced Ferry solo albums, and she would later muse that 'there was more to David's songs than Bryan's songs'). Nobody remembers why the Ford-conducted 20-piece orchestra was added to no more than two tracks ('just for contrast, I suppose', guessed Punter himself), but they added a 'magnificence' and a 'maturity' to the band's sound, with the interplay between band and orchestra in the album's closing minutes particularly gripping. Those two adjectives are by Reynolds, but Dean (this was the last full Japan album on which he would play guitar) put it more prosaically: 'It was a rush. It kind of gives you a stiffy. You had no idea what it would sound like, and then suddenly, there was this lushness flooding through all this music you've been working on.'[119]

Just as other bands would soon ape Japan (we'll return to Duran Duran in a moment, for example), so did *Quiet Life* seem to wear its influences on its sleeves. Although, in retrospect, the album shines with originality, at the time, its influences overshadowed its evaluation. In Napier-Bell's view, Sylvian 'went from Marc Bolan/David Bowie to Bryan Ferry overnight; Hansa Records went completely berserk.' According to Punter, the band 'wouldn't exactly say' what piece of which Bowie or Roxy track they wanted to emulate; 'well,' he added, 'maybe they would...' So, does the rhythm on 'Alien' echo the opening of Roxy Music's 'Out Of The Blue' (as Reynolds suggests)?[120]

It certainly does to my ears. And I cannot hear that very first word of the first track – 'boys!' – repeated as a leitmotif through much of the song and even the album, without hearing Bowie's big hit single of the previous spring, 'Boys Keep Swinging'. For some later critics, the new Sylvian croon wasn't Ferry at all but 'equal parts Scott Walker and *Low*-era Bowie.'[121] Sylvian even now looked like Bowie, with his dyed-blonde hair and blue suits hanging off his too-skinny body; not the Bowie of 1979, but the Bowie of a few years later, of *Let's Dance*. Was Bowie's look indebted specifically to Sylvian? Perhaps. Sylvian certainly arrived at it before his idol did. But the look was not unique to them. Bowie's look was arguably new romantic Lite, and thus indebted to all those who created that music-

and-fashion moment that swept London in 1980-83 – Sylvian included, more so than he himself wished and seemed to recognise at the time.

The irony was that while Japan had now entered a three-year, three-album creative chase after the experimentalism of *Low*, in those same years, Bowie pivoted away from the early Berlin albums to the pop-rock of *Scary Monsters* and then the post-disco pop of *Let's Dance*. Not that the larger story was so straightforward. By the end of 1980, the field of new synth-pop bands who were using the new affordable synthesizers to process the influences of Kraftwerk and Berlin-Bowie through disco-meets-punk filters was becoming crowded. Where would we put our money if we could go back in time to that moment and bet on which artists would continue to push away from pop into post-pop? (The contrivance is absurd, as how could we predict what was to happen without anticipating post-pop? Well, indulge me.)

We would want to acknowledge the distinction being made around 1980 by the likes of Stevo (Steve Pearce, then the teenage creator of the Some Bizzare [sic] label) and Daniel Miller (creator of the Mute label, discoverer and early producer of Depeche Mode) between the guitar-and-synth bands that would later be dubbed new romantic and the all-electronic bands that they dubbed Futurist.[122] We might have bet on Japan, noting their expulsion of guitarist Dean during the recording of their next album in the autumn of 1980. But I doubt we could have foreseen their struggle – both musical and in terms of their image – with the amorphous cultural movements of Futurism and new romanticism, let alone Sylvian's solo direction. Other obvious candidates would have been Gary Numan, the newly resurrected Ultravox and former member of that band, John Foxx – who mixed the ingredients of dystopian synthpop to stunning effect on 1980's *Metamatic*.[123] Visage would qualify, and perhaps also B-Movie and Blancmange; German acts such as electronic pioneers Kraftwerk (so-called Krautrock) and newer artists like DAF; and early electronic bands from Japan (the country), such as Yellow Magic Orchestra. Depeche Mode might also be considered, as Dave Gahan joined that year (recruited after the others heard him sing "Heroes") and their first single was recorded in December (released early in 1981).[124]

Kate Bush's discovery of the Fairlight, introduced to her by Peter Gabriel towards the end of recording sessions for her 1980 album *Never For Ever* – resulting in some experimental elements on that album – might have made her a candidate. The album is certainly 'startling, strange and original.' But only in retrospect does *Never For Ever* mark the birth of the artist we now know as a post-pop pioneer. Surely nobody predicted in 1980 how fast and far Bush would lean into sampled-sound experimental art-pop on the sequel (1982's *The Dreaming*, to which we shall return). Vince Clarke, having left Depeche Mode after one album, acquired a pricey Fairlight, inspiring former bandmate Gore to spell out 'Fairlight' in duct tape on the back of his far cheaper synthesizer for the *Top Of The Pops* performance of 'Get The Balance Right' (a mix of sour grapes and Basildon humour?).[125]

In the end, however, I suspect I would have bet that post-pop's founders would be Orchestral Manoeuvres in the Dark (OMD), based on their rapid shift from relatively simple synthpop to dark, experimental pop within a matter of months in 1980. Their first two albums came out that year – the eponymous debut in February and *Organisation* in October, both in the UK and Europe only. They revealed a tug-of-war between two connected genres: pure synthpop, almost as plink-plonky as the earliest Depeche Mode, exemplified by hit singles like 'Electricity' and 'Enola Gay'; and a kind of proto-post-pop, in which Kraftwerk-inspired experimentalism threatened to sink pop beneath moody musical noise (as suggested on 'The Misunderstanding' and 'Stanlow', which bracket side two of *Organisation*). A remark by Paul Humphreys, who founded OMD with Andy McCluskey, now oft quoted (it is even highlighted on the band's Wikipedia entry), memorably captures that tug-of-war: 'Musically, we were pushing boundaries as far as we could. At one Virgin meeting, the head of A&R asked us, 'Come on guys, are you Stockhausen or ABBA?' Andy and I said together, 'Can't we be both?"[126]

How to make post-pop? Take ABBA and add Stockhausen until you can hardly taste the ABBA: a serviceable, if simplistic, recipe. And how was OMD's cooking? Their two 1980 albums were not released in the US, and if you only know OMD from their US hit albums – the mid-1980s pair of *Crush* and *The Pacific Age* – you will already know that, as Humphreys later put it, 'We got scared and thought, 'Let's abandon Stockhausen and become ABBA for a bit.'"[127] Had I bet on OMD, would I, therefore, have lost my shirt? In a later chapter, we shall return to the topic – and to artists like Numan and Foxx, to Kate Bush in particular, as well as to influences like Karlheinz Stockhausen – and find out.

6: Swing

'Swing' Japan (1980, 6:23)

In the wake of Japan's messy divorce from Hansa, Napier-Bell found the band a new label home at Virgin. The marriage would be brief but happy, as new signings Japan and The Human League thereby saved the label from bankruptcy. Furthermore, the majority-female staff at the label – obliged to prove their worth in a male-dominated industry – were skilled and hard-working promoters of the band. Both Virgin and Japan (and, for that matter, The Human League) also benefited from lucky timing, as 1980 was the year that a new pop culture wave began to build.[128]

Right after their summer signing, Virgin rushed Japan into the studio. As *Quiet Life* had been such a positive experience, Japan returned to AIR – the studio above London's Piccadilly Circus – with John Punter again behind the mixing desk. But Sylvian's increasing confidence with all aspects of the creative process – from songwriting and singing to arranging and producing – created friction in the studio. 'There were disputes between Dave and myself', Karn later noted, claiming that Sylvian spent three days trying to record one word of 'Methods Of Dance' to his satisfaction. The singer admitted that he caused the problems – 'I tend to be too much of a perfectionist.' But that was small consolation to Rob Dean, who was excluded from most of the sessions without explanation (he would leave the band in 1981). Dean's guitar ended up on a few tracks, but, in his words, 'the band were moving towards electronic music, with YMO, Eno and Kraftwerk being the strongest influences.'[129]

Coming only nine months after *Quiet Life*, the DNA of *Gentleman Take Polaroids* was half that of its predecessor and half something new and alien. As Dean recalled, it 'would turn out to be a rather cold, albeit more sophisticated, album.' If *Quiet Life* was 'a turning point' (in Karn's judgement), *Gentleman Take Polaroids* was 'the maturing.' Decades later, it would be lauded as a 'seminal post-punk album.' Despite the often-fraught studio atmosphere and the move to another London studio to break that tension, the album was created and recorded in three months, quickly mixed and mastered, and released in November to catch the UK's Christmas buying market. It reached number 45, merely respectable. But, as the band's biographer noted, the album 'was hugely influential' and set them up 'for their one true masterpiece, *Tin Drum*.'[130] It showcased a style that achieved cheese-free balladry, sax-propelled Roxy-ness and

Orientalist musical tourism with coherence and originality. 'Filtering rain-swept romanticism through layers of lush Barbieri synths and that insanely brilliant rhythm section, Japan were the thinking person's pop visionaries, more Leonard Cohen than Duran Duran.'[131]

The album's title track was released as a single in October 1980, a month before its parent album dropped. With its complex bass and keyboard work combined with Sylvian's melodic croon, it revealed a band rapidly but not dramatically evolving – 'a clever musical bridge' between their third and fourth albums. The opening line – 'there's a girl about town, I'd like to know' – even reminded listeners from the very start that the horny teenagers of the first two albums had only just entered their 20s. But again, the goal was urban romance rather than suburban sex; gentlemen don't just take polaroids, 'they fall in love'. Although 'Gentlemen Take Polaroids' only reached number 60, it was their first single to chart in Britain.

Moreover, the album's release revealed the song to be both the eponymous opening track and the prelude to the most stunningly artful song that the band had yet created. On 'Swing', the ingredients with which Japan had been experimenting for the past year or two were mixed to perfection. From Jansen's drum patterning to Karn's bass groove to the layers of synth, guitar, saxophone and Sylvian's croon, the song is a masterclass in art pop restraint. 'I think 'Swing's epic structure is well-honed and entirely successful', Dean later said. Punter agreed: 'To this day, I see 'Swing' as the zenith of Japan's recorded career.'[132] Those first two of the album's eight songs are, indeed – 'to this day' – 13 and a half riveting minutes.

So, how did *Gentlemen Take Polaroids* – and, therefore, the still-evolving Japan, as of the end of 1980 – fit into the larger scene? The music press was as keen as ever to pigeonhole both album and band. For some reviewers, the Roxy Music connections, however superficial, made it easy. Japan had been widely compared to Roxy Music since *Quiet Life* came out at the start of the year, partly because both that album and *Polaroids* were produced by Punter (who, as mentioned earlier, had produced Roxy's *Country Life* and Ferry's *Let's Stick Together*). Roxy's latest, the smooth, moody, poppy *Flesh And Blood*, was the UK's number-one album for much of August. The lazy verdict in *NME*, for example, was, therefore: 'Japan's current sound is one long diffuse outtake from Roxy Music's *Flesh And Blood*.' *Melody Maker*'s variation on the theme was, 'If Roxy Music were not alive and well, it would be necessary to invent them, and Japan might fill that vacuum. But Roxy are still with us...'[133]

One suspects that these critics, tasked with wading through piles of new vinyl in an era when the music papers were published weekly, jumped to the cover version of 'Ain't That Peculiar' on side two of *Gentlemen Take Polaroids*, latching onto its imitation of the lounge-lizard persona of Ferry's solo albums. To Japan's credit, their cover sounds nothing like Smokey Robinson (who co-wrote the song) or Marvin Gaye (who had a hit with it in 1965). It is, however, very Ferry. Barbieri later called it 'the strangest track on the album', which I take to be a compliment (after all, weren't Japan aiming for strange?). Still, to my mind, 'Ain't That Peculiar' is a distraction that would have served the band better as a B-side, replaced on the album by 'Some Kind Of Fool' – which was left off at Sylvian's insistence, to the irritation of Punter and Napier-Bell. Remarked the latter, 'David was afraid of producing anything that sounded crassly commercial. So, we all had to learn – if something sounded like a hit, for God's sake, say nothing or perhaps tell him it sounded a bit 'obscure' or 'difficult'.' 'Some Kind Of Fool', recently and rightfully called a 'gorgeous, lilting torch song', might well have been a hit.[134]

Dropped at the last minute, 'Some Kind Of Fool' was replaced by 'Burning Bridges', which sounds like an updated version, with vocals, of a missing track from side two of Bowie's *'Heroes'*. It would be easy to dismiss the track as 'shamelessly derivative' (a phrase used in *NME* to bang on about Japan's Roxy influences), but I think that would miss the point. 'Burning Bridges' is a fascinating manifestation of Sylvian and his bandmates working through their influences to achieve something different – not a detour, but a necessary step on the journey through pop's various forms to an as-yet-unknown destination. Similarly, 'Swing' succeeded in 'out-Roxying Roxy Music on a track that somehow managed to advance many of the ideas Bryan Ferry toyed with on the albums *Stranded* and *Manifesto*' (as Sylvian biographer Martin Power put it).[135]

It is hard to convey now, over four decades on, how extraordinarily *new* the *Polaroids* album sounded in 1980. Not in the obvious in-your-face way that punk had sounded new, nor in the obviously clever way that stark synthpop, showcased on the two 1980 OMD albums, seemed new. Rather, this was music with its influences made transparent – yes, unabashedly Bowie and Ferry – but resulting in something subtly and artfully novel.

If side one of *Gentlemen Take Polaroids* reflected where Japan had come from, side two suggested different directions in which they might be moving. The first of the vinyl and cassette side's four tracks was the seven-minute 'Methods Of Dance', whose melodies and rhythms gave the impression of a step forward from side one. In retrospect, the song seems like classic Japan, largely because it anticipates the next album, *Tin Drum*, particularly in its reflection of Yellow Magic Orchestra influence (Dean specifically cited their 1979 *Solid State Survivor* album). Here was another manifestation of that irony of the band's name – chosen on a whim, and with Bowie, not the country, in mind, but leading to an abiding interest in East Asian music and culture. Japan and YMO were, by all accounts, mutual fans, and it was just a matter of time before they formally met. As it happened, YMO's Ryuichi Sakamoto was in London that summer, recording his solo album *B-2 Unit* in AIR studios. A friendship was struck up immediately, one that would last a lifetime, especially between Sylvian and Sakamoto.[136]

The influence of Sakamoto and his band was thus even more direct on side two's closing track, 'Taking Islands In Africa', which Sylvian composed in AIR with Sakamoto. The Japanese musician would only later become fluent in English, but the language barrier worked in their favour, said Sylvian: 'All the communication that really worked was musical.' 'Taking Islands', Barbieri recently confessed, 'isn't a Japan track for me. It just doesn't sound like Japan.' Karn later complained that this first Sakamoto-Sylvian composition was 'boring' and 'mismatched the rest of the album' (he claimed 'Steve even fell asleep while playing it in concert one night'). This may have been sour grapes, especially in retrospect (both Karn's and ours); the track anticipated Sylvian's compulsive yearning to work less with his old schoolmates in the band and more with anyone who might help take him creatively in new – primarily avant-garde, or 'obscure' and 'difficult' – directions. It is also easy to see the band beginning to divide along creative lines, with Sylvian resisting the collective desire of his bandmates, their manager and their producer for a pop breakthrough. Karn seemed to suggest as much when he judged *Gentlemen Take Polaroids* for having 'a slight loss of focus.'[137]

But I would argue that the loss of focus was restricted to side two of the record and that the conflicting desire for pop success vs. creative experimentation was more complex than a Sylvian vs. the rest divide. For example, the pre-album release of the 'Gentlemen' single featured two instrumental B-sides that were recorded during the album's sessions but left off it: 'The Experience Of Swimming' was the B-side in the UK; 'The Width Of A Room' was used for the German release; while both were included on a British EP release.[138] Neither were pop pieces. And while it is tempting to hear them as previews of Sylvian's later experimentation with ambient, sampled and electronic sounds, they were, in fact, written respectively by Barbieri and Dean. Indeed, it is not hard to trace a solid line of creativity from 'Swimming' through four decades of Barbieri's solo and collaborative work to his 2021 album, *Under A Spell* (to which we shall return later).

And then there is 'Nightporter', somewhat buried on side two between 'Ain't That Peculiar' and 'Taking Islands In Africa'. A seven-minute piano-based ballad, it is unlike any other track on the album, tending to divide critics and fans (but, from the very start, one of my favourite Japan songs). Its inspirations and references make it art pop. The relatively simple arpeggiated piano chords that underpin the entire piece were crafted by Sylvian (played by him and Barbieri in tandem) as a transparent nod to the French composer Erik Satie (1866-1925); 'I was influenced an awful lot by Satie', said Sylvian, later confessing to having 'milked him dry after 'Nightporter'.'[139] The title referenced the 1974 Italian film *The Night Porter*, a Nazisploitation drama about a sadomasochistic relationship between characters played by Dirk Bogarde and Charlotte Rampling.[140] But the song is merely moody where the film is disturbing; one is unpleasant to watch, the other soothing to listen to – especially with the light orchestration that builds to a gentle climax, lending the song a low-saccharine, pop-ballad feel.

As soon as *Tin Drum* came out, 'Nightporter' started to sound like an anticipation of 'Ghosts'. Sure enough, as both Hansa and Virgin sought to capitalise on the band's impending breakup in the autumn of 1982, 'Nightporter' was released as a single (lightly remixed by *Tin Drum* producer Steve Nye). It became a modest yet unlikely hit, peaking at number 13 in Ireland and at number 29 in the UK at the end of November, a couple of weeks before the band's farewell concert in Nagoya (Japan). It surely would have fared worse without 'Ghosts' to pave the way earlier in the year – ironically, considering that 'Nightporter' is far closer to conventional pop than 'Ghosts'.

One other incident complicates the impression that it was only Sylvian trying to 'pull away from 'muzak'' as he said at the time. According to Karn, he and Barbieri had been approached by a band they'd never heard of called Duran Duran via 'a cassette that arrived in the mail.' The tape came with a request that they produce the song planned as the band's first single, 'Girls On Film'. They declined on the grounds that it was 'a bit too poppy for [their] liking.' Not long after that, Japan found themselves across the hall at AIR studios from Duran Duran, who were there to record their debut album. Duran Duran had seen Japan play in their home city of

Birmingham, and they were big fans. Tellingly, Japan were less impressed, dismissing the newcomers' pop aesthetic as 'terrible.' Even more tellingly, when one of them told Barbieri that 'we'll be bigger than you because we want it more', nobody apparently cared enough to disagree.[141]

Clearly, then, the dilemma over whether to pursue pop success or nurture a more overtly obscure creativity was one that challenged the whole band, not just their singer. By the end of 1980, as reflected in the band's evolution towards and into *Gentlemen Take Polaroids*, even Sylvian had not internalised that dilemma to a degree that would destroy the band.

Yet, Karn's reference to Duran Duran would prove to be an unwitting anticipation of a fork in the road, taking the two bands in dramatically different directions. In 1980, Japan could decline to produce a song by an unknown band. In 1981 and 1982, they would face an uphill battle to resist being associated and compared to that band. In 1983, Duran Duran would become one of the biggest acts in the world (and *the* biggest British band), reducing Japan to a kind of cult precursor to the deified fivesome from Birmingham.

The Japan-Duran Duran connection took two forms. One was direct. Just as he was taking up the bass, John (born Nigel) Taylor saw Japan live in 1978, flogged their records ('Oh, I loved *Obscure Alternatives*!') and was inspired to think of creating a band that fused punk with funk. He saw what the critics didn't, that the boys in Japan instinctively grasped how those two genres could be reduced to their essences of attitude and sound, then built back up together into something original.[142] As the Birmingham band lagged in time slightly behind the Catford boys (making their debut in AIR as Japan made their fourth album), they were able to mix Kraftwerk, Roxy and Chic with both 1978-Japan and *Quiet Life*-Japan. That list of influences varies from interview to interview, but Japan is almost always present, and the end claim is always the same. For example, Roger Taylor (Duran's three Taylors are unrelated): 'We had all these various influences that we were pulling on, from Japan and Roxy to Chic and the Sex Pistols. When it was all combined, it created this force that was totally unique.'[143] Sometimes, that work of combining was quite transparent; if you know Duran Duran's back catalogue better than Japan's, the phased helicopter sound that opens 'Quiet Life' will be familiar – it was borrowed for the start of 'Planet Earth'.[144]

The other form of Japan-Duran connection was indirect, being the nexus of common teenage obsessions, most notably Bowie and Roxy Music. Taylor and Rhodes first bonded over their idolisation of the 1972 *Top Of*

The Pops appearances by Bowie and Roxy that so impacted Karn and the Batt brothers. As drummer Andy Taylor would later declare, 'We were the children of Bowie.'[145] The story, of course, was a larger one and not merely restricted to the world of popular music. New romanticism was less a genre of pop music than a pop culture phenomenon, originating at the turn of the decade as a tiny party scene in London, which then set off a tsunami in the early 1980s, drawing Japan into its pull. Confusingly, Japan seemed to be a cause of that tidal wave, partly through their ties of influence to Duran Duran. New romantics idolised music, fashion and pop art – all things that mattered with increasing urgency to Sylvian and his bandmates – and Japan and Duran Duran seemed to be making the right kind of music and fashion. And yet, from 1980 through 1982, new romanticism seemed to be taking popular culture in a direction that held little appeal for Japan – all of them, not just Sylvian. The band's dissolution and a public retreat were the only ways to get off that highway and pursue different journeys.

In which case, was the new romantic movement, created to a small degree by Japan, the cause of their demise?

The surviving veterans of the dawn and heyday of the new romantic scene in London differ on which of its elements was most important, although the argument that there were three – 'fashion, music and a base of operations' – is persuasive. Moreover, it was the fusion of those elements that underpinned new romanticism as a pop cultural and musical movement, combined with – perhaps counter-intuitively – the denial by its most visible protagonists that they had anything to do with it. In other words, the new romantic story was one of hybridity and its discontents.[146]

Taken in a loose chronological order, the first of those elements was a new embrace of fashion, conceived by a group of young London clubgoers in reaction to punk – whose look had, by 1979, become almost conventional. As the *Daily Mirror* commented in March 1980, the new youth fashionistas, still without press consensus on what to call them, 'make the punks look normal.'[147] The punk look, so shocking just a couple of years earlier, was now just 'easy fashion' – as Adam Ant put it in his 1981 number-one hit 'Stand And Deliver' – the 'clumsy boots, peek-a-boo roots' of 'a scruff', of which the likes of Adam Ant were 'so sick'.[148] 'I spend my cash on looking flash and grabbing your attention' perfectly summed up the fashion ethos of this post-punk (yes, post-punk more than anti-punk), neo-glam, retro-futuristic generation. The aim was not to shock but to dazzle. Everything from hair and makeup to footwear and home-bespoke clothing – a modernist mishmash of 18th-century frills and 1920s cabaret – was carefully chosen, customised and applied.[149]

Requiring a place to meet and be seen, where their look could dominate the room, the future new romantics began gathering on Tuesday nights, at first beneath a Soho brothel but then at Covent Garden's Blitz wine war (hence their early moniker, the Blitz Kids). The club was a safe space for those wishing to flaunt or defy the norms of gender and sexual orientation, and its fashion aesthetics reflected that fact – one that was of crucial importance to the club regulars (by most accounts, a majority) who came from the working-class, socially conservative neighbourhoods of London's Green Belt. At Blitz, the faithful convened to preen and seduce, drink and dance. The success of the scene soon made it a movement and it jumped from Tuesday nights to colonise the rest of the week, likewise spreading to other venues. London examples were Club for Heroes (as in *'Heroes'*) and Le Kilt. There were also satellite new romantic scenes in northern English cities (where it was, for a short while, called 'Futurism'), such as Leeds (birthing Soft Cell), Sheffield (The Human League), Manchester and Birmingham – whose Barbarellas club inspired five ambitious teenagers from the city's suburbs to call their new band Duran Duran.

The high-volume soundtrack was a carefully curated selection of synthpop, preferably from the continent (like Kraftwerk and Telex) or further abroad (Yellow Magic Orchestra), mixed with retro-futurist hits (Grace Jones' 'La Vie En Rose' and Queen's 'Flash Gordon'), and the latest efforts by British bands to create something new out of glam, punk and disco (The Human League and early Ultravox).

Above all, revered as icons of fashion and worshipped as gods of sound were David Bowie and Roxy Music. A Bowie night had been the Soho genesis of the club ('Fame, fame, fame – what's your name?' asked the flyer). And at Blitz, Bowie's catalogue covered – indeed, inspired – all the bases, from the glam of Ziggy to the disco of 'Fame' to the Euro-synth gloom of the flip sides of *'Heroes'* and *Low* ('Warszawa' was a favourite). The fact that Bowie's Berlin Trilogy of albums were co-created by Roxy refugee Eno added an extra layer of appeal, as the Eno-era art-pop albums of Ferry's band were especially venerated.

But what made the new romantic scene something of lasting cultural significance was not the music played over the Blitz sound system but the music that the scene produced, with the club serving as fertile ground for a 'scenius' (Eno's amalgamation of 'scene' and 'genius', a concept we shall revisit in a later chapter). The cloakroom attendant was George O'Dowd; he and his friend and Blitz regular Peter Robinson showcased the androgynous beauty look, and they were destined for international fame as new romantic pop stars Boy George and Marilyn, respectively. Another group of regulars from modest backgrounds – from the rough council estates of the Angel, no less – used their musical ambitions to start playing live music at Blitz. They soon had a name, Spandau Ballet, and became the house band. Meanwhile, the club's founder and DJ, Rusty Egan, formed a band of his own with the bouncer Steve Strange.

As gatekeeper, the influence of Strange (born John Harrington, 1959-2015) on the scene's fashion standards was sizeable; he would deny admission to VIPs (Mick Jagger's rejection became famous) but let in anyone who looked convincingly like Queen Elizabeth (the original, not the one then on the throne) or Robin Hood or a spaceman (Gary Numan's look of choice). But Strange's musical influence was significant, too. Although his band with Egan, Visage, did not have lasting success, its biggest hit, 'Fade To Grey', was a top ten hit in ten countries in the autumn of 1980.[150] Two of the band's other members, Midge Ure and Billie Currie, would also help remake Ultravox into one of the most successful synthpop bands of the early 1980s. Furthermore, the sound that Visage and Spandau Ballet were forging at the turn of the decade – later characterised as a kind of European Dance Music, with a Bowie/Ferry croon laid over 'the jagged edges of punk smoothed down by soaring synths [and] four-on-the-floor disco rhythms' – was elemental to the new romantic sound that would storm the world.[151]

An interlocking trio of developments allowed new romanticism to build from a wave washing over London's musical scene to a global cultural surge. One was the jump by the best-looking and most eye-catching musicians – labelled new romantic whether they liked it or not – from the music press to the British tabloids to the mainstream press, first in the UK and then all over the world. Another was the advent of MTV, propelled by the spread of cable television and the increasing affordability of videorecorders. With their emphasis on visual image and the need for a flashy video to run on *Top Of The Pops* when the band were touring too far away to appear in person, British New Rom bands had content for MTV before most US acts developed the habit (lending irony to that famous Duran Duran kiss-off line at the start of 'Planet Earth': 'like some new romantic looking for the TV sound').

The third was the Second British Invasion: the swamping of the US charts by UK bands, starting in the summer of 1982; by 1983, a third of

US record sales were by British acts, headed by Duran Duran. In March of that year, Duranies Nick Rhodes and Simon Le Bon co-hosted an hour of MTV. Prior to premiering the new video for 'Save A Prayer', they played videos by David Bowie, Kate Bush and Japan.[152] And in November, Boy George, who had been checking coats at the Blitz just a few years earlier, was on the cover of *Rolling Stone*. The special issue on the invasion was titled 'England Swings'. The phrase might have been a reference to a song from a band that, three years earlier, had helped start the movement that would change the course of pop history, even though, by then, that band had broken up and missed the trans-Atlantic assault boat.[153]

The multiple waves of the Second British Invasion flooded the US charts for years; for the middle half of 1985, for example, roughly 80% of the number one and top ten hits were by British acts. In the late 1980s, both American metal bands and global superstars like Prince, Madonna and Michael Jackson deployed music videos more effectively than British Invasion pioneers, gradually reclaiming the charts. By this point, the new romantic label had become defined by the Invasion and thereby rendered meaningless. The first wave, of course, had been headed by former Blitz Kids like The Human League, Culture Club and Spandau Ballet, as well as bands from various parts of England 'that had started off in small clubs alongside Duran Duran – The Cure, Depeche Mode, Psychedelic Furs, Echo & the Bunnymen – [and] would amass large, enduring American fan bases.'[154] But most of the British acts with huge mid-1980s hit albums in the US – such as Genesis and Dire Straits – had no new romantic origins or associations at all. Had Japan not missed the boat, they may well have evolved into a band that were big in America, falling halfway in between those with undeniable new romantic origins and those that had persevered since the 1970s.

If the Blitz scene seems to echo Japan in numerous ways – from the carefully applied makeup and big hair to the worship of Bowie and Roxy to the germination of a new kind of Europop – that is because it did. The music press made the connection immediately. 'I heard it said', Karn later remarked, that 'we all frequented the Blitz regularly.' In fact, Karn insisted, that was surely 'a case of mistaken identity in an environment comprising of new romantics.' He recalled being taken to the club once, wanting to leave as soon as possible and the future Boy George maliciously throwing a coat at a departing customer, spitting, 'Keep your hair on, you big poof!' and 'I'll show the lot of you one day.'[155]

'The new romantic era', Karn repeated, 'never had anything to do with us.' That was just the press using 'the slender threads of fashion' to tie Japan together with the likes of Adam and the Ants, Orchestral Manoeuvres in the Dark and Spandau Ballet. Sylvian concurred: 'We genuinely did not feel a part of any movement or genre. We were a very self-contained group of people, socially.'[156] That mature assessment echoes what Sylvian said back in the day, complaining that 'I don't like to be associated with them' – a denial of attachment to new romanticism that was frequently aired in the press as part of his increasingly infamous standoffish public persona. 'Their attitudes are so very different. For them, fancy dress is a costume, but ours is a way of life. We look and dress this way every day.'[157] In the short run, such supercilious declarations merely gave the impression that Sylvian was staying in character, for he refused to ever appear anywhere without his trademark glum-glam look: full hair and makeup over a studiously bored facial expression.

In the long run, Sylvian was willing to distance himself from new romanticism and everything that it represented by throwing the baby out with the bathwater. After all, Duran Duran objected to being 'put into a category – hence the remark in 'Planet Earth'', keyboardist Nick Rhodes has said of the media labelling them 'as first Futurists and then later new romantics.' But – in strong contrast to the Sylvian and Japan attitude – 'that worked both ways for us', admitted Rhodes. 'We saw it as an opportunity because people were writing about us.'[158] Japan, Napier-Bell later mused, 'kind of benefited from the whole new romantic thing, even though they had nothing to do with it.' Japan were both a huge influence on new romanticism, as well as exemplars of its look and sound, just preceding the Blitz scene.

As Napier-Bell himself noted, 'Eventually, they became the most influential group, as Duran Duran stole their hairstyles and Gary Numan stole David's voice.' As Japan's manager, Napier-Bell can be forgiven for seeing things in proprietorial terms. After all, by the time Duran Duran's global smash *Rio* came out, Japan had fulfilled the 'Ghosts' prophecy and imploded. 'In hindsight,' noted Annie Zaleski, '*Rio* feels like a passing of the torch to a band fully ready to continue the creative work of their heroes.' And Napier-Bell, with no apparent hard feelings, had to hand it to the band: having all 'copied David's looks, so you had five David look-alikes,' Duran Duran then 'very sensibly went off, and instead of making esoteric Japan music, they recorded good, old-fashioned four-to-the-floor disco music. So, in the end, they got the hits with the Japan look.'[159]

If Napier-Bell could shake off that cruel irony (he soon moved on to manage Wham!), it would be harder for ex-Japan members like Karn who did not go on to enjoy solo success similar to Sylvian's. If Sylvian's mid-1980s career was something of a spectral presence for his former bandmates, they were surely haunted even more by the ghosts of new romanticism as it exploded into a massively lucrative global phenomenon.

Although Sylvian, Karn and their bandmates had shunned new romanticism, protesting all association with the movement that they had unwittingly helped to create, they were still seen as rivals by the English bands nipping at their heels. It was one thing when Japan's singles were hovering outside the top 40 (by the early summer of 1981, their highest chart showing was only number 48 with 'The Art Of Parties'). But the band's rapid evolution from a critic-bashed, cultish, reluctant new romantic founder to a critical and commercial monster in 1982 (with six top 30 singles, a trio of charting albums and numerous magazine covers that year) made them frightening competition. Their sudden dissolution by the end of 1982 prompted sighs of relief among the bands riding the new romantic wave. As one pop writer recently noted, 'Duran Duran and Spandau Ballet were so in awe of the music the Catford-birthed band smuggled into the top 40 that they threw parties to celebrate their rival splitting up.'[160]

I like to think that at those parties, it was Sylvian's voice wafting from stereo systems, crooning 'relax and swing'.

7: Visions Of China/The Dreaming

'**Visions Of China**' Japan (1981, 3:37)
'**The Dreaming**' Kate Bush (1982, 7', 4:09)

'How do you know when it's time to pull the plug on the band you started as a teenager? Is it when you get married and have kids and buy a house in the deep New Jersey 'burbs? Or when you have a job so serious that they move you to Singapore for two years? Or when you turn 50?' The details here – New Jersey and Singapore – are specific to the band discussed in the article that began with these questions.[161] But the implication that rock bands fade and fold for the mundane reason that they are incompatible with domestic life is universally applicable. And, as we shall see in later chapters, more relevant to the Sylvian, Hollis and Bush stories than their creative struggles might at first suggest.

But in 1982, Sylvian was not yet there. (And Hollis, to whom we shall turn in the next chapter, was even further from it, just as Bush was still far from the hiatus that was her equivalent to a domestically driven band breakup). So why did Japan break up? The question matters because, whether the reasons were mundane and simple or profound and complex, the band's demise was potentially a crucial step on the journey from pop to post-pop. In fact, I think the causes were many and can be classified in various ways, but here are seven interlaced factors.

First, the rapid rise of new romanticism placed enormous pressure on the band, whose attempt at a neutral position – benefiting from the tag's publicity but denying the association to the extent of dampening that publicity – was becoming untenable. The Catford boys would sooner or later have been forced to either give in or fold completely; they chose to fold, and sooner. A second, closely related factor was that of the American market. Japan had played six gigs in the US in November 1978, but at that point, they lacked the material and momentum for those concerts to establish a foothold stateside. Making it in the US was notoriously hard work and a huge financial and psychological risk, but with immense rewards. It was and remains the world's most lucrative music market. But for some artists, the risks weren't worth it, and managers tended to see that reluctance as a big red flag. It was widely believed that ABBA's global fame was not matched in the US because the band hated touring there, refusing to invest anything close to the amount of time invested in Europe and Australia. Some saw that as sowing break up seeds. ABBA would effectively dissolve right when Japan did (at the end of 1982), partly because Agnetha Faltskog had developed a set of touring- and fan-based phobias. Her fears of flying, crowds and open spaces, and her terrifying visions of 'being suffocated by the sheer weight of people' would force her into decades of a reclusive life on a remote Swedish island.[162]

Kate Bush refused to play in America and, as a result, was almost completely unknown there, even as her star rose across Europe and the Far East. Turning down an offer in 1978 to support Fleetwood Mac on the final American leg of their *Rumours* tour, Bush instead toured Britain (with a few European shows) in 1979 and then never toured again. The hit album that trounced the conventional wisdom on touring America, *Hounds Of Love*, would not come until 1985 (and a tour would have made it a far bigger hit; arguably, *Hounds* was an exception that proved the rule, benefitting from the timing of the Second British Invasion and the rise of MTV – with Bush, 'an early and enthusiastic proponent' of music videos, directing her own from the mid-1980s on). The *Whamerica! Tour* was only eight dates and organised despite George Michael's extreme reluctance, much to manager Simon Napier-Bell's frustration – Wham! broke up months later. Napier-Bell suffered the same frustration in 1982 as, of course, he was also Japan's manager. 'They'd made themselves the biggest group in Britain and most of Europe,' he lamented. 'But just when America looked within their grasp, they decided to break up.'[163] Indeed, the 1982 combination of Japan's strong trio of recent albums (from *Quiet Life* to *Tin Drum*) and the onset of the Second British Invasion made massive success in the US a realistic prospect, one that might have kept the band going for a few years longer. But after that handful of concerts in 1978, Japan never again played in America.

A US tour, of course, would have meant an enormous commitment of hard labour on the band's part, and they were already feeling the weight of sudden success and the sheer grind that came with it. As one of their biographers puts it, Japan were 'actually insanely hard-working. (All five of their studio albums appeared within a four-year spell.).' Looking back now, Barbieri has said that he is amazed at 'how fast things progressed. We worked so, so hard. In between making those albums, there was touring, writing, rehearsing and all the press. It was so full-on!'[164] One would imagine that 'working 16 hours straight every day' would take its toll, and perhaps it did, making burnout another simple explanation for Japan's demise.

That leads us to a fourth factor intertwined with the three above – the allure and illusion of fame. Our three main protagonists, Sylvian, Hollis and

Bush, all came quickly to hate it; the two men railed against it for decades, and Bush, stung by it in ways that spared the men, retreated rapidly from its toxicity.[165] And there is no shortage of comments by musicians and other public figures on fame's false appeal. 'Fame, fame, fatal fame,' sang Morrissey a few years after Japan ended, 'it can play hideous tricks on the brain'. For an aspiring artist to crave it is as normal as it is for a successful one to be appalled by it. There are even children's books that use the cliché as a life lesson (I recently read one to my youngest child about a pony that gains global fame as a unicorn but soon craves a return to the peaceful anonymity of pony life).[166]

As early as the 1950s, psychologists observed how quickly fans developed proprietorial attachments to actors and other celebrities, dubbing such imaginary personal partnerships 'parasocial relationships.' The music industry paid attention. Ever since 'the machine' took on its modern form in the 1960s, the top of the pop charts has been a battlefield 'littered with superstars audibly struggling to survive the perils of fame.' Joni Mitchell famously wrote of the dangerous hubris that it is 'an almost inevitable byproduct of the starmaker machinery behind the popular song' – the latter phrase taken from her 1974 song about David Geffen and the industry – 'which shoves the artist into a dizzying gauntlet of exposure and acclaim, always urging her further along the path of total self-absorption – photo shoots, interviews, TV appearances, concerts, radio station visits and so forth, always with the same message: buy my album because I am great.'[167]

The public were the target, but the problem was the industry, or what Donna Summer called 'the machine' (even before Pink Floyd released 'Welcome To The Machine', one of Roger Waters' scathing commentaries on the music business). The machine made possible the success that all these artists had sought and then enjoyed, but its commodification of their bodies, their lives and their every move was stifling. The profound sexism of the industry made the experience worse for women. Summer, promoted in the 1970s as a hypersexual fantasy, found escape in the 1980s and 1990s by increasingly embracing evangelical Christianity.[168] Kate Bush escaped by creating her own micro-machine, controlled by her (as we shall see later). Such was the context behind industry survivor Robyn Hitchcock's wry remark that Nick Drake, who died decades before his work found a wide audience and made him famous, surely 'found success easier to handle from beyond the grave.'[169]

In view of such comments, it is chilling to hear Syd Barrett – a notoriously tragic case of the deleterious effects of mixing fame with mental illness

– enthusing over the prospects of success for a fledgling Pink Floyd. The band's debut was 'not like jazz music,' Barrett told a radio interviewer, "cos…' – cut in Roger Waters – 'We all want to be pop stars, we don't want to be jazz musicians!' Added Syd: 'Yeah! Exactly!' Bandmate Nick Mason said that when the first record came out in 1967, 'we were heading down the *Top Of The Pops* road.' That was exactly the road that George Michael ached to take around the time Japan were at their peak, and Talk Talk were on the rise. He was, he later mused, 'incredibly ambitious', convinced that he and Wham! bandmate Andrew Ridgely would be 'the biggest stars in the world.' But he soon found the endless publicity hunt to be 'just horrible', a mind-numbing routine of 'chasing your own tail.'[170]

Jump a few more decades to the present one, and comments on both sides of the phenomenon are still easily found in interviews. Maria Kelly, for example, as an ambitious 23-year-old rapper named Rico Nasty, insisted it was her destiny 'to be 'can't walk around' famous. That's what I want to be. I want to be 'swarming my hotel' famous. I want to be all that; I definitely do.' But actress and TV personality Keke Palmer had already been there. Having been famous for most of her young life, by 27, she concluded that 'fame is nothing to fool with. It's not a game. It's not fun. Yes, it has a perk to it at times, but it's nothing that you should ever be in pursuit of.' If you want to pursue 'being the fastest runner in the world' or 'the best person in science', then 'that's one thing. But fame in itself is going to bring so much trauma to your life.'[171]

Fame's false lure is Sylvian's warning in 'Ghosts'. And thus, his reaction to the factors above is our fifth causal factor. 'The seeds of ruin were probably sewn' as far back as *Quiet Life*, Sylvian later recalled, when there developed 'an enormous amount of tension in the band'. Then, 'with greater success came more pressure to tour, hence more friction. And I was already more drawn to melancholy pieces of music, about which the band were less than entirely enthusiastic. My heart was calling me as a writer to conceal myself less, to strip things away. With *Polaroids*, I was just beginning to get there. With *Tin Drum*, the door really opened, and I saw a path ahead that resonated.'[172]

In other words, Sylvian's response in 1982 to everything he found distasteful about Japan's newfound success and his sudden fame was not to retreat – not yet – but to seek a kind of compromise as a solo artist. What did that mean, exactly? Napier-Bell, who stuck with Sylvian for a couple of years after Japan ended, found out. 'In future, I want to be thought of like a minor Left Bank poet in postwar Paris – a celebrity but not famous', Napier-Bell later recalled the singer saying when they met in Berlin during the making of his debut solo album. The quote may be accurate, or perhaps Napier-Bell remembered a prolix statement by Sylvian through the filter of his own wry succinctness. Either way, that confession was, for Napier-Bell, the last straw: 'I didn't want to be a minor Left Bank manager.'[173]

If 'Ghosts' predicted Japan's demise, its parent album may have helped bring the end. After all, with such a rapid evolution to such a critical height, where could the band then go? After years of rough treatment from the British music press, *Tin Drum* prompted the *NME* to concede that 'Japan now have to be taken seriously; there's no other way. Be haunted by 'Ghosts' and hear what I mean.' That was onetime Japan-hater Paul Morley, who tagged the album 'gorgeously erotic' and 'perfectly evanescent.' Decades later, another critic noted that the Japan legend had faded due to Sylvian's 'refusal to engage with his past', but 'It shouldn't: even now, it's still impossible to fully grasp the meanings of their complex, grandiose material.'[174] Barbieri recently mused that while *Quiet Life* is the Japan album 'I enjoy the most, my personal favourite', it was part of a progression for the band and a product 'very much of its time.' By contrast, '*Tin Drum* is not of any time. You couldn't say what period in time that album comes from.' Of all Japan's projects, '*Tin Drum* is without doubt the best work.' The accolade by Roland Orzabal is not surprisingly often quoted: the Tears For Fears songwriter has said that their debut, *The Hurting*, was strongly influenced by *Tin Drum*, calling it 'an absolute masterpiece from lyrics to artwork ... just *everything*.'[175]

The irony of the success that *Tin Drum* brought Japan – numerous magazine covers and sold-out concerts, albums and singles charting in multiple markets – was that it was farther from conventional pop music than the band's previous two albums. Far from accidental, that was Sylvian's goal, to a degree that infuriated Napier-Bell: David 'was terrified of being condemned for being commercial.' In Sylvian's words, 'If we wanted to be pop stars, why would we put ourselves in for hard times? Why would we go through the chores of making this type of music?' And yet, handed the result of those chores, fans were far from put off, sending the album to number 12 and keeping it in the top 75 for a year. It was 'especially perplexing', as one critic later put it, 'that this beguiling, elliptical record would be their best-selling album' and 'its third single, the defiantly uncommercial 'Ghosts', would become their biggest hit.'[176]

Not only that, but right at the peak of new romanticism, which made Japan seem the height of fashion, the band had slipped into unfashionable isolation. In the crucial, creative years leading up to the completion of *Tin Drum* in the autumn of 1981, 'Catford's finest', as a veteran critic and fan recently put it, were 'a self-contained, self-absorbed outfit', not 'as 'in vogue' as most assumed.' Confirmed Barbieri, 'We weren't listening, around then, to what was going on around us.' While maintaining a punishing non-stop schedule of touring, writing, recording and promoting, they listened not to their contemporaries but to 'a combination of world music and weird stuff like Stockhausen. Mick especially was playing Turkish pop and Arabic music. We got into Chinese traditional music and film soundtracks.'[177]

In other words, the art-school Orientalism that was woven deep into the album's textures, making it 'experimental and absorbing, alien and distant, exotic and literate', was not simply a result of Ryuichi Sakamoto's influence.[178] If there was irony to the unplanned turn of events that led the Batt brothers from pulling 'Japan' out of the band-name hat before their first gig, to becoming big in Japan before any other country, to Sakamoto being their guide into Japanese avant-garde pop, then *Tin Drum* was the icing on that irony cake. While the album was overtly East Asian in multiple ways, there was, in fact, almost nothing Japanese about it. Instead, its influences and imagery were all Chinese (I was surely not alone in finding this at first confusing, then amusing, and eventually fascinating). On the cover, the juxtaposition of the band name in red (the only touch of colour on the whole sleeve) next to a portrait of Mao Tse-tung sets the iconographic tone. Beneath it, Sylvian eats with chopsticks in a room decorated sparingly with stereotypically Chinese objects – a bowl of rice, a bamboo hat, a small volume that one imagines to be Mao's Little Red Book. The track titles follow suit, from 'Visions Of China' to the closers of each vinyl side, 'Canton' and 'Cantonese Boy'. Lyrically and musically, the whole album might be described by the closing line of the sixth track: 'We're building our visions of China'.

Inevitably, journalists wanted to know why Japan had made a Chinese album. 'It's not really a Chinese album,' said Barbieri, 'but it's got a lot of Chinese influences on it.' Sylvian insisted many of the Chinese references in the words and sounds were humorous in intention and that the album 'isn't political at all' but based on a timeless impression of images of China. The track title of 'Visions Of China' was taken from a 1981 coffee-table book of the same name, comprising images shot in Maoist China by French photographer Marc Riboud (1923-2016). Sylvian – overtly aware that such sources might constitute 'cultural tourism' and that their use in pop music might seem 'trite' – responded that the band had thereby been inspired 'to invent instrumentation; and that, as kids, is an exciting development.' Furthermore, an element of respectful authenticity was implied by the fact that 'Japanese and Chinese people who have heard [the album] actually thought it was taken from original music.' He also offered a frank admission that *Tin Drum* was indeed a manifestation of cultural tourism: 'Of course it is. That's obvious.'[179]

Orientalism in the postwar West increasingly fixated on the country of Japan rather than on China for various reasons – not least of which was the fact that Western music acts increasingly toured and sold records in Japan, beginning in the 1960s, whereas that process did not start in China until the 1980s (and only then relatively slowly after Wham! played there in 1985). We would expect, therefore, that an English rock band becoming fascinated with East Asian culture in the late 1970s and early 1980s would channel that interest into a kind of latent Orientalism rather than a manifest Orientalism; in other words, lacking a direct knowledge based on serious study and travel, that band would indirectly receive, absorb and reproduce cultural elements of otherness and exotic difference. That is exactly what Japan did and what Sylvian meant in his comments on the album's Orientalism, and that context makes sense of the otherwise confusing mix of Chinese and Japanese references.[180]

East Asian preoccupations were hardly unique to the band; as biographer Reynolds put it, 'the early 1980s pop scene in Britain was infused with cod Orientalist musical flavourings and pseudo pentatonic piddling – the aural equivalent of soy sauce with fish and chips.'[181] Indeed, in late August 1981, as Japan worked on 'Ghosts' and 'Visions Of China' in the studio, the number one single in the UK was 'Japanese Boy' – sung by Scottish folk singer Mary Sandeman under the name Aneka, put out on Japan's old label, Hansa. And yet, 'Japanese Boy' and the new album by the boys in Japan were worlds apart. Karn and Jansen had already been exploring music shops in London's Chinatown, buying East Asian instruments, and for months, the whole band had been immersed in Chinese music. The catalyst, everyone agrees, was Japanese photographer Yuka Fujii.

Fujii had first met the band in 1979, shooting them for *Music Life* and serving as translator for 20 young Japanese fans who had flown to London to meet Jansen and Karn. Eleven years older than Karn and Sylvian, Fujii's previous romantic partner had been legendary jazz pianist Chick Correa (1941-2021), but it was the boys in Japan with whom she became involved in 1981 – moving in with Karn in the summer of *Tin Drum's* creation. She was 'obsessed with all things Chinese', Karn recalled, and gave her credit for bringing 'the first Chinese records home', influencing not only Karn but the whole band: 'We were all hooked.' The records 'had generic titles like *Chinese Orchestral Music* [and] *Songs From The Himalayas*', remembered Barbieri, inspiring long band discussions on how 'the unusual instrumentation ... somehow still produced commercially driven music.'[182]

The impact on the band was profound, particularly on the rhythm section. 'They broke all the rules', says Gavin Harrison, drummer and Barbieri's future bandmate in Porcupine Tree. Instead of Karn's bass following Jansen's bass drum, they 'made up weird, quirky rhythmic patterns where Mick would play between Steve's notes.' Jansen's zigzag drum patterning is especially effective on 'Talking Drum' (which Sylvian would see 'as a personal favourite and as the key track on the album'), while 'Sons Of Pioneers', the sole track for which Karn was given co-writing credit, was so Karn-based that Sylvian remarked (being snarky or candid?) that it could be characterised as 'just a bass line over and over again with just a few things thrown on top.'[183] Or take 'Life Without Buildings', recorded prior to *Tin Drum* as the B-side to the pre-album single, 'The Art Of Parties'. Credited solely to Sylvian, it nonetheless clearly developed from a musical conversation between Jansen and Karn (Sylvian has a single line to deliver, dropped in about two-thirds through the track). The track is less compelling than any of the eight on *Tin Drum*, deserving of its B-side relegation, but its starkness – its relative lack of melody and the near-absence of Sylvian – draws attention to the album's foundation and framing, as created by Jansen and Karn.

Although Sylvian admitted that 'you always think, when you've finished an album, should we bother carrying on?', it seemed clear that the whole band now felt this way. Arguably, '*Tin Drum* was so bold, so outré, so different from anything else before or since' that it closed off the path for Japan to continue. If so, while 'Ghosts' clearly announced Sylvian's solo trajectory, the album's other seven tracks do the same for the rest of the band just as strongly. Even the Karn-less 'Ghosts' does more than anticipate Sylvian's first solo album, made in effect by a Karn-less Japan, in its anticipation of Barbieri's long, future career in ambient music, art pop, and prog rock; his big influence on *Tin Drum*, he says, 'was Stockhausen, especially the abstract electronic things he was doing in the late 1950s. Listen to a track like 'Ghosts', for example, and you'll hear these metal-like sounds that hardly have a pitch, yet subconsciously suggest a melody.'[184]

Even at the time of *Tin Drum's* release, music journalists sensed that Japan had painted themselves into a corner from which they could not leave together. They had 'reached the zenith of their creativity with nowhere else to go', a *ZigZag* review declared. 'The sterility of perfection has left them out on a limb.'[185]

What if you don't have a band to break up? Without the public drama of a group split, with its contractual renegotiations and rebooted expectations, how does an artist escape 'the machine' and begin anew? Is the only option to buy that metaphorical (or actual) 'house in the deep New Jersey 'burbs'?

Not if you already have such a house. Kate Bush burst onto the pop music and pop culture scene in the first weeks of 1978 with the release of the extraordinary 'Wuthering Heights'. In mid-February, with the single at number 27, she made her first *Top Of The Pops* appearance; although she was 'a bag of nerves' and the performance was poor, it was as unconventional and striking as the song, as its videos (made soon after) and as young Kate herself. Within a few weeks, 'Wuthering Heights' was number one. By the year's end, her first two albums were hits (mostly top ten) in the UK, in half a dozen European nations, in Australia and in Japan. The speed of her rise to fame, in the year she turned 20, was dizzying (and dazzling – as a 14-year-old schoolboy, I was utterly mesmerised). The following year, she gave numerous interviews and television appearances, putting on an elaborately theatrical costumes-and-dancers six-week tour of the UK and Europe. Her third album pushed Bush from a new and novel star to a well-established global one; *Never For Ever* was her first UK number-one, birthing three hit singles in 1980 in her home country, giving her chart success all over the world (save for the US).[186]

But such fame came with a price. The music press of the day, snarling and soaked in toxic masculinity, pounced. A doctor's daughter from a middle-class London suburb, Bush seemed both sheltered and naïve, as well as calculatingly coy and suspiciously clever – what Simon Reynolds has called 'an odd combination of artiness and artlessness.' Punk offered one of the few ways for a woman to be admitted, albeit grudgingly, into the boys' club of critically acceptable music, and Bush was about as far as one could get from Siouxsie Sioux. As *Melody Maker* noted (when 'Wuthering Heights' was still number one), 'her father is a GP and she had quite a comfortable childhood' and 'she comes from a 'good' family', one that 'was always musical.' That meant folk music via her Irish mother and prog rock favoured by her older brothers – including Pink Floyd, whose David Gilmour discovered Kate through a Bush family friend and famously became her mentor. She was still 19 when her debut *The Kick Inside* was released, and only 20 when *Lionheart* came out just nine months later; like their creator, neither album had the sharp edges that were then so in vogue. 'James And The Cold Gun' (from *Kick*) and 'Don't Push Your Foot On The Heartbreak' (from *Lionheart*) stood out because their lean into rock made them atypical tracks (but arguably closer to what we now call classic rock than end-of-the-1970s new wave). More typical, and far more impactful in terms of Bush's reputation, was her second single 'The Man With The Child In His Eyes', a jaw-droppingly beautiful gem of a pop song, earning an Ivor Novello Award for 'Outstanding British Lyric' and rightfully garnering much attention for being written when she was 13. She recorded the demo for Gilmour when she was 16.[187]

Called 'sweet little Kate Bush' (*Sounds* in 1978), 'cuddly and submissive' (*NME* in 1979), she was condemned as child-like, her music 'dismissed as a middlebrow soft option, easy listening with literary affections.' At the same time, her body was subjected to the media's relentless leering gaze. Critics seemed unable to get over the fact that Bush was not only female but young and beautiful, and they succumbed quickly to the sexist logic that she could be little else. The observation in a 1978 *Melody Maker* interview that she 'has a pretty face with curves to match' was one of the more restrained remarks. Journalists ignored or glossed over the fact that 'I wrote my own songs [and] played the piano', as Bush herself put it in 1982. 'The media just promoted me as a female body. It's like I've had to prove that I'm an artist in a female body.' 'It was very scary for me', she recollected decades later, 'because whatever I wore, whatever I did, people were putting this incredible emphasis of sexuality on me, which I didn't feel.'[188]

Her label (EMI) was part of the problem, promoting her first album with the now-infamous leotard photographs. Men leered, women jeered; the comedian Pamela Stephenson lampooned Bush on the BBC with a helium-shriek chorus of 'people bought my latest hits, 'cause they liked my latex tits.' Even when interviewed by a woman (as in the *NME* in 1982), the words 'breasts' and 'tits' predictably, yet again, came up. That interview ended with the line, 'We should stop bugging her', but it was clear that would never happen, and that the initiative had to come from Kate herself.[189]

As biographer Doyle noted, 'From 1978 and on into the 1980s and beyond, Kate Bush slowly regained utter control of her career: inch by inch, record by record, video by video.' Having already set up her own publishing company (Kate Bush Music) and management company (Novercia), Bush resolved not to repeat the exhausting experience of her 1979 tour (which had been required by her contract with EMI). The closest she has since come to touring was a single series of 22 concerts in London's Hammersmith Apollo in 2014, ending a 35-year run without performing one full gig. She also quickly stepped up her control over the processes of recording and promoting. She built her own studio on her family property, later followed by a bigger studio very close to home, co-producing *Never For Ever* and then – starting with 1982's *The Dreaming* – producing all her albums herself. Choices of singles became hers (she was still fuming decades later over the lie that in 1978 she had 'burst into tears' when EMI tried to block the release of 'Wuthering Heights' as her debut single). Press interviews and television appearances became fewer and more guarded. By the mid-1980s, Bush, still a young woman in her 20s, 'was responsible for every aspect of her career, an unprecedented feat for a UK female artist.'[190]

That extraordinary achievement was a challenge every step of the way, both when an album was deemed a misstep or even a critical and commercial failure (*The Dreaming*, now highly regarded) and when an album was hailed as a great success – as was *Hounds Of Love*, which, along with the hits compilation, *The Whole Story* (quickly released by EMI in 1986 on the heels of *Hounds*), pushed her global star status even higher. *Hounds* even broke in the US, where it reached number 30, despite not a single concert or television appearance there – although Bush's above-mentioned channelling of her theatricality into videos, right at the height of the MTV-driven music-video era, made all the difference (and *The Whole Story* was successfully given a parallel, extended-release as a video album). That challenge – keeping the outside world at bay while also reaching it with new music – became easier in later decades, especially when Bush went into a 12-year hiatus (1993-2005), followed by the release of an album that pushed her art pop and progressive pop tendencies into new territory (we shall return to that album, *Aerial*, later on).[191]

So, how was this retreat from the pop world reflected in Bush's pop music as she moved to protect herself from the machine's exploitative intrusiveness? *The Dreaming* is usually cited by critics as the turning point, 'accelerating [her] quest to align her musical voice with a form of authentic self-representation.'[192] As mentioned earlier, the album was preceded the year before by its lead single, 'Sat In Your Lap'. Released some months before 'Ghosts', 'Sat In Your Lap' anticipated the Japan song's core lyrics with the line, 'I must admit, just when I think I'm king'. But in contrast to Sylvian's defeatism, Bush followed with 'I just begin'. In other words, Bush wasn't quitting; she was starting over again with new rules – or starting again by throwing the rule book out the studio window.

The result, *The Dreaming*, is not post-pop, but it contains many of its elements, with Bush experimenting with dismantling conventional pop songs and using the Fairlight and other studio techniques to create stories that are sonically unexpected. Dare to call Kate cuddly and submissive? This is your slap in the face. This album 'wants you sat bolt upright', as one writer recently put it: 'It's the 20-coffee all-nighter to *Never For Ever*'s hypnotizing waltz; an anxious, questing and imposing work.' In using the Fairlight synthesizer and other experiments 'in pursuit of sound and atmosphere over song', Bush's bold step towards post-pop confounded record-buyers and 'scared the babooshkas out of the record company back in 1982.' The title track, for example, has no discernible verse-chorus structure and its vocal line is highly processed. Like all the songs on the album, the verse and chorus of 'The Dreaming' do exist but aren't immediately obvious, here lost amidst the unsettling use of a didjeridu, animal noises and percussive sounds of uncertain origin to evoke the theme of Aboriginal Australian dispossession. Pop music is built upon predictable elements, with the assurance and anticipation of those elements central to its definition, but 'The Dreaming' is a kind of chant that leads the listener off somewhere unknown (into the outback?) without any sense of where or when the trip will end.[193]

Highly unconventional as a 7', 'the oddball single to end all oddball singles' (*Smash Hits*) and 'the weirdest damn record I've ever heard' (*Melody Maker*), it was only Bush's massive popularity in 1982 that allowed 'The Dreaming' to reach as high as number 48 in the UK. Future Pet Shop Boy Neil Tennant famously called its parent album 'very weird', writing in *Smash Hits* that Kate was 'obviously trying to become less commercial' – a wry, if unwitting, reference to the impulses that would push pop stars into post-pop experimentation. Bush herself called it her 'I've gone mad album.' Having said in 1982 that, enduring 'depression during the album', she 'ended up feeling quite pleased with it', she then remarked in 1993 that 'I look back at that record and it seems mad.' But over time, critics and fans increasingly came to appreciate the method to the madness. The

Melody Maker anticipated the album's future, remarking that, 'initially, it is bewildering and not a little preposterous', but a listener who can 'hang on through the twisted overkill' will find 'there's much reward.' As one fan put it recently, the album is 'pure genius and it contains 13 mins 43 seconds of utter escapism with 'Night Of The Swallow', 'All The Love' and 'Houdini' as a three-track sequence'. Escapism, indeed; those three tracks follow the title track on side two, which packs as much emotional punch as any side on a Bush record. But are the emotions hers or those of the characters whose stories she tells?[194]

The autobiographical element in Bush's lyrics has tended to be muted (at least in her 1978-93 albums). She herself has said that 'most of my songs aren't autobiographical.' She could be the protagonist in a few songs on *The Dreaming*. She called 'Suspended In Gaffa', for example, 'reasonably autobiographical', as it is about 'reaching for' and 'seeing something that you want' but then 'I become aware of so many obstacles', remembering being told in school about purgatory ('I caught a glimpse of God'). If Bush is playing herself, singing 'I want it all' but suspended (that is, wrapped or tied up) in Gaffa (that is, gaffer tape), the autobiographical metaphor may be her yearning and struggle to complete her first self-produced album and to escape the purgatory of protracted studio time ('it all goes slow-mo', she laments). In fact, the whole album could be seen as a meta-metaphor: a metaphor for 'my frustrations, my fears, my wish to succeed, all that went into the record', as she put it a few years later. As she sings in 'There Goes A Tenner', 'I'm having dreams about things not going right'.

But that is hardly the strongest of autobiographical links. Moreover, she's in character, not playing herself, in 'Tenner'. *The Dreaming* is an album full of characters, and she deploys a wide array of them – some borrowed from fiction or history ('Houdini'), most invented by her (the female bank robber in 'Tenner', the pilot's wife in 'Night Of The Swallow', the Viet Cong soldier in 'Pull Out The Pin' and the title's track's van-driver in the Australian outback). The technique allowed her to achieve a kind of multifaceted subjectivity, creating distance between her own emotional expression and the listener and thereby asserting some control over how the media and the public – so often intrusive, even ogling – perceived her. The character-creating, story-telling technique also enhances the paradox of her pop songs as being both remote and intimate, both enigmatic and conventional, both musically experimental yet also hook-filled and melodic.[195]

If the result isn't yet post-pop, it certainly leans into an experimentalism that is often included in discussions and definitions of progressive rock; indeed, I would argue that *The Dreaming* is Bush's first step towards prog-pop, which she then fully embraces on side two of the sequel album, *Hounds Of Love*. *The Dreaming* is still a ten-song pop album, but it has always drawn comments on its 'proggy' features (as they are sometimes called): its shifting time signatures; the use of the studio to create experimental sounds from vocal loops, samples, unusual percussive sources and everyday objects; the emphasis on constructing a work of art, one that gradually reveals its intricate ingredients over multiple listens, rather than compiling a set of catchy tracks that are instantly hummable or danceable. Prog tends to be complex, musically and lyrically, and Bush spent many months in multiple studios constructing sounds to match the inventive poetry of each song on *The Dreaming*. It may not be a concept album comprising long-form compositions, but its sequence of stories lends it a coherence of imagination as if each track were an episode of a diverse yet singular narrative vision. 'I wanted to try and create pictures with the sounds by using effects', Bush later explained, and 'all the ideas are aiming towards the same picture.'[196]

Indeed, there is no filler. No tracks stand out as weaker or stronger or comprising the creative core (I chose the title track to title this chapter, and others have seen it as the album's experimental 'apex', but I might have picked any of them; the author of a short book on the album picked 'Night Of The Swallow' as its 'epic ... cornerstone'). There are no dominant hit singles ('Sat In Your Lap' was a remix of the single released 15 months earlier, the amusing 'There Goes A Tenner' was shunned by UK radio and stalled at number 93 and it was surely the above-mentioned anticipation that gave the title track a moment in the top 50). 'I've always been an album-oriented artist,' declared Bush weeks after the album's release. 'I'm not interested in making singles.' That was far from obvious in 1978-80 when she enjoyed eight UK 7' hits. But with *The Dreaming*, she seemed to be making the point with a vengeance. Unlike its three predecessors, but like its sequel, it was very much an album, made to be played and appreciated as a whole.[197]

The story of Bush's first five years in the business is heavily threaded with skirmishes and battles for control; in essence, a familiar industry narrative but, in this case, deeply gendered. Gail Colson – who knew Bush through her friend Peter Gabriel, whom Colson managed – offered a deft distillation of Bush's victory: 'Kate told me after *The Dreaming* that they sat her down at EMI and said they wanted her to have a producer, that she couldn't produce herself. And she was so angry that she went home and built a studio and made *Hounds Of Love*.'[198]

The reality, of course, as Colson knew herself, was that Bush had endured years of patronising dismissals and deceits, with every step taken towards control over her product and promotion being hard-fought. And, in the end, she only avoided being dropped into obscurity by EMI and the men of 'the machine' by creating the critical *and* commercial triumph that was *Hounds Of Love*. 'They left me alone from that point', Bush later recalled. 'It shut them up.'[199]

Bush offers, in other words, a crucially important variation on a theme. Her upbringing in London's Green Belt, not far from the same suburban neighbourhoods that produced so many of popular music's transformative artists, from Bowie to the Batt brothers, might at first seem to place her outside the pattern. After all, far from suffering a childhood of working-class disaffection, Bush enjoyed a middle-class upbringing and the full support of her family – parents and brothers involved in both the creative and business sides of her careers, but, by all accounts, never compromising her primacy and control. But in an era when the sexism of the music industry, popular culture and society at large was deep-rooted and blatant, gender substituted for class as a factor of disadvantage.

The two are not the same, of course, nor are the opportunities for overcoming their disadvantages. But Bush's response was to double down on her femininity – to neither deny her gender and act manly nor to surrender to male demands that she be a sex symbol, but instead to be an artist who embraced and expressed her identity as a woman without compromise or apology. She also used her songs and their videos to explore gender roles with a fluidity that now seems ahead of its time. While most of the characters she created and inhabited are women, some are men and some could be either. In the 'Cloudbusting' video, she plays the scientist's son as an androgynous son/daughter. And, of course, the song that is now her best known is entirely about gender-shifting: the sub-titular 'Deal With God' is for a male-female couple to swap bodies, to 'exchange the experience' of their sexes. She had anticipated such a concept as early as 1978 when she told an interviewer that as much as she really enjoyed 'some female writers ... I feel closer to male writers. Maybe I want to be a man.' If *The Dreaming* channelled Bush's resentment over being boxed in as a woman – 'There's a lot of anger in it,' she later mused, 'there's a lot of 'I'm an artist, right!"' – then *Hounds Of Love* saw her outside that gender box, not trying to escape like Houdini but already doing her deal with God. That sense of fluidity did not compromise her feminism but became a defining part of it. It is hard to overstate just how significant that was, and is, both for popular music as a whole and for the development of new intertwined genres such as art pop, prog-pop and post-pop.[200]

Japan's breakup stemmed from, and consequently sheds light on, issues to do with fame, creative freedom and the music industry's historic commodification of artist and product. As such, it helps us to see how some artists sought to flee what they had so eagerly pursued not long before, in rare cases ending up on the path from pop to post-pop.

Yet, that said, there is also a simpler, more mundane explanation (isn't there always?). (I said I'd offer seven Japan breakup causes; this is the seventh.) The members of Japan all saw the breakup differently – the kind of Rashomon slippage between memories, deepening over time, that we would expect. Amidst those differences, Karn's version stands out starkly. Sylvian has often conceded that 'Mick and I were pulling apart', but for Mick, there was a clear catalyst.[201]

Tin Drum was officially composed by Sylvian. But for Karn, it was a collective creation, with his live-in girlfriend, Yuka Fujii, playing a crucial role. He saw the record as developing through the group's interpretation of the sounds and images introduced to them by Fujii, and later resentfully recalled: 'This is where I get so angry at almost all the tracks on *Tin Drum* being credited solely to Dave.' That, however, would turn out to be the least of it. In December 1981, as the old Sylvian-Karn friendship fractured, both agreed to complete the planned tour – but as the last thing the band would do. The night before they boarded the tour bus, while Karn was – by his own telling – ranting against Sylvian, he 'was cut short by Yuka delivering the shocking final blow: 'I will be moving out while you are on tour and moving in with Dave."[202]

Because Karn and Sylvian lived in the same building, Karn's flat offered a view right into the living room of what was – after they'd returned from a tour on which they barely spoke to each other – Sylvian and Fujii's place. The latter pair soon moved, but Karn stayed, and instead of taking down the framed photo of Sylvian and him that hung on his bedroom wall, he took to sleeping on the sofa. During both that tour and the larger one that the band reluctantly agreed to complete in 1982, the tension between the two childhood friends 'was a massive elephant in the room', as Jansen put it. 'It was painful to witness.'[203]

Karn later conceded that while the betrayal 'was not on its own reason enough to split', it left him forever distrustful and bitter – feelings that made a Japan recovery in 1982 impossible, that kept him off the solo projects on which the rest of the band would collaborate and that compromised the reunion of the foursome at the end of the decade. The romantic relationship between Fujii and Sylvian would last ten years, and their working collaborations would continue beyond that; they remain friends to this day. 'I hadn't only lost my companion and partner,' lamented Karn, 'I'd also lost my best friend.'[204]

Although the others later insisted that the band's breakup was inevitable anyway, Napier-Bell claimed that what Sylvian had done, and how he acted afterwards ('being a prick'), was a hard thing for Karn to live with, and he 'couldn't stand it.' The result was 'chaos', said the manager. 'The group just couldn't function together in any way at all.'[205]

So, in light of all this, how might Napier-Bell have kept Japan together? He could not, of course, and the futility of such efforts is amusingly illustrated by a conversation Napier-Bell had a year after Japan's breakup, discussing with a Chinese politician in Canton the prospects of a concert in China by Wham! (another group whose breakup Napier-Bell was powerless to prevent). Napier-Bell later recounted their exchange, beginning with the Chinese official's reaction:

'I never hear of Wham! How about The Beatles? I think The Beatles would be better for a concert.'

'They broke up.'

'Oh really?' He seemed genuinely surprised. 'I thought The Beatles were very good for England. Why did the government let them break up?'

I laughed. 'In England, people can do as they want. How could a government keep a pop group together if they wanted to break up?'

'Maybe put them in jail?'[206]

8: Talk Talk

'Talk Talk' Talk Talk (1982, 7', 2:58/3:23)

Do brothers play crucial roles in the post-pop story? Or is it just coincidental – it is hardly unusual, after all, to have a brother – that for each of our three main protagonists, a brother was a seemingly invaluable source of support or inspiration?

The presence of Kate Bush's two older brothers, Jay (John Carder) and Paddy (Patrick), runs throughout her life and career. Paddy, for example, played or sang on every Bush album from her 1978 debut through to 2005's *Aerial*. Kate's album artwork has often featured Jay's photography, and it is hard to imagine how we would see her without his photographs. Their encouragement was not only artistic; they made the family both an emotional support network and a financially secure business corporation. She probably would have still had a musical career without them, but it surely would have unfolded very differently and less smoothly. Likewise, if he'd had no younger brother, David Sylvian might well have still teamed up with Karn and Barbieri to form a band. But it wouldn't have been the same. The Batt brothers were inseparable from the very earliest moments of musical interest, and they have remained musical collaborators throughout their lives. The dissolution of Japan was not a breakup of brothers; the post-Japan careers of Sylvian and Jansen are as inextricable as their Japan days were.[207]

As for Mark Hollis, he was the middle of three boys, but it was his older brother, Ed, who played a crucial role in his musical life.

Eddie and the Hot Rods were an Essex pub band that formed in 1975, becoming part of the emerging London punk scene the following year ('often thought of as a bridge between pub rock and punk'). Indeed, they became a famous footnote to that scene when The Sex Pistols, playing their very first London gig, opened for Eddie and the Hot Rods at the Marquee Club – and then proceeded to destroy the Rods' equipment on stage. The stunt earned the Pistols their first notice in the *NME*, which made no mention of the headlining act, although the following week's edition did note that the Rods had 'dismissed' the Pistols as support band (''S what you get for mixin' with real punks'). Whether the Hot Rods were real punks or not, they were real musicians, supposedly unlike the Pistols, whose theatricality centred on their admission at that Marquee Club gig that they couldn't play ('So what?') and were 'not into music' but instead 'into chaos.'[208]

The Sex Pistols' planned performance of chaos was, of course, infamously successful, whereas the Hot Rods endured several years of changes in name, personnel and record label, achieving one minor UK hit in 1977 before imploding in 1981. That one hit, 'Do Anything You Wanna Do', was credited to Graeme Douglas (who had left the Kursaal Flyers to join the Rods) and Ed Hollis, the band's manager.[209] Ed was the closest thing the band had to someone called Eddie, as the original 'Eddie' was an on-stage dummy used as a gag when the band were starting out.

Ed was also Mark's older brother, thereby exposing Mark in his early 20s to the highs and lows of the music business. Ed wrote and produced, as well as managing and touring with his own band – bringing back tales from the US, for example, where Eddie and the Hot Rods supported The Ramones and the Talking Heads as 'Special Guest Stars from England' in the autumn of 1977, playing in legendary clubs such as Chicago's Aragon Ballroom. His brother's experiences seem to have instilled in Mark a deep scepticism regarding the industry, one that helps explain the rapidity of his transition from delight to disillusion once he himself became a success. But it also nurtured the one aspect of the business that most attracted him: writing songs. Indeed, the first Eddie and the Hot Rods single, 'Writing On The Wall', a 1975 flop, was credited to 'Hollis' as one of two writers. The Hollis in question may have been Ed, who produced the song, but a later publishing contract specified that it had been Mark – he would have been 20.[210]

When Mark was born in the north London neighbourhood of Tottenham in 1955, his brother Ed was three. Their parents were Londoners who had met during the war, aged 14 and 12, while billeted in Cambridge. They married as teenagers in 1944, moving back to London when the war ended the following year. Future father Dennis took up the trade of a greengrocer, specialising in fruit. Working life in a war-wrecked London was not easy, and the family moved frequently, settling in Essex by the time the youngest boy, Paul, was born in 1962. There, Dennis became a 'receiving agent' for London newspapers, delivering them to local newsagents, a job that allowed the three Hollis boys to grow up in the towns of southernmost Essex.[211]

As a schoolboy in one of those towns, Rayleigh, Ed was nicknamed 'One Thousand Eddie' for his remarkably large record collection. He was, in the words of his brother Mark's biographer, 'a music obsessive to an almost absurd level.' As the Hot Rods drummer later recalled, 'everything Ed did in life was to excess', and that meant, above all, music and drugs; both would impact Mark in profound, but very different, ways.

'If you've got an older brother, you'll know', said Hollis in 1984, explaining that his brother 'just listens to a phenomenal amount of records' and that he had done so 'all the way through', using his massive collection to 'guide me into things I should be listening to.' That meant exposing a young Hollis not only to the psychedelic rock of the late 1960s and early 1970s (with Pink Floyd, Traffic and The Doors as enduring favourites) but also to less obvious genres such as 1940s blues, modal jazz and modern classical (most notably, Shostakovich, Stockhausen and John Cage).

Leaving school at 18 before taking his A-level exams, Hollis continued to study part-time while apprenticing in an industrial laboratory. At 20, he passed the exams, quit the lab and enrolled at the University of Sussex – he lasted a year. That might seem like the history of a young man failing to find his place and purpose in the world, but, in fact, he *had* a purpose – music. And Ed was his guide. In 1975, having started managing the Hot Rods, Ed secured them residencies in Central London pubs frequented by A&R scouts, leading to the band signing with Island Records. 'I'd watched Ed at work and thought it all very exciting', Hollis later recounted. Seeing the bands play, meeting them and 'talk[ing] to them about the pop business' made him 'determined that it was all I wanted to really do.'[212]

Leaving his new girlfriend, Felicity, to finish her degree at Sussex, Hollis dropped out to be a roadie for the Hot Rods. Felicity, known then and since as Flick, was destined to marry Hollis, have two sons with him and be widowed by him over four decades later. In her last year at university, Flick supported Hollis, who was based in southern Essex, bouncing between factory jobs and Hot Rod gigs and dying every day 'to get home and start writing songs and lyrics' (as he later said). He also observed the Hot Rods make a studio album, then a live EP and watched his brother produce other bands and then persuade Island to give him his own label. In homage to the heroin-cocaine cocktail that had become his drug of choice, Ed named the label 'Speedball'. Despite the grip of addiction, Ed managed to keep producing, thanks in part to colleagues in the business: the sound engineer on the second Hot Rods album, recorded in 1977, was a young Steve Lillywhite (later to become an award-winning industry giant, working on over 500 albums by the likes of U2, Simple Minds and The Rolling Stones). As band members remembered it, Lillywhite was 'the brains behind it'; 'really, *he* was the producer, and Ed was out of his fucking tree.' Ed would not produce subsequent Hot Rods albums. After a year, Speedball Records was shut down by Island.[213]

Hollis, meanwhile, studiously avoided falling prey to hard drugs, refusing to follow his brother down that path while also leveraging his brother's connections into forming a three-piece band and grabbing studio time. He called the band The Reaction, giving them the then-fashionable punk-new wave sound but with some throw-back psych-rock flavouring. They started opening in Essex pubs and clubs for the Hot Rods, whose drummer remembers them as 'a really good, high energy, psychedelicy band.' Ed also wrote a song for his brother's band, produced a recording of it and succeeded in getting it included on a 1977 punk compilation titled *Streets*. The song was titled 'Talk Talk Talk Talk'. Although Ed 'was already getting himself into a bit of a state' – in the words of Island managing director Tim Clark – he was able to get The Reaction a six-album deal in April 1978. Days before, Japan had released their debut album. The Reaction, it seemed, were about to catch them up.

With Ed producing them (and, unofficially, managing them), The Reaction recorded a two-minute single, 'I Can't Resist', which failed to trouble the charts that summer. They performed opening gigs, as well as their own modest shows in London and in Essex, their repertoire including three songs that would end up on the first Talk Talk album: 'Candy', 'Have You Heard The News?' and a less-punk Hollis/Hollis version of 'Talk Talk Talk Talk', now called 'Talk Talk'. A full album of tracks was recorded but not finished before Island A&R executives – hearing sample tracks – decided the band were not marketable and dropped them. Rightly or wrongly, Ed, as producer, was blamed. The Reaction soldiered on, their setlist growing with new Hollis compositions – including 'Mirror Man', destined for the Talk Talk debut, and an early version of 'Renée', which would end up on their sophomore album. In 1979, an A&R man for CBS was impressed enough to give them studio time to lay down nine demos. But that led nowhere, and by the year's end, The Reaction had folded.[214]

The 1980s began, Hollis turned 25 and his ever-influential older brother seemed to have guided him into a career in the music business that was a dead end. Without a band or a deal of any kind, Mark was done with Ed, professionally speaking, and vice versa. But then, in a last-minute twist, Ed found himself in the Island offices – he had tried, in vain, to secure the production job for the next album by The Damned – and on his way out, dropped a cassette on the desk of the new creative director, Keith Aspden, muttering, 'I've got this tape by my little brother.' A 16-year-old office junior played it, loved it and persuaded Aspden to listen, too. As 1980 gave way to 1981, Hollis was offered a songwriter deal with Island. Lacking a band and somewhat dispirited by his experience with The Reaction, he now envisaged a career as a songwriter, not a performer ('I thought of it primarily as a publishing thing', he confessed a year later).

But through London's network of musicians and record shops, he met Simon Brenner, a keyboardist and recent graduate of Warwick University, and they started writing songs together. Suddenly, Ed was back. While talent-spotting in the Hollis home ground of southern Essex, Ed came across a teenage rhythm section that he thought were a perfect match for his brother and Brenner: Lee Harris on drums and Paul Webb on bass. The boys took the train into London, Brenner picked them up in his orange Mini and they helped Hollis and Brenner record initial demos. It 'very quickly turned into creating a whole set and forming a band', said Webb, in just 'a few weeks.' Claimed Hollis himself the following year: 'It was a real band after the first week.'

The foursome laid down three formal demos at Island, with Ed producing. But Aspden 'was hugely disappointed', as he later said, blaming Ed's production, insisting Hollis' brother be removed completely from the project. Impoverished by his protracted efforts to get a music career going, Hollis and Flick had meanwhile become homeless and were sleeping – with Aspden's tacit approval – in Island's rehearsal room. It was as if Ed had once again led his thirsty brother to a river from which he could not drink.[215]

Facing another dead end, Hollis persevered and another lucky break helped him push on. Island's Aspden was hooked (as was that teenage office junior, Clive Black) and they persuaded Jimmy Miller – famous for his work with Traffic, The Stones and Motörhead – to go into a small London studio with the unnamed band to record three demos. The relatively simple renderings of 'Candy', 'Mirror Man' and 'Talk Talk' expertly showcased the sonic elements that each band member contributed: a rhythm section betraying the influence of Japan, with Webb using a fretless bass like Karn and Harris drumming with a lack of fuss reminiscent of Jansen; Hollis' distinctive and plaintive vocals; and Brenner's keyboard melodies. Aside from Brenner's later replacement with various musicians (none of whom became official band members), this structure would underpin the band for a decade. 'The sound was basically a four-piece jazz quartet playing pop songs', Brenner later noted, articulating Hollis' own vision for the band. The demos allowed Aspden to shop the band around, soon settling on a publishing contract with his own bosses at Island, simply adding the others to Hollis' publishing deal – one that Aspden later admitted was 'an awful deal' for the band but 'the sort of standard of deals which was given to people starting out as songwriters.' The band were finally given a name: 300 Cubs.[216]

Clive Black was puzzled by the name. But as he had recently introduced Hollis to the profane comedy of Derek and Clive (created by Cook and Moore), much to his subsequent regret, he received this response: 'I remember saying, 'Mark, why 300 Cubs?' He said, 'Exactly, you cunt, that's right. How many? *How* many, you cunt?!' He was fascinated by Peter Cook and Dudley Moore and the dark side of the humour.'[217]

Black never found out where the name came from, and within a couple of months of the Island contract being inked, it was re-issued with the band now named after its signature song – the song that Ed Hollis had written for his brother, who had revised it for The Reaction and then rewritten it for the foursome now called Talk Talk. The Ed connection to the new name soon proved ironic, as this was the moment when Ed finally slipped away from direct involvement in his brother's music career. The press release announcing the new name stated that Talk Talk were 'currently working with producer Ed Hollis.' But Ed's official role as producer and unofficial role as manager were already fading, and very soon after this, Aspden decided to leave Island to manage Talk Talk himself. By the end of that same year (1981), Aspden had secured the band a record deal with a major label, they had opened for the already-massive Duran Duran and the Durans' producer was signed on to make Talk Talk's debut album. Ed was gone for good. Although, as Brenner later recalled, Hollis 'never really talked about his past. Except Ed.'[218]

If the association with Duran Duran had haunted Japan – from Japan's influence on the Birmingham boys to the press' insistence that both were core new romantic bands – to the extent that it contributed to their self-destruction, then Talk Talk's association with the Durans was equally fraught with anxiety and resentful ingratitude. Indeed, the story of Talk Talk's first two years (1982-84) and first two albums is arguably centred on how they handled – or mishandled – the break that Aspden delivered to them at the close of 1981. After years of false hopes and starts, being lumped in with Duran Duran was a crucial turning point for Hollis and it happened to be exactly the path down which he did not want to journey.

Feeling the pressure, during the autumn months of 1981, as the band's new manager with no other job, Aspden shopped the band around as 'gamekeeper turned poacher.' When the Miller demos and the band's showcase performances in London secured competitive bids from London Records and EMI, Aspden went with the latter; EMI made the best offer, they were the most established UK label, they had international reach and they had just scored big with Duran Duran. Colin Thurston had produced the Duran debut, which reached number three in the UK in 1981, going top ten in numerous countries stretching from Sweden to Australia; it would remain in the British charts for well over two years. Meanwhile, in January 1982, Thurston would enter EMI's AIR studios to record the sequel, *Rio*, whose global success would dwarf that of its predecessor. Hollis was sceptical, even dismissive, of Duran Duran, despite the latter agreeing to let Talk Talk open for them on their home turf – those three December 1981 nights at the Odeon in Birmingham, following shows in other English cities throughout that month. But Thurston had worked for Tony Visconti as sound engineer on *'Heroes'*, whose title track 'is one of my all-time favourites', said Hollis, and so 'I thought he'd be good.'[219]

Before turning to *Rio*, Thurston spent a fortnight with Talk Talk at the residential studio in the picturesque Cotswolds' village of Chipping Norton. The session was productive, and a few days into February, EMI put out 'Mirror Man' as the first Talk Talk single. But Hollis wasn't happy. 'If the geezer can't deliver, then he isn't worth it', he complained. 'The immediate problem was that he was trying to lay back our sound', explained Hollis; in Thurston's hands, the album 'had lost all its oomph', said Brenner. A solution was quickly found: Hollis liked how a live session on BBC Radio 1 had been handled a few months earlier, so the same in-house engineer, Mike Robinson, was hired to rework and remix the album. When the album came out in July, Robinson was given the credit.[220]

Except, according to Aspden, Thurston enjoyed 'a rubbish contract that EMI did with him' that gave him the full royalty payments anyway; he was paid for Robinson's work despite having 'nothing at all to do with any of the success of that first album.' Furthermore, Robinson's credit was merely 'mixed by', not 'produced by', and on 1990's *Natural History* compilation (the best-selling record worldwide in Talk Talk's catalogue), it is Thurston who receives credit. A 40th-anniversary white vinyl re-release of the album was likewise promoted as 'produced by Colin Thurston', with the attached tag: 'better known for producing Duran Duran's first two albums.'[221]

If the tenuous Duran Duran connection worked to give *The Party's Over* credibility in 2022, the effect was the opposite in the music press of 40 years earlier. When the first single, 'Mirror Man', fell instantly on barren ground, EMI put out the title track in April. 'I'm afraid it's in the same category as Duran Duran', wrote Lynval Golding of Fun Boy Three in *Melody Maker*. 'A mite too close to Duran Duran for comfort' and 'watery reflections of Duran Duran' were the lazy phrases that appeared in *Smash Hits* and *Record Mirror*. An interview with Hollis in the latter was subtitled 'Self-styled pretty boys TALK TALK have been billed as the next Duran Duran.' An exasperated Hollis veered characteristically between sarcastic humour ('I mean, sure, we're all *pretty!*') and derision for those who failed to hear his music properly ('If I had some ears to graft onto them, I would do it' was also not without intended humour, as Hollis was conscious of his own unusually large ears).[222]

The Reaction's punk-pop 'Talk Talk Talk Talk', in its reincarnation as 'Talk Talk', enjoyed 'a smoother delivery and production to match – slap bass, luscious soft synths and a driving, sparkling piano – [that] made for a more palatable listen.' But that spring, it still only reached number 52 in the UK. The negative reaction of the all-powerful music press was partly indolence – as in their earlier treatment of Japan, the apparent Duran Duran connection made the band low-hanging fruit – and partly due to the fashionable suspicion of major labels. Reviews routinely mentioned that Talk Talk were signed to EMI, implying or outright alleging that the label had manufactured the band, refined its sound 'to the point where there is no real substance left' and bused in fake 'rent-a-crowd' fans to gigs. Aware of this prejudice against them, the majors had, by 1982, created over a dozen independent labels on which to place bands to whom they wished to give 'indie' credibility. The ruse worked surprisingly often, but it was not used for Talk Talk. In Aspden's verdict: 'There's no doubt about it, EMI did screw up.'[223]

Hollis, however, did not help matters. A year or two before, Duran Duran and Japan had reacted very differently to the publicity opportunity of the new romantic phenomenon, with its sequel in the form of the Second British Invasion: the Durans had reluctantly embraced the new rom tag, then enthusiastically pursued the US market; Japan eschewed both, then broke up. But whereas Japan's first two albums were born into the conflicted world of punk and disco, and their next two at the dawn of new romanticism, Talk Talk's debut arrived as new romanticism became mainstream and began to go global. Pushed into things by EMI, albeit without much thought or backing, Talk Talk attempted a kind of middle ground. But their efforts were compromised by Hollis' discomfort on stage, read by one critic as 'asinine aloofness', and his suspicion of interviewers manifested in piss-taking humour or non-cooperative sullenness. His sidekicks, Webb and Harris, took their cue from Hollis. But Brenner found his attitude self-defeating, and Ian Curnow – who played keyboards with the band on tour – found it perplexing: 'The thing I never got to the bottom of is if you're that private a person, why did you become a pop star?'[224]

The answer, of course, was that Hollis wanted his pop music to be heard without him being a pop star, a contradictory position that matched his contrarian personality. Had he heard or read Sylvian stating that precise ambition? Perhaps. Or Bush, who had already begun articulating her ambition as neither fame nor money, but 'making something interesting creatively' that nonetheless had to be heard – otherwise, 'you could almost say it doesn't exist.'[225] Either way, the pop cultural context of 1982 was thus both an opportunity for the kind of success that had eluded Hollis for years and also a reason to ponder other paths.

Meanwhile, with the first two singles failing, EMI decided to try one last time, releasing a third single, 'Today', and its parent album, *The Party's Over*, on the same day in July. Both limped into the lower reaches of the charts. The press was ready with predictable potshots. They either gave Thurston production credit, accusing EMI of a 'rather depressing' effort 'to repeat the formula' that had worked with Duran Duran, or they noted Robinson's role and derisively accused the band of trying 'to redeem themselves after two successive single flops by a change of producer.' Nonetheless, 'Today' spent the summer slowly working its way up the charts, taking two months to peak at number 14, thereby saving the band's contract; 'I was going to drop you if that didn't happen', EMI's head of A&R later told Aspden.[226]

The slow but crucial turnaround may have partly been a result of last-ditch efforts by EMI to push 'Today' on BBC Radio 1. But it was also partly a reflection of the way that *The Party's Over* found an audience among Japan fans (who were coming to terms with the likelihood that there would be no sequel to *Tin Drum*) and partly the way that the album contained evidence of future potential. Just as *Quiet Life*, in retrospect, pointed the way towards *Tin Drum*, so did songs like 'Have You Heard The News?' and the title track suggest that Talk Talk might rapidly evolve in creative ways.[227] That said, the biggest factor may have been the band's reception outside the UK. Just as Japan found success in the country of Japan first, and then a following in continental Europe before full acceptance at home, so did the 'Talk Talk' single slowly open doors for its band on the continent (first in France and Portugal), in Australia and New Zealand (the only country where the album would go top ten) and in Canada and the US – where the timing of the Second British Invasion worked in Talk Talk's favour.

While 'Today' was keeping Talk Talk afloat in Britain, the band were touring the United States in support of Elvis Costello. The debut album, released stateside in October, and its title track single both only reached number 75 in the US. But that was considered respectable enough – combined with reasonably positive reviews of the tour – for EMI and Aspden to plan a second album and US tour. Modest but encouraging international success also prompted EMI to commission a reworking of 'Talk Talk' by Rhett Davies – Hollis's choice, based on his work with Ferry and Roxy Music. The remixed version, now as long as the album track, did much better in the UK. Helped by a spirited appearance on *Top Of The Pops* at the end of November, the single peaked at number 23 (but it hit number one in South Africa, another sign of how much the band's international profile dwarfed their home reception). The relentlessly snide UK music press inevitably used Talk Talk's US tour against them, accusing them of money-grubbing hypocrisy: 'like Duran Duran,' sniped *Record Mirror*, 'they've cottoned onto the fact that most of the spondulicks repose there. What fine motivation for a group so concerned with their art.'[228]

Although Talk Talk now had worldwide momentum, and Hollis had been gradually accruing new songs (including some written while on tour in the US), that momentum was slowed by the disconnect between EMI's pigeon-holing of Talk Talk as a moodier Duran Duran and Hollis's emerging vision of a pop band that were trying not to be one. A placeholder single, 'My Foolish Friend', was their sole 1983 release, stalling at number 57 in the UK. That same week, Duran Duran were number one, 'Is There Something I Should Know?' having entered the chart at the top position the previous week. The whole Duran thing riled Hollis so much that he cold-shouldered Simon Le Bon at an EMI event and 'sort of made fun of him' behind his back, recalled keyboardist Phil Ramocon. Confirmed Brenner, Hollis insisted that 'we were always meant to say disparaging things about Duran Duran.' With every step of EMI's marketing of the band, Hollis chafed at the bit. The previous year, he had selected white suits for the band to wear in videos and promotional stills, seeing them as a nihilist statement that would direct people to the music. When EMI promoted the look as pretty-boy new romantic chic, Hollis demanded – in vain – a break with the label.

EMI then booked studio time for the band to work with Rhett Davies on their second album. That worked at first, although Davies introduced Hollis to the randomising creative methodology behind Brian Eno's 'Oblique Strategies' deck of cards. Combined with his recent reading of Luke Reinhart's novel, *The Dice Man*, which entranced Hollis with the concept of 'decision-making through dice throwing' (in his words), the new album began to coalesce as a concept album called *The Chameleon Hour*. It is unclear whether EMI or Hollis were dissatisfied with the Davies sessions or if he was simply called away by a prior commitment to work on what would become Bryan Ferry's *Boys And Girls*; either way, around the time that EMI had hoped to release the new album, a new producer, Tim Friese-Greene, was hired to re-record and produce it.

Friese-Greene and Hollis hit it off immediately. A songwriter and a musician before moving into producing, Friese-Greene would become an unofficial member of the band for its duration. Although his privileged background placed him on the other side of London's tracks, Friese-Greene shared both Hollis's profane sense of humour and his passion for a wide range of jazz and classical music. Curnow, who did some writing with Hollis in 1983, resulting in one song ('The Last Time') that would end up on the second album (*It's My Life*), saw that the band's new producer rapidly developed 'a very special relationship with Mark, which even Paul and Lee didn't really get inside of.' For Hollis, songwriting was the core creative activity, more viscerally necessary to him than recording and far more so than performing. As Friese-Greene immediately became an effective writing partner – he would co-write two of the singles for *It's My Life*, the title track and 'Dum Dum Girl', and go on to co-write Talk Talk's entire third album with Hollis – their bond developed fast and firm. That partnership, combined with their shared tastes in music and humour, meant that – as Hollis's biographer insightfully notes – 'it's not hard to imagine how Friese-Greene might have reminded Hollis of a more middle-class version of his brother.'[229]

As 'Talk Talk', the earliest iconic song in the Talk Talk/Hollis catalogue, had been co-written by the Hollis brothers, it was thus symbolically significant that Hollis co-wrote with his new studio brother 'It's My Life'. It was the next song to attain that status – indeed, to become the best-known and best-selling Hollis track of his career, making possible both the non-commercial later albums and the complete absence of albums in the decades after that. The pair only grudgingly accepted all that the song would do for them for the rest of their lives. Said Friese-Greene 23 years

after the writing of the song on the piano in his London living room:
'It's one of the truisms of life that you're going to get remembered for something you least want to be remembered for; I don't think 'It's My Life' is a crap song, but you certainly couldn't say it's one of the best. As a song, it's serviceable and shows little touches of what was to happen later, but it's nothing to get excited about.'[230]

Placed at the centre of the album, as the closing track of side one, and destined to be made over-familiar by the success of the No Doubt cover, 'It's My Life' can easily overshadow the rest of its parent album. But skipping it allows the listener to focus on the songs around it – the 22 minutes of 'Dum Dum Girl', 'Such A Shame', 'Renée' and 'Tomorrow Started' – and thereby better appreciate the creative leap made between the first and second albums.

The Party's Over is good, but *It's My Life* is great. The debut is a two-dimensional album, very much of its time, suitable for awkward teenage dancing (which is, of course, an awkward confession by me), ideal as background pop in the dorm room while hanging with friends, perhaps cranking the volume to drown out the music coming from other rooms. Its sequel served those purposes, too, but it was three-dimensional, a headphones album, best appreciated in a deep armchair or in bed, lights out, eyes closed, cans on. As subsequent Talk Talk /Hollis albums would all be, this one was a sonic world into which the listener stepped, one with space in which to settle and dissolve into the music.

For me, 'Tomorrow Started' has always been the most exciting entrance on *It's My Life* to that world. From the moment I first heard it, a few weeks after the album's release – around the time I was ceasing to be a teenager in March 1984 – I was entranced by the way the song was pop – in its structure, its melodic core, its expression of emotion – and yet it leaned into a creative space that was beyond pop.

If anyone was using the term 'art pop' in the early 1980s, it was likely an inversion of pop art to suggest musical manifestations of the art movement of the 1950s and 1960s. Pop art drew upon popular and commercial culture for visual elements that were then incorporated into artworks – seemingly low-brow ingredients for a supposedly high-brow medium. One might imagine art pop, then, as an inversion of that process, with high-brow musical elements and references incorporated into popular music's supposedly low-brow genres. Hearing 'Tomorrow Started' in the year of its release, I could not have conceived of it in those terms, but in retrospect, it seems to have art pop aspirations from its very start.[231]

After 45 seconds, the song stops, and there is a full three seconds of silence (more like five, if the volume is low) before it begins again with Hollis's plaintive opener, 'Don't look back until you try, a line so openly a lie'. In the slightly slower, elongated version recorded live in Rotterdam in 1984, that pause happens three times, filled with audience whistles and yells of anticipation. The emotional tension is rock, and its attachment to melody is pop, but the track's foundation is full of subtle allusions to other genres. The references to jazz and classical music are more transparent in live versions, both of this and other tracks from *It's My Life*. When playing 'Call In The Night Boy' on tour in 1984, keyboardist Ramocon would go into a John Coltrane riff while the band chanted 'a love supreme', extending the jazz jam up to 20 minutes. Such references are still discernible on the studio versions. At the time of its release, Hollis alluded to the influences that he attempted to channel into 'Tomorrow Started', all of which make sense now but which prompted derision from the music journalists who knew less about music than he did: 'The intro reminds you of Erik Satie, the verse is maybe closer to Pharaoh Saunders, and then this sort of Marvin Gaye rhythm vibe comes in. And that is all just a reflection of the fact that my whole life has been one long process of being into lots of different types of music' – not just 'being into' but also absorbing and using those 'types of music' to move along the path towards post-pop.[232]

Hollis does not mention his brother Ed, but it is hard not to hear him thinking and remembering how it all began with the fraternal sharing of a record collection by One Thousand Eddie.

9: Tomorrow Started/Brilliant Trees

'**Tomorrow Started**' Talk Talk (1984, 5:57/6:42 live)
'**Brilliant Trees**' David Sylvian (1984, 8:39)

What do you get if you cross 'scene' and 'genius'? The answer, mentioned earlier, is 'scenius', a term coined by Brian Eno to describe 'the communal form of the concept of genius.' In Eno's thinking, this goes beyond the collaborations between band members and their producers (which is why the concept only really becomes relevant at this point in our story). 'Genius is individual, scenius is communal', Eno has explained. And, on another occasion, 'scenius stands for the intelligence and the intuition of a whole cultural scene.'[233]

In terms of the creative process that produced albums, various arguments could be made regarding the potential relevance of 'scenius', but my interest is in its *functional* relevance to the journey towards post-pop taken by pop artists. The initial impression of that journey is one from group to solo work – the very opposite of a journey that draws or relies upon a scenius. Kate Bush's commitment to controlling the process of production, from her withdrawal from touring to the creation of her own studio and label, would seem to make her the quintessential solo artist. Sylvian would seem to be the poster boy for breaking up a band at its peak, their biggest hit being his song warning them of his imminent act of destruction. And the cover credits on the Talk Talk/Hollis catalogue – five band albums and one solo one – disguise the reality of a steady band-to-solo transformation across the 1980s and 1990s. But we don't have to dig very deep to see that none of those artists were seeking creative isolation; on the contrary, as they seemed to become more solo, they simultaneously sought to widen the collaborative net to draw upon what Eno called 'a whole cultural scene.'

Far from rejecting the other musicians, artists and influential predecessors that constituted such cultural scenes, Bush, Hollis and Sylvian are notable for the enthusiasm with which they sought them out. The more they read and studied and listened to past writers and composers, painters and photographers, the more they sought out current artists with whom to collaborate, the further down the path from pop to art pop to post-pop they travelled. The catch is that such connections could not be allowed to compromise their paramount need: freedom of creative expression.

The compatibility of creative freedom with a scenius is only possible without the purse-string-holding intrusion of a corporate record label –

manifested in roles played by A&R men and producers hired by labels – and without the potentially paralyzing democracy of a band of equals. It is easy to exaggerate the conflicts that Bush and Hollis had with EMI – neither were as confrontational as the battle between Sony and George Michael, for example – but the fact is that there were conflicts, and they were manifestations of this larger pattern. Likewise, we saw the messy way in which Japan dissolved, with the breakdown of the Sylvian-Karn relationship playing a central role. And we turn in a moment to the relationship between Hollis and Brenner, which was so crucial to Talk Talk rising from the ashes of The Reaction, to see how their connection began to fray before *The Party's Over* was even finished.

In other words, scenius was crucial to the development of post-pop; artists, such as those followed in this book, could not and did not take that journey alone. But scenius only functioned effectively by not undermining the freedom, control and centrality of each core artist.

Not all those who have written about music see the flow of influence, collaboration and competition between artists as positively as scenius implies. Such relationships, 'among the most powerful forces in the continued development of any art form', are sometimes seen in darker terms – as cannibalistic, for example, given 'the penchant' among popular music artists 'for feeding off of each other (and for occasionally devouring one another).'[234]

Metaphors of cannibalism may go too far. But there is no denying that craving and consumption, dependence and destruction, characterise artistic collaboration. For decades after I first fell for 'Tomorrow Started', I believed that the chorus line, 'I'm just the first that you take', was, 'I'm just a bus that you take'. The real line is better poetry and has the advantage of being what Hollis actually wrote. But my version, imagined for so long, is a clunky metaphor for a person being used by another. And that, in essence, is how the recording studio sceniuses created in 1983 by Hollis and Sylvian functioned.

Throughout his biography of Hollis, Ben Wardle grapples with the 'dichotomy' of Hollis's personality, recognising that he was a 'loner genius' but one who, at the same time, 'loved pubs, swearing, fast cars and golf.' In an interview with German pop magazine *Bravo* in 1984, Hollis confessed that his recent purchase of blue mirrored sunglasses had changed his life. He'd bought them in New York, simply in response to the bright summer sun, but to his delight, he found that, as a result, people 'were moved away and kept at a distance. I instantly felt better.' The interviewer inferred that 'Mark is a typical loner. When other people get too close to him, he quickly feels pressured.'[235]

That conclusion did not stop the editor from titling the piece 'Talk Talk singer Mark is the target girls throw bras at.' That irony would resonate for years, as the mirrored shades became Hollis' signature look, giving him a 'perma-cool, often stoned, rock star' image that 'was not only at odds with his own personality but also with what he wanted to portray in Talk Talk's music.' Going on stage wearing the sunglasses with his own simple clothes was Hollis' way of trying to keep people away, but the effect was very different; as an *NME* critic mocked in a concert review, Hollis' image said, 'Look! I'm just the same as you, but *I'm* a popstar.'

All this carried over into the contradictory way in which Hollis approached collaboration – from writing to recording to performing. On tour, Hollis was infamous for not talking to the other bands. In the studio, many found him amiable, funny and even caring. But he also tended to be exacting and focused to a degree that could be alienating to invited musicians. According to manager Aspden, Hollis saw that he had to work with others in order to relieve 'the pressure to deliver', to achieve his creative goals and to tap into the talents of others (that is, to access the scenius). But he did it with great reluctance, stubbornly committed to his vision and to having 'his own way about most things.' Said Aspden, 'He's someone who needed to collaborate but, in essence, he really hated to collaborate' and 'He *needed* other people, but he didn't *want* other people.'[236]

Such was the context behind the breakdown of the relationship between band founders Hollis and Brenner. As Brenner later explained, 'Mark was very of his place. I was brought up a nice Jewish boy in Northwest London; it was a very different world to me.' Hollis's 'place' was working-class southern Essex, and he remained true to his roots throughout his life, his cockney accent never changing (in contrast to Sylvian, whose accent changed as his life did).[237] Essex boys Webb and Harris shared Hollis's affinity for the profanity-laced piss-taking humour that wore thin on Brenner. During the recording of the first album and the subsequent touring of it in the US, UK and Europe, that humour seemed more and more like Hollis bullying Brenner, with the teenage rhythm section as his sidekicks.[238]

'It's true there were occasions when he could be a bully', Wardle concluded. The pranks played on other bands while on tour were often poorly received; the teasing of those who worked with the band (like the young Clive Black) tended to ignore the sensibilities of those getting hazed. Hollis's 'pursuit of his goals sometimes showed little regard for those upon whom he depended for their realisation', with the most oft-cited example being the tying of Ian Curnow's fingers together, forcing him to play for hours 'in considerable discomfort.'[239]

Hollis decided that Brenner's time with Talk Talk was up. But without telling him that, Hollis auditioned a new keyboard player, Phil Ramocon, who was primarily a jazz pianist. For the final months of 1982, Ramocon toured with Talk Talk, making it a five-piece; he played piano and Brenner stayed on synth. But Hollis was miserable being on the road, tensions mounted and when the band entered the studio the next year to make *It's My Life*, Brenner was finally fired (he'd receive co-writing credit on one of its tracks, 'Call In The Night Boy'). He would never be replaced, not by Ramocon – a highly versatile and talented Afro-Londoner who made uncredited contributions to *It's My Life* and who would go on to contribute to the careers of numerous pop and jazz artists – and not even by Friese-Greene, who remained an unofficial band member.[240] Harris and Webb stayed – the inseparable duo whose rhythms underpinned *It's My Life* and its sequel, *The Colour Of Spring*. But their roles were relegated increasingly to that of session musicians on the final two Talk Talk albums, and in the 1990s, they committed themselves to their own band, .O.rang.

Brenner's departure thus reduced Talk Talk to a tight trio, like a jazz outfit, allowing Hollis to bring in other musicians to help create specific moments on specific tracks. Hollis insisted he did not see these hired guests as 'session people' because 'we allow them to come in and play with freedom.' His goal, in other words, was to forge a scenius. Robbie McIntosh, for example, who had worked with Friese-Greene on 'The Lion Sleeps Tonight', contributed guitar despite having just joined The Pretenders. He would go on to an extraordinary career as a session guitarist, still finding time to pop up on future Talk Talk/Hollis albums. This was also the start of Ian Curnow's role as one of Talk Talk's keyboardists, both in the studio and on tour. Percussionist Morris Pert (1947-2010), who had played on a couple of Kate Bush albums and would contribute to *Hounds Of Love*, lent the opening track (and thus opening seconds) of *It's My Life* a distinctive rhythmic sound. Jazz veteran Henry Lowther improvised the trumpet solo on 'Tomorrow Started', a crucial addition to that song; he would play on future albums right through to Hollis's solo record.[241]

Brenner's departure also gave Aspden and Hollis the pretext to rework the band's publishing deal, creating a new company – Hollis Songs – establishing him as Talk Talk's sole writer. Hollis surely remembered how, a few years earlier, his brother Ed's relationship with Eddie and the Hot Rods had soured when they discovered he'd taken credit for half the album's songs, which they considered a group effort, as Wardle biographer put it, 'Ed's publishing land grab backfired.'[242] The challenge for Hollis, then, was to ensure he wasn't caught between a disgruntled band and a company skilled in the art of avarice. Luckily for him, he had Keith Aspden as manager. As a former Island executive ('gamekeeper turned poacher'), Aspden was aware that songwriting and recording contracts with record companies were 'designed to rip people off' and he ensured Hollis's new deal was no such thing. But it excluded not only the likes of Ramocon but also Harris and Webb – who had received credit on over half of *The Party's Over* but who would be uncredited on all four remaining Talk Talk albums. Referring to these arrangements by Aspden and Hollis, Phill Brown (sound engineer on the second half of the Talk Talk/Hollis catalogue) remarked that 'Keith and Mark are both ruthless.'[243]

It remains unclear if the deal caused lasting resentments. Ramocon was certainly convinced that his contributions to 'Such A Shame' deserved a songwriting credit, and it being denied, he refused to work on the next two albums, only returning a dozen years later to play on Hollis's solo album with firm promises (he would be credited with co-writing opening track 'The Colour Of Spring'). Brown noticed that, around 2005, all those involved with Talk Talk in the 1980s began refusing interviews, from Aspden himself to Friese-Greene (who did so adamantly and angrily) and Harris (and, to a far lesser extent, Webb); Wardle speculated that the timing of this shift, right when No Doubt's 'It's My Life' made Hollis a newly wealthy man, suggested the 1982 publishing deal may have been a root cause.[244]

Either way, the contract is significant to the history of post-pop. Post-pop is, by definition, less commercial than pop, even resolutely non-commercial. But it can be as expensive to create – in Talk Talk's case, even more expensive. The success of *It's My Life*, especially in continental Europe, paid for *The Colour Of Spring*, whose European success, in turn, effectively paid for the subsequent shift into foundational post-pop albums. And, as we shall see again near the end of the book, the later success of 'It's My Life' made possible Hollis's ultimate move: his *post*-post-pop life (or his post-career).

That pattern was evident and similarly important to the parallel history of Sylvian's solo career, increasingly non-commercial and sporadically post-pop, funded in part by the fact that he received the lion's share of Japan's royalties. Napier-Bell, as the band's manager, had 'explained it away as being simpler', an impoverished Karn later grumbled. Clarified Napier-Bell in one of his memoirs: 'As you climb the pop hierarchy, you get better contractual conditions as you go, moving from a bottom-rung deal where you're ripped off by every technique a record company knows, to a higher-rung deal where you're ripped off with greater subtlety.' Added the veteran manager, 'That's the fun of the music business.'[245] Neither Sylvian nor Hollis, however, seem to have found any part of the *business* of music to be fun. Excluding their bandmates from their own publishing companies was seen as a necessary contingency, not something they relished having to do. But did it they did.

Like it or not, Hollis was now on the industry conveyor belt, and it was extremely difficult to get off it while also releasing music to the public. He could slow it down, and he did, with increasingly long gaps between album releases that were unusual for the era – 19, 24, 31 and 36 months. One gets the impression that such gaps were not only so Hollis could get every track right but also because he knew that at the end of recording came something he increasingly loathed: touring and promoting. And in 1983, as he and Friese-Greene laboured to complete *It's My Life*, Hollis's solution to the problem of touring (to quit it) was still a few years away, while his solution to that of promotion (to be uncooperative or take the piss) would resume after the album's release.

Under the momentum of the partnership with Friese-Greene, the earlier *Dice Man* theme of the album gave way to a new leitmotif, one that would run through this and future albums: the natural world. The seagull cries on 'It's My Life' are the best-known example of bird and animal sounds in Talk Talk songs, but the percussion on 'Dum Dum Girl' has a similar effect, as do the elephant noises embedded in 'Such A Shame'. The original idea was to use recordings of animals made at the London Zoo, but background interference (such as 'children arguing with parents over ice cream') obliged the band to turn to Curnow's expertise with his Roland Jupiter-8 synthesizer. That artifice carried over to the videos for 'It's My Life', mentioned earlier, with their odd use of zoo footage and their reflection of the fact that 'for all his artistic aspirations', Hollis was grudgingly and 'unfortunately, in the business of selling records.'[246]

That leitmotif also carried over into the album art. Aspden had introduced Hollis to James Marsh, an illustrator who had worked with record labels since the 1960s (the original connection was that Aspden's girlfriend had been to school with Marsh's wife). All five Talk Talk album covers – along with the sleeves of all 14 singles – were designed and painted by Marsh, giving the catalogue a visual cohesion rare in the music world. Both Aspden and Marsh were avid naturalists and birdwatchers, with representations of animals, birds and insects featuring heavily in the latter's work. When the sophomore album's title had been *Chameleon Hour*, Marsh's mock-up cover riffed on his design for the debut album, showing an eyeball as a clock. Then, given only the new title of *It's My Life* and not the music, he reworked an earlier book cover design with puzzle pieces featuring animals more heavily than people. By pure chance, it matched the album's content well. Marsh's evocative artwork, combined with the absence of band members on any of the record covers, contributed to the mystique that Hollis sought ('I want to separate image from music', he explained, 'All I'm interested in is writing songs'). 'Beautiful, mysterious and absorbing' in the words of The Brian Jonestown Massacres's Matthew Tow: 'Each album design was a perfect complement to the rich-textured atmospherics [of] the Talk Talk sound.'[247]

As 1984 dawned, 'It's My Life' was released in the UK, peaking a few weeks later at number 49. A few weeks after that, *It's My Life* came out, appearing in the British charts at number 35. That same week, The Thompson Twins' *Into The Gap* entered at number one (as Wardle notes, that band's Tom Bailey was, like Hollis, turning 30, having spent his 20s making experimental pop). The next week, *Into The Gap* held onto the top spot, while *It's My Life* turned around and slowly slipped out of the charts. Reviews in the UK press were mixed, better than for the first album, but there were still judgements such as 'crushingly, excruciatingly average' (*Smash Hits*), 'limp and whiney where it tries to be plaintive and yearning' (*Melody Maker*) and 'no, no, no … it's the Duran Spandau Leaguoo' (*Record Mirror*). Some daily papers ran more favourable notices, including one in the *Birmingham Evening Mail*, surely penned with a sideways glance at the charts: 'The urgent vocal delivery, swinging rhythms, general moodiness and imagination make this band's material a cut above that of the likes of the Thompson Twins.'

However, signs of a small shift in the critical appraisal of Talk Talk were not matched by chart success in the UK. The singles to follow did even worse: 'Such A Shame' peaked at number 49 in the spring and 'Dum Dum Girl' reached a pitiful number 74 in the summer. When Talk Talk went on the road in April, *Sounds* taunted them with the headline 'Shamed Into Touring'. None of the UK gigs sold out, as the press were quick to point out, but some critics did admit that a passionate fan base seemed to be developing. For example, a third of the seats were empty in London's

Lyceum, but the band worked those who did attend into a frenzy of 'wild adulation which demanded three encores.'

If the story had ended there, with Talk Talk developing a fanatical cult following in the city where they lived, Hollis might have found a satisfyingly limited fame. After all, Talk Talk were never massive at home: of their 14 singles released in Britain between 1982 and 1991, only 11 charted (between 1982 and 1988), with an average peak place of number 54. That their albums did better (an average peak of number 21) only served to underscore that their fanbase was solid and dedicated but not vast, like that of a prog rock outfit rather than a band of pop stars. But there was more to the story than that. Talk Talk were, in fact, entering their imperial phase – elsewhere in the world.

Days after the UK tour, the band jumped to Italy, Germany, the Netherlands and elsewhere, finding all across continental Europe exactly what had eluded them at home: sold-out shows of screaming fans, eager and respectful (if not always well-informed) press and huge chart success. They needed additional security details in Germany, France, Spain and Italy – including police escorts in the latter. Almost everywhere, the album did better than in the UK, going top four in five European markets, charting well in a dozen others there and around the world – including places the band would never play, like New Zealand, where the album sat in the charts for over four months. Outside the UK, album sales were strong through 1984 and 1985. The singles did equally well, even better in some markets, especially 'Such A Shame', which hit number one in Switzerland and number two in Germany, settling for weeks into the Dutch and French top tens. At one point, there were three Talk Talk singles in the German top 50 at the same time. When 'Such A Shame' was finally released in France in January 1985, it didn't leave the charts until the summer.[248]

I spent some time in France that spring and summer, and I was struck by the huge popularity of a band that I had perceived as relatively obscure and only modestly successful. 'Such A Shame' was particularly inescapable on French radio. I don't remember meeting a single person my age (I was 21) who wasn't a fan, and some, upon realising that I was from London, immediately made a *'comme Tok Tok!'* comment. It all rubbed off on me: I left France a Tok Tok fanatic.

With the Second British Invasion in full swing in the US, the singles received airplay and the album sold fairly well stateside – both it and its title track charted higher (number 42 and number 31) than in the UK. That success was helped by the band's willingness to tour there, and in

Canada, supporting the band Berlin in the late summer of 1984. Hollis hated the touring, even complaining about American food, but he was willing to lump American record-buyers in with Europeans, all of whom 'are more concerned with music' – in contrast to the British, who were more 'preoccupied with image and trend.'[249]

The week that 'It's My Life' squeaked into the US top 40, *Billboard* noted that the 'Talk Talk Single was Hot Hot' (the small article's title) but that Americans were stymied by 'the group's uncategorisable musical quality.' The fact that the single was number 40 on the Hot 100 but 'number seven on the Dance/Disco chart may not make the band easier to label.' In the end, it seemed enough of an explanation just to repeat that Talk Talk were British – this was, after all, 1984. Hollis was reluctant to be reassured by that – and rightly so, as the Second British Invasion would play itself out before long, while, back home, critics continued to struggle with a band refusing to be pigeon-holed. 'The English press has had difficulties placing us', Hollis grumbled 'resignedly' to *Billboard*. 'They've compared us to 24 bands.' It would be many years before Talk Talk were deemed to be quite simply beyond compare.[250]

Sylvian's first solo single after Japan's split would prove to be his most successful, at least in terms of chart positions – it would be downhill from then on. 'Forbidden Colours', released in June 1983, became Sylvian's sole number one. But it only hit the top spot in Iceland, with its highest peak positions elsewhere being number 15 in Ireland and number 16 in the UK – where no subsequent single would reach higher. Not that such numbers ever bothered Sylvian. In the 40 years following Japan's demise, he only released 15 singles, each with minimal publicity, and no album of his has spun off a single since 1999 – all in keeping with an artist determined to keep recording while also staying out of the limelight, determined to maintain no more than the muted renown of 'a minor Left Bank poet.'

The relative success of 'Forbidden Colours' was due to a combination of factors. One was the knock-on effect of Japan's posthumous popularity; that same June saw the release of *Oil On Canvas*, which became Japan's highest-charting album in the UK, entering at its peak position of number five – an extraordinary feat for a double live album by a defunct band.[251] Another was the fact that the song was from the soundtrack to a successful film, *Merry Christmas, Mr. Lawrence*, whose cast included David Bowie (then at a career peak of global commercial success) and Ryuichi Sakamoto – who also wrote the film's score. Indeed, as Sakamoto wrote and played the keyboards on 'Forbidden Colours', produced the track, then released it under his name, too, it was arguably not really a solo Sylvian single. Nonetheless, because of Sakamoto's role – not despite it – the song was a firm and revealing step between the final Japan studio album and the first Sylvian solo album, illustrating the increasing relevance of scenius.

'Forbidden Colours' is a beautiful composition (another factor explaining its immediate and enduring popularity). Sylvian delivers his own lyrics in a croon that is less Ferry and more evocative of Bowie's balladeering. Had Bowie sung 'Forbidden Colours', it might have been a bigger hit, borne aloft by his star power. But – if 'God Only Knows' on *Tonight* is anything to go by – Bowie would have over-sung it; Sylvian's delivery is subtle and intimate, believably emotional, the momentary rasp in his voice a gentle tug at the heartstrings.[252] It is the style previewed on 'Nightporter', honed on 'Ghosts' and perfected on the solo albums to come. The poetic pairing of the film's theme of forbidden love with Sylvian's chosen metaphor of spiritual angst is inspired and affecting, as is the string arrangement by Ann O'Dell (who had worked on *Quiet Life*).

In 1983, I bought and wore down the 7' single of 'Forbidden Colours', finding it so convincing that, despite having seen the movie whose plot it reflected, I wondered if Sylvian himself might be nurturing a forbidden love. Was he secretly singing to Sakamoto?

That was obviously not the case – at least not in the sense of the illicit homosexuality that is artfully depicted in *Merry Christmas, Mr. Lawrence*. But Sakamoto had been an influence on Sylvian since the latter had discovered the early Yellow Magic Orchestra albums. Their collaboration had begun in 1980, with the *Gentlemen Take Polaroids* track 'Taking Islands In Africa', and continued in 1982 when they wrote and recorded (with Jansen on percussion) the sibling tracks 'Bamboo Houses' and 'Bamboo Music'. Although Japan had yet to formally dissolve, it was clear – certainly to Sylvian – that the band would record no more studio albums, so he and Sakamoto released the tracks as a double-A-sided single. 'Forbidden Colours', then, was not the first Sakamoto-Sylvian collaboration, and it would be far from the last. While the 'Bamboo' tracks reflect one side of Sakamoto's influence, evoking the Orientalist art pop of *Tin Drum*, 'Forbidden Colours' reflects another. Its exquisite piano intro and orchestral outro, composed by Sakamoto, signal the Japanese musician's future as a writer of film soundtrack scores more than pop songs; yet such use of classical music elements in a pop song anticipated where Sylvian was also heading.[253]

Above all, Sylvian's collaborative impulse proved to be crucial to his journey through various pop genres and into post-pop. Indeed, in terms of his output of recordings, he was seldom travelling alone, despite the fact that his declared intention to move from Japan onto solo work was 'to walk a path that is entirely my own' – a statement about ownership, not solitude.[254]

For example, as much as Japan's split seemed to come at the close of 1982 as a hard stop (even if it was an agonisingly protracted hard one, lasting all that year), time revealed it to be a soft one. His brother Jansen played on every Sylvian solo album through the 1980s and Barbieri also played on most of them – making them, in a sense, half or three-quarters Japan records. The same could be said of the other projects by ex-Japan members: Sylvian played and sang on Karn's 1987 solo album; the other Japan members had played on Karn's first solo album five years earlier; and, as we shall see in a later chapter, in 1989, all four band members reunited to write and record another album.

It is hardly surprising, then, that Sylvian's first solo album featured Sakamoto on three of its seven tracks, Barbieri on two of them and Jansen on all of them. It is certainly a Batt album, and much of it is a three-fourths Japan album. In retrospect, it is indeed 'as much the last Japan album as the first David Sylvian one.' But there was a distinction that was crucial for Sylvian, who explained that 'Richard and Steve are guest musicians', which was 'totally different to being part of a group.'[255] So, ex-Japan or not, brother or not, Jansen and Barbieri were in the same boat as Sakamoto and the nine additional musicians whom Sylvian brought to the studio in Berlin. They all reflected Sylvian's influences, the directions in which he was headed, and the sceniuses he sought to draw upon.

Strengthening the connections to *Tin Drum* and to Sakamoto, Steve Nye came back, this time as co-producer of the album (with Sylvian), as well as one of its keyboardists on piano and synthesizer (a parallel to the pairing of Hollis and Friese-Greene). Nye, Sakamoto and Sylvian re-recorded 'Forbidden Colours' for the album, but at the last minute, it was dropped to make room for the newly written 'The Ink In The Well', whose languid jazz-pop suited side one perfectly.[256]

Indeed, just as Hollis would increasingly reach into a jazz scenius, so did Sylvian do the same. Wayne Brathwaite (sometimes written Braithwaite) played bass in the New York City jazz, reggae and R&B scenes and would go on to write and play with Billy Ocean, among many others (dying in his early 30s in 1991). Jazz and funk guitarist Ronny Drayton (1953-

2020), also a Black New Yorker, flew to Berlin with Brathwaite to join him in making crucial contributions to two of the side one tracks that would become singles ('Pulling Punches' and 'Red Guitar'). The meeting of Jansen's Japan-like drumming with the finger flairs of Brathwaite and Drayton was unique alchemy – said Drayton of 'Punches': 'Man, that track swings.' Drayton was Nona Hendryx's musical director at the time, and Hendryx vouched for Sylvian, as they had become friends during his 1979 New York visit; plus, 'I knew David's work', Drayton later said. 'Me and my crew in New York loved all that English techno-pop. Japan were cool.' The acoustic six-string on those two tracks was played by Phil Palmer, of London music pedigree (The Kinks' Davies brothers were his uncles), who had already begun to build an extraordinary track record as a jazz, rock and pop session guitarist.[257]

Bass on the other single on side one, 'The Ink In The Well', was played by English double bassist Danny Thompson, a connection to England's folk-jazz scenius. Having begun his career in late 1960s London playing blues with Alexis Korner, Thompson had been a founding member of Pentangle, and he'd played on Nick Drake's debut album, as well as John Martyn's string of 1970s albums. It is hard to imagine the spare folk-pop of Martyn records like *Solid Air* and *One World* without Thompson's bass, as Sylvian was surely well aware, for he sought to create on the record an intimate musical atmosphere that was in part reminiscent of that forged in the previous decade by the likes of Drake and Martyn. Thompson also connects Sylvian to Hollis and Kate Bush: he had played on *The Dreaming*, and he would go on to play on *Hounds Of Love* and *50 Words For Snow*, as well as on Talk Talk's *The Colour Of Spring* and *Spirit Of Eden*. If Sylvian, Hollis and Bush were architects of different forms of art pop and post-pop, Danny Thompson was one of the builders.

No less than four horn players were brought to the *Brilliant Trees* sessions in Berlin, all making significant marks on the album and on Sylvian's creative development, connecting him to a broad scenius network of jazz and experimental music. Canadian jazz trumpeter Kenny Wheeler (1930-2014) of the jazz-fusion trio Azimuth played ethereal flugelhorn parts on two side one tracks ('Ink' and 'Nostalgia'), while legendary trumpeter and composer Mark Isham, whose career had begun touring with Van Morrison, played on two others ('Pulling Punches' and 'Red Guitar').[258]

Another Canadian jazz trumpet player, Jon Hassell, played an even more important role. Having recently worked with Brian Eno, he was, by 1983, 'a major player on the ethnic jazz-fusion scene.' Side two of

Brilliant Trees was the more experimental one, its three tracks showing Sylvian edging away from art pop towards a more avant-garde sound; Hassell's contributions were strong enough on the two longest tracks, 'Weathered Wall' and the title track, that he received a co-writing credit on both. The studio Sylvian had chosen in which to make *Brilliant Trees* – Hansa – was where Bowie had made Sylvian's favourite Bowie album, *'Heroes'*, with Eno. So Hassell was the second link to Eno. In which case, the fourth horn player invited to Berlin, Holger Czukay (1938-2017), was a link back to one of Eno's influences. Czukay, a founding member of German experimental art-rock band Can, had been a student of Karlheinz Stockhausen (1928-2007) – the above-mentioned Cologne composer and theorist whose groundbreaking use of electronics in the creation of classical music was often mentioned by key figures in the post-pop story, from Eno to Sylvian and Hollis.[259]

In fact, Hassell, too, had briefly studied with Stockhausen, so he and Czukay were old acquaintances – enhancing, for Sylvian, the sense of a complex scenius into which he had tapped. Sylvian confessed that 'although I'd discovered the work of Stockhausen as a teen', and it had influenced how he and Barbieri created 'Ghosts', Czukay took Sylvian far deeper into the pioneering German's work. Noted Sylvian, 'The significant shadow of Stockhausen' was omnipresent at the *Brilliant Trees* sessions. Czukay's use of tape slicing on his recent solo albums had inspired Sylvian to write him a fan letter with a gentle invitation, an approach that struck the German as 'very proper!' A friendship developed ('we got on famously', said Sylvian), with Czukay collaborating on multiple Sylvian projects, beginning with *Brilliant Trees* – to which he contributed some French horn parts, a little guitar and some Dictaphone samples.[260]

Amusingly, a battered old IBM Dictaphone 'salvaged from a skip' (dumpster) was the only instrument Czukay brought to Berlin. But he knew how to manipulate it in creative ways, turning it into 'a marvellously flexible instrument' (said Sylvian). Two decades later, Sylvian would note that 'I've always enjoyed incorporating sounds into a work that were kind of unidentifiable' – an old avant-garde technique that was central to post-pop – and he reminisced about Czukay's ability to manipulate sound sources with the Dictaphone in a way that was 'technically superior to anything that was on the market in terms of samplers.' Sylvian saw that 'very evocative' sounds whose source 'you couldn't place' could create 'an emotional intensity' within a composition. Thus, even more important than specific contributions, Czukay opened up for Sylvian the world of sampling techniques and the use of tape improvisations. Likewise, Czukay was 'someone to bounce ideas off', in Sylvian's words: 'I wanted one wild card, something unpredictable, and Holger Czukay was that person for me.' The German polymath helped him 'to create a sense of space, a sort of unspecified aural landscape.'[261]

As a result, *Brilliant Trees* is a brilliant sequel to *Tin Drum*. A significant step forward in Sylvian's songwriting, the Orientalist theme of Japan's last studio album is replaced by the twin themes of pastoralism and spiritual searching. Both lyrically and musically, the album is 'a richer, more emotionally complex world' than was that of Japan, incorporating 'elements of jazz and atonal improvisation.'[262] More than mere mid-1980s art pop, the album is a musical expression of the various genres and scenius networks that Sylvian sought to access through controlled collaboration – from jazz to classical to ambient to experimental electronic music.

Simon Napier-Bell was still Sylvian's manager when the recording sessions for *Brilliant Trees* began in Berlin in the summer of 1983. Pondering 'whether to continue managing him or not', Napier-Bell travelled to the Cold War-divided city to hear the new songs, which he later described – with characteristic candour – as 'wonderful but uncommercial; dreamy rather than focused, with large periods of improvisation between rambling vocals.' Although he recognised that Sylvian was now reaching new 'emotional areas', Napier-Bell lamented what he perceived as a loss of discipline – such that he made the 'hard decision', after going 'through a lot together' over seven years, to let Sylvian go. 'There was no animosity that I remember', said Napier-Bell. After all, Sylvian would have taken no issue at his departing manager's observation that he had now embraced 'a very un-commercial attitude.'[263]

All that said, 'Red Guitar' would have made a great Japan single, with Brathwaite's funky bass helping us to forget that Karn was the only missing Japan member on the record. Sylvian's brother Jansen contributed a subtle but important drum part ('recorded in a stone stairwell at Hansa', he recalled). One wonders if the song's upbeat tone stemmed in part from Sylvian writing it 'in a rather drug-induced state' (as he later confessed). As it was, it was a great Sylvian single, reaching number 17 upon its release in June and hanging around in the singles chart, while *Brilliant Trees* enjoyed its early weeks on the album chart. It was sufficiently jazz-leaning to fit the album and Sylvian's new direction, but it retained the pop elements to which he'd repeatedly return ('even employing a key change in the final chorus – a classic Pop song device').[264]

Follow-up singles produced diminishing returns ('The Ink In The Well' hit number 36 in August and 'Pulling Punches' only number 56 in November). But the album reached number four, a career peak for Sylvian. *Brilliant Trees* was a refreshingly avant-garde presence in the top four compared to the mainstream pop albums immediately in front of it – Elton John's *Breaking Hearts* and Spandau Ballet's *Parade*. This was surely more than a reflection of the persistent popularity of Japan. After all, when Virgin's Japan retrospective double-LP came out five months after *Brilliant Trees*, it only reached number 45. (Its title, *Exorcising Ghosts*, was a reference not only to Japan's biggest hit but to a line from 'Nostalgia', a track on the new solo album, in which tree-branch cutting is a metaphor for Sylvian cutting out memories 'to exorcise the ghosts from inside of me.')

Furthermore, the press, who had only come around to appreciating Japan at the end, raved over the 'totally triumphant debut' (*Soundcheck*), which 'glimmers with expectations and glows with success' (*Sounds*). This 'masterpiece' (*Melody Maker*) was 'an astonishing statement' from 'an uncanny talent' (*NME*). Betty Page (*Record Mirror*) declared she could 'wallow indefinitely' in an album so 'splendidly sensual' and 'oh-so-fragile but meaty at the same time.' Even Napier-Bell conceded that he 'did rather like the album' – while noting that 'several tens of thousands owed to the record company for recording costs and advances', with 'no chance of David playing gigs at a profit', meant that *Brilliant Trees* 'certainly isn't a commercial success.' No matter: while Napier-Bell was turning Wham! into a cash cow, Sylvian was jubilant over the acclaim for the album and indifferent to its lack of profitability. The album steadily found an audience in other corners of the world, going top 40 in Sweden and New Zealand, top 20 in Japan and top ten in Italy and the Netherlands. Like Talk Talk, Sylvian would find an enduring following in continental Europe, where critics and consumers were less likely than the British to find moody pop 'un peu pretentious' (as Page put it – and she was a Sylvian fan).[265]

If *It's My Life* was pop music that invited the listener into a kind of living space, *Brilliant Trees* did that even more so. Eno has often talked of ambient music as 'a space, an atmosphere, that you can enter and leave as you wish.' In the later Japan years, Sylvian (and Barbieri, too) had begun to think of pop music as having that potential, and one can experience Sylvian's career-long efforts to realise that potential beginning here. It is evident on the more pop-flavoured side one of the album, especially in 'Nostalgia', whose 'atmospheric sound' – in the choice words of one Sylvian biographer – 'relied as much on the space between chords as the chords themselves.' There is yet more atmosphere and space on side two's track trio, especially 'Brilliant Trees', which achieves a delicate beauty without being precious and a sonic sublimity without being predictable. The 'Ghosts' theme of self-doubt is here again – 'When you come to me, I'll question myself again' and 'Every plan I've made, lost in the scheme of things' – but the context is one of learning from the experience, of hope, of anticipating a future of possibilities. In the end, Sylvian concludes with cautious optimism, 'My whole life stretches in front of me.'[266]

The whole of side two showcases Sylvian's genius for combining a restrained sonic intricacy with lyrical poignancy; both held just shy of the difficult darkness into which he would later evolve. The title track, in particular, the longest and most brilliant on the album, stirringly shows how effective controlled collaboration can be, with Sakamoto and Hassell allowing Sylvian to achieve his vision, or, in Arena's words, 'according to the lines of counterpoint, Sylvian and Sakamoto oppose each other (Jon Hassell also plays a part).' It is a masterful ending to 'a superb record' (as *The Sunday Times* rightfully deemed it).[267]

Brilliant Trees was an early milestone on the post-pop journey, combining traditional pop/rock features with acoustic jazz and electronic experimentation, infusing its lyrics with literary, philosophical and art references, and weaving 'high and low elements across each other.'[268] The album revealed that travelling from pop to art pop and beyond required the inspirational fuel provided by the numerous evolving musical genres – and the scenius networks of musicians who developed them – of the 1960s, 1970s and early 1980s. The journey to post-pop, it turned out, was more collective, more scenius-driven, than the Sylvian and Hollis stories might at first suggest.

Side C (1985-91)

10: Happiness Is Easy/Let The Happiness In

'**Happiness Is Easy**' Talk Talk (1986, 6:30)
'**Let The Happiness In**' David Sylvian (1987, 5:36)

Is post-pop hauntological? The term 'hauntology' was originally coined by philosopher Jacques Derrida as a portmanteau of 'haunting' and 'ontology' that thereby serves as a pun on the latter (their French cognates, *ontologie* and *hantologie*, the 'h' being silent, are close to homophones). Derrida's neologism only appears a few times in the 1993 book for which he created it, but it underpinned his argument that Marxism and communism have 'haunted Western society', creating an ontological disjunction – that is, a disconnection between Europe's political and social nature in the present and its perceived nature as affected by the haunting presence of *Specters Of Marx* (his book's title). Derrida's made-up word was subsequently applied very effectively by English music writers – first Mark Fisher and then Simon Reynolds – to refer to a similar disconnection in postmodern popular culture between visions of the present and nostalgic obsessions with an often-imaginary past (Reynolds called it 'retromania'). As mentioned earlier, it was Fisher who first hit upon the hauntological nature of Japan's 'Ghosts' – an observation that, once made and shared, seems utterly palpable.[269]

I would go further than that, however. The creative journeys of Sylvian and Hollis were ones that envisioned and then endlessly probed a troubling disconnect between the present and spectral elements of the past. They sought to make something new, but always in reference to the old. And they did so *because* of the old because some things old – ghosts if you like – never ceased to bother them. One of those things was, of course, pop music itself. So, post-pop is indeed, by definition, hauntological.

Post-pop's ghosts tend not to be happy ones. As noted in an insightful study of Nick Drake's final album, 'Art and depression are common, if unfortunate, bedfellows'; the links between artistic creativity and altered brain chemistry, including mental illness, are, somewhat paradoxically, both vague and 'so familiar it's practically a cliché.' Drake's family and fans have long been divided over that album's relationship to his death, officially ruled a suicide. But whether that ruling was wrong or not, and whether the album likewise presages such a death or not, it certainly plays 'like the product of an extraordinarily uneasy mind.'[270]

The same might be said of the work of Sylvian and Hollis. The term 'angst' has come up already, mostly applied to the two of them, as they battled against the restrictions imposed on them by success – by record companies, by bandmates, by fame. The implication of that context is that such angst would dissipate once an artist could achieve complete creative freedom. One imagines the end goal being something like the world that Kate Bush created for herself – a solo artist producing her own songs in the studio she built in her home, eventually even releasing the results on her own label. But Napier-Bell, ever droll and insightful, put his finger on the problem. Explaining to a friend why Sylvian and George Michael were determined to end Japan and Wham! respectively, 'just when we've achieved what we set out to achieve', and why he consequently chose to stop managing them once they became solo artists, Napier-Bell sighed, 'It wouldn't change anything. I think they have angst in their souls.'[271]

'I am never a person that sits back and feels very comfortable with life', Sylvian said in the late 1980s. 'If I'm happy, there is always an undertone of doubt, nervousness and sadness.' In another interview around this time, Sylvian stated that his compositions of the previous five years were often designed 'to produce a sense of unease. Because the unease is there, it's in me.' He confessed that 'the past two years have been very difficult, a period of transition', adding what strikes me as a frank self-reflection on depression: 'There are days when I wake up and wonder whether it's worth it, what am I doing here and so forth.' And yet, just when Sylvian seems to be the archetypical tortured artist, he pulls back from the brink; his next line in that interview was: 'But you soon come to your senses.' He then declares his determination 'to have a purpose and a fascination with all aspects of living.'[272]

That ambivalence towards happiness was part of a cycle whereby Sylvian seemed to take such pleasure from the gloomy wallowing that his mood lifted – temporarily. 'I'm not a depressive', he insisted at the time of *Tin Drum*, 'I enjoy my depressions. I actually find 'Ghosts' optimistic, not pessimistic.' The power of 'Ghosts' is indeed that it is paradoxically both despondent and hopeful. Sylvian claimed there was 'a feeling of hope' throughout *Tin Drum*, but Paul Morley rightfully observed in *NME* that the album's vocals conveyed a persistent tension 'between confidence and gloom' and 'love and loss.' Sylvian, dubbed 'the mandarin of melancholy' by *Sounds*, would soon be paired by the music press with Scott Walker 'as two of pop's great melancholics.' But there was a difference, one that would become clear over the ensuing decades. Gloom and loss were stiflingly omnipresent on Walker's halting journey into avant-garde pop/rock: his only 1980s album, the half-hour *Climate Of Hunter* (released a few months before *Brilliant Trees*), barely hinted at the suffocating, discomforting post-rock of *Tilt* (1995), *The Drift* (2006) and *Bish Bosch* (2012). Walker didn't journey into post-pop; he left pop pleasures behind in order to periodically express pain in novel musical ways. Whereas Sylvian always remained aware of the pleasures afforded by pop, never surrendering hope, always using it to balance despair.[273]

Napier-Bell had, years earlier, noted 'a profound disquiet' within Sylvian, but, as one of his biographers put it, that was 'part of the charm' for his manager and for his fans. This was not the charm of Morrissey's miserabilism, however. Where Morrissey's gloom was delivered with uniquely dry, often dark, humour, Sylvian offered his gloom with an earnest intensity; where comedy lightened the shadows cast by Morrissey's emoting, Sylvian's were lightened by glimmers of heartfelt hope. 'Why were The Smiths 'important'?' asked Simon Reynolds in the wake of their breakup. 'Because of their misery. Never forget it.' As Reynolds predicted, that condemned Morrissey to forever live out the pantomime of his miserabilism. But Sylvian – whose early solo career of 1984-87, with its cluster of experimental and masterful albums, exactly coincided with the era of The Smiths – was not deemed 'important' by the music press. Thus, his supposed irrelevance gave him the freedom to be earnest, to explore genres and to experiment in presenting his personal journey through the pleasure/pain paradox.[274]

That journey underpins his entire catalogue, rearing its head regularly, propelling him through genres and into different forms of pop – and towards post-pop. *Quiet Life*, to pick one example, would surely lack its enduring appeal were it not for how Sylvian explores his melancholic impulses on tracks like 'The Other Side Of Life' and 'Despair'. 'Nightporter', on the next Japan album, may have stumbled over its production in ways that 'Ghosts' did not, but it still conveyed the same sense of self-doubt, regret and an aching longing for a happier place – defined vaguely enough for the listener to connect emotionally.

Lest fans feared that the upbeat first single from the first solo album signalled a lighter Sylvian, he clarified that 'Red Guitar' did more than convey that music was his art, his 'means of expression' and his life's preoccupation; it was also destined to forever give his life 'the most pleasure and the most pain. It's that simple.' Both single and parent album reflected the problem of Sylvian's periodic bouts of depression and his self-medicating solution: 'I had this illness, a mental problem, which meant I was always exhausted,' he confessed in the mid-1980s, 'the doctors couldn't do anything, so I used coke.'[275]

The result was hardly music fuelled by cocaine, which Sylvian appeared to use relatively sparingly – enough to get him into the studio to explore that pleasure/pain dialectic, not to make albums that were 'the sound of five men in a studio on coke, not giving a fuck' (as Noel Gallagher famously said of Oasis' *Be Here Now*). On *Brilliant Trees*, even where the music was 'light and agreeable', as on 'The Ink In The Well', the words were not, offering a pastiche of disturbing images to evoke the Spanish Civil War – the song's inspiration being Sylvian's viewing of Pablo Picasso's *Guernica*. He croons 'fire at will' as though he is singing a line from a love song, rendering the surprise of the gloomy theme all the more unnerving. Nestled in among those side one tracks destined to be singles was 'Nostalgia', a key Sylvian song. In line with post-pop's hauntological nature and its intrinsic spirit of nostalgia (as it yearns with contradictory ambivalence for the pop it has – almost – left behind), the song serves as a kind of sequel and 'companion piece to 'Ghosts'.' Just as his memories had been like ghosts, growing increasingly wild and threatening, now his nostalgia threatened to drown him. The only solution was for memories, like tree branches, to be 'ruthlessly pruned.'[276]

The trio of tracks on side two of *Brilliant Trees* comprise a less ambiguous step towards post-pop territory. They were a clearer signal to Japan fans that unpredictable new forms of pop music were liable to leap out and spook anyone following Sylvian on his creative journey. While some fans were likely to 'be forever left behind clutching worn copies of *Quiet Life* and *Gentlemen Take Polaroids*', others were given enough of a pop top-up to keep them going – at least until early in the next century, when Sylvian finally stepped into the darkest neck of the post-pop woods. Furthermore, while the music of side two of *Brilliant Trees* was new territory, the lyrics were replete with Sylvian's signature self-doubt.[277] All three tracks tell of loss of some kind, suggesting a weariness against which Sylvian struggles as he tries to get back up, feet firmly on the ground. He gets there in the end, but it isn't easy; the closing lines of the title track and the album are: 'My whole life stretches in front of me, reaching up like a flower, leading my life back to the soil'.

One of Sylvian's biographers interpreted *Brilliant Trees* as a concept album on existentialism and as such a big step on his journey of spiritual exploration.[278] Sylvian later admitted that the album came at the start of a spiritual journey, that during its making, he was 'on the brink of discovering' Jewish mysticism and the Kabbala, as well as the Tree of Life and other aspects of Buddhism. The references in the album's lyrics are largely literary, risking the snarky accusations of affectation made in the press; Picasso was one thing, but there was a pretentiousness (or fearlessness, depending on your perspective) in Sylvian's nods to Jean Cocteau's essay on 'The Difficulty Of Being' to Cocteau's startlingly avant-garde 1930 film *The Blood Of A Poet* and to no less than three novels by Jean Paul Sartre (*Nausea*, *The Age Of Reason* and *Iron In The Soul*, all titles incorporated into the album's lyrics).

Spiritual journeys are not intrinsically angst-filled – even if that is often how they end up. But Sylvian lends his an air of despair by lashing it to his parallel journey through genres of pop music. At heart, pop is personal – 'the personal as the realm in which the meaning of your life is resolved', as Simon Reynolds once put it. That resolution is the aching hope that defines Romanticism, with its faltering 'dream of the redemptive love that will bring heaven-on-earth, resolve all difference, end alienation.' The triumph of pop in the late-20th century revived and repositioned early-19th century Romanticism (or, in Reynolds' words, 'replaced religion as the opium of the people').[279] Thus, Sylvian's twin quest for spiritual enlightenment and personal happiness is rooted in the Romanticism of pop, allowing him to push against the defining boundaries of pop so as to, well, let the happiness in.

How far could Sylvian push and still create a coherent work of art? *Brilliant Trees* succeeded because its deeply personal nature was both transparent and complimented by musical consistency. Its two sequels drifted off that path, signalling that Sylvian's journey would not in future be the sure-and-steady building on *Tin Drum*, Japan's spectacular swan song, that *Trees* had been. Sylvian was also reading Milan Kundera and Mishima, alongside Sartre and the existentialists, and the resulting 'music began to buckle under the pressure of ambient, mood and tone poems.'[280]

A true artistic sequel to *Brilliant Trees* would come in 1987 – the most fully realised masterpiece of Sylvian's solo career, *Secrets Of The Beehive* – but not before a sequence of confusing releases. Late in 1984 and through 1985, Sylvian continued to compose, first inspired by a trip to Japan, where he wrote two instrumentals for a documentary film about his own career: the cod-Orientalist 'Preparations For A Journey' and a 19-minute soundtrack piece co-written with Ryuichi Sakamoto, titled 'Steel

Cathedrals'. Back in London, drawing upon his ever-expanding scenius of top-notch session players and jazz/rock veterans, Sylvian added to 'Steel Cathedrals' Wheeler, Czukay, his own brother Jansen, ex-Japan guitarist Masami Tsuchiya and Robert Fripp (more on him in a moment). He also turned again to Hassell to play on three further compositions (giving Hassell and Jansen co-writing credit on one). Sylvian hoped all this would amount to an album, but it didn't quite work. Cutting their losses, Sylvian and Virgin cobbled together these various projects into two releases. One comprised the three pieces Sylvian had made with Hassell, released as a 14-minute EP called *Words With The Shaman*. The other took that same material and added the other two instrumentals just mentioned, creating a short album (under 37 mins); released on cassette only at the end of 1985, *Alchemy: An Index Of Possibilities* was clumsily titled, vocal-free and unsatisfyingly fragmented.

'Velly Intelesting, but shurely shome mistake?' was the reaction in *Sounds*, complete with period racism. 'An EP that's really a 12' single and an LP that's a mere EP only available on cassette. Added to which – nowhere can the golden larynx of the former 'world's most beautiful man' be located.' The writer was still entranced by the result, which he called 'a beautifully gentle and hypnotic experience' ('I have one word for this shy, retiring young man: Banzai! ... I mean Bonza!'). But the complete absence of Sylvian's voice broke his journey from pop, comprising a detour towards the territory that Sakamoto had begun to explore (and in which he would triumph for decades): film soundtrack composition. And that was not where Sylvian wanted to go. 'I was aiming for something between pop music and avant-garde music', he told *Record Collector*. He rejected the label 'new age' as 'a marketing term for record companies.' For Sylvian, 'making instrumental music' – which is exactly what he had just done – posed a problem. The results, 'if they are to work, must convey a sense of fascination', rather than the soothing effects of being gentle and hypnotic; 'I'm interested in the unease in music.'[281]

Sylvian's solution to the challenge of conveying that 'unease' was to keep making both avant-garde pop and electronic instrumentals through the collaborative process but to keep them separate. He primarily chose two partners. One was Czukay, whom he joined at the Can Studio in Cologne at the end of 1986, rapidly recording a pair of instrumentals, roughly 16 and 18 minutes in length, featuring shortwave radio samples. Due to contractual complications, the work was not released until 1988 – as an album titled after the two pieces, *Plight & Premonition*. In that year, Sylvian and Czukay reunited in Cologne to make a second pair of instrumentals, averaging 19 minutes each, with one of them ('Flux') featuring Stockhausen's son, Markus, on flugelhorn and two members of Can – drummer Jaki Liebezeit (1938-2017) and guitarist Michael Karoli (1948-2001) – thereby connecting Sylvian tightly to the decades-old Cologne scenius. The second pair were released as *Flux + Mutability*, credited to 'David Sylvian and Holger Czukay'. The tone of the four pieces was, however, one that was fast becoming recognisably Sylvian's. 'Low-key' and 'sleepy' was how *Q* magazine described them, concluding that these "ambient' instrumentals drone along pleasantly/pointlessly in a doomy, gloomy sort of way.' 'Vacuous' was the verdict in *Rolling Stone*. Years later, music press views on the albums remained similar, although British music magazine *Fact* spotted echoes of the pleasure/pain paradox that was Sylvian's late 1980s focus: 'While *Plight & Premonition* felt like a study in unease, wracked with paranoia, *Flux + Mutability* admits the possibility, if not any certainty, of earthly bliss.'[282]

The pursuit of that paradox was precisely what Sylvian sought in following up with another collaborator, leading to a firm musical friendship with Robert Fripp. As a founder of King Crimson, whose 1969 debut album *In The Court Of The Crimson King* was seen as a – if not *the* – cornerstone of progressive rock, Fripp was English prog rock royalty. This fact, plus his connections to Eno and Bowie, along with his experimental guitar work, all appealed in obvious ways to Sylvian. In turn, Fripp would later say of Sylvian that 'he writes wonderful lyrics, he has a gorgeous voice and the sounds he makes from his keyboard are stunning. And then you move on to the third [sic] point: I like being with him.'[283]

On Sylvian's next album, the double LP *Gone To Earth*, released nine months after *Alchemy*, his voice was back but restricted to disc one, with the soothing potential of his signature croon offset by Fripp's angular guitar playing; disc two was entirely instrumental. If *Gone To Earth* 'forms a pair' with *Brilliant Trees*, as one music historian has written, it is only in the sense that Sylvian's spiritual journey was continued here, or to quote Sylvian's own website, it was his next step in the intermingling of 'the personal with the themes of Gnosticism and alchemy.'[284] Fripp's role was prominent (he played on over half the tracks, and he was given a co-writing credit on the title track on disc one and two of the disc two instrumentals), lending the album a somewhat oppressive and angsty tone. That stymied reviewers a little. One saw disc two as Sylvian being 'a bit philosophical', with disc one full of arty love songs, but with a catch:

Right: The cover of Japan's 1982 single 'Ghosts' depicted its writer and singer, David Sylvian. (*Virgin*)

Left: A frame from Japan's performance of 'Ghosts' on *Top Of The Pops* on 18 March 1982, showing David Sylvian, his brother Steve Jansen and Mick Karn. (*BBC*)

Right: Following *Top Of The Pops* rules, Sylvian mimed the words to 'Ghosts', yet still managed to stun viewers with the song's unique sound and emotional impact. (*BBC*)

Left: Although Japan's third album prompted them to be dropped by their label, *Quiet Life* would later prove to be an influential stylistic breakthrough. (*Hansa*)

Left and above: Sylvian alone graced the covers of the final two Japan albums, *Gentlemen Take Polaroids* (1980) and *Tin Drum* (1981), the other band members relegated to the back cover or inside artwork. Allegedly, they arrived for the *Tin Drum* photo shoot only to discover that Sylvian had completed the task early with his latent Orientalist vision. (*Virgin*)

Right: Japan and Sylvian were featured repeatedly in the Japanese music magazine *Ongaku Senka*. This example is from 1978, long before they received similar attention in their home country. (*Author's collection*)

Left: A 1982 promotional shot of David Sylvian showing his post-1979 look, inspired by early-1970s David Bowie – who, in turn, adopted this look in 1982. (*Steve Rapport for the Sounds Fan Library*)

THE DREAMING
KATE BUSH

Left: Kate Bush, as Houdini's wife, uses a kiss to pass Houdini the key to his escape on the cover of 1982's *The Dreaming*. (*EMI*)

Above: It is not hard to avoid the objectifying and infamous leotard photographs of Kate Bush; this stunning yet tasteful alternative is from 1982. (*Guido Harari*)

Right: James Marsh created the distinctive covers to all five Talk Talk albums, beginning with the 1982 debut, *The Party's Over*. (*EMI*)

Left: Marsh's artwork never depicted the band, but the photographs inside the *It's My Life* CD showed Talk Talk reduced to a trio, with Hollis in a separate frame from Harris and Webb. (*EMI*)

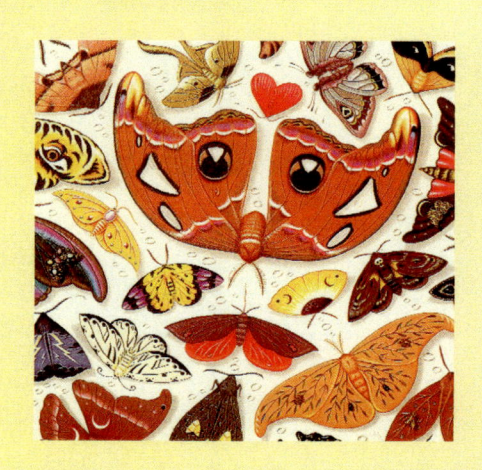

Right: Marsh's use of both nature and a stylised face on 1986's The *Colour Of Spring* served as a visual link between the first Talk Talk album cover and the last two. (*EMI*)

Above: The Talk Talk trio (Mark Hollis, Paul Webb and Lee Harris) performing in their mid-1980s heyday. (*Getty*)

Below: Talk Talk were very popular in France, while Sylvian's solo work was bigger in Italy and the Netherlands, but both artists were more popular in continental Europe than at home. (*Author's cassette*)

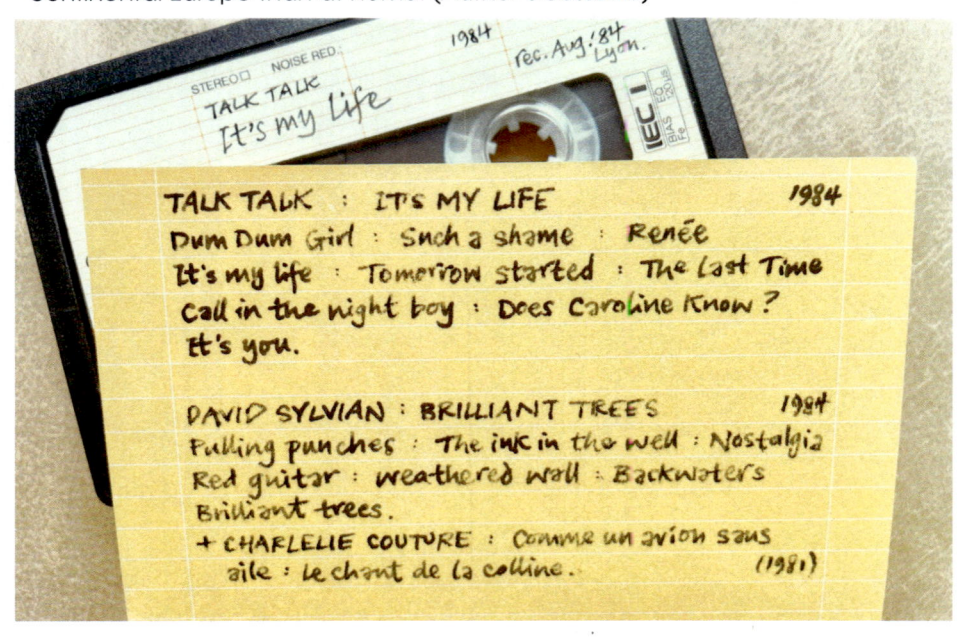

```
TALK TALK : IT'S MY LIFE                           1984
Dum Dum Girl : Such a shame : Renée
It's my life : Tomorrow started : The Last Time
Call in the night boy : Does Caroline Know?
It's you.

DAVID SYLVIAN : BRILLIANT TREES                    1984
Pulling punches : The ink in the well : Nostalgia
Red guitar : weathered wall : Backwaters
Brilliant trees.
  + CHARLÉLIE COUTURE : Comme un avion sans
     aile : Le chant de la colline..        (1981)
```

Right: *Brilliant Trees* successfully launched David Sylvian's solo career in 1984, but no subsequent album would do as well. (*Virgin*)

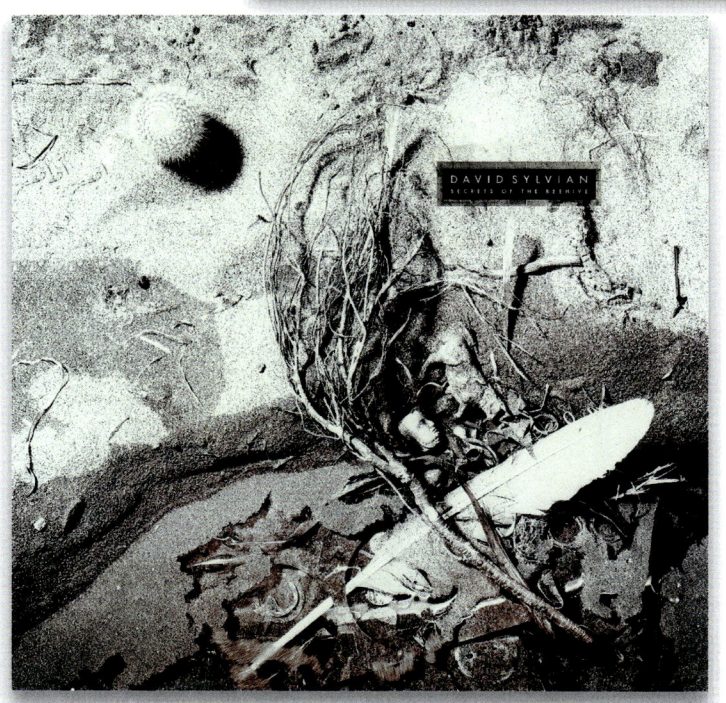

Left: The self-effacing cover, designed by 23 Envelope, of David Sylvian's 1987 *Secrets Of The Beehive*. (*Virgin*)

Above: Ryuichi Sakamoto and David Sylvian during the 1986 recording of *Secrets Of The Beehive* in France. (*Yuka Fujii*)

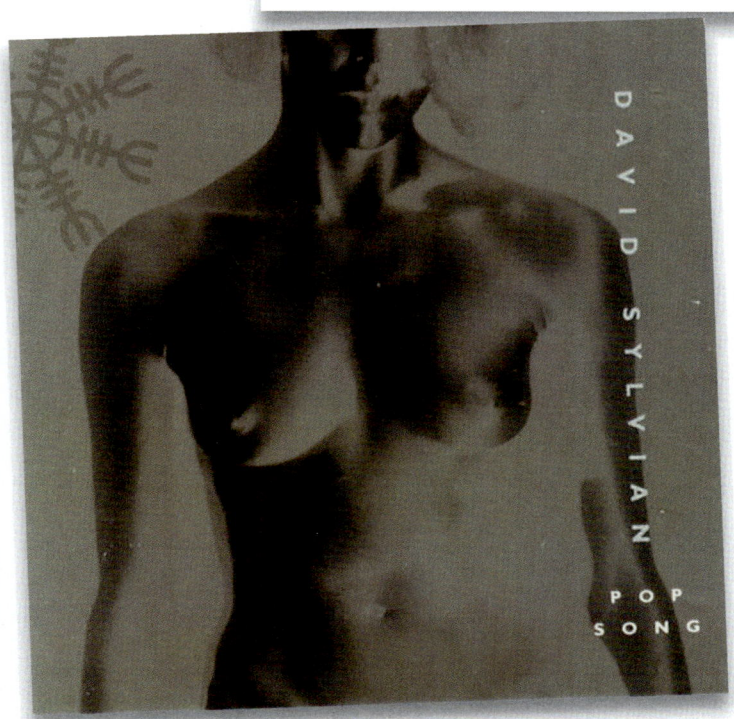

Right: In 1988, Talk Talk's Spirit Of Eden stunned fans, critics and label executives with its indefinable sound. (*Parlophone*)

Left: The cover of David Sylvian's 1989 CD single 'Pop Song' contrasted with the artwork of his albums. (*Virgin*)

Above: Although he famously loathed having to promote his records, Mark Hollis could be a jovial jokester. (*Getty*)

Right: The enduring reputation of Kate Bush's Hounds Of Love as her greatest masterpiece helped cement the iconic status of this 1985 cover. (*EMI*)

Kate Bush

Hounds Of Love

TALK TALK

LAUGHING STOCK

Left: Now a duo of Hollis and Harris, with producer Tim Friese-Greene an unofficial member, 1991's Laughing Stock took Talk Talk deep into post-pop territory. (*Verve/Polydor*)

Above: Though not particularly prolific (nine original studio albums in 33 years), Kate Bush is a compellingly unique talent. (*Alamy*)

Right: A Japan album in all but name, Rain Tree Crow was Sylvian's choice for both record and band monicker over the objections of bandmates and label. (*Virgin*)

Left: The cover of Mark Hollis's 1998 solo album was as understated and odd as the album itself. (*Polydor*)

Left: David Sylvian and Ingrid Chavez, the actor, singer, songwriter and poet to whom he was married from 1992 to 2004. (*davidsylvian.net*)

Right: The look of a post-pop star? Hollis, resembling a high school history teacher making a point, during a 1998 interview for French magazine *Magic*. (*snowinberlin.com/markhollis*)

This page: The marital joy expressed in 1999's *Dead Bees On A Cake* (Virgin) contrasted chillingly with the pain that David Sylvian channelled into his divorce album, 2003's *Blemish* (Samadhisound), and into his challenging final post-pop work, 2009's *Manafon*. (Samadhisound)

Left: The birdsong soundwave on the cover of Kate Bush's *Aerial* (2005). In 2010, its second disc, 'A Sky Of Honey', was retitled 'An Endless Sky Of Honey', its nine tracks dissolved into an unbroken, prog-pop tour de force. *(EMI/Columbia)*

Right: *Aerial*'s blissful summer theme contrasts with the exquisite and eccentric beauty of winter concept album *50 Words For Snow*, Bush's 2011 swansong (so far). *(Fish People)*

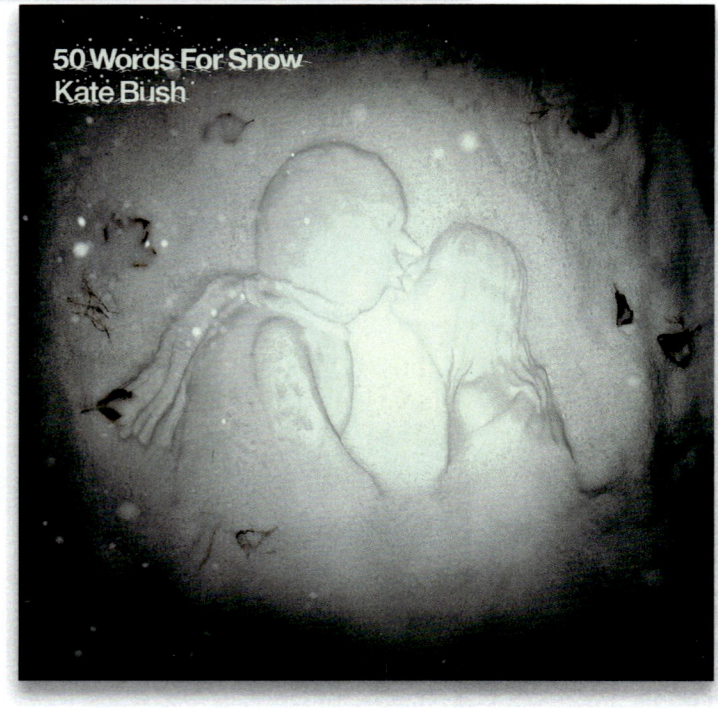

Sylvian was 'a subversive romantic', his love songs favouring 'dissonant chords' as much as 'soothing lilts', used by Sylvian to convey 'the stress of personal relationships' (his phrase).[285]

Sylvian confessed that the 'so raw' title track to the album was an expression of 'anger and frustration' over the conflict between one's 'desire to understand' and 'anger at the inability to understand.' This existential angst resulted in what Rob Young called 'a muddy, atonal duet between Sylvian's voice – a crevasse at the song's heart – and Fripp's mangled-steel guitar.' The Fripp-Sylvian composition is preceded by 'Before The Bullfight', deemed by biographer Power to be the 'centrepiece' of *Gone To Earth*. Almost ten minutes long, 'Bullfight' has a funereal tension that grates as much as it grips.[286] The song's production, like that of the whole first disc, is far from a wall of sound, yet lacks the breathing room that helped make masterpieces of *Brilliant Trees* and *Secrets Of The Beehive*. Sylvian's self-flagellation – 'when all's forgiven, still every fault's my own' – combined with the relative lack of space in a track like 'Bullfight', contributes to disc one's claustrophobia. *Gone To Earth* has its virtues and its supporters, but neither at the time nor in retrospect does it quite succeed as a manifestation of Sylvian's exploration of the pleasure/pain paradox.[287]

But the following spring, Sylvian was back in the studio, again with a sterling cast of supporting musicians, and in ten weeks, he had recorded a new album, released that autumn of 1987. *Secrets Of The Beehive* – 'melancholic, acoustic and atmospheric' – was arguably his best yet, and, to my ears at least, one that would not be topped. He confessed that 'the path I'd been pursuing since *Brilliant Trees* had been exhausted. It had come to a conclusion.' And while he would not cease to pursue collaborations, some fruitful, some not, he would not make another solo album for 12 years.[288]

If we see Sylvian's journey of 1984-87 as a pursuit of the ultimate expression of the pleasure/pain paradox, the degree to which *Secrets* succeeded was a matter of taste. When Sylvian toured the album in the US the following year, he found a very small but rapturous following of fans, critics and fellow musicians. The American composer and producer Anton Sanko, for example, enthused that '*Secrets Of The Beehive* is one of the greatest records ever made', one he played over and over trying to figure out 'how he did it', how Sylvian created a musical and lyrical environment 'so exciting, idiomatic and iconoclastic.' Back in the UK, the *NME* deemed *Secrets* 'a fabulous and mercurial record', but while a reviewer for *Sounds* admitted that some 'find Mr Sylvian's music quite ravishing', he found it 'dank, depressing and po-faced.' Its mood of 'misery and self-pity' inspired the reviewer to imagine Sylvian pacing 'a lonely room, waiting for phones to ring and friends to drop by just so he can remind them of what a terrible time he's having.'[289]

We might smile and then dismiss such a panning as a cheap laugh, but the metaphor of the room was close to home. Sylvian's response to accusations of miserabilism was barely a defence, admitting that listening to his albums was like 'being alone in a room with yourself, or even a step worse than that.' *Secrets* was 'introspective in a way that makes some people really nervous. The kind of people who immediately turn on a television when they are alone don't enjoy my music; it makes them terribly uncomfortable.'[290]

If that was most of the record-buying public, those fans who relished that discomfort were a loyal minority, placing *Secrets Of The Beehive* in the UK top 40 in its first week – but at number 37, after which it dropped to number 67 and then disappeared. Perhaps it was thus in recognition of the select nature of Sylvian's following by 1987 that 'Let The Happiness In' was chosen as the lead single to *Secrets*, the sixth 7' of Sylvian's solo career. For it would otherwise have been an odd choice, surely predictable that it would make no more than a modest chart appearance (it entered at number 66) and soon disappear (as it did the following week). Yet it faithfully whetted the appetites of the faithful for the album, which followed just weeks later. The song's beginning is without rhythm, just a gentle dirge of brass and synths, over which Sylvian begins to croon despondently that he is 'waiting on the empty docks'. The ships he awaits are a metaphor for – what? – spiritual enlightenment? God? Joy? Love? As one biographer put it: 'Sitting on top of the orchestral soup was a positively suicidal sounding vocal from Sylvian: 'I'm waiting for the agony to stop, oh, let the happiness in'.'[291]

But this is Sylvian: instead of mere miserabilism, we are led into the pleasure/pain paradox. Noted Power: as 'Let The Happiness In' progressed, 'a hymn-like optimism began to invade' and what had 'sounded so despairing but a moment ago began to exude a real sense of joy.' *Secrets Of The Beehive* as a whole achieved a delicate balance between dark and light, 'conveying the same sense of joy and sorrow as an old blues record' and that accomplishment resonates most effectively across side two's four tracks.[292] The first two, 'When Poets Dreamed Of Angels' and 'Mother And Child', act as a pair, their innocuous titles and gentle arrangements thinly disguising a disturbing theme of domestic violence and abandonment. The contradictory emotions invoked and provoked by those songs set up the listener for the paradox of 'Let The Happiness In', which itself prepares us for the beautiful agony of the closing track.

'Happiness' and 'Waterfront' also form a pair, but in the latter, the ship is no longer anticipated: it has sunk. The sound is simple and gorgeous: Sylvian's refined croon, tinged with an emotive rasp, balancing Sakamoto on piano, his strings swelling but spare. Under a minute into the song, it stops. The pause offers us five seconds of silent anticipation. Then the strings return, and Sylvian delivers one of the most agonising pleasure/pain lines of his career: 'On the waterfront, the rain is pouring in my heart'. The spectre of 'Ghosts' is close, brought closer by the next line: 'Here the memories come in waves'. There are two more pauses, three seconds before the verse-chorus cycle repeats, and seven seconds before that heartstring-tugging chorus returns.

And then, if that isn't enough, a single line at the end, a musical and lyrical coda, a so-very-Sylvian moment of poignant self-doubt: 'Is our love strong enough?' You listen, you cry and you don't know why. But you do know that Sylvian has done a number on you.

If Sylvian's call to let the happiness in lacked conviction, leaving us still aware of whatever state of misery inspired such a plea, Hollis's assertion that 'Happiness Is Easy' similarly undermined itself. The phrase employs one of Hollis's favourite rhetorical techniques in everyday speech, although one not often found in his lyrics: sarcasm. 'Happiness Is Easy', far from being a carefree love song, is a biting denunciation of religion and its self-serving manipulation of the innocent with lies about the afterlife. Hollis even deployed a children's choir from Acton – whose adaption of 'Little Ships Of Galilee' haunts the song's chorus – to make the point unflinchingly. The easy happiness of the song's title is presented as a sham, a false promise designed to fool the faithful and keep them sheep-like. 'Take good care of what the priests say', warns Hollis: 'After death, it's so much fun'.

'Happiness Is Easy' and 'Let The Happiness In' do not explore psychological states of depression or euphoria in the way that Bowie's 'All The Madmen' or Elton John's 'Madman Across The Water' or Pink Floyd's *Dark Side Of The Moon* portray and critique the contemporary concept of madness.[293] Instead, they offer contrasting examples of how pop's angst potential can be used to express contradictions and paradoxes inherent to happiness – both personal and spiritual. The exercise is all very pop – as Power notes, the 'romantic pop outsider' is an old trope of pop/rock, even of popular culture in music and literature going back to 19th-century Romanticism. But its gloomy earnestness also leans into something beyond pop.[294]

It was an old notion that the words written by Hollis, his style of delivery and his discomfort on stage and with journalists all constituted a stew of gloom. Even *It's My Life*, an admittedly moody record but hardly a depressing one, had been denounced in *Record Mirror* as 'one long negative river of regret, a gluttony of guilt, a tribute to torpor.' The theme also appeared in European music magazines, despite their generally favourable view of the band; for example, *Humo* characterised the second Talk Talk album as 'endless sorrows whimpered by Hollis', whose voice combined 'a death rattle with the call of a rutting snow hare' (an animal not found in the Netherlands, the magazine's home country).[295]

The Colour Of Spring may now be seen as 'ethereal and enigmatic', but at the time, those qualities were taken by some critics to mean gloomy and pretentious. If 'Happiness Is Easy' was sarcastic, the second track, 'I Don't Believe In You', was unabashedly downbeat: 'Now the fun is over', it begins. I could not agree more with a recent verdict that Webb's melodic bassline anchors and inspires a song that sees 'Hollis at his most poignant and plaintive', with a searing synthesised guitar solo taking 'the track to fresh heights.' But the album was denigrated as 'cumbersome, allegedly "impressionistic" waffle' in *NME*, with Hollis accused of sounding 'like a man yawning with a mouthful of glue.' A *Sounds* review titled 'Spring Bored' complained that, after a few tracks, the album's 'melancholia' began 'to wear thin.'[296]

Significantly, the only truly upbeat track on *The Colour Of Spring* did not emerge from the album's sessions but was created afterwards by Hollis and Friese-Greene in a spirit of perverse irony. Faced with the record label's clichéd reaction to what they had recorded – 'there isn't one hit on this album!' declared EMI's Dave Ambrose – they laughingly rose to the challenge. That meant doing the opposite of what Ambrose feared they would. Friese-Greene admitted that his and Hollis's 'first, immediate reaction was to go, 'Fuck 'em!'.' The song they wrote went against the grain of the album, its spirit of composition and its mood. This was the late summer of 1985, and the UK charts were packed with pop (in mid-August, Madonna was both number one *and* number two). But this was Hollis, and so for a template, he picked Kate Bush's 'Running Up That Hill', which reached its number three peak at the end of that month. 'If she can write a song with one chord in it', declared Hollis, 'so can I!' They began with a drum pattern inspired by the Bush hit, over which Hollis played 'Green Onions', and a few days later, they had 'Life's What You Make It'.[297]

'Mark absolutely hated it as far as I know', said Robbie McIntosh, the Pretenders guitarist who played on most *Spring* tracks. Hollis conceded it was 'a good choice for a single' – it would enter the top 25 in a dozen markets and become the second biggest hit, after 'It's My Life', of the band's career. But he resented how it differed from 'the rest of the stuff on *The Colour Of Spring*', where he was 'getting far more in a modern classical feel.' And if 'Life's What You Make It' was the exception that proved the rule – the album was musically a step too far from upbeat pop and lyrically gloomy to boot – even its hit single was tinged with fatalism; the line that followed the title phrase was 'you can't escape it'.[298]

The public and press perception of Hollis as a depressive was partly based on his demeanour on stage – the above-mentioned sunglasses, hair flopping over his face as he hunched over the microphone, seldom acknowledging the audience. That look was a symptom of his dislike of touring.[299] This was something else he had in common with Sylvian and Bush. Her absence from the stage was notorious (as mentioned, she toured once, in 1979, and never again). Sylvian endured touring as a hazing ritual of up-and-coming bands, but he imposed limits on tours before Japan had made it big, refusing to return to the US after one brief visit. In the wake of Japan's collapse, Sylvian told a writer for *Juke's* that after a couple of years of doing something, 'then you realise the things you're doing don't make you happy. You don't enjoy it and wonder why you're doing it. For myself, it's touring.' He understood that it was what bands did, especially when they were starting out, but – in Karn's words – 'David hated it. Absolutely hated it.'[300]

By 1988, Sylvian had not toured for almost six years, avoiding the chore completely while he forged his solo career. But in March of that year, he began a tour titled *In Praise Of Shamans: Around The World In 80 Days*. He did it either because he had promised himself he would, once he had at least three albums out (as he later claimed), or because he'd forgotten his disdain for live performance as a torturous trick played on the audience, 'misguided into believing that I'm giving them something.' The touring band was three-quarters Japan, with Jansen and Barbieri included but without Karn – although musicians who had recently played with Karn, David Torn and Robby Aceto, were recruited (much to Karn's annoyance), as was Mark Isham (to handle the brass parts that he and others had played on Sylvian's albums). The success of the tour in the US, where he'd not played for a decade, was significant and somewhat unexpected, but its success in Japan was less surprising – as was the warm reception he received in Italy, the Netherlands and other European markets, as well as at the tour's finale in the UK.[301]

And yet, Sylvian's demeanour before so many loyal fans was similar to Hollis's, with a few sentences at most muttered to hungry audiences. The band's defence of this attitude was touching but unconvincing; for example, 'he takes his work seriously', Isham argued. Yet, he and most of the others would never play again with Sylvian. Conceding at the end of the tour that he 'sort of' enjoyed it, then claiming in 1990 that 'it was worth it', he admitted four years later that the tour 'was a mess. I was a mess at the time. The whole entourage was beset by problems.' The fact that the tour had been a hit, raising his international profile to new heights, was grounds for Sylvian – in the tradition of 'Ghosts' – to retreat, which he did – from touring, from making solo albums and even from living in England.[302]

As the sun set behind the 18th-century buildings that enclosed the Plaza Mayor of the spectacular Spanish city of Salamanca, the lights came on the elaborate stage that had been constructed on one side of the square, and 389 musicians and choristers began to line up or take their seats. It was June 2022, and in the video recordings of the concert, I think I can see myself, with my youngest daughter on my hip, standing in the crowd as the orchestra and choir fill the plaza with the stirring pomp of the *Carmina Burana*. It is hard to think of a better setting for the majestic sounds of this famous cantata, composed in the 1930s by the Bavarian Carl Orff (1895-1982), its libretto mostly in Latin and based on medieval poems. This was not my first visit to Salamanca; I spent part of my childhood living in Madrid, and so I had first set foot in the city's Plaza Mayor a half-century earlier when cars were still allowed in the square and General Franco still ruled the country. But I had never seen or heard the plaza like this.[303]

And yet, there remained in my mind another connection to Salamanca's Plaza Mayor, a specifically musical one. Had I seen a concert there many years ago? Was I imagining something based on a music video I had once seen or something I'd read? It took a few months, but eventually, the penny dropped. In September 1986, Talk Talk played their final ever gig in this very same plaza. I was not there, but I found footage of the concert, which was very blurry but with surprisingly good sound. The concert ended with a poignant nine-minute rendition of 'Such A Shame'. Hollis was never one to engage audiences or do much more than stand and sing, and here he hides behind sunglasses (although this was a nighttime outdoor concert), clutching the microphone with both hands, giving the impression of defeat. He seems unable to draw energy from the audience – although, unlike the Orff concert audience 36 years later, they are all on their feet, many jumping up and down, arms in the air, singing along and cheering. Before the 'Such A Shame' encore, Hollis merely says, twice, 'thank you very much', and after the song, repeats the phrase twice again, then offers a slightly downhearted smile before muttering 'thank you' and 'goodnight' as he turns from the microphone and the crowd. It is all terribly affecting.[304]

Have I invented the heartbreaking atmosphere of that September night in Salamanca? After all, the crowd were having a blast; continental Europe in the mid-1980s was the heartland of Talk Talk's massive success, the setting for their imperial phase, and the audience could not have known that neither Talk Talk nor Hollis himself would ever play a concert again – not in Spain, not anywhere. But I know that now, and it is impossible to watch the footage from 1986 without remembering that fact, without allowing that knowledge to merge with the melancholic power of the final song. Add to that the knowledge that Hollis himself is now gone, plus the emotional resonance for me of the Salamanca setting. So, perhaps I did imagine something.

Or perhaps not. Hollis's biographer Wardle has watched the footage, and he, too, saw how Hollis 'cuts a forlorn and exhausted figure on stage.' Compared to earlier recordings, 'his voice has less power; its appealing fragility appears genuinely as if on the point of cracking.' Wardle also spoke to Chris Beale, the sound engineer whose five years of experience touring with Talk Talk would end in Salamanca. By that night, although it was unspoken, 'everybody knew that Mark wasn't coping very well' with touring, that he 'wouldn't be doing it again.' 'It was gutting when it ended', said Beale. 'It was the saddest show that we did.'[305] Such a shame, indeed.

Hollis was a fan of the *Carmina Burana*; on several occasions, he mentioned it or Orff himself when discussing how he valued and was influenced by certain examples of modern classical music. He surely would have loved the performance of it in Salamanca that summer of 2022. But, equally surely, he would not have been able to forget the setting as that of his final concert. Would those memories have been happy? Or more mixed and complicated than that? After all, as Lana Del Rey reminded us, with a dark pop sensibility that surely owes much to Bush, Sylvian and Hollis, happiness is a butterfly. Happiness isn't usually easy, and it can't always simply be let in.

11: April 5th/September

'April 5th' Talk Talk (1986, 5:51)
'September' David Sylvian (1987, 1:17)

'We say that we're in love' is a classic Sylvian phrase. It seems at first to be a typical pop song line, tapping into pop's Romanticist motherlode. And yet, the prefixing of the words 'we say' suggests artifice, planting a seed of doubt that is immediately fertilised by the phrase that follows: 'while secretly wishing for rain'. This insertion of a slightly sinister ambiguity at the heart of romantic love is a fine example of Sylvian's preoccupation with the pleasure/pain paradox. It comes in the middle of the nine lines that comprise the lyrics to 'September', the stripped-down miniature song that opens *Secrets Of The Beehive*. It is both delicately beautiful and stunningly effective as an introduction to the musical and lyrical tones of the album.[306]

As much a product of a scenius as were all of Sylvian's 1980s solo albums, 1987's *Secrets Of The Beehive* succeeded far more than the other albums in keeping the contributions by all those musicians restrained, subtle, even minimal. The resulting sense of control over sound and space echoed Talk Talk's 'April 5th', anticipating where Hollis would go the following year, even as Sylvian himself would pull back from the brink of post-pop minimalism for the next decade (while Kate Bush was leaning away from prog-pop and, with *Sensual World* and *The Red Shoes*, closer to more mainstream pop). Just as 'September' feels fully realised, despite its 1:17 running time, so does its parent album feel rich and complete, despite being a mere 34 minutes, almost entirely acoustic, with the sparest of Sakamoto's string arrangements.

'September' lets the listener know that the album is pop, but not in a conventional sense; as *Secrets Of The Beehive* unwinds, it reveals its jazz and minimalist classical influences. Yet, calling it jazz-pop or art pop seems inadequate. By viewing it as a stage in Sylvian's journey from commercially successful pop to various forms of experimental pop and post-pop, perhaps we can classify it as 'A Step Towards Post-Pop' – a new category tag for websites and streaming services to consider, perhaps?

'September' was reputed to be inspired in part by 'April 5th', which is likewise unconventional as a love song and as a pop song. Both songs are spare and intriguing, prompting the listener to ponder issues of genre. 'April 5th' taps deep into the pastoral theme of *The Colour Of Spring*, being ostensibly about the arrival of that season. Hollis, like Bush, was drawn to how English composers like Frederick Delius (1862-1934) musically expressed a connection to nature (Hollis would have heard Bush's 'Delius (Song Of Summer)' on 1980's *Never For Ever*). But there is more here: spring is also a metaphor for love's onset in the form of Hollis's wife Flick, whose birthday was 5 April (after almost a decade together, the two married in 1985, a few months after 'April 5th' was written and recorded). Without that knowledge, the larger meaning of date and song remains opaque. With it, lines such as 'Come gentle spring, come at winter's end' and 'Here she comes, laughter in her kiss' become mutually illuminating. Sequenced at the end of side one of *The Colour Of Spring*, 'April 5th' forms a musical pair with the penultimate track on side two, 'Chameleon Day', which Wardle called 'a Trojan Horse, leaving the door ajar for Talk Talk's future manifestation.' [307]

The metaphor works well for both songs, which could fit comfortably on the next album, *Spirit Of Eden*, despite the latter's reputation for being a jarring, great leap forward (a leap off the cliff of commercialism). They sound very different from the other six tracks on *The Colour Of Spring*, especially the four that were singles. They are the only two tracks lacking Lee Harris's drumming, a motor that memorably drives the rest of the album and gives it (six-eighth's) coherence. Other cues that these might be pop songs – such as obvious verse-chorus structures – are also missing or unclear. Both tracks (along with 'Happiness Is Easy') feature the Variophon, an electronic wind instrument that processes imitated reed and brass instrumental timbres. Invented at the University of Cologne in 1975, the Variophon connected Talk Talk to the same experimental electronic musical legacy that Sylvian sought to access. As mentioned earlier, Stockhausen was educated at the University of Cologne, where Czukay later studied under him in the 1960s.[308] The Variophon would be played by Hollis – which, he said, 'sounds right weird' – on both *Spirit Of Eden* and *Laughing Stock*. The instrument is thus inseparable from what would eventually be heard and conceived of as the sound of post-rock (and, as I am arguing here, post-pop).[309]

Why is post-pop a necessary category? Consider how much the Talk Talk albums have confounded efforts to squeeze them into genre boxes. A 1988 review of *Spirit Of Eden* in a Florida newspaper argued that the album 'can't be classified as rock, pop or New Age', but its songs 'effortlessly segue from one style to another.' The format of Wikipedia does not allow for a 'can't be classified' category, and so contributors to the relevant pages (or are algorithms making a laughingstock of us?) have gamely attempted to catch all the subtle shades of genre, classifying *The Colour Of Spring* as 'new wave/art pop/progressive pop/experimental pop', *Spirit Of Eden* as 'post-rock/art rock/progressive pop', with *Laughing Stock* simply (?) 'post-rock/art rock'.[310]

By 2021, there were 83 genre categories up for grabs at the annual Grammy Awards, with each nominated album's genre 'debated, often hotly, by nomination committees.' Those committees cannot satisfy everyone; that year, Justin Bieber complained that what he called his 'R&B album' was nominated in the Best Pop Vocal category, while Tyler the Creator, in winning Best Rap Album, opined that 'rap or urban' were 'just a politically correct way to say the N-word. Why can't we just be in pop?' Genre labels were once crucial to selling records – indispensable to record store employees, radio programmers and marketing departments – and record companies are still obliged to provide such metadata for every release. But 'it's pretty archaic', according to Nabil Ayers of British label 4AD; trying to assign albums to 'one of these big buckets' is outmoded, not just because Grammy's 83 genres (or Music Genre List's 49 primary and 337 sub-genres) aren't enough, but because younger listeners simply 'don't think about it.'

Genre may be increasingly irrelevant to how we create and consume music. Genre only works if it is static and if it reflects a listener's expectations (marked by a 'typified rhetorical action', as scholars of rhetoric put it). That makes genre poorly compatible with the streaming age, the era of Fisher's 'strange simultaneity', in which cultural time has 'folded back on itself.' In the streaming age, playlists are consumed more than albums – playlists that often privilege mood or other expansive categories over genre, generated by algorithms, by music editors working for companies like Apple and Spotify, and by genre-careless listeners themselves.

If that means we now live in a post-genre world, where does that leave pop music? Of all the old genres of music, pop, above all, defied the inertia of a firm definition. It demanded, in Petrusich's words, 'a kind of endless, purposeful reinvention' acting as a crucial motor that helped keep the Album/Singles Era in perpetual motion. Post-pop, then, as itself a kind of genre in motion, has been a symptom and manifestation of the journey into our post-genre world. But we still need genre in order to contemplate the music we have. As genre is 'inherently backwards-looking', we require it as a tool, however imperfect and imprecise it may be, to do everything from understanding music history to organising records on a shelf.[311]

The impulse to organise, categorise and label everything may be a natural human tendency, or it may be a particularly Western one – a function of European acquisitiveness in the age of empires. Either way, the evolution of popular music since the mid-20th century has been accompanied by endless efforts to invent and identify genres, label bands and fit them all together. That is possible if we pick a moment, freeze time and inspect the state of the things in stasis. But popular music is never in stasis; it is constantly in motion, a ceaseless flow of influences and stimulations. Our collections of music, however large or small and in whatever formats, reflect that fact. In Questlove's words, 'a collection starts as a protest against the passage of time and ends as a celebration of it.' When the fictional Rob Fleming reorganises his record collection in Nick Hornby's *High Fidelity*, he unwittingly recognises the futility of a perfect curation based on content. We love – we need – to see music as classifiable, as orderly as a record shop (or our own collections because, admit it, yours is organised, too). 'When you're a collector, you're creating order' out of chaos, observes Sonic Youth's Thurston Moore. 'We think, therefore we sort', as one historian of our curatorial impulses puts it.[312]

But popular music is only easily sorted if we view it strictly through our own lives; Rob Fleming arranges his records in the order that he acquired them, thus subordinating music history to his personal history ('because this, after all, is who I am'). Viewed in its totality, music is more like a vast delta, with rivers and streams and tributaries constantly merging and branching off, bursting or draining, perpetually flowing. Yes's Steve Howe once said this of the genre he helped to create, but it could apply to any genre: 'Prog is about influences merging in an indescribable sort of way, the folk, the blues, the rock, the jazz, the classical – in my case flamenco – but not being allowed to dominate.'[313]

One way to look at the creative output of Sylvian, Hollis and Bush in the 1980s is to highlight their interrogation of genre. Loosely speaking, four genres outside pop influenced their journeys through that delta: classical music (especially, but not strictly, minimalism); jazz (especially modal jazz); progressive rock, or prog; and experimental electronic music. Considering that the primary influences on all of them were the rock/pop artists of their teen years (Hollis turned 13 in 1968, Sylvian and Bush in 1971), it might seem as if I'm making a point too broad to have insight – that they were influenced by every genre they could lay their hands on. To an extent, that is true: experimental pop artists were inspired initially to make music more or less in the genre that first grabbed their youthful attention, to be their own version of – for example – David Bowie. But equally important was their simultaneous, voracious appetite to discover other genres, leading them to experiment with making something novel in genre terms.

That experimentation has tended to take two forms. One was the exploration of hybridity, the attempt to create music with elements borrowed from multiple genres, but still – in most cases, but not all – identifiable as having pop foundations. The other form was to adopt a loosely post-modern approach to music making, seeking inspiration in genres that were themselves, by definition, post-genre experiments. Sylvian, Hollis and Bush did not go back to the canon of artists that defined the classical core – such as Beethoven and Mozart (Hollis's comment to 1990s collaborator Laurence Pendrous that 'Mozart was a cunt' was his way of expressing suspicion of anything canonical).[314] Instead, they delved into the work of those who consciously composed both in respectful reference to, but also against, that canon in a way that was post-modern (even before postmodernism was officially born in the middle decades of the 20th century). Such an interest in 'post' music is an active one because the concept was culturally and technologically dynamic to an unprecedented and dizzying degree throughout the 20th century; it quickly took our post-pop travellers from Delius to Stockhausen to Eno.

For the same reasons, modal jazz interested Sylvian and Hollis. Artists such as Miles Davis, John Coltrane and McCoy Tyner forged in the late 1950s and 1960s a new kind of jazz that was structured horizontally (that is, improvisation based on scales, exploring melody and rhythm in novel ways) rather than vertically (improvisation tied more conservatively to chords). Modal jazz was, in a way, post-traditional (although not usually described as such) and, adding to its appeal in this post-pop context, it tended towards hybridity, as strictly modal jazz pieces were outnumbered by compositions or live improvisations that combined modal sections with more traditional chordal sections.[315] As for prog rock, it developed closely in the wake of modal jazz and postmodern classical music (broadly defined). The high profile of bands like King Crimson and early Genesis, right around the time that our future post-pop explorers were entering their teens, made prog an accessible example of how genres might be combined. Finally, the technological changes of the 1960s and 1970s made possible a new genre – experimental electronic music – that drew heavily on the core concepts of hybridity and post-genre.

Those concepts only worked as sources of creative inspiration because genres were conceived, promoted and even policed as separate. Sylvian, Hollis and Bush grew up in a society in which classical music and pop music were seen as completely distinct. Moreover, classical was the precursor to pop, a reluctant parent to its bastard offspring, the 'old' music for older listeners, in contrast to the 'new' music for the young. This separation was enshrined in radio programming all over the world, but the example of the BBC is particularly illustrative: the Light Programme ran 'light' entertainment and non-classical music from 1945 to 1967 when it split into Radio 1 (music for younger listeners; think *Top Of The Pops*) and Radio 2 (music for their parents; think Sinatra), with classical siloed in Radio 3 – a trifurcation that persists to this day. The teleological vision of the relationship between genres/stations is amusingly captured by Chuck Berry's 'Roll Over Beethoven' and its joyful use of rock 'n' roll (and 'rhythm 'n' blues') to rally the teen rebellion against the older generations (tell Tchaikovsky the news: 'my local DJ' and the jukebox aren't playing him anymore!).

But while those boundaries may make sense from a programming and marketing perspective, they oversimplify both the history and creative development of classical and pop (and jazz, for that matter, with its own fraught and undervalued relationship with classical music). Both classical and pop evolved in parallel in early modern Europe, constantly cross-fertilising each other. The opera boom of the 17th century, for example, anticipated long-form orchestral compositions, catchy pop songs about romance, pop's theatricality and arena rock. The 20th century's technological revolution permitted listeners to cross the boundaries between genres – from passive listening in childhood to the active pursuit of music in adulthood. When those listeners became songwriters, pop music became redirected. Pop/rock's roots in folk songs and hymns, jazz and blues are obvious, but the full array of late-20th-century genres is inconceivable without classical's continual influence, from prog rock to power ballads, ambient to metal.[316]

Even the treatment of 'Roll Over Beethoven' shifted in the years between Berry's 1956 original (faithfully covered by The Beatles in 1963) and the 1973 Electric Light Orchestra version. Over eight minutes long and beginning with the famous opening bars of Beethoven's *Fifth Symphony*, Jeff Lynne incorporated Beethoven's riff into Berry's song, turning what at first seems to be a statement about displacement into one about hybridity.[317]

As the rock era aged, that influence became more, not less, transparent. Thanks in large part to the influence of prog rock, popular music went from 'Roll Over Beethoven' to 'A Fifth Of Beethoven'. The former proclaimed that rock 'n' roll had replaced classical music; the latter appropriated and celebrated it with a disco homage, a US number one single that was no doubt a first introduction to the two-century-old German composer for many fans of the hit's parent movie soundtrack, *Saturday Night Fever*.[318] Working-class boys from the suburbs of Greater London, like Sylvian and Hollis, were exposed to classical music before 'A Fifth Of Beethoven' climbed the UK charts in 1976, but they may have perceived it as the pretentious music of 'the toffs' – the soundtrack to lives that were allegedly cultured but in the minds of non-toffs (and, to some extent, in reality) were 'all about cocktail parties, going to hunt balls, getting plastered and shagging other people's wives.'[319]

In the extraordinarily creative 1976-84 period, amidst a great swirl of interacting genres, classical music was all over the pop charts – from a purist viewpoint, bastardised into low-brow disco, reggae and all manner of cheap ear candy. On their important 1979 debut, Madness included – of all things – a two-and-a-half-minute 'Swan Lake', effectively a cover of the 1968 reggae cover by The Cats. Tell Tchaikovsky the news, indeed. 'Trying to do a beat to a classical song isn't that easy. I made a right cock-up', confessed drummer Dan 'Woody' Woodgate, but 'it was a mistake which seemed to work.' One might say the same of *Hooked On Classics*, a 1981 album by London's Royal Philharmonic Orchestra that sold millions worldwide, earned Grammy nominations and spawned a hit single (number two in the UK, number ten in the US); retitled *Classic Disco* in Germany and Austria (hitting number one in both countries), the album worked commercially, if not artistically. If classical-pop hybrids by the likes of Walter Murphy and Madness were just good fun, and albums like the *Hooked On Classics* series (the first spawned four sequels) were a justifiable way to keep orchestras funded, there were more earnest campaigns to bring classical music to the masses via the pop charts. Johann Sebastian Bach's 'Toccata And Fugue In D Minor', for example, composed in the early 18th century, reached number five in the UK charts in 1980, reworked as 'Toccata' by Sky. An instrumental group helmed by Australian guitarist John Williams, Sky's seven albums of 1979-87 showcased the 'classical crossover' end of the prog rock spectrum.[320]

By 1980, the ghost of Bach was no stranger to new hybrid genres such as prog rock and electronic music. Wendy Carlos's *Switched-On Bach* had been a milestone in the history of musical genres because – in the words of Robert Moog, inventor of the synthesiser used to create the album – 'in 1968, most people thought that electronic music was an avant-garde endeavour that had little connection with traditional musical values.'[321] The popularity of *Switched-On Bach* may not have convinced classical musicians to exchange orchestras for Moogs, but it was welcomed by the wide array of musicians who would end up influencing our purveyors of post-pop. Stockhausen said as early as 1958 that he could only imagine the kinds of oscillating sounds and pitch manipulations one might create from a machine, one not yet invented (and thus lacking the name synthesiser), but 'one may expect that someday such an instrument will exist.'[322] It was thus with great enthusiasm that avant-garde minimalists, rock and jazz keyboardists and Cologne-influenced experimentalists embraced rapidly evolving synthesiser technology in the 1970s. Just as classical music became somewhat untethered from its class associations through prog rock, a parallel untethering took place through the development of electronic music.

'Prog bands had demoed the electronics, pioneered the found sounds and use of empty space. They tweaked the synthesisers and parodied the three-minute pop song.' So proclaimed one prog rock historian, not alone in seeing the end of the 1960s and early 1970s as the period when English bands took the experiments of 'people like Delia Derbyshire and Stockhausen' – in the words of one BBC producer – 'and launched it into space in terms of popular music.' Adding 'it's pop music of a different order', he was thinking primarily of Pink Floyd's debut, but the phrase anticipates later developments, including journeys into post-pop. These prog accolades could equally apply to the pioneers of art pop, experimental pop and prog pop in the 1980s. Indeed, when Robert Fripp later spoke of 'the remarkable explosion of the creative impulse in popular music', he was thinking of the 1980s as well as the decade before it.[323] And the notion of experiments that 'parodied the three-minute pop song' would certainly have appealed to Hollis, and – with an emphasis more on metamorphosis than caricature – Sylvian and Bush, too.

Although both Hollis and Sylvian mentioned Stockhausen as a direct influence, as well as various impressionist and minimalist classical composers also favoured by Bush, more contemporaneous musicians served as crucial intermediaries. Suburban Londoners in their pre-teens would not have heard LPs like Steve Reich's 1966 tape-loop experiment *Come Out* in real time, but as teens, they were exposed to Kraftwerk's seeding (beginning with 1974's *Autobahn*) of a genre that would one day 'take over the entire world' (as Underworld's Karl Hyde would put it). Brian Eno, meanwhile, was ubiquitous as an influence because he channelled the likes of Reich and Kraftwerk *and* the likes of Roxy Music and Bowie *and* classical composers like Satie.[324]

Gone To Earth, for example, was both indebted to Eno and – through Eno – to classical music: Eno's *Discreet Music* (1975) comprised a 31-minute side of foundational ambient music ('two overlapping tape loops of serene electronica') and a flip side of variations on Johann Pachelbel's Canon In D Major. But where Eno's album reflected minimalist classical music's origins in (early modern) chamber music and (modern) electronica, Sylvian's album displayed, in its two discrete halves, its origins in art pop and ambient instrumentals. The problem with Eno's original ambient compositions was the ironic inevitability that they would birth the kind of spa muzak Eno was trying to write against – perhaps not a problem, in that Eno has often said he's 'proud to have been partially responsible' for almost every genre of music cited by interviewers as ambient-influenced.[325]

Still, as one critic, Richard Gehr, long ago noted of Eno's late 1970s ambient albums, 'this occasionally sublime hissing of digital lawns was a dead end, of course.' That necessitated the absorption of the genre in the 1980s, of which *Gone To Earth* is a prime example. Its side two meets the Eno requirement of ambient, that 'it must be as ignorable as it is interesting.' It functions both as background sound and as a space in which the listener can enter and be soothed by the music's 'restful, rural contemplation of nature' (as Gehr described Eno's ambient pieces).[326] Sylvian's solution to the potential problem of instrumental music as more ignorable than interesting was Fripp – a former Eno collaborator.

I earlier called Fripp prog rock royalty of the early 1970s. But when the rapidly shifting music scene of the late 1970s made the prog tag unfashionable, Fripp, 'as ever, found a sideways path to the new trend.' From the closing of the 1970s through the 1980s and beyond, he established himself as an exemplar of the scenius musician, collaborating with Peter Gabriel, Daryl Hall, ex-Police guitarist Andy Summer, Bowie (on *'Heroes'* and *Scary Monsters*) and Brian Eno – with whom he had been working on and off since their seminal 1973 album, *(No Pussyfooting)*.[327]

Fripp and Eno developed a recording technique that they dubbed 'Frippertronics', in which Fripp's guitar playing was passed through a tape loop delay of three-to-six seconds. The result is both a little harsh and often beautiful – and thus, it is easy to see why it appealed so much to

Sylvian. It was also *not* a way to play blues guitar; indeed, Fripp's guitar technique is notable for being distinct from the British blues movement that coalesced in the late 1960s, instead drawing upon classical (especially minimalist) and avant-garde 1950s-and-1960s jazz traditions. As already noted, Sylvian had hoped that Napier-Bell could get Fripp to produce Japan's second album back in 1978; they collaborated in the late 1980s, and while Fripp failed to persuade Sylvian to join a new iteration of King Crimson as the band's vocalist, they did record a pair of early 1990s albums, one in the studio and the other live.[328]

The journey to post-pop is thus a journey through genres, with each step defying easy genre classification. How might we tag the albums of Sylvian's peak solo years of 1984-87? In 1988, the *Los Angeles Times* summed them up as 'atmospheric esoterica that falls somewhere between old-line progressive rock, post-punk experimentation and soft-centred New Age dreaminess.' Not long ago, a *Classic Pop* piece enthused that the albums 'defined the sub-genre of art pop completely.' Just as Wikipedia struggles with Talk Talk's catalogue, placing their five albums in varying grab bags of multiple genres, so are the four Sylvian records, from *Brilliant Trees* through *Secrets Of The Beehive*, dizzyingly classified as 'art rock/avant-pop', 'electronic/ambient/world music', 'art rock/electronic/ambient' and 'art rock/chamber rock', respectively. Apple Music understandably throws its hands up and simply classifies all those Sylvian albums as 'alternative', with the Talk Talk albums all 'rock' – save for *Spirit Of Eden*, whose classification as 'pop' confusingly belies its reputation as foundational to post-rock.[329]

Clearly, then, the journey to post-pop is itself a genre category; my suggestion above – that algorithms include 'A Step Towards Post-Pop' as a genre – is not entirely tongue-in-cheek. In that context, the classification of *The Colour Of Spring* as post-rock, art rock and progressive pop is a reasonable assessment of how a listener might hear the album's elements. Those three tags are also a reasonable summation of how the album hit my ears the first time I heard it, which I still remember well – even if, at the time, I had none of those labels to help me articulate my response.

In the spring of 1986, months before I was to graduate from university, I rode my scooter two miles to the apartment where my sister lived with her boyfriend. Their place was always very welcoming, all floor cushions and beanbags, top-quality hashish and low-quality beer (brewed, literally, under a bed) – an idyllic setting for listening to music. The latest Talk Talk album was played on the turntable that evening as we passed the record sleeve back and forth, sharing looks and comments of amazement and puzzlement as we pondered how Hollis had done it – how he had created something that was connected to the past, to its predecessor and its influences, while also anticipating a brave, unknown future.

My sister and brother-in-law no longer remember it, but the moment stuck with me – not simply the pleasure of discovering music together, but the notion, one that has never left me, that *The Colour Of Spring* is a treasure trove of creative contradictions. Hollis's biographer wrote decades later that 'to German, Italian, Spanish or Dutch fiftysomething music fans, [Hollis] is an 80s superstar – a Boy George or a George Michael; to younger musicians, journalists and music obsessives all over the world, he is a visionary akin to Scott Walker, Nick Drake or Syd Barrett.'[330] To me, in 1986, he was both, even if I was not able to articulate it in that way.

If I had managed to articulate such a thought in 1986, it would have been an extraordinarily prescient one, considering that Hollis had yet to birth the albums that would years later be hailed as foundational to post-rock. But, meanwhile, there were plenty of conundrums to ponder regarding how *The Colour Of Spring* was made and what kind of pop music it consequently was. Every track featured melody, as one would expect of pop, but the melodies moved like butterflies between instruments, floating and elusive, entrancing.[331]

In retrospect, it is easier to see two methodological features borrowed from the nexus of genres underpinning the album – minimalist classical, modal jazz, prog rock and electronic experimentalism – that broadly influenced Hollis, Sylvian, Bush and other travellers on journeys to post-pop. One is the use of scenius; the other is the exercise of a kind of perfectionist minimalism.

Like Sylvian, Hollis issued studio invitations that allowed him to tap into a wider world of music culture that included artists and technicians whose past work he admired. For Hollis in 1985, that meant Traffic's Steve Winwood, whose organ playing on three songs on *The Colour Of Spring* helped evolve the Talk Talk sound; Robbie McIntosh of The Pretenders; the Average White Band's Alan Gorrie, who drummed on 'Happiness Is Easy'; and Danny Thompson, the Pentangle founder whose double bass playing grounded much of *Brilliant Trees*, and whose work on Sylvian and Bush albums helps connect the three artists together and link them back to English pastoral folk and prog roots. Harmonica player Mark Feltham made crucial contributions to the sound of *The Colour Of Spring*, with the 'explosive blues notes' from his diatonic harmonica on 'Living

In Another World' being particularly memorable; he would continue to play on Hollis's compositions through the final album. In all, at least 13 (and perhaps as many as 20) musicians were hired to play on the album, counting neither Talk Talk's members nor any of the choristers.[332]

There were two choirs hired for the making of *The Colour Of Spring*: the children's choir from the Barbara Speake Stage School in Acton (for 'Happiness Is Easy') and the Ambrosian Singers, who had been known in the 1960s as the London Symphony Orchestra Chorus (for 'Time Is Time'). Valued for their skills at both reproducing the polyphonic choral sound of Renaissance music and creating the dramatic but subtle choral backing to operatic recordings, singers from the group lent the album's 8:14 closer a controlled, full-bodied intensity. Pop features, such as the waxing and waning of the song's sound, combined with deft key changes, were dramatically enhanced by singers from the ensemble. Wardle's suggestion that the track is 'reminiscent of Hollis favourite *Carmina Burana*' is surely right and not coincidental. 'Time Is Time' isn't yet post-pop, but it is a far cry from the relative pop simplicity of 'Talk Talk'.[333]

The use of such a large cast was intended to maximise the 'organic' way the album came together in the studio, allowing Hollis and Friese-Greene to compile sonic fragments – often very small ones – in ways that tended to disguise the details of the creative process. Hollis was militantly opposed to using synthesisers as convenient substitutes for expensive, time-consuming session players. Insisting he'd always hated synths – a reflection in part of the punk roots of Talk Talk's ancestor band, The Reaction – Hollis took advantage of the larger budget that EMI gave him to create a scenius in the studio. But that didn't mean synths were banned, especially if they could be used in surprising ways. 'One of the banes of my life', McIntosh later said, 'has been 'I love the solo you do on 'I Don't Believe In You', which is, of course, a synthesizer! It's Ian Curnow with a Prophet-5 and a fuzz pedal.' The synth was played 'through guitar amps', Curnow confirmed; 'I think Mark liked the irony of this.'

As for that perfectionist minimalism, a good example is the treatment of a full brass section that was recorded for use on 'I Don't Believe In You'. Hollis's reaction at the end of the session was a preview of how his subsequent albums would be painstakingly assembled: he threw out every note, save for 'a trumpet player blowing spit from his mouth at 0:46 and a squeak at 2:15.'

During the year that it took to make *The Colour Of Spring*, Hollis listened to the impressionist classical composers whose understated and subtle work would serve as a precursor to minimalism. The Frenchman Erik Satie has already been mentioned as an influence on Hollis and Sylvian, as has his English contemporary Frederick Delius as inspirational for Hollis and Bush. Add to these composers others of the same era and genre, such as Claude Debussy (1862-1918), Maurice Ravel (1875-1937) and Béla Bartók (1881-1945). Whether out of trusting naiveté or unthinking enthusiasm, Hollis revealed to British music journalists these influences. Unwilling or incapable of connecting Hollis's admiration for what he called 'the textural quality' of such music to the new album – and responding to his cockney-inflected talk of 'the impressionist period' as if he were waving red banners – the journalists charged like bulls.

'Bartok's A Great Geezer' headed a feature in *Record Mirror*, quoting a line of Hollis's. Sneering that 'Debussy and Sibelius are well good lads, too, according to Talk Talk's classical connoisseur Mark Hollis', the piece fed Hollis some of his own sarcasm but with classist brutality. *Smash Hits* made fun of Hollis's cockney, too, assuming readers would agree that claiming knowledge of high-brow music using a low-brow accent was hilariously absurd. Because he had also praised Delius's 1912 tone poem 'On Hearing The First Cuckoo Of Spring', *NME* titled a savage review of the album with 'HARK! FIRST CUCKOO!'. As if having ideas above his station wasn't bad enough, the *NME* condemned *The Colour Of Spring* as 'bestriding the huge empty husk of progressive rock' like 'those crappy dinosaur groups that we can all do without being reminded of, thank you very much.'[334]

In stark contrast, on the continent, the theme was picked up with some respect. A Dutch interview titled 'Met Dank Aan Bartok' ('With Thanks To Bartok') took Hollis's discussion of classical influences seriously, while an Italian piece, headed 'Parole Di Primavera' ('Spring Talk') was likewise free of snide derision. When Hollis, Webb and Harris clearly decided to act the fool throughout an interview for French *Salut!* magazine, the interviewer simply played along, titling the piece 'Gangant' ('Winners') and concluding good-naturedly that the band were 'vraiment frappés mais terriblement fun!' ('truly bonkers but awfully fun!'). There was no editorial sarcasm inserted when Hollis told another Dutch magazine that 'I've always loved classical composers like Debussy and Bartok. In addition, I also idolise jazz master Miles Davis. It's perhaps not immediately audible, but these elements are incorporated in Talk Talk's music.'[335]

Little did anyone – Hollis included – know the ways in which such elements would be incorporated on the albums to come.

12: Desire

'Desire' Talk Talk (1988, 7:08)

'Desire' is my favourite punk song.

That takes some explaining. Side one of *Spirit Of Eden* is a single composition, over 22 minutes, presented as three tracks – 'The Rainbow', 'Eden' and 'Desire' – that are best understood and heard as parts of a whole. (On the original CD version in the UK, side one is a single track, as Hollis intended.) 'The Rainbow' is a minimalist symphony of discord, of noises whose origin and nature are uncertain, whose combination shouldn't work yet rivetingly does. As the album's first vocal line warns us, 'the world's turned upside down'. 'Eden' likewise begins with its pieces disassembled, laid out like the first page of an assembly manual, only randomly and with the instructions incomplete. As the pieces come together, as we know they must, the crescendo is still somehow surprising. What might be a love song of sorts ('everybody seems someone to live by') turns out to be, perhaps, a theological critique ('rage on omnipotent'), an ambivalent theme threaded throughout the album. A minute before its end, 'Eden' eases into a quiet, low-key rhythm, gliding smoothly into 'Desire', the mood gentler and more hesitant, with a similar rhythm gradually generated by what sounds like strumming on a guitar of some kind. Like so many other moments on the album, the listener isn't sure if the playing is deliberate or accidental, virtuosic or amateur. But whatever is happening, it succeeds in soothing you while at the same time creating tension.

At 1:53 into 'Desire', Hollis intones, 'desire, whispered, spoken', and then, 'rivers, oceans', like a free-form poem that is as fragmented as the music. Then, around 2:38, there's a split second of feedback and in crash a band – cymbals, drums, bass, screeching guitar and a wailing Hollis. His words are as distorted as the music, so one can barely hear him insisting, over and over, 'That ain't me, babe!' What turns out to be a chorus of sorts ends with 'I'm just content to relax, than drown within myself' (which I've always heard as '*and* drown within myself'). Suddenly, there is a second of silence before the gentle start of the song again, unexpectedly following the customary pop/rock structure, meaning that, this time, the listener expects the raucous chorus. First a surprise, then a thrilling reassurance, as the song thrashes on, now extended like a punk song embedded within a prog rock piece before a closing 30 seconds of gentle, rhythmic piano chords.

The whole seven minutes is viscerally gripping, artful and controlled, yet channelling punk's spirit of fuck-you amateurish noisy protest. It's Hollis all in one track – embracing pastoral minimalism, murmuring about rivers and oceans over delicately placed notes, yet equally committed to denying any part of it because, *babe* (does he really mean 'babe', or is that a sarcastic cover for the c-word?), that is who he is and yet that also ain't him. 'Desire' works on its own, but it works best as the climax to side one of *Spirit*; for more than 18 minutes, we wait in giddy anticipation for Hollis to break loose and yell at us. I love the parts to side one that anticipate the middle-aged Hollis of his 1998, but I also yearn for the Essex punk of 1978 to be loud and in my face.

'Unanswered mysteries always have legs', says Martin Ditcham, guitarist on the second half of the Talk Talk/Hollis catalogue, in specific reference to the question often placed at the heart of discussions of Hollis: 'What led Hollis to reject fame in favour of music so esoteric and fastidious?' The phrasing is by music critic Wyndham Wallace, who poses a pair of contrasting solutions. One sees Hollis as bravely facing down the machine of the music industry in order to promote the noble cause of creative freedom. The other sees his motivations as simply selfish to the point of indulgence; as Aspden put it not long ago, 'Mark had his cake and ate it all himself.'[336]

The question matters here, for it is more or less this book's core query, used to explain the directions taken by Sylvian and Bush, as well as Hollis. And the answer is, well, book-length. But it includes the twin theories above, which I would argue are mutually compatible. Indeed, Wallace phrases the question in a way that suggests such an outcome. Hollis (like Sylvian and Bush) was appalled by the trap and trappings of fame. However, he was not yet willing to give up the opportunity to compose, record and release music. His bloody-minded response was to make exactly the kind of music he wanted, which partly coincidentally and partly *not* coincidentally was music so discordant with considerations of marketing, promotion, audience and popular taste as to relieve him of fame's trappings. Or most of them – the royalties from his earlier compositions continued to flow.

Asked about Talk Talk's relationship with prevailing trends – as *Spirit Of Eden* seemed so completely disconnected from popular music in the late 1980s – Hollis rather modestly claimed that 'it's just a consequence of taking so long to make these albums. I mean, it's quite hard to be part of any trend if you're sort of two years between each album.' But would he prefer to be aligned with current trends? 'No, definitely not', said Hollis, with an embarrassed smile, adding that the success of *It's My Life* 'enabled us to make *The Colour Of Spring* and this one [*Spirit Of Eden*] increasingly more on our ideal terms.'[337]

In interviews like this, Hollis did little to encourage the later legend of him heroically pursuing creative freedom for its own sake, as if he were an artistic David facing down the money-grubbing Goliath of the record industry. Instead, he is very transparent about the commercial utility of the band's earlier pop albums, each one essentially funding the next, as Hollis leads the band down the path to post-pop. Hollis would not have used that phrase, of course, but his description of how *Spirit Of Eden* was created evokes the paradoxical nature of post-pop and is worth quoting at length:

> What we've tried to do here is to put together two things that don't normally exist on record, that I've never actually seen exist anywhere on an album before. Always for me, you have these two areas of music which sit apart from each other. One is this thing with sort of spontaneity and freedom, and the other is this thing of having a very textured depth of arrangement. And what we've tried to do with this album is just bring these two things together for once. And, you know, that is why it takes so long. The approach to making this album is one where everyone who comes and plays on this album is given absolute freedom, has no direction at all in what they play and will play maybe for days. And then you just take a few seconds, and you assemble an arrangement from that. So, you end up with something which is very tightly constrained but everything within it that has been played is completely free and completely loose. What you do is just talk in the absolute basics and fundamentals of what music should be, which is just in its attitude and not in its technique.[338]

If '*The Colour Of Spring* hinted at an unsuspected ethereal potential,' in Simon Reynolds' words, '*Spirit Of Eden* was something else again: a pellucid, meditational, uninterrupted suite of songs' influenced not by the rock and pop that preceded it in the 1980s but by John Martyn's *Solid Air*, Miles Davis albums like *Sketches Of Spain* and the minimalist jazz of earlier decades. Indeed, *Spirit Of Eden* picks up specifically where 'Chameleon Day' and 'April 4th' left off. But whereas those tracks were nestled in *The Colour Of Spring* among pop songs, like a pair of cuckoo eggs, the six tracks of *Spirit Of Eden* are more like the movements of classical compositions – or of a single composition, a 41-minute suite that *should* be heard as one, uninterrupted.[339]

If there was a cuckoo-and-warbler-eggs contrast within *The Colour Of Spring*, it was replaced by a contrast that was woven throughout *Spirit Of Eden*, manifested within each track. *Spirit* contains more moments of peace and quiet, of sombre reflection, where Hollis's voice fades to a whisper and where the music slides into classical minimalism. But there are also more moments of jarring dissonance, in which Hollis raises his voice in apparent distress or insistence, with processed guitar parts approximating distortion and expressing alarm.

Two elements of Hollis's and Friese-Greene's method of composition and recording were carried over from *Colour* to *Spirit* to an excessive degree. One was the use of a vast musical scenius. The growing community of guest musicians on the previous albums was here taken to an extreme that has become legendary. 'An army of musicians', more than 50 (by Hollis's own estimate), were brought into the studio over a two-year recording period.[340] The other methodological element became equally legendary: the way in which these musicians were treated and used.

At no stage in the process – before, during or after their time in the studio – were session musicians given instruction from Hollis or Friese-Greene. 'They wouldn't let me hear the music!' exclaimed Ditcham. Instead, he'd lay down multiple tracks 'of percussive ideas', which they'd later cherry-pick or discard, with Ditcham only finding out what was used when he listened to the final record. Arriving musicians were kept in the dark in every respect – including literally, as there was minimal lighting from a couple of anglepoise lamps and an old oil projector. They were 'brought in with a torch [flashlight]', the album's sound engineer, Phill Brown, later recalled. The many bemused, confused and sometimes annoyed guests were sat down, 'given headphones, then we'd play them the track.' What they then played would likely end up being discarded, as countless hours of notes and noise recorded over two years resulted in a record of just 41 minutes. 'Once, we spent five 12-hour days perfecting a guitar sound', recalls Brown. 'It was an extremely unusual way to work.'[341]

The method was hard on the young rhythm section of Harris and Webb, recruited six years earlier to record different music in a different way. They were now at the mercy of Hollis and Friese-Greene's absolute commitment to a tortured combination of spontaneity and perfectionism, spiced with the old studio banter that, under these circumstances, turned dark more quickly. 'It was World War III', Harris later told the album's art director. Sometimes 'it was just nasty. Paul left because of that', he added, referring to Webb's departure at the end of the *Spirit* sessions. In Brown's telling, Webb was worn down by giving his all, playing 'everything that he'd been asked to play' and then being told to do it all again; in the end, he just 'put his bass down...'

There are differing stories and memories regarding how much of *Spirit Of Eden* was preconceived or demoed. Either way, it is clear that, as Hollis claimed, '80% of this album is spontaneous', so much so that a live performance would have been impossible: 'There is no way that I could ever play again a lot of the stuff I played', he added, 'because I just wouldn't know how to.' Significantly, this album, later hailed as foundational to post-rock (and, as I'm arguing, post-pop), was inspired in counterpoint to pop and in more specific ways than the end result reveals. For example, 'Wealth' was originally labelled on the studio tape boxes as 'Rocket Man' because its piano-and-vocal opening was reminiscent of Elton John's signature pop hit (an echo that surely few would hear unless it was pointed out, but 'Wealth' may never sound the same to you now). And Duran Duran, whose superficial Talk Talk connection was used for years by journalists as a torture tool on Hollis, came up occasionally during the *Spirit* sessions; predictably, Hollis made fun of Simon Le Bon's lyrics, but there was also a group singalong of the Durans's Bond hit, 'A View To A Kill', with Le Bon's 'famous bum note' at Live Aid a particular target of parody.[342]

In the historical context of the century-long arc of changes in recording technology and the resulting shifts in recording culture from the 1920s to the 2020s, *Spirit Of Eden* was made at a significant middle point. As Petrusich recently noted, in the early decades of that period, 'it was possible for a curious listener to identify each of the constituent parts of a pop song.' Then, in the second half of the 20th century, multitrack recording gradually undermined that transparency. By this century, the increasing flexibility and affordability of digital technology caused 'that sense of pliability' to balloon, rendering instrumentation – potentially every single sound on a recording – opaque.[343]

But, in 1987, the technology to achieve that opaqueness was still years away; the DAW (digital audio workstation) only became commercially available at the end of the decade, with Pro Tools turning studios digital a couple of years after that. Hollis noted that the album could not 'have existed in an earlier time' due to the 'absolute freedom' afforded by 'digital recording technology'; but he could not have known how far and fast that technology would develop. He, Friese-Greene, and Brown thus unwittingly anticipated the future with a painstaking and visionary use of analogue tools – many of them antique, as Hollis had already begun his lifelong passion for collecting vintage musical equipment. As Brown later noted, 'It's very hard to tell exactly what is playing what' on almost the entire record. Today that is expected; back then, it was astonishing.

Wardle put his finger on what Hollis and Friese-Greene were doing in the studio: 'effectively,' he concluded, they were '*sampling* live musicians' (his emphasis). There was thus a purpose to having musicians repeat passages for hours without any intention of keeping a single take. Danny Thompson, for example, who later told Brown that *Spirit Of Eden* was 'the worst session of his life', gave eight takes of a five-minute passage on his double bass; three notes ended up on the record. After a series of takes on a guitar, Friese-Greene got up and tripped over the cable (the studio being dark); his takes were deleted, but the accidental crashing sound was kept and placed elsewhere on the album.[344]

Instrument inventor Hugh Davies, who had begun his career in experimental sound as an assistant to Stockhausen in the 1960s, brought in hack saws, an egg slicer, saucepans and other elements of what he dubbed Shozygs (after the *SHO- to ZYG-* volume of an encyclopedia, hollowed out to store some of his 'instruments'). The point for Hollis was not to show how to make music from kitchen implements but to show how sounds created from unknown sources could be carefully selected to create music; no listener could guess that Shozygs were used (or even existed) without being told. Hollis liked to talk about this method as embodying the spirit of punk. As 'punk said technicality is unimportant,' he told *Melody Maker* during the promotion for *Spirit*, 'everyone in this world, if they wanna be, is a musician.' That, plus Hollis's unique vision, grim determination and generous studio budget, all contributed.[345]

The result, proclaimed *Sounds*, was 'uncommonly beautiful.' For Barbieri, *Spirit Of Eden* and its sequel were works of 'exquisite beauty' ('there's magic at work'). The record is 'a plea and a blow for a new dawn', gushed *Melody Maker*. A reviewer for a Florida newspaper gave the album kudos at the expense of a fellow Londoner: 'Talk Talk has achieved what singer David Sylvian has been trying to do in vain on his albums: subtle music worth the listener's effort.' But other reviewers, stymied by its genre and unwilling to concede that the album might have founded a new one, fell back on one of the era's routine insults: Talk Talk were 'trying to raise the ghastly spectre of progressive rock all over again', accused Ireland's *Hot Press*. In a way, Hollis conceded the point, arguing to a *Q* critic that the album only seemed radical in 1988's context, 'not radical compared to what was happening 20 years ago. If we'd delivered this album to the record label [then], they wouldn't have batted an eyelid.'[346]

'Brutally non-conformist' is how Depeche Mode's Alan Wilder describes one of his 'favourite albums.' Enthused Guy Garvey, 'The first time I heard *Spirit Of Eden*, I just kept saying, 'What the fuck is this? This is amazing.' I'd never heard music that dynamic while being organic. It's such a brave record. To this day, I can hear its influence.' That was said years after the album had made its impact on Garvey's own band, Elbow, and numerous others. Doves are one example, added Garvey, and 'you could tell that Radiohead knew that record and loved it, too.'[347]

In other words, whatever bands we might cite and whatever genres we may tag them with – from indie to art rock, prog pop to post-rock, even post-Britpop – the list is potentially very long. The fact that few anticipated that impact when *Spirit Of Eden* came out has only added to its legend. As music writer Jack Chuter noted, nobody called *Spirit Of Eden* post-rock when it came out, and even when Reynolds did coin the term five years later, he did not mention Talk Talk. But Chuter is right to note that 'the album opened the door post-rock would eventually walk through.'[348] To borrow that metaphor, it kicked wide open the door that post-pop had already nudged ajar.

'*Spirit Of Eden* was said to be loathed by the label who'd paid for it and largely scored by critics – neither rumour is entirely true, but legends are always popular.' The legend of Talk Talk has indeed been popular and long-lasting. As with most enduring legends, it grew from distortions and exaggerations of things that were actually said and done. While Aspden loved *Spirit Of Eden* from the start, for example, as the band's manager, he was 'pissed off that there was no hit single' – in Webb's words. The bassist remembers Aspden's first reaction to hearing the album: 'Oh my God! What have you done?' The reaction at EMI was similar: appreciation of the album but concern over how to market it. EMI's Tony Wadsworth later told *Uncut* that 'we honestly loved it. We all felt as if we were working on something special.' However, whether his colleague, Nick Gatfield, 'broke down in tears' upon hearing the album or not – that was the story that Brown heard – there was genuine alarm at the label. So did Wadsworth and Gatfield end up in court, representing EMI, because – as legend has it – the label sued Talk Talk? Not exactly.[349]

As Wardle clearly outlines, the court case stemmed from a difference of interpretation over the timing of the album's delivery. Aspden argued that Talk Talk had fulfilled their obligations to EMI and that the band were thus free to walk away – without paying their debts to the label – and to negotiate a new contract with another label. Far from trying to get rid of Talk Talk, and regardless of the commercial viability of *Spirit Of Eden*, EMI insisted that they had exercised their right to the band's next album. Both sides dug in their heels, the dispute went to court and EMI won. The week of the ruling – in November 1988 – *Spirit Of Eden* dropped out of the UK charts, having leapt in a couple of months earlier at number 19. Hollis insisted he was oblivious to the court case, but the *Q* journalist, whose review had been titled 'Come On, *Market* Me!', claimed that a few weeks later, Hollis accosted him at a concert venue, called him a 'wanker' and claimed that the article was 'going to cause me no end of problems.'[350]

But the story wasn't over. EMI had, in the meantime, managed to shoehorn the unconventional material into a conventional promotional campaign (albeit with the weak tagline, 'An Album For 1988'). Hollis mostly cooperated. Having flat refused to edit any of the tracks into singles, he conceded that 'I Believe In You' (rightly called 'a song of such exquisite elegance' by one critic) could be cut in half and a video be made for it (Hollis later, and quite rightly, regretted both). EMI highlighted the song's reference to heroin in their press release, allowing Hollis to mention how much of a scourge the drug was ('a wicked, horrible thing'). Journalists quickly made the connection to Ed Hollis, whose decade-long addiction had left him ravaged; in May 1989, it took his life. That same month, Aspden won the band's appeal in court. Talk Talk were free.[351]

Yet still, the story was not over. As distorted as is the legend of *Spirit Of Eden*, there had indeed been a protracted court case, resulting in Talk Talk leaving EMI. Talk Talk were now a band in name only, with Webb leaving and Harris excluded from the contract that Aspden procured for Hollis. Fielding generous offers, they signed with Polydor, whose million-pound advance – actually a 'superstar deal' of £2 million for two albums – allowed Hollis to begin creating a sequel. *Laughing Stock*, in terms of both its recording method and the resulting sound, was much like its predecessor but several steps deeper into the post-pop/post-rock woods – thereby further adding to the legend.

Meanwhile, EMI were left with the band's back catalogue, which they immediately proceeded to milk. As already mentioned, the *Natural History* compilation was a worldwide million-selling smash, hitting number three on the UK album charts; a re-released 'It's My Life' reached number 13. Talk Talk were enjoying more commercial success than they'd ever had. Hollis hated it: it overshadowed the release and reception of *Laughing Stock*, drawing attention to what he considered a very different and now outdated musical past; he detested the remixes that EMI commissioned of the singles pulled from the compilation album. But new digital mixing technologies and the rise of the new club culture made multiple remixes irresistible to record labels, inspiring EMI to go several steps further and release an entire CD of them, *History Revisited*. The mix of what had been finely crafted recordings with bog-standard dance beats was 'a terrible bodge', to put it mildly. 'It's outrageous,' fumed Hollis. 'They've bastardised my work without my knowledge. They should be ashamed of themselves.' EMI were again taken to court, and again, the label lost – all unsold copies of the remixes, even the master tapes, had to be destroyed.[352]

Meanwhile, rumours circulated that *Laughing Stock* had given Polydor executives heart attacks the way that *Spirit Of Eden* had supposedly hit the suits at EMI. After all, it was released on Verve, an old jazz label owned by Polydor, giving the impression that they were unsure what to do with an album of 'perverse genius' – as *Select* magazine called it. The same review raved that 'Talk Talk despise the music business and all its machinations.'[353] The legend of Talk Talk was taking on a life of its own. Certainly, it was driven by the legal battles with EMI coinciding with the band releasing albums that seemed willfully uncommercial and avant-garde. But there was also a larger context in which lawsuits between labels and bands were increasingly a part of how business was conducted, drawing more and more attention to the exploitative nature of the industry – the 'machinations' of 'the machine', as it now had been called for decades.

For example, when vinyl had ruled, artists in the US typically received 75 cents on every record sold; in the CD era, labels charged consumers almost $8 more per album, but the typical artist royalty only rose to 81 cents. In the US alone, industry profits from CDs rose from $17 million in 1983 to $103 million in 1984 (on sales of 6 million), then $13 billion by 1999 (on sales of 942 million). In 1992, the year that Talk Talk sued EMI to stop selling *History Revisited* (whose costs the label had taken from the band's royalties), George Michael sued Sony, and the following year, Prince sued Warner – both very public battles. As Napier-Bell described it, referring to the CD era of the 1980s and 1990s, 'an artist who sold 200,000 copies of a first album would still be in debt to the record company, despite the record company having made a million dollars profit.' Or as

Courtney Love put it in a widely read *Salon.com* article titled 'Courtney Love Does The Math': a top band receives a million-dollar advance to record an album that sells a million copies, but as the costs come out of the band's share, they end up with $180,000 (split among band members), while the record company takes $4.4 million.[354]

These numbers were not imaginary, and for thousands of recording artists, they spoke the truth about their experiences. But as a back story that fed the legend of Talk Talk, they contained considerable irony. In 1999, *Laughing Stock* was re-issued, along with the previous year's *Mark Hollis* solo album, on Pond Life – a new label founded by Aspden. Both albums had been deleted by Polydor. The re-issues prompted reviews that resurrected the old legend, adding new details: *Spirit Of Eden* had been recorded in 'an abandoned church', lit only by candles while incense burned; EMI had sued and then dropped Talk Talk; Polydor had deleted *Laughing Stock* from their catalogue after only three months (that was, in fact, how long the label had kept *Mark Hollis* listed), 'an album produced from artistic struggle,' declared *The Times*, 'the work of men fighting to claim the peripheries of their pop remit.' As Hollis faded from public view in the new century, the band's legend took on further mystique; a 2008 article in *The Guardian* added 'stories of hedonistic, opium-laced sessions' during the making of the final albums, 'though nothing was ever proven.' Hollis was now a mythical hero, 'one man against the system in a bid to maintain creative control.'[355]

As Wardle remarked, none of these articles 'mentioned Hollis pocketing two million pounds.' Brown estimated that *Spirit Of Eden* and *Laughing Stock* had cost about £700,000 to make, paid for with million-pound advances from EMI and Polydor – the latter paying another million for the *Mark Hollis* album, which they had tried, in vain, to have released as a Talk Talk record in an effort to recoup some of their losses. The point is not to begrudge Hollis his success at paying for these albums and making a living besides, but rather to emphasise how pop pays for post-pop. Each Talk Talk album made the next one possible, in financial terms, with record labels willingly financing Hollis's increasing creative freedom. Rather than impoverishing him, that system permitted him to then take the next creative step chosen by him: retirement. In the years after *Mark Hollis*, with No Doubt bringing 'It's My Life' back into the charts, the royalty income from Hollis songs jumped from tens to hundreds of thousands of pounds a year. Pop, having funded post-pop, also funded life after post-pop.

13: Pop Song/The Ninth Wave

'**Pop Song**' David Sylvian (1989, 4:30)
'**The Ninth Wave**' Kate Bush (1985, 26:21)

As the 1980s drew to a close, Virgin issued *Weatherbox*, comprising David Sylvian's four solo albums of 1984-87, packaged as five CDs in a small box, each one labelled with a natural element (not quite *the* four elements). The first was straightforward: *Tree: Brilliant Trees*. The second took the hitherto cassette-only five-track album, *Alchemy: An Index Of Possibilities*, and re-packaged it as a six-track, lumberingly labelled *Stone: Alchemy: Words With The Shaman (Songs From The Treetops)*; two tracks were added, with one of the album's original tracks removed. The third and fourth CDs comprised Sylvian's 1986 double album, labelled as *Earth: Gone To Earth* and *Water: Gone To Earth Instrumental*. Last came the brilliant *Light: Secrets Of The Beehive* (with sound quality oddly inferior to the original release).

Weeks before the box came out, a new Sylvian single appeared. Titled 'Pop Song', it was viewed by the label as a promotional aid for the box set despite not being included in it. Instead, its two B-sides were the two new tracks added to the box's *Alchemy* CD. A 'Weatherbox Sampler' CD was another packaging of the single, as 'Pop Song' headed its five tracks.

If you are confused, that's because it is confusing and contradictory. The limited run of *Weatherbox* (5000 copies) and its beautiful packaging and artwork – most notably featuring art and photography by Russell Mills – suggested it was aimed at hardcore fans. Yet, the handling of *Alchemy* and *Beehive* suggested it was more suited to casual fans willing to catch up on Sylvian. Furthermore, such fans would have found a bewildering mixture of pop music, experimental art pop and ambient instrumentals. They might have been intrigued, even thrilled, by Sylvian's post-Japan ambivalence towards commercial pop, his apparent vacillation between his pop star past and what promised to be an obscure non-pop future. Or they might simply have found it baffling, even disdainful of listeners.

The new single embodied these contradictions even more blatantly. The cover of the CD single was arty and provocative, but in a way that had become almost mainstream by 1989. Women's breasts had adorned record covers from *Electric Ladyland* and *Country Life* through to albums released just the year before, like *Surfer Rosa* and *Bummed*.[356] The image was a far cry from the covers of Sylvian's solo albums, such as his most recent, *Secrets Of The Beehive*, with its monochrome, high-brow reference to shamanistic artists like Joseph Beuys.[357] Sylvian seemed to be reaching for a different kind of audience reaction with 'Pop Song'. Indeed, it was praised in Britain's *The Sunday Times* as 'an unusually perky and assured single' and 'a remarkable single even by Sylvian's standards' in *Melody Maker*. The interviewer in that music weekly went further, calling it 'witty and lovingly crafted', suggesting it was 'deliberately commercial' and 'a highly infectious single that openly grades its mastery of the pop form, a soft, insistent beat and a dry, sardonic lyric that should return Sylvian to the place he's been eager to escape from for the last decade – the top 40. 'Pop Song' will sound brilliant on daytime radio.'[358]

But was 'Pop Song' a pop song, let alone an infectious one, destined to be a hit? Virgin's Simon Draper later claimed that he had agreed on a budget for studio time for Sylvian to record 'a pop song.' But Sylvian insisted that Draper had misunderstood; 'It's *called* 'Pop Song'. It is not *A* pop song.'[359] In fact, the song clearly *is* pop. It bounces along through a series of verses and repeated choruses, radio-friendly in both its core sentiment ('I'll tell you I love you, like my favourite pop song') and its length. But it isn't particularly catchy. Not surprisingly, it failed to get much play on daytime radio, entering the chart at number 83, dropping a few places the following week and then exiting. That was surely the inevitable result of Sylvian trying to have his cake and eat it, too.

'It's a strange piece, a real one-off', he said. The lyric is 'playful' yet takes a stab at 'what I see in popular culture which is, basically, a waste of creative potential and a willingness on the part of the public to be a party to that.' In other words, the song's purpose was to wag a finger at the DJs who played the song and the listeners who bought it, to play at 'being subversive from within.' Did Sylvian want 'Pop Song' to be a hit? 'Of course, because the whole point of it was to make a statement from within the media that I'm criticising.' Did he expect it to be a hit? 'I don't think it stands a chance of doing anything in commercial terms.'[360]

That deliberate creation and embrace of a pop paradox was, of course, classic Sylvian and was part of his larger attitude towards pop as a genre. At the time of 'Pop Song', he placed his 1980s solo work within that genre while laying claim to an avant-garde space at its edge. As recounted in *The Sunday Times*: "How can I put this without sounding pretentious?' Sylvian ponders, inhaling a French cigarette and adjusting his dark glasses. 'I wanted to write from experience, to make the work a by-product of the learning process of my life. So, I went for the basic form of pop, which, for me, is the ballad'.[361]

That was far from the only time that Sylvian defended pop as a genre while articulating his own complex relationship to it. 'I wouldn't dismiss pop music. It's easy to generalise and say it's all superficial and meaningless, but I don't believe it is', Sylvian said on another occasion, adding that he conceded that 'a great deal of it is just based on ego and image and style ... but in a way, people need that. It lifts them up for a moment.'[362]

A typically backhanded compliment from Sylvian to the genre, to be sure, but, nonetheless, a recognition of pop as an art form – one that is arguably as valid as any in music. After all, pop has an undeniable, and possibly unique, power to channel and express emotion, to package and communicate it in a few intense minutes: 'Out of nowhere, some otherwise innocuous radio song floors you with its emotional power. It is why hits exist, and why pop ultimately counts as a true art form (rather than some camp, poor relation of 'deeper' music).'[363]

Intrinsic to its power is pop's unmistakable structure. Pop songs tend to be built around verses and a chorus, both immediately clear to the listener, defined by lyrical contrast (the chorus is, by definition, repetitive) and by melodic contrast (the chorus is set to the catchier melody). More than that, the verses are a commentary on the chorus, which in turn conveys most directly the song's subject. This structure is primal in origin, rooted in ancient human rituals of performance and audience: for us – as for our ancestors, perhaps as far back as the very dawn of human language – the chorus is where we sing along, where we join in. Hence, the sheer joy that is so often pop and why singing along to songs in the car is 'one of the most genuinely life-affirming rituals invented by the 20th century.'[364]

'I'm a creature that just deals with chords, melody and halfway decent lyrics', says Jimmy Webb, one of the great and consummate composers of pop songs of the Album/Singles Era. 'Those are all the things that I'm interested in – I mean, incredibly interested in. Totally absorbed with, dedicated, in the deepest part of my being.'[365] Webb objects to the modern machine that generates pop hits – the algorithms and software, the code-writers and DJ-producers – not to post-pop. But in identifying the three elements of pop songs that matter to him, he unwittingly puts his finger on three elements – chords, melody, lyrics – that potentially become obscured, if not lost altogether, when artists consciously try *not* to make pop songs.

It is revealing, too, that Webb seldom uses 'pop song' in talking about his own work, and others tend more often to refer to his songs as country; rock is even occasionally used. Sparing Webb the limitations of genre-tagging is perhaps fair (he is, after all, the only artist to win Grammy Awards for lyrics, music *and* orchestration). But he also entered the business in the 1960s, when the gender – and gendered – divide between rock and pop was being created. That divide has roots that pre-date rock's invention by centuries, and it has a long and complex history into this century. Suffice to note here that pop has long been forced to battle the perception that it is not a serious genre of music, a perception that is tinged with sexism and homophobia (rock is for men, real men; pop is for women – and gay men). Here's Debbie Gibson, commenting recently (aged 51), after decades of having to defend the genre: 'I was always not ashamed to say that I love a catchy pop song. I think there's such a brilliance to it.'[366]

Gibson was derided by critics in her imperial phase, not just because she was a female pop artist but because her fans were female – teenagers, no less, and 'few things are more aligned and diminished than the tastes of teenage girls.' That tradition of misogyny stretches forward into this century (consider the treatment of Taylor Swift, for example) and back into the 1960s, in between catching any male artists who happened to make pop music that appealed to young women. 'Let's not mince words,' says Rob Sheffield, 'Duran Duran are famous because girls like them.' Consequently, a band like Duran Duran were treated as if they were female, seen as 'all style, no substance.' When Annie Zaleski writes the following about Duran Duran, she could have been writing about any female pop artist (as she well knows): for detracting critics, the band members 'couldn't be both handsome [substitute pretty or sexy] and talented; their songs couldn't be commercially oriented and also innovative; the band couldn't be ambitious and artsy.' In other words, (mostly male) critics not only policed the pop/rock divide but gave it a gendered hierarchy.[367]

Hollis became aware of this phenomenon through his experience of the music press in the early Talk Talk years. Rockist prejudice underpinned the negative view of his band when it was perceived as a bunch of pretty-boy Duran-wannabe upstart-pop stars. But *Spirit Of Eden* seemed antithetical to the tastes of teenage girls, allowing it – and thus now Talk Talk – to fall on the 'right' side of the pop-rock line. In that sense, Talk Talk's rehabilitation was equally tainted by rockism.[368]

Sylvian likewise became increasingly conscious of all this in the early 1980s. The tag of 'most beautiful man in the world', cooked up with remarkable success by Japan's management team, infuriated him, as did the appeal to teenage girls – first in Japan, then in Europe and the UK – of his elaborate coiffe and heavy make-up, which he had adopted in part as a childish emulation of Ziggy-era Bowie and in part as a mask behind which to hide. Escaping his teen-pop fanbase became harder as he himself became emulated; remember Napier-Bell's above-quoted boast of Japan's influence: 'Duran Duran stole their hairstyles and Gary Numan stole David's voice.' In the 1980s, Sylvian sought to flee from his own gendered pop self. Even as Japan moved into new, experimental pop territory, their fanbase continued to lean heavily toward teenybop. As one critic spotted, 'it was as if Japan embarrassed him.'[369] Breaking up the band wasn't enough; the music itself needed to be pushed deeper into art, prog, jazz and ambient, taking that untrod path into post-pop, all in order to escape the gendered pop world that critics had defined.

This is not to suggest that Sylvian was himself disdainful of fans because they were teenage girls or that he internalised the misogyny of the pop/rock police. The point, rather, is that the larger context – music critics, the 'machine' of the industry and the popular culture of the 1970s and 1980s – meant that artists could not easily cherry-pick genres, styles, images and fans. Any decisions they made in the hope of gaining something resulted in losses, too. If pop stars gain something when they consciously try *not* to make pop songs, they also lose something. Awareness of that fact fuels pop's inertia. The efficacious simplicity of its structure and its power to convey emotion tend to pull artists back into pop, even if they have received critical acclaim (and perhaps commercial success) for moving into the avant-garde territories of sub-genres like art pop, experimental pop and prog pop. For some artists, the often-prejudicial gendering of pop by music critics and buyers adds to that inertia, be it due to female identity, feminist commitment or simply a contrarian impulse to flip a finger at the genre police.

'Pop Song' was not only a manifestation of that push-pull effect, but it was also the climactic point of Sylvian's five-year experiment in navigating pop's inertia as a solo artist. After 1987's *Secrets Of The Beehive*, he would not release a solo album for 12 years, nor would he release a solo single for a decade after 'Pop Song'. He would struggle through the 1990s with pop's push-pull effect, facing challenges in his attempts to collaborate and compose, paralleled with dramatic changes in his personal life, until emerging finally into a new period of productivity – and a new engagement with post-pop.

Kate Bush likewise felt the inertia pull of pop, her journey to post-pop being a similarly long and winding road. Like Japan and Talk Talk, her first step had been to achieve mainstream pop fame (in her case, it came as a sudden explosion, as we saw earlier). Then, when her chance came to be queen in the conventional popstar sense, she retreated. She saw how misogynistic prejudice against pop had trapped her, forcing her to conform to gendered genre expectations. She escaped by abandoning touring, by moving steadily towards total control over her product and promotion and by making an album that was so experimental as to seem willfully uncommercial. But 1982's *The Dreaming* was hardly a joyful expression of freedom; it was, rather, a manifestation of her *struggle* to be free. The symbolism of 'Houdini', about the famous escapologist, was obvious – except Bush adopts the role of his wife, both in the song and on the album's cover. In effect, she is both Harry *and* Bess, helping herself to escape, trying to communicate with her own dead self. 'Houdini' and the song that precedes it, 'All The Love' (with its opening line, 'The first time I died...'), are the emotional core of a record that is 'terribly sad', imbued with 'a very metropolitan melancholy.'[370]

Indeed, it was the last record Bush would make in London; the following year, she escaped its 'air of doom' (her description of the city at the time of *The Dreaming*), moving out to an old farmhouse in Kent. Having made it from the Green Belt and into the centre, she then fled back out and into the country – both metaphorically and literally. Pastoral themes would feature increasingly in her work. That same year, she built a new 48-track studio on her parents' property back in Welling, where she had grown up, where, at her own pace, she crafted *Hounds Of Love*. Having made 'my "I'm very angry" album', one that was 'all mental' ('fuck you, record companies! Trying to pin me down!' she later laughed), Bush could flee to her rural haven to create whatever she wanted.[371]

Creating whatever she wanted might have resulted in something even more experimental and less commercial than *The Dreaming*, which is exactly what EMI feared. But the label's efforts to impose a producer on Bush were rebuffed by her, despite the fact that she seemed to internalise the label's belief that an album's commercial viability was incompatible with an artist like her having complete creative control. By insisting on producing herself, she believed she had decided 'that no, fame didn't matter to me as much as making a good album did.' Yet, the result was the most commercially successful album of her career, a come-back smash that brought her greater fame than ever. It had been three years since her last album, five since her last hit album, 'an eternity in the rapid-turnover context of the 1980s', making her close to a has-been in the UK – while she remained virtually unknown in the US. The immediate success of 'Running Up That Hill', then *Hounds Of Love*, then three more singles from the album, made Bush 'a returning elder stateswoman of pop' in her home country (although she had only turned 27 in that summer of 1985); the album even broke into the US market – against the odds and industry predictions. Yet, despite drawing such sales, it also retained 'all of the individual idiosyncrasies' that had originally shown Bush to be 'a talent distinct from the pack.'[372]

How did she do that? How did *Hounds* avoid the fate of Sylvian's 'Pop Song' – which tried both to be and not to be a pop hit, thereby falling into the cracks between the two – and instead manage to bridge the commercial and the idiosyncratic, the conventional and the experimental, pop and something beyond it? Superficially, the answer lies in the two sides of the album. Arguably, the buoyant energy of the thrilling 21-minute first side (titled, a tad confusingly, 'Hounds Of Love') – four of its five tracks upbeat hit singles – was the Trojan Horse that Bush used to slip onto turntables and CD players the experimental second side. A 26-minute seven-song cycle (titled 'The Ninth Wave'), its allegorical tale of the possible rescue of a girl lost at sea, at night, carried a distinct 'concept album' aura (Bush called it 'my first novella' and 'the concept side'). One might view 'The Ninth Wave' as 'an album within an album', and if 'there's a strong case' that *Hounds Of Love* is Bush's 'masterpiece', 'there's an even stronger case that it's two'.[373]

Yet, the album is remarkably coherent. Streaming or on CD, the flow from side one to two, from the stirring 'Cloudbusting' to the gorgeous 'And Dream Of Sheep', is completely seamless. And that reflects Bush's triumphant use of the same scenius technique that Hollis and Sylvian were developing. Bush was in charge. She was the writer, composer, vocalist, pianist, Fairlight synthesizer operator and sole producer; she exercised full control over 18 musicians, plus a string sextet and a choir, two arrangers and seven sound engineers. Although that included her two brothers, her romantic partner Del Palmer (1952-2024) and old friends who had played on previous albums (like guitarist Brian Bath, bassist Danny Thompson and drummer Stuart Elliott), those musicians were not a band but session players following her instructions as she painstakingly constructed her vision. 'Every individual musician would come down and play their parts separately', remembered Youth (who played the propulsive bass line on 'The Big Sky'); it was all 'quite unusual', a method that brought to mind the German experimentalists, 'people like Kraftwerk and Can.' In testimonies by the musicians and engineers, Bush comes across as a gentler version of Hollis – less teasing, more cups of tea – giving instructions that were 'experimental' and without clear details on 'notes or sounds or harmonies of melodic structures' yet conveying 'an extremely clear impression of the atmosphere she wants to create'.[374]

If Bush's vision, combined with her ability to direct her scenius of professionals into realising that vision, connect the two sides of *Hounds*, its two halves are also tied together by thematic concerns that repeatedly crop up in her work. One is that preoccupation with pastoralism, here manifested in bold manifestations of nature: big skies and portentous clouds on side one; endless ocean waters on side two. Another is the theme of escape, picked up from *The Dreaming*: escaping the corporal confines of one's gender on side one; waiting to escape the waves and ice and danger of drowning on side two. One of the album's most memorable lines, delivered with such passion – the title track's 'take my shoes off and throw them in the lake' – is surely a wonderfully exuberant expression of escape. And yet another unifying theme – perhaps the most important of all – is love: in the opening tracks, between lovers; but then, after side one shifts to 'Mother Stands For Comfort', love between parent and child. 'Mother' is followed by 'Cloudbusting' and its exploration of a boy's perception of his father's troubled life and work (the real-life Peter and Wilhelm Reich), and the above-mentioned seamless transition into 'The Ninth Wave' is thus facilitated by the gradual realisation that the greatest fear gripping the girl lost at sea is the prospect of permanent separation from her parents.

In a way, then, side one of *Hounds Of Love* is an exploration of those themes through pop songs, and side two is their exploration through a prog pop (not quite post-pop) masterwork. 'The Ninth Wave' comprises seven songs, but to be fully appreciated – and understood as a crucial step on Bush's journey into post-pop – it should be heard the way it was conceived: as a single piece of work. Thus, *Classic Rock* magazine's listing of 'The Ninth Wave' as number one in their list of Bush's 'Top 25 songs of all time' is a forgivable cheat (like my use of it in this chapter's title). Significantly, that issue of the magazine was devoted to 'Prog'. As the issue states, 'The Ninth Wave' is 'simply spellbinding', an arc from misty-eyed beauty to menace and angst and back to peaceful poignancy, from the glimmering hope of the first line ('Little light shining') to what we optimists take to be the relief of the last line ('How much I love them' – her mother, her father, her brothers). I say 'we optimists' because the ending is admittedly ambiguous, with the girl's rescue from the water not made explicit. And yet I think Bush biographer Graeme Thomson is right that 'The Ninth Wave' is 'a story about not dying, not going under, but instead riding the waves and, somehow, keeping going.' 'I think the woman lives', says David Mitchell, who helped stage 'The Ninth Wave' as part of the 2014 live show, *Before The Dawn*. 'The last track, 'The Morning Fog', has too much light and air to be a watery grave'.[375]

Thomson was not willing to go further than vague optimism, conceding that while it is tempting to see 'The Ninth Wave' as 'a highly stylised, oblique dramatisation of much of the difficulties Bush had undergone in 1981 and 1982', that would ultimately be 'overly simplistic.' But others could not resist the autobiographical possibilities, seeing the 'sink-or-swim scenario' as 'an extended metaphor' for the protracted process of extracting just the right sounds from the many members of her studio scenius in order to complete the album she envisaged – be it *The Dreaming* or *Hounds Of Love* or both. In the end, of course, 'The Ninth Wave' has many interlocking meanings, being a creative expression of Bush's childhood dreams (and nightmares) about water and the seas, *and* a story about being 'at the mercy of your own imagination' (in Bush's words), *and* a metaphor for fears of separation from her family, *and* a metaphor for the drawn-out effort to stay afloat while making a complex and sophisticated record. Perhaps we might also see it as a metaphor for Bush's engagement with genre, her sensing of pop's push-pull effect and her ambivalence over the journey into post-pop. I must admit that I have tended to see that journey as a metaphorical walk in the woods, complete with paths and clearings, my mind surely influenced by the Bush, Hollis and Sylvian fascination with nature; but perhaps it is also a journey at sea, an experience less linear and more floating and drifting, fighting the fear of drowning, hoping to 'get out of the waves, get out of the water' (from the exquisite penultimate track, 'Hello Earth') and be 'born again into the sweet morning fog' (from the last track).[376]

Sometimes, the buying public responds positively to a song or an album that is so obviously an expression of sheer genius – so catchy and memorable and resonant – regardless of genre and fashion. And *Hounds Of Love* was not a conventional mid-1980s pop album. Its resurgence in 2022 – fuelled by 'Running Up That Hill' hitting number one in eight countries in the wake of its deft use in the hit television drama *Stranger Things* – was partly made possible by its timeless production. The role of 'Running Up That Hill' (or 'RUTH', as even Bush took to calling it) in multiple *Stranger Things* episodes was powerfully effective, but that cannot explain why the song was the most-played track *worldwide* in the summer of 2022 ('the whole world's gone mad!' exclaimed Bush on the

BBC's *Woman's Hour*). 'RUTH' was streamed 6 million times a day through June on Spotify alone. It hit number one in the UK (Bush's second number one at home, after 'Wuthering Heights' 37 years earlier), quickly selling over a million CD singles, and it reached number three in the US (where it had previously been her biggest hit, peaking at number 30 in 1985). The newfound popularity of the song and then its album was neither prompted by, nor did it spawn, a 'retro' moment or a burst of 1980s nostalgia. On the contrary, 'RUTH' and *Hounds* thereby became as much 2022 as they were 1985; which is to say, they are neither and both.[377]

The further explanation that such virality requires lies within the song itself and its crafting as 'plainly weird pop music' – that is, a song that is recognisable as pop yet leans towards something experimental and strange, something beyond conventional pop. Like the best pop, 'RUTH' is open to interpretation, permitting it to become, for example, a trans anthem. Its theme of gender-swapping is expressed poetically enough for it to be ignored or treated lightly as an amusement in the vein of 'swap' movies like *Freaky Friday*, but it can also be embraced as a radical rumination on sex and a challenge to heteronormative, boy-meets-girl culture – whether in the 1980s or 2020s context. And 'RUTH' is just the beginning of its parent album's interpretive potential. The millions of new fans led in 2022 by that song to *Hounds* thereby encountered that album's experimentalism, especially when they reached 'The Ninth Wave'.

Hounds Of Love is not simply a pop album, then, but nor is it quite post-pop: it is art pop and prog pop, taking some of the elements of progressive rock and presenting them in a gorgeous pop wrapping. One critic recently placed it in the 'small coterie of auteurist art-rock albums' of its era ('including classics by Peter Gabriel, The Blue Nile and Talk Talk'). In 1985, *Hounds* seemed to anticipate a kind of post-pop that could not yet be articulated; in the 2020s, it seems like a foundation stone, and it has rightly been received as such by millions born since 1985 as if it were a thrilling new discovery emerging from an inspired archaeological dig.[378]

'The spirit that fuelled progressive rock from the early 1970s later 'cropped up in Kate Bush's idiosyncratic approach to song arrangement on *The Dreaming* and *Hounds Of Love*', claimed one historian of prog rock, and 'reared its head unashamedly in the expansive sounds of the so-called post-rock groups like Godspeed You! Black Emperor and Sigur Rós.'[379] Those two bands seem like a far cry from Bush's work after *Hounds*, and indeed, they are part of the genre flow of prog rock/post-rock that features countless artists from the 1990s to the 2020s – Bush not included.

But her true sequel to *Hounds Of Love* would not come for 20 years. Instead, Bush felt the pull of that inertia inherent to pop music, partly as a result of the global success of *Hounds*. The two albums that followed – one coming after four years (*The Sensual World*) and the next four years after that (*The Red Shoes*) – did not lack for inventive and imaginative elements and contained some of Bush's most stirring compositions. But they were pop albums, lacking the conceptual coherence and prog pop captivation of what came before and after. Having taken a big step towards post-pop, Bush stepped back. One explanation is that despite the positive critical and fan response to 'The Ninth Wave', it was the singles from *Hounds* that gave Bush her global imperial phase – as a pop star. Including 'Experiment IV' (not technically an outtake from the *Hounds* sessions but originating in them and sounding very much like a side one *Hounds* track, recorded in 1986 as a single to add to *The Whole Story* compilation), there were five hit singles with lives as records, as videos and as tracks with the highest visibility on Bush's two biggest albums (*Hounds* and *The Whole Story*). It may be, therefore, that discovering she could be a world-famous pop star without touring anywhere, and with minimal public exposure, she continued to make pop records – hardly mainstream ones, but, nonetheless, not ones that were spawned by 'The Ninth Wave'. But I think there is another explanation, too, one relating to the way in which Bush's creative mind loops back through older influences, preoccupations and genre styles in order to engage them again in new ways. As a result, in terms of the relationship of her albums to pop and post-pop, *The Sensual World* is really a sequel (skipping over two albums) to *Never For Ever*, while the sequel to *Hounds Of Love* (again skipping two albums) is *Aerial*. More specifically, 'The Ninth Wave' found its sequel in the multi-track long-form second half of *Aerial*, titled 'A Sky Of Honey'. That pairing was made explicit in 2014's *Before The Dawn* (its recording released in 2016), in which the two conceptual works were performed in their entireties, back-to-back, as the show's heart.

But that was all in an unpredictable future. After *The Red Shoes*, Bush would not make another album for 12 years. It seemed as if she had bypassed the making of post-pop albums and gone straight to the destination claimed by her friend Mark Hollis: reclusive retirement and musical silence.

The push-pull phenomenon was experienced by a minority of 1980s pop artists, and even most of those found the commercial tug of pop too strong to resist. After all, part of what defines the journey to post-pop is that most pop artists never started – or even contemplated – it. Few imagined that their creative future might involve the conflicting influences of Stockhausen and ABBA. Familiarity with Stockhausen and an indifference to how uncool ABBA were in the 1980s made the likes of Paul Humphreys and Andy McCluskey a small minority.

It was OMD upon whom I suggested earlier I would have bet in 1980 as future post-pop pioneers. I would thereby have lost my shirt – but not immediately. OMD's 1980s trajectory was less a winding road than a zig-zag between those two poles, although those poles were less extreme than the ABBA/Stockhausen contrast suggests: the experimental electronic pole was closer to Kraftwerk and some of the Stockhausen-influenced Cologne artists, like Can; while the pop pole was closer to 1980s synth-pop bands that, in the circular irony that was central to pop history, were themselves influenced by early OMD – such as Depeche Mode, Howard Jones and the Pet Shop Boys.

Humphreys and McCluskey followed their groundbreaking pair of 1980 electro-pop albums with a zig into pop; 1981's *Architecture & Morality* was a great commercial success, buoyed by three massive international hit singles, and despite mixed reviews at the time, it is now rightly considered one of *the* classic synth-pop albums. The duo then did what Bush, Sylvian and Hollis would all do when faced with commercial success: they used the financial windfall to make a defiantly non-commercial album, not to be bloody-minded but simply because they felt creatively and financially free to do so. 1983's *Dazzle Ships* was thus a zag into electronic experimentalism. Like Bush's *The Dreaming* (released six months earlier), *Dazzle Ships* was less extreme than was claimed at the time – it contained pop moments, such as the single 'Telegraph', just as *Architecture & Morality* had included tracks (like 'Sealand' and the title track) that would have sat comfortably on the more experimental albums that came right before and after it. Nonetheless, *Dazzle Ships* anticipated where post-pop would go, with its use of shortwave radio samples, its juxtaposition of synth-pop melodies with electronic soundscapes and its use of sonic and mood shifts to undermine pop's predictability.

But OMD, like Bush, found little support for such a journey. As one writer recently put it, 'Suddenly, this brave new music that had taken over the charts had limits imposed upon it.'[380] For the music press, being pretentious was even worse than being pop, and being both was simply uncool. *Dazzle Ships* was panned as 'the worst kind of futuristic nonsense' and 'redundant avant-garde trickery'; its 'soundtrack-like effects' serve to 'clutter what decent electropop baubles there are here.' Despite their failure to anticipate how innovative and influential the album would later be seen, such critiques correctly identified the two poles between which OMD zig zagged. As did their label, Virgin, who used contractual obligation to pressure the band to zig back into the pop lane. OMD did so willingly because, as McCluskey later admitted, they deliberately 'decided to dial down some of the experiments and dial up some of the melodies. We had to think, 'This is our job, this is how we pay the bills, so we better be more careful'.[381]

The result, 1984's *Junk Culture*, was an imaginative synth-pop album positioned, in terms of poles of genre and influence, very close to *Architecture & Morality*. From that point, OMD did not look back. They moved on to make two polished pop albums produced by Stephen Hague, deliberately aimed at breaking a US market that was still in the grips of the Second British Invasion. *Crush* (1985) and *The Pacific Age* (1986) reached a respectable number 38 and number 47 respectively (going top 20 in the UK), each producing a top 30 US single, sandwiching the number four smash, 'If You Leave' (from the *Pretty In Pink* soundtrack). In the very years when Hollis and Sylvian were exploring ways into post-pop, OMD travelled firmly on the pop path. There were hints at post-pop possibilities on the experimental tracks buried on their albums, but they were few and far between. By the end of the 1980s, they were a mainstream pop band who could have an international hit album called *The Best Of OMD* – very ABBA, not even remotely Stockhausen.

OMD were far from being the only electronic or synth-pop artists whose early experimental leanings were abandoned in favour of mainstream pop success. One notable example is Depeche Mode, who slowly evolved their synth-pop sound during the 1980s, then doubled down on their dark side, producing a pop masterwork that still stuns (1990's *Violator*), and becoming the biggest pop-rock band in the world in the early 1990s. Others explored progressive pop in the 1980s and theoretically might have journeyed closer to post-pop but never quite did – examples include Tears For Fears, The Sundays, Cocteau Twins and ZTT artists like Art Of Noise and Propaganda.[382]

In 1984, Propaganda began a collaboration with Sylvian, who contributed some ideas to 'Duel' and a couple of other tracks on their debut, *A Secret Wish*, having been invited by the German act to produce the album. But although the band's Claudia Brücken later said, 'It was amazing when

David came in', he suddenly and inexplicably left the project. One cannot help but wonder if Sylvian's full commitment might have nudged a fine synthpop album further into art pop, even post-pop, territory.[383]

There was similar potential in the wake of the temporary dissolution of the original Ultravox lineup (earlier styled Ultravox!). A phoenix trio emerged from those ashes, but synth-pop outfit Visage imploded early, while the new Ultravox – despite the innovative elements of synth-pop-rock masterpiece *Vienna* (1980) – were led by Midge Ure into increasingly mainstream pop territory. Six months before *Vienna*, ex-Ultravox frontman John Foxx released his solo debut, *Metamatic*. To my mind, the album remains undervalued and often overlooked as a crucial step between groundbreaking 1970s electronic pop by the likes of Kraftwerk and the mainstream synthpop of the 1980s – itself an important influence on the world-dominant EDM of later decades.

Metamatic 'blew everyone's minds', recalled one member of the Basildon circle of friends surrounding the emerging Depeche Mode – 'Vince [Clarke] loved that.' Foxx had self-financed *Metamatic*, then sold it to Virgin and used the funds to convert an old warehouse in Shoreditch, in London's East End, into a studio. Called The Garden, early electronic pop bands like Depeche Mode would record there. The title of *Metamatic* was borrowed from the name of a painting machine invented by a Parisian artist in the 1950s (*le métamatic*). Foxx's album achieved a kind of machine-cold pop – catchy and melodic but dispassionate and metallic, lacking pop's emotional warmth. A unique statement and a possible signpost for one journey to post-pop, it proved impossible to top. Three sequels, *The Garden* (named after Foxx's studio), *The Golden Section* and *In Mysterious Ways,* yielded diminishing critical and commercial returns; rather than building on the style created for *Metamatic*, those albums reached back to 1978's *System Of Romance*, the last album by the Foxx-helmed Ultravox. Seeing a dead end, Foxx sold his studio and quit the business, returning to work and teaching as a graphic artist under his birth name, Dennis Leigh. By the 1990s, he appeared to have chosen to journey to the place where Hollis would eventually settle (a place that Sylvian and Bush have periodically visited): complete, public, musical silence. (We shall return later to Leigh's re-emergence as Foxx.)[384]

What musical journeys, meanwhile, had the other former members of Japan taken in the years between the band's dissolution in 1982 and its troubled restoration in 1989? Sylvian's brother, Steve Jansen, left adrift by the collapse of the band he had co-founded as a teenager, clung to his ex-Japan friends – and especially to his brother, playing drums on all of Sylvian's 1980s solo albums. He also stayed close to Richard Barbieri, making two albums with him. *Catch The Fall*, released in 1987 under the name The Dolphin Brothers, drew on some of the session musicians who also played on other records central to the post-pop story – percussionist Martin Ditcham, for example, who played on all three of the later, post-pop, Talk Talk/Hollis albums; and the ubiquitous bassist Danny Thompson, who (as we saw earlier) played on various Sylvian, Talk Talk and Bush albums (including *The Dreaming* and *Hounds Of Love*). Despite those connections, *Catch The Fall* is pure 1980s synth-pop, sounding more like Level 42 than Japan – a far cry from the avant-garde records made around this time by Sylvian and Hollis.[385]

However, two years earlier, Jansen and Barbieri had made a very different record. *Worlds In A Small Room*, released as Jansen/Barbieri, was pure ambient instrumentals – less experimental than the ambient disc of Sylvian's *Gone To Earth*, bearing the influence of Eno's more melodic instrumental work. The album was appropriately spacey, commissioned to soundtrack NASA footage of the Space Shuttle. Whereas Sylvian spent the 1980s trying to find ways to reconcile or juxtapose avant-garde pop with experimental instrumental music, Jansen and Barbieri took a far simpler and less experimental approach: they separated them completely. While they'd never make another pop album or use The Dolphin Brothers name again, they would continue to make instrumental albums together throughout the next few decades. Like Jansen, then, Barbieri did some session work in the 1980s but otherwise stuck close to his former bandmates in terms of his career (he, too, played on some Sylvian albums and on Sylvian's 1988 world tour). Not until the 1990s would Barbieri find another band home (with Porcupine Tree) and not until this century would he develop a catalogue of solo albums.[386]

Mick Karn was the first member of Japan to release a solo album, beating Sylvian by a couple of years by putting out *Titles* in November 1982, just before Japan fully dissolved. Jansen and Barbieri played prominent roles, technically making it a three-quarters Japan album, helping it to chart. But it wasn't nearly Japan-sounding enough, peaking at number 74 and quickly disappearing. *Titles* had the virtue of showcasing Karn's unique style. As Duran bassist John Taylor later noted, he played 'with great beauty and verve, punching delicate holes in the fabric of the songs; in Mick Karn's basslines, no notes were ever wasted.' But that was not enough to sustain *Titles* – the sound of a 24-year-old musician with considerable talent but no experience as a solo artist. Karn recorded each track in the order that they were sequenced on the album, a curious technique that is rare – for good reasons.[387] Side one was instrumental; side two was all songs – a bifurcation whose precedents were the Eno and Bowie-in-Berlin albums that Karn and his Japan bandmates idolised and which Sylvian would soon follow on *Gone To Earth*. But those examples worked because the contrasting sides spoke to each other, illuminating each other in subtle ways – a conversation unrealised on *Titles*.

Karn's self-defeating problem was that he found instrumental music to be incomplete (nothing 'to sing along to, no story or subject matter spelt out to the unimaginative'). But lacking confidence in his lyric-writing and singing, he needed a collaborator – and yet he never 'felt happy about writing with someone else' and never found the right partner. He had played on two Gary Numan albums in 1981 and 1982, but their friendship had been awkward and did not produce a full-length collaboration. His friendship with Midge Ure produced one modest hit, 'After A Fashion', which reached number 39 in the UK in the autumn of 1983, the highest showing of Karn's post-Japan career, but the track was really Ure's ('more his song than mine', Karn conceded).[388]

Napier-Bell had introduced Karn to Peter Murphy of the recently defunct Bauhaus, and in 1984, the two released *The Waking Hour* under the name Dali's Car – rendered on the record as 'Dalis Car', the missing apostrophe symbolic of the project's inconsistency. Karn's bass playing, often described as rubbery or slippery, is notably elastic on *The Waking Hour*. But the album is a clear example of what happens when the ingredients are evocative and engaging – Karn's forefronted bass riffs and noodles hint at keyboard melodies that would have found happy homes on Numan, Foxx or even Japan albums – but in need of additional ingredients to make the tuneless morsel of an album sound whole.

At the time, my reaction was terribly obvious: this needs the other three members of Japan! Yet, decades later, even after the gorgeous purple vinyl 2022 reissue of *The Waking Hour* had spun a dozen times on my turntable, I couldn't shake that same thought. One of the problems was that Karn and Murphy lacked chemistry, thus failing to create or draw upon a scenius – 'we simply didn't like each other', the bassist later explained. One track is instrumental because Murphy didn't bother adding his vocals ('he'd already given up'). Dismissed by one music journalist as 'the world's most pretentious collaboration', Karn's defence was to quip that 'if Peter had his way, it would have been a lot more pretentious.'[389]

Karn's second solo album, 1987's *Dreams Of Reason Produce Monsters*, had the potential to move into more experimental pop territory, especially with Jansen playing on every track (and writing one of them, the ambient-pop instrumental 'Land'). But the album caused Karn to be 'dropped from Virgin for the third time' (his words). The verdict in *NME*, that some songs were 'repetitive ramblings, lacking focus or real direction', could be said of the whole album – and, uncharitably, of Karn's entire post-Japan career.[390] Where the lack of focus seemingly shown by Sylvian (and by Hollis and Bush) appears as exploratory journeys into forms of post-pop and beyond, Karn's seems more like a simple lack of focus.

The ghosts of Japan certainly haunted *Dreams Of Reason*, as Sylvian co-wrote and sang on its two best tracks, including the single 'Buoy' – his voice helping it spend three weeks on the charts (peaking at number 63 in January 1987). 'I couldn't have been more pleased,' Karn said of Sylvian's vocal, 'one of the best I've heard him deliver.' The song's significance to the larger story was that it and the other Sylvian/Karn track led to the longer reconciliation that made possible the Rain Tree Crow project (to which we now turn). But it also reflected the fact that, as much as Karn was reluctant to devote himself to a career as a session player, his most successful recordings were made playing bass behind vocalists with the kind of presence and profile of Sylvian: Joan Armatrading, for example, two of whose successful early 1990s albums featured the rhythm section of Karn and Jansen; and 'dear Kate Bush', as Karn later referred to the friend with whom he played at a fundraiser in 1982, going on to play on a track on 1989's *The Sensual World*. It has often been noted that both via Japan and after it, Karn's bass playing 'would continue to exert an influence on the pop scene.'[391] To be fair, then, albeit in largely indirect ways, he also influenced the development of the post-pop scene.

14: Cries And Whispers/After The Flood

'**Cries And Whispers**' Rain Tree Crow (1991, 2:31)
'**After The Flood**' Talk Talk (1991, 9:39)

Was *Laughing Stock* really a Talk Talk album? Billed as Talk Talk, it was credited as created by Hollis and Friese-Greene – that is, one band member and a producer who was not a band member. The sole other band member was Lee Harris, but he was treated the same way that session players were. In fact, he had been treated that way for much of the *Spirit Of Eden* sessions, as had Paul Webb – which is why Webb then quit the band. If those were Talk Talk albums, then Sylvian's 1980s solo albums were Japan records – credited to and directed by one band member, but with three-fourths of the band playing on them. In other words, the sequence of artist names on these albums disguises the real creative story: the run of seven or eight albums from around 1980 to 1991, credited to Japan, then David Sylvian, then Rain Tree Crow, were all, in fact, band projects in which Sylvian exerted increasing control but with all or most other band members making varying contributions (some credited, some not). Similarly, Talk Talk was a Hollis creation, and their five albums between 1982 and 1991 were increasingly created and controlled by him, with a declining number of band members making contributions (again, some credited, others not).

It is easy for me to make such assertions – organising my LPs and CDs accordingly – but it was far from easy for such issues to be resolved by band members, let alone by managers and label executives attempting to work with band members. The mix of ego, resentment and potential living-wage profits was a heady one. Haunting such wranglings was the increasingly obvious fact that the labelling of records and the crediting of songs determined who could subsequently afford to make the music they wanted.

When, therefore, the four ex-members of Japan met in the spring of 1989 to discuss recording together again, one of them hoped the reunion would allow him to continue on his explorative musical journey – and the other three hoped it would financially support them in a way that had been denied them since Japan dissolved. As Jansen recalled, his brother 'said, 'I may not have mentioned it, but if this does happen, it has to go out under my name.' So, we backed off immediately.' That might have been the end of it, but Sylvian seemed willing to compromise that summer, reconciling with Karn and suggesting the four simply jam together and take equal credit for any music that might emerge. There was one small catch: if an album came together, it would not be a Sylvian solo effort, nor would it be released as a Japan record.[392]

The plan predictably floundered on the rocks of Sylvian's perfectionism and his privileging of process over product. For seven months, Karn, Barbieri and the Batt brothers jammed in one studio after another, moving from Miraval in the south of France to Italy to two studios in London and, finally, to the Tears For Fears studio in Bath. When they asked Virgin for more funds, the label agreed on the condition that the end result be released as a Japan album – a reasonable position that, as we shall see, paralleled the negotiations that Hollis would have with his label.

'The 'improvised' album was about as improvised as a synchronised swimming team', Karn later wrote. In his telling, Sylvian's initial concession to split the royalties four ways was 'a gesture to put right the wrongs of the past in a small way.' But 'Dave now insisted on having more than the equal percentage', increasingly asserting both creative control and financial primacy. Of the four, Sylvian was the only one who flat refused Virgin's conditional offer. He pointed out that their studio costs had not consumed *all* of the advance from Virgin due to (in Karn's words) 'a small fraction that we'd set aside for ourselves to live on.' As Sylvian could live off his income from the Japan catalogue, he wanted to use those funds to finish the album, insisting the others do the same – which they could not afford to do. How to break the impasse?

Sylvian's solution was brilliantly Machiavellian: to pay for the mixing of the album himself, but only on the basis of him reaping the lion's share of the songwriting royalties, and with the rest of the band excluded from the mixing sessions – 'the final insult from the biggest, baddest Sylv', grumbled Karn. 'The bottom line', Jansen said, was that his brother 'believes he's right in what he's doing, he believes in himself to such a degree' that he was willing 'to abuse his friends' and to 'take [the album] away from us.' What 'an incredible manipulator', exclaimed Barbieri. 'Charismatic, charming,' he conceded, 'but he wants control over everyone, including his friends.'[393]

As such comments reveal, Sylvian's commitment to creative freedom was total; for the other three, the issue was lifelong friendship on the rocks. The resulting record – mixed by Sylvian without their input, released under a new band name created by Sylvian alone, Rain Tree Crow – reflected that emotional and psychological divergence. The album, also called *Rain Tree Crow*, was both a Sylvian album and a Japan album.

Imagine, as I suggested above, that Sylvian's solo records of 1984-87 were Japan products without the original bassist, but with him returning on *Rain Tree Crow*. The album then makes sense as an evolution of the *Tin Drum* sound through those Sylvian albums, especially *Gone To Earth*.[394]

Musically, at least, that was the result – and a fine result it was. The Orientalism of *Tin Drum* was here replaced by a hint of Americana, using three guitarists to lend the album a tinge of Mississippi blues, 'reminiscent of the work of Daniel Lanois in its evocation of big skies, barren landscapes and rocky terrain.' That lent the album a 'classic rockishness', and, as a recent review put it, that also helped make it 'stark, desolate and beguiling.' A third of the tracks were instrumentals, with 'New Moon At Red Deer Wallow' particularly effective – 'really exceptional', Sylvian enthused at the time. 'The track realises the potential that this group always had that was never realised before.' There was even a single, the somewhat somnolent 'Blackwater', which sounded nothing like the UK singles chart of spring 1991, evoking both late Japan and mid-period Sylvian but without obvious 1980s or turn-of-the-1990s production. Not surprisingly, it only peaked at number 62, but it surely helped draw Japan and Sylvian fans to the album, which reached number 24 (with more modest showings in Europe and Japan). The review in *Q* called the album 'a strange grower', not suitable for playing at parties but 'pretty well everywhere else. It would seem a shame if this is only a one-off project.'[395]

The melancholic potential of the album was exacerbated by the lyrics, which were infused with phrases of desolation and heartbreak. Many of the songs seemed to reflect a sad realisation by the band that 'a one-off project' was all this could be. 'Feel like crying, the jokes gone too far' sang Sylvian on the beautiful 'Every Colour You Are'. 'A shattered dream on a bed of lies' began 'Cries And Whispers', an equally lovely but ultimately gloomy composition. The closing track to the album, 'Cries And Whispers' is its emotional core, channelling the subdued pain of the protracted end to a long and profound relationship.[396] For Sylvian, there were two layers to that pain, as his personal relationship with Yuka Fujii was coming to an end, while his boyhood band was again crumbling – this time, once and for all.

Sylvian later confessed that the end of the decade was 'a dark period' in which he battled depression. He had admitted that this was an issue earlier in the 1980s, too, but in 1991, he dated the problem to the years after *Secrets Of The Beehive*, stating that he was in therapy 'for about two years' and that the Rain Tree Crow project was 'both a symptom and cure' for 'what's been happening to me for the past four years.' In other words, the entire three-year project was a kind of therapy, resulting in the permanent death of the band – over which Sylvian said he felt neither 'particularly negative' nor did he 'rejoice over it.' But the 'cure' left a bitter taste in the mouths of the rest of the band. Karn later said he mostly remembered 'the incessant arguing between Dave and Steve over religion at every single dinner break' and that after Sylvian had taken over the project's mixing and launching, he promoted it 'as basically his project from start to finish', with the cover art's crow 'symbolically representative of himself.' The bad ending was hard on Jansen, who said he saw his brother 'change into this awful person again' and he hated how it was 'no fun for our parents knowing we're avoiding each other.' But there was catharsis in it all for Karn: 'It really felt as if it was the final killing off, if you like, of the Japan days. It really felt as if it was something we had to do before we could really move on.'[397]

That mixture of personal, fraternal and band angst – the conflicts in, outside and after the studio sessions – no doubt 'contributed to making *Rain Tree Crow* an important album' (as one critic later put it, but the sentiment is Karn's, too). In the middle of the album is a 45-second morsel of a song, titled 'Boat's For Burning', that offers a devastating epitaph, perhaps to the Sylvian/Fujii relationship, but certainly to Japan/Rain Tree Crow. Sylvian croons, 'We were wrong, there's no love, all sense has gone', and then the line that really got to Tears For Fears' Roland Orzabal: 'Strike a match, stand well back, this boat's for burning.' 'It's like ... fuck. Incredible. Just too perfect a pop group.' Orzabal admitted he was 'crazy about *Rain Tree Crow*' when it came out. 'An unbelievable album. I love every track. You can tell they'd all been listening to *Spirit Of Eden* by Talk Talk.'[398]

In the autumn of 1991, I was living in Los Angeles, spending far too much time in record shops. I justified my steadily growing vinyl and CD collection with the dubious logic that I was saving money by mostly buying cut-outs, easy to find in one of the music industry's capital cities. (As rationales go for collecting records and CDs, that was relatively rational; it's a low logic bar.) Although *Laughing Stock* was brand new, I soon found a discounted vinyl copy with a hole punched through the sleeve. My initial reaction to the album is eclipsed in my memory by the reaction of the college-aged pop music fan who was, at the time, a brother-in-law of mine.

This was a different brother-in-law from the one who had first played me *The Colour Of Spring*, but he was, nonetheless, a fan of pre-*Spirit* Talk

Talk. He came over soon after I had bought *Laughing Stock* – perhaps the same day. 'Here, listen to this, it's the new Talk Talk album!' The needle dropped. He frowned, shaking his head a little at the fragmented sounds that comprised the beginning of the first track, 'Myrrhman'. Then, as Hollis started to sing – keening, murmuring – my brother-in-law started to laugh. In disbelief, he grabbed the record sleeve. Seeing the album's title, he laughed harder. He had assumed that *Spirit Of Eden* was, like Bush's *The Dreaming* or OMD's *Dazzle Ships*, a way of Talk Talk working something out of their system – a need to experiment, a need to flip the finger at the label and industry – before remembering their fans and returning to the pop fold. But this was no step backwards; it was a resolute step forward along the same path.

'It can't *all* be like this, surely?' he questioned. To which I flipped the disc and 'Taphead' began. Whereas 'Myrrhman' starts as if several musicians are warming up, 'Taphead' begins with a slow, solitary guitar line, perhaps also a warm-up, before Hollis begins another murmuring, slurred lyric. My brother-in-law was appalled and amused in equal amounts, convinced that the joke was on us, Hollis making a laughingstock of everyone.[399]

Laughing Stock was, indeed, all like that. It was like *Spirit Of Eden*, but with 'more edge to it', as Friese-Greene would later note. The loud parts were louder and the quiet parts were quieter. The guitar was more prominent, as Friese-Greene 'wanted it noisier', lending the album its 'abrasive, lo-fi feel.' If it was Friese-Greene who was responsible for the rough edges, Hollis was a master of the opposite – 'silence is the most powerful instrument I have', he said in interviews for the album. *Laughing Stock* was full of paradoxes: loud and quiet, anarchic yet meticulously crafted, cyclical yet lacking pop's repetitions (as Hollis said of 'Myrrhman', 'no part of that track will ever repeat itself'). As Chuter put it, this was 'a sculptural work, chiselled away through the application of retrospect.'[400]

Studio conditions were even more harrowing than they had been on the previous album – 'marriages were collapsing, there were breakdowns, people resigning', recalled Brown (who returned, with trepidation, as sound engineer). For harmonica player Feltham, the sessions 'were possibly the most draining, intense and physically exhausting' of his 30-year career. Harris, obliged to repeat the same drum patterns for weeks, developed 'stress-related flu symptoms and had to take some time off'. With nothing but desk lamps and that old oil projector lighting the studio, Brown found the darkness oppressive, and 'the process of listening to the same songs over and over again put me in a very dark emotional state.'[401]

That emotional atmosphere carried over into the album – too much so for some reviewers. 'Mark Hollis' music has slipped into a vat of dark, brooding melancholy so deep that even David Sylvian would join Right Said Fred rather than partake of its glummo brew', moaned the *NME* review. But the relentlessness of the studio method also permitted the same meticulousness that had lent *Spirit Of Eden* its paradoxical feel of chaos and control. Brown's comment on *Spirit* – that 'the album feels like seven guys playing live in a room, but every 'note' is placed where it is' – applies equally to *Laughing Stock*: 'The album is an illusion!' When bands self-produce, they can 'spend an inordinate amount of time obsessing over small details.' As Bryan Ferry realised during the making of *Avalon*, the studio becomes the band (or up to '90% of it'). As engineer, Brown was at the mercy of that obsessiveness by Hollis and Friese-Greene – as the writers, creators and producers. Decades later, deep into the digital age, such a method would be seen as the musical equivalent of molecular gastronomy. As described in 2013 by Glaswegian hyperpop musician and producer Sophie Xeon, 'It's about getting to the molecular level of a particular sound – realising what that sound is actually made of and why it behaves a certain way when processed or cooked. Then you use those molecules to build new forms, mixing and reappropriating those raw materials, and, of course, it should be bloody delicious.'[402]

But the taste of *Laughing Stock* was bitter-sweet rather than bloody delicious. It was full of contradictions and contrasts, 'a brilliant achievement', as Rob Young exclaims, a 'hitherto unknown' blend of 'fluidity, abstraction and hushed, tensed power.' On an album of starkly juxtaposed moods, the centrepiece – the masterstroke – is 'After The Flood'.[403] The track is a gripping study in contrasts: beautiful and grating, jazzily improvised and relentlessly rocking, artfully constructed and accidentally happening. It knows not what it is, and yet it is completely comfortable in its own skin. It is an essential post-pop track.

The 7' edit of 'I Don't Believe You' had killed the impact of the loud/quiet contrasts within that otherwise powerful *Spirit Of Eden* track. Mindful of that, Hollis and Friese-Greene recorded a separate version of 'After The Flood' for Polydor/Verve to release as a single. Called 'After The Flood (Outtake)', it was limited to only a few markets. The 7' holds up, but it 'doesn't have the mad solo in the middle', as Brown put it – the purging one-note flood of sound that Hollis forced out of a malfunctioning Variophon. A minute long, that solo's pleasure-pain delivery feels longer and better, making the 9:39 album version indispensable.[404] Neither version of 'After The Flood' has a recognisable chorus, nor, in fact, does any track on the album. The record hits your ears more or less as rock/pop, yet paradoxically, the reassuring structures and signals of rock and pop are missing or misplaced. It unswervingly delivers the disorientation of post-pop.

If 'After The Flood' is one of post-pop's foundational moments, it also represented a kind of endpoint for Hollis. There would be one more album after *Laughing Stock*, but Hollis's musical journey, taking him from the age of 21 into his mid-30s, from The Reaction's 'Talk Talk Talk Talk' to Talk Talk's 'After The Flood', was a creative development that was extraordinarily relentless and single-minded. He had followed the 'sorrowing masterpiece' of *Spirit Of Eden* with an album that was 'a scorched-earth tilt at the finish line' (in Rob Young's words). 'I remember thinking, this is the end; this is as far as we can go', recalled Friese-Greene; 'after one note, there are no notes.' When Hollis died, Elbow's Guy Garvey characterised that journey with resonant hyperbole: to go from playing punk songs 'to writing some of the most timeless, intricate and original music ever is as impressive as the moon landings.'[405]

And where do you go after landing on the moon? Home to your family. As 1991 drew to an end, and the music world slipped into a CD-centred future dominated by grunge, Britpop, hip-hop and EDM, this appeared to be the end of the story told here. Bush had reverted to making pop music and then stopped making music at all. Sylvian had reunited Japan only to sacrifice it again on the altar of his own ghosts. He'd now buried the band so deeply that it could never again be disinterred; a new solo album was not planned and nor would one emerge as the 1990s unfolded. Hollis had also sacrificed his own band, taking it on an excruciating creative journey, only to emerge with a pair of albums that confounded as much as they amazed. With sighs of relief, the remnants of these bands parted ways with their mercurial leaders, with the pioneers who had hacked a path into territory that had yet to be named. But the genre labelling and debating would be left to others. For the pioneers, it was time to settle down. Their journeys were over.

Or were they?

Side D (1992-2024)

15: Heartbeat

'Heartbeat' Ryuichi Sakamoto featuring David Sylvian & Ingrid Chavez (1992, 5:18)

'You'd be surprised how quickly you could get back to being anonymous if you stopped singing, started to live a normal life, got married, had children, grew a paunch', Simon Napier-Bell told George Michael soon after he stopped managing David Sylvian. 'It would take less than a year and there'd be no more kids hiding behind the bush taking photographs, no more journalists hounding you.'[406]

Napier-Bell was right, of course: disappearance has proved remarkably quick and easy for many a pop star (no doubt to their surprise). Hence the rarity of being able 'to watch popular performers grow older through their creative work, singing material that reflects who they are in their advancing years, in front of an audience willing to pay attention.'[407] That quote comes from an essay on ABBA and Adele, both of whom have revealed their ageing in very limited ways. ABBA skipped 40 years between penultimate and ultimate albums, giving us a then-and-now rather than an insight into the process. As for Adele, she's older but far from old; so far, her latest age-stamped album is *30*. As with Michael's masterful *Older*, released when he was only 33, ruminations upon the passing of one's 20s resonate less with older listeners than efforts to express the impact of middle age.

Michael is one example of why we seldom get 'to watch popular performers grow older': some are taken from us. Others permit us to watch them age, but not 'through their creative work.' That is, we get to revisit the songs of their and our youth as we all nostalgically age together (think Billy Joel). Others disappear, temporarily or permanently, as was the case with Sylvian, Hollis and Bush. Indeed, disappearance is a logical destination in the journey out of pop stardom into the relative obscurity of post-pop. If perpetual public presence is inherent to fame, its opposite is total absence. As Jenny Fabian, famous groupie and *Groupie* co-author, noted of Barrett, 'Where would Syd have gone through the 1970s, 1980s and 1990s? Would he have become some kind of ancient ambient trance musician? When you look back, he did absolutely the right thing: he flipped out and disappeared!'[408]

Looking back from the 21st century, there is certainly a logic to seeing a figure like Barrett as having only those options – disappearance or making ambient albums (or a slow toggling between the two). At the end of the day, Napier-Bell saw not only that the extraordinary life of a popstar was incompatible with ordinary married-with-children life but that the latter was, for some, a relief and a refuge – not a compromise reluctantly made. In 1992, Hollis turned 37 and Bush and Sylvian turned 34. In the years that followed, all three would devote themselves to domestic life with romantic partners and children. Their public lives would pale in comparison to their experiences of the previous 15 years, while their creative output would shift and slow.

In 1993, Bush's romantic relationship with Del Palmer ended (he had been her bassist and boyfriend since her late teens) and a new one began (with guitarist Danny McIntosh, later her husband and father of her only child). That same year, she released her only album of the decade, *The Red Shoes*, often ranked as her weakest. Hollis had, in 1985, married the woman he'd been with for many years; by 1992, they had two sons, then aged about two and five. From that year until his death, 27 years later, he made only one album, devoting infinitely more time to child-raising than to music-making. Sylvian, meanwhile, met and married Ingrid Chavez and then went even further than Napier-Bell imagined: he left London permanently, settling in a modest home in the suburbs of Minneapolis, Minnesota, where he and Chavez raised two daughters (born in 1993 and 1996). I've found no evidence of paunches, but Sylvian, like Hollis and Bush, otherwise lived Napier-Bell's 'normal life.'[409]

Sylvian continued to write music and seek collaborators, even while living the life of a young Dad in suburban America. That is partly a testimony to his creative compulsion but perhaps a reflection, too, of the fact that his wife was also a songwriter and musician. The professional and the personal thus coincided, although not in a way that led to Sylvian's best work – and not to a solo album until the end of the 1990s. It was thus ironic that Sylvian and Chavez met in the studio where Sakamoto had invited Sylvian to contribute to the Japanese star's new solo album.

Having worked with Lenny Kravitz and Prince (she sang and acted in his *Graffiti Bridge* movie), Chavez released her own debut album in 1991. Impressed by an advance tape, Sylvian invited her to the Sakamoto sessions, resulting in her singing with Sylvian on the title track to what would be Sakamoto's ninth solo album, 1991's *Heartbeat*. By the time the song was released and charted as a single (it was a UK number 58 in June 1992), Sylvian and Chavez had been married for several months. Their wedding took place in her hometown of Minneapolis, where they bought a house. (Sylvian never moved back to England, living in various corners of the US ever since.)[410]

I've always enjoyed 'Heartbeat (Tainai Kaiki II)'. After *Rain Tree Crow*, it's a virtual banger, buoyed along by a gently chugging beat and a playful interaction between Sylvian's croon, Chavez's 'seductive background murmur' and Bill Frisell's guitar. But it is Sakamoto's song, not Sylvian's, fitting better into the former's impressively varied catalogue. As a reflection of Sylvian's creative journey, it shows him happily distracted, but it also symbolises the mixed results of his attempts to collaborate productively in the wake of the final collapse of Japan. Sakamoto would seem to have been the ideal candidate. They had intended to make an album together as far back as the 'Forbidden Colours' days when they had achieved a profound musical understanding. 'Despite being unable to speak each other's language', they were able to communicate productively 'via the keyboard keys' (as one observer put it). 'They are not so far from each other', Czukay said of the pair after all three had first worked together on *Brilliant Trees*: 'somehow, they are brothers in mind.' Sakamoto had himself put it in such terms a few years earlier, asserting that 'Sylvian and I are like brothers' on the same 'spiritual journey.' But that mental brotherhood proved insufficient, and no Sylvian/Sakamoto album emerged, several attempts notwithstanding.[411]

Despite being a self-confessed 'anti-social', Sylvian was seemingly now unable to compose on his own. While periodically trying, in vain, to create a full album with Sakamoto, he pursued other potential writing partners. Sylvian had been compared to Scott Walker, a 'fellow pop melancholic', as far back as the 1980s. Flattered by such a pairing, he visited Walker in the studio. But the talked-about collaboration never materialised.[412]

Sylvian also turned to an old collaborator, Robert Fripp. Declining Fripp's offer to join King Crimson, the two did end up creating an album together – the rapidly assembled *The First Day*, released in the summer of 1993. But, as with Sakamoto and 'Heartbeat', the result reflects Fripp's musical journey more than Sylvian's. 'The record came out rather more loud than if I had been working by myself, which is rather exciting in a way', Sylvian told *Creem*, an understated admission, considering how dominant Fripp's guitar playing was ('his fleet-fingered solos tumbling over each other like towels in a dryer', as Power evocatively put it).[413]

Rather than being a further step towards post-pop, *The First Day* was a side trip into art rock. It garnered generally positive reviews, jumping into the UK charts at number 21. But Czukay put his finger on the problem when he 'called up David and said, 'I don't think [Robert] understands your special qualities and moods." The record was too rockist, too 'general', just plain 'traditional'. Fair enough. Czukay sensed that Sylvian had original creations ahead of him and that *The First Day* was an excursion, one more rooted in the moment than Sylvian needed to be. The album even spawned a couple of singles, one of which, 'Darshan', was remixed into an extended EDM track by Dave Ball of Soft Cell and The Grid – a Sylvian fan ever since he bought 'Life In Tokyo' and saw 'Ghosts' on *Top Of The Pops*. Another version of the single by The Future Sound of London, a very 1993 trip-hop mix, was far enough removed from its parent that it was retitled 'Darshana'.[414]

But newlywed Sylvian was happy to explore outside his wheelhouse and even to do something he'd always hated – go on tour. Despite becoming a father for the first time in September 1993, the following month, he flew to Japan with Fripp and a small touring band, kicking off a world tour that crossed North America and Europe, ending in London – where performances at the Royal Festival Hall were recorded and released in 1994 as *Damage*. The live album was dedicated to Sylvian's infant daughter. His second daughter's birth was still two years away, but in the meantime, Sylvian went back out on the road again. His 1995 *Slow Fire* tour took in Japan, Italy, Belgium and England, all markets where he had developed an ardent fan base. More deeply engaged with Eastern religion than ever, he dedicated the tour to the Hindu philosopher and guru Mata Amritanandamayi Devi. On stage, he wore a traditional Indian silk shirt and suit. Journalists at the London concert were both amazed and a little appalled by the imagery and the fan response as people rushed to the stage 'to rest their foreheads on his palms.' *Mojo* feared that he'd 'become a guru, a god', while *The Independent* writer jibed that 'I swear I saw him turn somebody's mineral water into Chablis.'[415]

There had, meanwhile, been some collaborations of a very different nature, including another with Fripp. The long-standing respect for Sylvian in Japan, combined with his friendships with Japanese musicians who had themselves become major cultural figures (such as Sakamoto), had made him in demand as a composer of ambient soundtracks for art installations. These tended to be as minimalist as their titles were not: *Ember Glance: The Permanence Of Memory* was written (in collaboration with the artist Russell Mills) and staged in a museum in Shinagawa in 1990; *Redemption: Approaching Silence* (written with Fripp) was part of an instalment in a Tokyo temple museum in 1994. The two compositions, running roughly 35 and 38 minutes respectively, were released in 1999 as a CD simply titled *Approaching Silence* – it was mixed by Sylvian in the Napa Valley, where he had moved with Chavez and their infant children.[416] 'Approaching Silence' (in its form as the title track to the 1999 CD) is the better of the pieces: brooding, ominous, timeless and cinematographic. It feels less like a signpost to more travel and more like an ending with a reckoning. It seems to anticipate where Sylvian will end.

But we are not there yet. Earlier in 1999, Sylvian had finally – after 12 years – released another solo album. This was the question, then, at the turn of the century: was the creative future for Sylvian, a family man in sunny California, best anticipated by his rockist excursions with Fripp, by his ambient electronic compositions or by a new solo album that may or may not have continued his journey towards post-pop?

It was Dave Ball who, in the 1990s, put his finger on the nature of Sylvian's journey, sensing where it needed to go. 'Japan were great abstract pop', said Ball, articulating something of the way that post-pop emerges from experimental and art pop: 'In David's solo career, he's gone for the abstract part of it but retained a great pop sensibility. The guy's matured in years, but also as a musician. You do your youthful pop thing, and then you hear something in your music and pursue that element. With Sylvian, it was the darker side of Japan.'[417]

Size and length matter. The width, speed and running time of singles and albums were well established by the birth of the Hollis/Bush/Sylvian generation for reasons pre-dating, by many centuries, the invention of their technologies. A modern pop song is roughly as long as its early antecedents were – the ditties of medieval European troubadours, the sung tales of African griots and so on – because two-to-four minutes contains a manageable amount of melody and lyric for most people to remember. The human attention span tends to wane soon after 20 minutes, which is not coincidentally the approximate length of later compositions (song collections, for example, or movements within symphonies) – as it is of one side of a vinyl LP. Two human attention spans thus make an album (as Fripp once put it, 'most responsible, good-hearted people will put up with 45 minutes of something they don't like').[418] When the cassette tape became popular in the 1970s, it followed suit; blank tapes varied in length, but pre-recorded albums reproduced vinyl versions, even shuffling tracks around to minimise the amount of tape used.

That was the cultural and technological world in which Bush, Japan, early solo Sylvian and early Talk Talk made albums. But then the CD arrived and 'had a profound effect on music' – but for a bizarre reason. The silver disc developed by Philips had, by 1979, overcome the challenges of emerging digital technology to shrink to 11.5 centimetres, enough to accommodate almost an hour of music and thus even the longest of single albums. But Sony had also developed a digital disc and neither company wanted a 'clusterfuck of different formats competing in the marketplace.' In the ensuing negotiations to establish a standard CD format, Sony president Norio Ohga pushed for a 12-centimetre diameter. Ohga's ambition as a student was to be an opera singer; he had studied music in Berlin and established a life-long friendship with influential conductor Herbert von Karajan. That extra half-centimetre was 'very important', Ohga insisted to Philips's François Dierckx, as it extended the CD's carrying capacity to 74 minutes, sufficient to accommodate von Karajan's recording of Beethoven's *Ninth Symphony*. Indeed, Ohga argued, having 'conducted a survey of classical music recordings', he could affirm that a 12-centimetre disc 'would accommodate 95% of the principal works.' Ohga's reasoning carried the day, as the decision-makers at both companies imagined that the expensive new CD players and their discs would be marketed to older listeners whose preference was classical music.[419]

Initially, that was the case. Then player prices came down and CD sales of back catalogues in all genres began to take off. By the late 1980s, new albums were routinely released on CD, and at the end of the decade, CD sales surpassed that of vinyl. As a result, albums grew longer, creeping towards the one-hour mark and then, as the 1990s wore on, often beyond it. CD capacity stretched to 80 minutes (by arranging data more closely on the same 12-cm disc, the original 650 MB was extended to 700). The decline of the CD in the 2000s only exacerbated the bloating trend: the shift to digital downloads and then streaming freed music formatting from its traditional lengths. By the 2010s, the *average* album length was an hour, with up to 90 minutes no longer unusual. Singles mostly grew shorter, front-loaded with hooks (as a streamed song counts as played after only 30 seconds), but albums expanded. Arguably, the resurgence of vinyl as a low-sales but high-profit prestige format helped retain some of the old sizes, as albums in the 60-to-90-minute range could be marketed as doubles. But I suspect that, regardless of shifts in technology, we will always prefer songs at roughly three minutes and albums at forty-and-change; human nature will persist as the foundational, deep-rooted reason for those sizes.

Does all this help us to understand why and how post-pop developed (and are the Hollis, Sylvian and Bush cases illustrative)? With respect to Hollis, mostly yes. He and Talk Talk kept within traditional length boundaries, even into the CD era: the first Talk Talk album was only 37 minutes, the next four averaged 43 minutes and his solo album ran to 47 minutes. But the number of tracks on each album shrank (from nine to six) as the songs grew longer. Even as Hollis leaned into longer-form pieces, as he shifted from pop to experimental pop to post-pop or post-rock, his increasing obsession with minimalism and perfectionism kept the albums from CD-era bloating. With respect to Japan and Sylvian, the impact of the format change is starker. The five Japan albums (all pre-CD) averaged 43 minutes, while Sylvian's solo and collaborative albums through to 1991's *Rain Tree Crow* averaged 39 minutes.[420] But then the two decades of albums that begin with 1993's *First Day* – itself a CD-era distended 63 minutes – all took advantage of being freed from vinyl's length limit, reaching a 63-minute average. As Sylvian moved away from pop into post-pop, ambient and other experimental genres, so did tracks and albums grow longer – made easier by digital formatting.

The point is not that the digital age led to post-pop but that it offered opportunities for increasingly experimental pop, for former pop artists to explore compositions at lengths outside vinyl's single or double LP standards. Let us linger on one more example, that of Kate Bush. Her first four (pre-CD) albums averaged 40 minutes. But the 1980s CD boom helped *Hounds Of Love* to be 48 minutes. Although her next album was a more conventional 42 minutes, its sequel, *The Red Shoes*, came out in 1993 when albums were ballooning, and it ran for 56 minutes. 'I'd made it long because I wanted people to feel they were getting their money's worth', Bush confessed in 2005. 'CDs were expensive.' But she regretted it, feeling 'really strongly' that CDs were too long, that artists had been 'forced into' the medium 'completely against the creative process.' Vinyl's 40 minutes was 'a good amount of time', with the added benefit of a 'natural space' or 'forced gap when you had to turn the record over' and 'go for a cup of tea or a pee or something.' Despite her strong feelings, Bush's release that year ran for 80 minutes. In double CD format, *Aerial* did, in fact, have that 'breathing space' – three such spaces in the vinyl version. But the vinyl release was, and remains, expensive (in the $50-100 range), while streaming obviously eliminates such spaces. Moreover, two oversized CD albums came six years later – the reworked songs of *Director's Cut* at 57 minutes and *50 Words For Snow* at over 65 minutes. The latter's seven tracks average more than nine minutes, its CD bloat reflecting its experimental, post-pop nature.[421]

As one musicologist has noted, digital formats gave artists the option of 'stretching the canvas and making it continuous.' While artists in mainstream genres simply dumped extra tracks onto albums, those moving into post-pop and related genres used that option to *change* their music. Certainly, 'long-form genres like post-rock and ambient techno feel intimately connected to the [CD] format's golden years' and one might argue that the most expansive and dramatic end of the post-rock spectrum – bands like Mogwai and Fly Pan Am – would not have made the records they did without the CD boom of the 1990s.[422] But it is equally clear that the technological shift impacted the culture of music production in multiple ways, helping to explain why artists like Sylvian and Bush evolved as they did.

There is a further element to this story, a twist in the digital tale: the CD boom ended very suddenly after Y2K and the public release of mp3 technology. In this century, therefore, experimental artists have been restricted neither by vinyl nor the compact disc. Indeed, this latest chapter in the digital revolution had an even greater impact on the popular music industry than previous format changes, ending the great Album/Singles Era.

I mentioned the Album/Singles Era earlier; the moniker is my own, as I have found others (such as the Album Era and the Age of Rock), while less clunky, to be too limiting. I see an era stretching from the mid-1960s, when two clear formats – the 7' 45rpm single and the 12' 33 1/3 album – emerged in a symbiotic relationship with each other, dominating music production and sales and flourishing through technological changes to the early 2000s. In fact, the lifespan of *Top Of The Pops* – although it aired in the UK, not in the US, and was dedicated to the singles chart – arguably matched the life of the Album/Singles Era: 1964 to 2006, with a popularity peak in the late 1970s and a steady decline around the turn of this century.

In the year surrounding the demise of that iconic TV show, the physical locations where people had bought singles and albums for decades likewise disappeared. Apple opened its iTunes Music Store in 2003 with a modest catalogue, but by 2008, it was the top music retailer in the US, selling over four billion songs worldwide. In that same five-year period alone, over 500 independent record stores closed in the UK, and the number in the US was in the thousands, while on both sides of the Atlantic, once-familiar high street anchors – like Tower Records, HMV and Virgin – were shuttered. As one of MTV's founders pointed out at the end of the 2000s, online retailers like iTunes were 'selling songs and not albums. I mean, you do the math.' In the 2010s, as streaming steadily eclipsed purchasing, playlist listening steadily eclipsed album listening – hitting 70% by the decade's end. 'Make no mistake, the album is fighting for its life', *Rolling Stone* had warned in 2018, and while the album has not – and surely never will – die, the Album/Singles Era is long gone.[423]

Just months before *Top Of The Pops* died, Mark Fisher asked, 'Is pop undead?' Not dead, he mused, 'because nothing ever really dies, not in cultural terms.' But undead, in that pop music seemed to have lost its 'capacity to *define* a time' and, thus, had 'reached its terminal phase.'[424] Pop has persisted, of course, as have singles and albums. But Fisher rightly saw that a new era had begun, one not easily defined by pop. In the larger cultural and commercial sense, the era is one of a new pop that is not anchored to a specific time. Chronologically untethered, it floats – metaphorically and literally – in the cloud. But in the more specific sense relevant to our journey here, this is the post-pop era.

16: A New Jerusalem/I Surrender

'**A New Jerusalem**' Mark Hollis (1998, 6:49)
'**I Surrender**' David Sylvian (1999, 9:29)

If 'Chameleon Day' and 'April 4th' were cuckoo eggs in *The Colour Of Spring*, unwittingly placed there by Hollis to anticipate the sound that would grow into *Spirit Of Eden*, then two tracks from *Laughing Stock* did the same for *Mountains Of The Moon*, the Talk Talk album that Hollis slowly developed during the 1990s. 'Taphead' and 'Runeii' stood out on *Laughing Stock* as being more minimal, intimate and lacking in rhythm than the rest of the album. The rest of the band were now gone – the last original member, Harris, had joined Webb in a new band project, and unofficial member Friese-Greene, an essential partner in the creation of all but the first Talk Talk albums, had also walked. Brown was approached after a few years; he agreed to come back but then almost immediately changed his mind. There was no question of yet another dive down the rabbit hole of recording, with Hollis losing himself in the studio for years, dragging others down with him.

Hollis had always needed a creative partner – from his brother Ed to Brenner to Ramocon to Friese-Greene. But he now fell back on occasional writing sessions with a series of collaborators, more protracted and less intense. Guitarist Dominic Miller worked with him for a while at his house in the Suffolk countryside – where he and Flick were raising their boys – and the product of the sessions would eventually turn into 'Westward Bound'. Engineer-producer Warne Livesey likewise spent time at the house, an experience he later called 'frustrating, but ultimately rewarding' (but in an unguarded moment, he called its pace of production 'torture'). In 1995, the Hollis family moved back into greater London, settling in Wimbledon, round the corner from Aspden. There, the gradual co-writing continued, now with a new collaborator, Laurence Pendrous, who ran the music program at the school where the Hollis boys went. Ramocon had briefly returned to write a song with Hollis, and Pendrous executed its piano lines with deft skill; the creak of the piano stool that can be heard on 'The Colour Of Spring' – what would be the new album's opening track – is also him.[425]

By the spring of 1996, Hollis had recorded enough for an album, and he was then able to persuade Brown to return – as all that was needed was the mixing. In fact, Hollis predictably wanted significant amounts of re-recording, but Brown found Hollis to be a new man, 'open and refreshing', chatting with the musicians, 'a whole different world. I mean, we had bright lights!' Nine months later, master CDs of Talk Talk's *Mountains Of The Moon* were delivered to Polydor. But while the label was figuring out how to market an album that was exquisite but completely out of sync with the late 1990s, Hollis decided that 'I honestly don't think this record can be considered a Talk Talk work.' His logic was sound, as he was the only member of Talk Talk who had worked on the album. But that also ignored the fact that the band had been steadily shrinking since its debut album and that Friese-Greene, whose absence he specifically cited as relevant (without mentioning Webb or Harris), had never been a band member. Polydor were understandably unhappy. As art director Cally Calloman remembered, it was a decision that would likely 'slash the sales by two-thirds', and after Hollis insisted the record be labelled as a solo album, 'I felt the light going out at Polydor every time I went in there ... you could feel the blinds being pulled down in offices.'[426]

For six months, the label stood their ground. Even after they conceded, it was another six months before the record was released – in February 1998, self-titled *Mark Hollis* – but only in the UK and select European countries. It received rave reviews – the best of Hollis's entire career – but sold fewer copies than any Talk Talk album. A step beyond *Laughing Stock*, it was an experiment in less, not more. It was a few minutes longer and had spent more years in gestation, but it drew upon a smaller scenius of session musicians and – most importantly – its sonic palette was minimalist and spare, 'so fragile it seemed translucent.' Reviews were littered with such terms – fragile, beautiful, restrained, minimal. A musician confessed in *The Irish Times* that the album changed his life, inspiring him not just to play 'with less notes, less noise' but to *live* that way. Hollis's music 'breathes as deep as a whale', revealing 'the richness of the space between' sounds. A review and interview in *Vox* worked hard to understand Hollis, calling him 'as anti-pop as it's possible to get.' The review ended on an apt note: stop trying to describe this music, it suggested, and 'just listen.'[427]

During the long making of the album, Hollis had become a passionate collector of vintage instruments, delving into their sounds and possibilities, learning how to play the clarinet and score woodwinds. His goal was 'to make music that can exist outside the timeframe', and to do that, he restricted himself to 'just acoustic instruments' that 'can't date', he insisted, 'by virtue of the fact that they've already existed for hundreds of years.' As a result, *Mark Hollis* was determinedly acoustic. Having been made at a snail's pace, its 'songs crawl at a snail's pace, and Hollis's vocal performance is a miracle of control.' There is none of the punkish angst that flared up on *Spirit Of Eden* and *Laughing Stock*. Instead, Hollis does the opposite, at times taking his voice so low that we have to lean in to hear him. Most of the time, he sounds like a quietly hesitant preacher. As Rob Young remarked, 'the confession box on *Mark Hollis* is thick with purification, repentance, atonement and redemption.' Not for the first time in the Hollis catalogue, the message seems religious, even specifically Christian. When Young put this directly to Hollis, he replied, 'I'm not a born-again Christian, but I would hope there's a humanitarian vision there, for sure.'[428]

That term – 'humanitarian' – Hollis used often when talking about the album. The term reflected the ambiguous attitude towards religion that had surfaced as early as *The Colour Of Spring* and which underpinned the lyrics on *Spirit Of Eden* – in which an angry cynicism regarding organised religion was offset by a yearning for faith, spirituality and a value system. Reynolds' view of *Spirit Of Eden* as 'a lament for paradise lost' works as a leitmotif running all through Hollis's work – a paradise not of blind faith but of human virtue.[429]

'Virtue' was thus a sibling term that also cropped up again in interviews at this time. Hollis had become a great fan of French and Italian cinema of the 1940s, such as *Les Enfants Du Paradis* and – in particular – the 1948 Italian neorealist film *Ladri Di Biciclette* (*The Bicycle Thief*, aka *Bicycle Thieves*). He identified two qualities about such movies that particularly appealed to him: 'What they deal with are character and virtue; they don't deal with narrative.'[430]

The first of these (virtue) translated into Hollis's lyrics, specifically his interest in morality. The second (dearth of narrative) was reflected in the musical structure of the new album. Pop music's structure has the reassuringly predictable quality of narrative, helping us to hear the cues of the beginning and the end, with the narrative progress of verse, chorus and bridge in the middle. But Hollis had already disassembled those elements and dispensed with pop's equivalent of narrative, and he continued in that vein here. Dig deep and you might make a case for a semblance of verse or chorus in some of the tracks. But they are not obvious and arguably aren't there. In other words, *Mark Hollis* is a post-pop manifestation of the narrative-free morality tale that is *Bicycle Thieves*.

Making 'music that can exist outside the timeframe' – timeless music made through taking his time – matched Hollis's lifestyle. For he now committed himself to a normal life with the same doggedness that he had shown in the studio through the 1980s to *Laughing Stock*. As a pop star, he no longer existed, lacking a band, never performing, giving no interviews. That changed only briefly in the months after the release of *Mark Hollis*. In retrospect, his embrace of a normal life really began around 1992, after the dust had settled from *Laughing Stock* and the lawsuit over *History Revisited*, and with the exception of the one solo album, it extended for almost three decades, as he and his wife raised their children into young men in their 20s. 'I have a wife and two sons', he said in 1998, during that brief emergence into public life, 'who I'm incredibly devoted to.' Approached to write, play or produce, he responded mostly indirectly – through Aspden or via his wife's email account – that he would 'only do something every seven years' (a renewable timeframe) or that 'he had retired from the music industry.'[431]

Not that Hollis became a recluse. In his post-post-pop life, he continued making music as a private affair, a hobby. He was a passionate follower of football, enjoying it with his sons. He travelled with his family. He channelled his attention to detail into motorcycles – collecting, tinkering, fine-tuning, devoting to his machines the same focus and tenacity that he had applied in the studio as a younger man. He rode, taking trips across Italy and the United States. Such trips were a pale reflection of his 1980s tours with Talk Talk, but with a crucial difference: anonymity replaced audience. It was as if he had recorded an album with a few mates in his garage and then gone out and played it live in picturesque, people-free settings. Even back home, the members of his informal motorcycle club treated him as a fellow enthusiast, not a pop star (although, apparently, one day, the penny dropped for one of them, as he connected this Mark to that Mark, gushing that Talk Talk songs were what he wanted played at his funeral – to Hollis's bemusement).[432]

Hollis thus committed to a normal life as thoroughly as he had committed to making Talk Talk's albums. When Gwenaël Brëes, a Belgian filmmaker, sought to make a documentary about him, the result – *In A Silent Way* (2020) – was essentially a film about Hollis's refusal to be filmed and forced into public. Hollis frequently commented, especially in interviews surrounding the release of *Mark Hollis*, on how much he appreciated silence – 'I like silence; I get on great with silence. I don't have a problem with it.' A review of the album in the London *Times* noted that Hollis was 'unusually interested in silence.'[433] The comment refers to his music, of course, but it also applies to his early and long retirement as an exercise in producing public silence.

As another reviewer noted, the album's 'hushed conclusion, 'A New Jerusalem' – its brittle acoustic guitars and softly struck piano embellished with otherworldly woodwind melodies – ends with 100 seconds of silence.'[434] And that is exactly how the final track on the final Hollis album should have ended.

We may want the musicians we follow to make music as if they are miserable, but we would like to think they are actually happy; there are surely limits to our embrace of *schadenfreude*. There is thus something deeply reassuring about Hollis's success at turning his back on something that both compelled and satisfied him but also frequently made him miserable. His normal life is a happy ending, making his death at only 64 particularly tragic. For the same reasons, Sylvian's journey into family life is reassuring and – after his open battles with depression, channelled so effectively into melancholic music in the 1980s – a pleasant surprise. In the years when Hollis was happily married and raising children in Suffolk and Wimbledon, Sylvian was doing the same in Minneapolis and in the Napa Valley.

Their stories diverged dramatically once the new century began, but we are not there yet. For now, we can enjoy the moment when – after a dozen years of collaborations, both successful and failed – Sylvian produced a new solo album, one reflecting his loving feelings for his wife and children. When the new album came out in the spring of 1999, he effused about his American life, first the 'wonderful break' in Minnesota, where 'I was away from the industry entirely … I saw it as something of a retreat.' Although he insisted that 'I enjoyed those long winters', after a few years, he and Chavez then moved to Sonoma, now a family of five (their two small daughters joined by Chavez's teenage son). There, he considered putting down roots; 'maybe this part of California could be our home.'[435]

Love and happiness: not exactly the flavours most associated with Sylvian. But, he asserted, 'This was a wonderfully rich and happy period of my life and I think the album reflects that.' And it does – on *Dead Bees On A Cake*, sunshine triumphs over rain, his signature 'slow-burning melancholy' is cut gently with contentment and everywhere there are displays of 'Sylvian's abiding love for his wife.'[436]

The key track on *Dead Bees On A Cake* is its opening and longest one, 'I Surrender'. The song is long-form spiritual art-pop, flirting with post-pop in the way that much of *Secrets Of The Beehive* did. The repeated phrase 'and I surrender' serves as a kind of chant, with the act of surrendering being a reference to Eastern religions, especially Buddhism. But he's also surely surrendering to his feelings for Chavez, to the joy of domestic bliss ('I've travelled all this way for your embrace, enraptured by the recognition of your face'). Who could have imagined that the angst-ridden creator of 'Ghosts' would now be releasing a nine-minute love song to his wife and mother of his children? Although the song has a compelling, even addictive quality to it, it made for almost as unlikely a top 40 single as 'Ghosts' had been some two decades earlier. Yet, 'I Surrender' squeaked into the UK charts at number 40 – a reflection of the buying power of Sylvian's devoted following. His highest climbing single since 1984, it would be his final appearance on the UK singles chart.

The dozen years between *Secrets Of The Beehive* and *Dead Bees On A Cake* disappear as soon as 'I Surrender' begins, *Bees* seeming to pick up right where *Beehive* left off. Even the album's title references its predecessor (albeit in a rather clunky way). But as *Dead Bees On A Cake* unfolds, it also reveals a subtle evolution in Sylvian's approach. The four albums of his imperial solo phase, 1984-87, in a recent review of their re-issue, were called 'staging-posts' on his 'ever more refined, rarefied musical journey, fuelled by his intuited truth: he had to absent himself from pop to find his strongest, purest voice.'[437] *Dead Bees* proved to be another staging post, with Sylvian not yet fully absent from pop; that is, the album contains the elements of those 1980s albums but is not yet the evolutionary step into coherent post-pop that would come later.

For every moment when Ryuichi Sakamoto did not emerge as Sylvian's partner in the writing and recording of an entire album, there seem to be several when he contributed to individual songs or parts of an album. *Dead Bees* is no exception. In the wake of another unsuccessful full-album attempt, he joined Sylvian to play a Fender Rhodes electric piano on 'I Surrender' and two other tracks, to assist in the use of guitar and other samples and to do what he did particularly well – arrange the strings and brass – contributing something to half the album's tracks.[438] Sylvian's brother Jansen was also back on drums, as was flugelhorn player Kenny Wheeler, both of them joining a scenius of musicians slightly different from the 1980s albums – most notably now including guitarists Bill Frisell (a jazz virtuoso) and Marc Ribot (known for his work with Tom Waits) and tabla drum maestro Talvin Singh. Still, as a reviewer for *The Independent* noted, Sakamoto was 'the most pervasive musician on *Dead Bees*, besides Sylvian' and the album benefited from having 'his signature' (as Sylvian himself put it).

At 14 tracks and 70 minutes, the album was paradoxically both too short and too long. That *Independent* reviewer suggested some track resequencing possibilities for the listener, one to create an eight-track 'eclectic, loose, creative album', the other to enjoy a seven-track 'smooth, easy-listening album.' It is not hard to see why some found the album compromised by a 'troubling inconsistency.' Arguably, the 2018 re-issue on vinyl solved the problem by adding two tracks; each of the resulting vinyl sides, running between 15 and 24 minutes each, cohere well.[439]

If the album was not Sylvian's best work, it was his best since *Secrets Of The Beehive*, and it holds up as his last enjoyably compelling work. 'Sometimes flawed, sometimes heart-rending', in Power's words, it amounts to a coherent claim that 'one does not fail by surrendering to the gift of love. Instead, one might prevail.'[440] One might prevail, but then one might not. With a little wishful thinking, *Dead Bees On A Cake* can be heard as nothing but an ode to marital bliss, but it doesn't take much digging to find the dark doubts of Sylvian's earlier work lurking beneath the surface, threatening to banish the sunshine and bring back that rain 'pouring in my heart'. In 1999, it was easy to miss the agonised apprehension of Sylvian begging, at the very end of the album, 'I don't ever want to be left alone with all my darkest dreaming'. Years later, in view of what then transpired, such lines are heartbreakingly prophetic.

17: A Fire In The Forest

'A Fire In The Forest' David Sylvian (2003, 4:14)

'Musicians have long fretted over the notion that getting married, having children or in any way embracing a more rooted lifestyle will stifle their ability to make interesting art', music critic Amanda Petrusich recently mused. 'It's a presumption that seems at least partially born of a very silly sort of misogyny, yet you would nonetheless be hard put to list many canonical rock records about a happy family. By contrast, there are plenty about a love gone wrong.'[441]

When he made *Blemish* and *Manafon*, Sylvian was 45 and 51, respectively. His separation, leading to divorce, occurred when he was 46. Anyone who has lived through their 40s knows that is when, to be blunt, shit happens. As Sylvian confessed in 2007, some months before turning 50, 'The journey has been long and there's been much suffering.'[442] We are willing to pay attention to that long journey not merely for a taste of *schadenfreude* but because it prompts ponderings upon our own journeys. And therein lies another potential solution to post-pop's mystery: might post-pop simply be, for some artists, where pop goes as it suffers through middle age?

A couple of years before he constructed *Blemish* – made in his home studio and released as the first album on his own label – Sylvian was already primed to channel his emotional life into his art. His aim in composing music was not to give listeners 'a cerebral experience' that 'might be interesting', but, instead, 'to break open your heart and open up a whole new dimension for you. That's the goal, to really pierce the heart and to open it up, to bypass the intellect, because music is one of the few mediums where that's possible. The mind is divisive, and the heart isn't. The heart just accepts what enters into it.'[443]

Doesn't everyone love a good divorce album? I certainly do. I think of divorce pop as its own sub-genre, and I look forward to discovering old divorce pop albums as much as I relish the release of new ones. Does that kind of *schadenfreude* come with any guilt? A little. Adele's *21* is better than her *25* because heartbroken Adele is more compelling than happy Adele, but I regret wishing her misery just so we can get another album like *21*. (And I feel bad for being disappointed that *30* was not more dripping in divorce angst). Such opinions were criticised in a cover story on Kacey Musgraves, written after her divorce and just before the 2021 release of her divorce-country-pop album (the wonderful *Star-Crossed*, a 'display' of 'really personal' thoughts on her dissolved 'union' with 'this other person', in Musgrave's words). It 'can feel charged in a way that only happens to female artists', asserted the writer. 'I've seen tweets in response to female artist breakups expressing delight about the music that will result, as though they're jukeboxes, not people.'[444]

It may be that there is such a bias in society at large, but my music-loving friends and I do not share it (or at least I like to think we don't). We enjoy Fleetwood Mac's *Rumours* for the breakup emotions expressed by both the male and female band members. The same is true of Richard and Linda Thompson's *Shoot Out The Lights*. The very best ABBA songs are those documenting the divorces of the group's two couples, sung by the (ex-) wives but written by the (ex-) husbands. For every great divorce album by a woman (from Carole King's *Tapestry* to Annie Lennox's *Bare* to Sharon Van Etten's *Are We There*), there are as many by men (to my taste, *Face Value*, *Tunnel Of Love* and *Ghost Stories* are the best albums in the Phil Collins, Bruce Springsteen and Coldplay catalogues). And I am particularly partial to Elton John's *Blue Moves*, much of which is a divorce album by John's lyricist, Bernie Taupin.[445] In all these cases, there is a broad emotional range expressed in both words and music, with hope and relief breaking through the grief and anger – sometimes through the juxtaposition of tracks, sometimes within a song (most obviously when gloomy lyrics are set to upbeat tunes). Musgraves herself articulated something of that yin-yang dynamic in 'Happy & Sad', a song – ironically – from her falling-in-love album, *Golden Hour*.

One might imagine it wishful thinking to expect a divorce record by David Sylvian to fit that mould. After all, the very notion of a Sylvian divorce pop album is almost tautological. His entire body of work is infused with the existential angst of separation. By the time he recorded *Blemish*, he had been making records for 25 years, many of them about divorce from someone or something; 'Ghosts' could be interpreted as an anticipation of divorce from Japan, even of self-divorce. Back in 1989, he recorded a track titled 'A Brief Conversation Ending In Divorce' as the B-side to the 'Pop Song' single. It has no words, spoken or sung, consisting only of three and a half minutes of dissonant piano notes and gentle waves of synthesised feedback. I am tempted to call it divorce-post-pop, except it bears no resemblance to pop of any kind, sounding simply like an excerpt from an avant-garde jazz or minimalist classical composition.[446] Or perhaps that's what minimalist divorce-post-pop is.

When 'A Brief Conversation Ending In Divorce' was originally released, Sylvian was processing the end of his relationship with Yuka Fujii – the very relationship that, according to Karn, had precipitated Japan's breakup. The track was reissued both in 2002 and 2003 when Sylvian's marriage to Ingrid Chavez was apparently on the rocks.[447] But despite its title, the track is not exactly breakup music; it is hard to imagine even Sylvian pulling off divorce-ambient if such a genre is even possible. In early 2003, Sylvian was inspired to do more than reissue an old track whose expression of breakup emotion was highly muted. Retreating to his home studio, he felt 'a certain sense of safety, of liberty, to deal with the emotions that were primarily negative and all to do with my relationship with my wife. I wanted to delve far deeper into them than I would in daily life.' The result was hardly easy listening (as one critic noted recently), but it was 'all the more compelling for the rawness at its heart.'[448]

A third of *Blemish* is taken up by the opening title track, a minimalist and disquietingly intimate glimpse into Sylvian's struggle with divorce's emotions. It is as if Sylvian is in the room with you, and now you're not so sure you're comfortable with that. 'Blemish' is a 14-minute experiment in hesitant poetry, loosely put to a gently pulsating music whose blemishes of noise are audible through its spareness – and yes, the brilliance of Sylvian's artifice is to prompt the listener to think of such sounds as blemishes. As David Topp put it in *The Wire*, 'Nothing is covered, removed, detached, enhanced. The voice is a naked man, seated in a room unfurnished except by tremulous, broken sound waves.'[449]

If that sounds unnerving, it is. Indeed, *unnerving* describes the whole album. Sylvian later described how while 'I was going through a breakup of a marriage' (note the distancing lack of possessive pronouns), 'and that was very painful', every day he'd walk into his home studio on the New Hampshire property where he and Chavez lived, 'shut the door, and I would allow myself into the darkest recesses of my heart and my mind to uncover what was there.' No wonder that *Blemish* is, 'without question, his most challenging' album, 'especially brutal.'[450]

But there is also beauty here, found in moments of melodic sweetness and occasionally reassuring phrases. The album's pearl comes at the end. 'A Fire In The Forest' is a song of exquisite yearning and deep melancholy all at the same time. 'There is always sunshine above the grey sky', begins Sylvian, but you immediately sense this to be a statement of aspiration, not discovery; sure enough, he adds, 'I will try to find it.' The song is both finely crafted and unstructured; it is slow, yet it passes quickly.

'A Fire In The Forest' is a marvel of quiet contradictions. Its flaws make it perfect; its flirtation with, but reluctance to embrace, the core elements of pop make it a fragile exemplar of post-pop. It is 4:14 long, but 'too short, too sad, giving up a meaning only reluctantly, the song demands to be played over and over.'[451] Sylvian's repetition of the final phrase, 'yes I will try', is an expression of hope that tugs so delicately on your heartstrings that you cannot leave it behind. Instinctively, your finger pushes rewind and the song plays again.

If the closing track of *Blemish* is exemplary post-pop, the album itself is as much an example of the genre as is *Laughing Stock*. The Talk Talk album has a rough edge to it, found when Hollis seems to momentarily lose control of his emotions, even if you know that those outbursts are, in fact, tightly controlled. That allows *Laughing Stock* to lean into the post-rock end of the genre, while *Blemish* leans into the post-pop end, its only hint of rough edges revealed in Sylvian's periodic flourishes of quiet sarcasm. The songs on *Blemish* are fragile, yet there are disquieting touches of which Hollis would have approved and understood – the virtuoso guitarists of past albums (the likes of Fripp and Frisell) are replaced by experimentalist guitarists Derek Bailey and Christian Fennesz, while spaces within the tracks contain 'disquieting buzzes, hums and clicks' that deny 'complacent listening.'[452]

Laughing Stock and *Blemish* are both milestones in the respective journeys that Hollis and Sylvian took out of pure pop and into minimalist, experimental pop-rock/pop. Both albums show how their creators took the elements of ambient music and embedded them within collections of pop songs, forging albums that were neither ambient nor pop – and yet somehow both.

There are some moments on *Blemish* when the music and Sylvian's voice, too, seem to fragment. One cannot be sure how much such moments are artful production touches, accidental glitches left in for the same effect or just emotive catches in Sylvian's delivery. But it doesn't matter. Those moments are metaphorical; their hint that the whole album might at any minute disintegrate reminds us of the disintegrating marriage that is the album's subject. We wonder, might Sylvian himself fall apart? But, once again, he reassures us that he 'will try to find' a way to let the happiness in. It is as if he has, at last, hit rock bottom, faced utter desolation and then miraculously found hope there. As a fully realised, coherent work of art – an essential post-pop album that is as 'deep, dark, cathartic' as Sylvian might have wished to take us, and certainly as far as we might like to go – *Blemish* could have been a final destination. If not a swansong equivalent to *Mark Hollis*, then at least the last stop on the journey through pop genres.[453]

Sylvian's post-*Blemish* output seemed at first to confirm that notion. Shortly before *Blemish*, two career wrap-up compilations were overseen by him, complete with him 'having a second crack at certain pieces' – the revisiting, re-recording or remixing impulse symptomatic of an artist whose perfectionism leaves him never quite satisfied.[454] He collaborated with his brother, co-writing two and appearing on three tracks on Jansen's first solo album, 2007's *Slope*. Meanwhile, they released an album together under the name Nine Horses, which featured German electronic music experimentalist Berndt (aka Burnt) Friedman as a third band member and Sakamoto on two tracks. Both 2005's *Snow Borne Sorrow* and *Slope* sound like variant evolutionary sequels to the Rain Tree Crow project – with echoes of some of Sylvian's other work and of Jansen's work with Barbieri – as if Sylvian was winding down the long journey of musical collaboration between the Batt brothers. As a *New York Times* reviewer deftly put it, *Blemish* was 'notoriously difficult' and *Snow Borne Sorrow* 'retains some of the bitterness of *Blemish*, but draws upon pop-song forms, making it more accessible.'[455] At the same time, Sylvian tinkered with *Blemish* itself, remixing some tracks and re-recording others with different musicians, releasing the result in 2005 (titled *The Good Son Vs. The Only Daughter: The Blemish Remixes*).

Then, finally, came the one-track 70-minute ambient soundtrack to an art installation in a museum on the Japanese island of Naoshima. Designed to be played in the museum in 2006 with island sounds heard in the background, Sylvian added some of those 'found sounds' to the 2007 release, *When Loud Weather Buffeted Naoshima*. The CD was given a limited release on Sylvian's own Samadhi Sound label (whose first release had been *Blemish*) and was then deleted. This now seemed like a perfect ending. Having taken pop to a dark and difficult post-pop destination, Sylvian had now moved completely beyond pop into 21st-century ambient electronic installation sound. That sound's location in – and sonic incorporation of – Japan seemed a resonant conclusion to a journey begun at that distant teenage moment of on-the-spot thinking up a band name.

But then came *Manafon*.

As early as 2004, Sylvian had begun to record improvisations with various collaborators, and for three years in studios in London, Vienna and Tokyo, he assembled the pieces that would be released in 2009. *Manafon* was – and remains to date – Sylvian's ending beyond the ending, the mining of a vein of emotional desperation that tilts his final post-pop album to post-pop's edge. Or, for some, over the edge.

Manafon is an apple that has fallen far from the pop tree. As a mature-period solo album from a former pop star, released on his own label, it makes no clear non-pop genre claim (it is not, for example, a soundtrack or ambient instrumental or jazz or spoken word). But with nine tracks, eight of them songs, spanning 50 minutes, it is also an album of pop songs that have been disarticulated so that they no longer resemble pop. The verses lack choruses, the melodies are stillborn and the songs start and end without builds or bridges. The album's musicality is highly attenuated, placing the lyrics at the forefront, delivered by Sylvian's mature voice with apparent – perhaps even mannered – discomfort; a sequel, in that sense, to *Blemish*. The inclusion of background studio noises, be they real or contrived, lends the album the feel of a poetry reading, accompanied by gentle fragments of music rather than a music-with-lyrics performance. One imagines the setting to be the dark corner of a bookshop or a basement bar, the stage minimal or non-existent and the experience either rivetingly visceral or just plain depressing – or some confusing combination of the two.

One cannot but sympathise with the disaffected fan who opined online that 'just because Sylvian no longer uses a verse, bridge and chorus doesn't mean that he isn't still a pop star. I know he'd like to be a South Bank poet, and he has disdain for the 'industry', so why is he still in it?' Arguably, Sylvian had been working hard for years *not* to be a pop star but instead to be an exemplary post-pop star equivalent of a minor Left Bank poet (yes, the fan moved Sylvian's ambition from Paris to London, which I take to be very witty, whether it was intentional or not). *Manafon* was named after the Welsh village where poet and doubting priest R. S. Thomas (1913-2000) had been rector, his 'lost sense of purpose' (in Sylvian's words) appealing to the troubled troubadour. But poet – whether major or minor, Welsh or English or French – was hardly a reassuring category for fans following former pop stars; in fact, just the opposite. The above-quoted fan continued by asking rhetorically why Sylvian could not 'revert back' to using skilled session musicians to forge beautiful albums. Instead, the artist had gone too far; 'Yep, he's lost me. The journey's over for me.' And he doubted he'd be the only fan 'telling the Emperor that I can't see his new clothes!'[456]

Sylvian was aware of how the album sounded to others. This statement – made less than a year after the album's release – is worth quoting at length:

> What happened with *Manafon* was that the work abandoned me. As I was writing and developing material, the spirit holding all these disparate elements together just left me. I sat stunned for a moment and then realised: 'It's over; this is as far as it goes...' In a sense, I'd been steadily working my way towards *Manafon* since I was a young man listening to Stockhausen and dabbling in deconstructing the pop song. Having said that, I don't think we only develop as artists practising in our chosen fields. For me, that meant an exploration of intuitive states via meditation and other related disciplines, which, the more I witnessed free-improv players at work, appeared to be crucially important to enable being there in the moment – a sustained alertness and receptivity.[457]

The image is a delicious one: Sylvian as young Dave Batt – and we might imagine here Mark Hollis, Dennis Leigh (before he was John Foxx), Paul Humphreys and many others, all barely out of boyhood – crouched over small record and cassette players in the 1970s, listening to Stockhausen and wondering how the pieces of pop songs might be disassembled and then put back together to create something new, but with the pieces still visible, tangible, audible, even if barely. Other boys did it with toasters. We are lucky that some did it with pop music.

18: A Sky Of Honey/Among Angels

'**A Sky Of Honey**' Kate Bush (2005, 42:00)
'**Among Angels**' Kate Bush (2011, 6:48)

In the first few years of this century, the music industry seemed to be facing the apocalypse that many had feared Y2K would bring. The digital revolution, having been embraced by the industry in the form of overpriced CDs, was now finally letting consumers into the promised land of unrestricted access. How artists would fare in this file-sharing paradise was as yet unclear. Few fans wanted to listen to those party poopers who rightly predicted that the industry would find a way to keep monetising the supply of music at the expense of artists. Likewise, discussions of how genres would fare in this brave new world were largely optimistic. Only in retrospect would it be apparent that the Album/Singles Era was expiring. Only later would we grasp the insight offered by music writers like Reynolds and Fisher, when they observed that culture was slowing down as daily life sped up, that in pop cultural terms the future was slowly being cancelled.[458] What they saw, in effect, was that the great 20th-century flow of genres, moving inexorably into the vast and complex estuary of rivers and lagoons and creeks, overlapping and interacting but mostly recognisably distinct, had finally reached the sea; the Mississippi of popular music had entered the Gulf.

Having anticipated such a world – if not in terms of technological change, but in terms of how genre needed to free itself from commercial restrictions – Mark Hollis chose to absent himself from it. David Sylvian both embraced it and, paradoxically, was oblivious to it: his descent, finally, from art pop into post-pop came precisely in those river-reaching-the-sea years, almost as if he had been waiting for genres to dissolve before making a record that lacked genre. And yet, that descent was also intensely personal, too personal to be contrived or clearly conceived, an agonising slide from music of inner peace to music of marital dissolution to music of inner turmoil. Meanwhile, Kate Bush – having not released an album since 1993 – seemed to be as absent as her friend and Green Belt neighbour, Hollis. Until, with almost no advance warning, *Aerial* arrived.

Like Sylvian's output of 1999-2007, Bush's 2005 double album was both very much of its moment and also so personal as to seem disconnected from the outside world, as if its timing was pure coincidence. *Aerial* is, in many ways, the true sequel to *Hounds Of Love*: just as the earlier album was conceived as two separate pieces, each with its own title, so was the new album, but as it is twice as long, each piece was given its own CD (and, later, vinyl record). 'A Sea Of Honey' is a seven-song cycle about family and domesticity and 'A Sky Of Honey' is a nine-part composition about nature, built upon the arc of a day from one afternoon through the night and up to the dawn. But the two themes bleed into each other, lending the whole album a musical and lyrical coherence. Deceptively simple at times, this is a complex concept album that has been hailed as a milestone of post-progressive rock.[459] To my mind, it is that, but it can also be understood as prog *pop*. As such, and because it seamlessly blends pop with extended moments in which the elements of pop are not fully put together, *Aerial* is Bush's post-pop masterpiece.

The three core elements of Bush's work, going back to her early albums, are fully manifested on *Aerial*, remaining intact despite her partial stepping into post-pop: femininity, nature and Englishness. Like Yes's prog rock classic, *Close To The Edge*, 'A Sky Of Honey' begins with sounds of nature and birdsong periodically seeps to the sonic surface throughout (the album cover is the soundwave of birdsong). The prog legacy is appropriate – *Aerial* has been called 'the most obviously progressive musical meditation on nature' since 1972's *Close To The Edge* – but so is the placing of Bush within a local pastoralist tradition of folk music. As Rob Young noted in his masterful study of modern British folk, 'Neither Nick Drake nor Kate Bush nor Talk Talk sang old folk songs, but their music resonates with Romantic yearning for an intense communion with nature and the desire to reclaim a stolen innocence.'[460]

Bush's love of gardening is notorious, used by the British press to deride her as a batty recluse – ironic, in view of her lifelong ability to imaginatively leap from the natural world around her to elements, life cycles and natural phenomena anywhere. It has been suggested that *Hounds Of Love* was in part inspired by the 1917 Mary Webb novel *Gone To Earth*, by its pastoral setting and its exploration of sex and nature. If so, that is another Bush connection to prog rock in the form of the 1977 album by the English pastoral prog band Barclay James Harvest, as well as to Sylvian's parallel post-pop journey, as his own double album *Gone To Earth* was being made when *Hounds Of Love* came out.[461] But *Aerial* builds upon *Hounds* and then goes further in its prog pop embrace of a panoramic vision ('we become panoramic') of the human-included natural world and its cycles of dark and light, birth and death, earth and sky.[462]

Indeed, the prog pop potential of 'The Ninth Wave' of *Hounds* was enhanced and more fully realised through its staging in the 2014 *Before The Dawn* concerts, where it was paired with the staging of 'A Sky Of Honey'. There were three acts to *Before The Dawn*, with 'The Ninth Wave' as Act II and 'A Sky Of Honey' as Act III. Pop star Bush began *Before The Dawn* – Act I's seven songs culminated in singles 'Running Up That Hill' and 'King Of The Mountain' – but the show completely ignored her pre-*Hounds* albums, devoting most of its time to post-pop Bush and her paired conceptual long-form pieces. Of the 27 songs, 22 are from *Hounds* and *Aerial*. Bush had always said that 'The Ninth Wave' was *seen* by her as if it were a film, and here it grew in visual-sonic form from 26 to 42 minutes, while the original 42 minutes of 'A Sky Of Honey' became a whopping 73 minutes (that included 'Among Angels' and 'Cloudbusting' at the end, but most of the extra minutes comprised the expanding of the original 'Honey' tracks and the addition of a new one). Thus, the combined conceptual journey into a dark ocean, out of it, and through a summer's afternoon and night, emerging into dawn, was driven by the embedding of pop song elements into an expansive post-pop canvas of sights and sounds. To dub *Before The Dawn* a post-pop concert would be going too far, ignoring how the pop hits and the added moments of dialogue and humour kept its feet fairly firmly in musical theatre territory. Yet, it was 'by no means a straightforward gig,' as Bush biographer Tom Doyle enthused, 'it was a soaring and uncompromising flight of imagination, an outpouring of surprises as rich and strange as the arkful of creatures that spilt from beneath Bush's dress on the cover of *Never For Ever*'. By expanding 'A Sky Of Honey', giving it a similarly expanded 'Ninth Wave' prequel, and adding theatrical elements, *Before The Dawn* represented a crucial further step on Bush's journey to post-pop. And the inclusion of that *50 Words For Snow* track at the end ('Among Angels'), along with 'Cloudbusting', completed the reference to her career's engagement with natural elements – water, sky and sun, and back to water as snow.[463]

Aerial has been called 'the biggest stylistic jump in Bush's career'; using this book's terminology, I'd call it her biggest step on the post-pop journey. As one critic put it, '*Aerial* is both typical of Kate Bush's work and completely different'. That's because it represents an evolution of the thematic, lyrical and musical elements of her career, but without the surprising jolts of experimentation or angst found in her 1980s albums; there's nothing jolting in *Aerial*, which, 'stately as a galleon', rides 'a largely calm musical ocean'.[464] If the above-mentioned core features of her work (femininity, nature and Englishness) remain so prominent, how is their continuity reconciled with her stylistic step forward, or is the difference primarily a musical or sonic one?

The musical origins of 'A Sky Of Honey' lie not in pop song composition but in free jazz improvisation – specifically, as drummer Peter Erskine recalled, in a series of 'very long pleasant days' in which he joined John Giblin on acoustic bass and Bush played piano with 'a jazz sensibility', doing 'delicate, interactive trio work' that fed into 'the conceptual song-suite' that became the second half of *Aerial*. Thus began, too, the next iteration of the Bush-centred scenius. Just as she had deliberately composed pop songs (but denying she intended to write singles) for side one of *Hounds Of Love* – in order to feel more free to experiment with 'The Ninth Wave' on the other side – so did she declare that disc one of *Aerial* was 'just Kate songs', so as 'to lessen the blow' of disc two. Hardly a 'blow', 'A Sky Of Honey' is, nonetheless, a 42-minute composition that demands to be consumed in one sitting – as the 2010 CD reissue made necessary, with its nine elements folded into one digital track (then titled 'An Endless Sky Of Honey'). Certainly, by accessing a different issue of the album, one can extract a song like the lilting groove of 'Somewhere In Between' for inclusion on a playlist. But that denies its full musical impact, its role in the unfolding journey from a meandering summer's-day start (echoes of that delicate, interactive jazz trio) towards a building of pace and the 'full-tilt melodic power' of the suite's final third – 'Nocturn' and 'Aerial'. Not just each song or track, but each musical element within each track needs the others to do its job. 'Somewhere In Between' is the bridge between that concluding pair and the suite's central pivot, 'Sunset'.[465]

'Sunset' never ceases to dazzle with its ability to express in music the gentle setting of the sun (turning the sky honey-coloured), tempered by an assurance – conveyed with a lovely shift into flamenco guitar, then an infectious beat, then prominent backing vocals by Procol Harum's Gary Brooker (1945-2022) – that the sun will rise again. 'Sunset' seems less to anticipate bedtime than it does dancing until dawn. But neither night nor dawn comes yet. First, there is the final birdsong of the evening (the one-minute 'Aerial Tal'), then the trio of tunes contained within 'Somewhere In Between' (with Brooker's voice again merging deftly with Bush's) – and, at its end, Bush's son Bertie murmuring 'goodnight sun, goodnight mum'. And then comes the gripping tension-builder of 'Nocturn' and 'Aerial', taking us through the night. The melodic pop potential of that inseparable 16-minute pair is nudged towards post-pop by a structure that defies pop's circular verse-chorus convention – 'dynamically, the songs are a masterclass' – as the song-pair weaves in birdsong and laughter, a turn by Brooker on Hammond organ, a guitar solo by Bush's husband McIntosh, Erskine and Giblin's dramatically developing rhythm section and backing vocals from 10cc's Lol Creme, all towards a crescendo whose euphoria celebrates not just the dawn but life itself.[466]

If the musical elements of *Aerial* are both familiar and novel, both recognisable as reflections of Bush's scenius and also surprising as a distinct manifestation and use of that scenius, so, too, are the album's lyrical influences. The above-mentioned Mary Webb (1881-1927) was an English writer, her novels all set in the English countryside, and she was roughly a contemporary of those English composers, loosely labelled as pastoralists, whom Bush regularly references – from Frederick Delius on her 'Delius (Song Of Summer)' of 1980 through to the appearances of Edward Elgar (1857-1934) and Ralph Vaughan Williams (1872-1958) on *Aerial*. Bush's interest in nature, then, is cosmically expansive but also locally specific: she is inspired by – and, in turn, has made significant contributions to – a tradition of *English* pastoralism. 'It is tempting', note music writers Hegarty and Halliwell, 'to over-emphasise Bush's Englishness', although I would argue that her career-long global awareness – from the Australian setting of 'The Dreaming' to the Bulgarian elements of *The Sensual World* – are all seen through an English prism, with English literary and classical musical references serving as the constant foundation to her world view. Young argues that Bush – along with Sylvian, Talk Talk and Julian Cope – sought to escape the confining expectations of 'commercial and popular success' by making 'hybrid, idiosyncratic sound environments' – more or less what I have been calling post-pop. But for Young, there is an additional key factor: as pop had become 'increasingly Americanised or homogenised for global consumption', those artists sought to 'maintain a distinctively British voice.'[467]

British, yes, but more specifically English, and more specifically still, the voice of London's environs – the Green Belt, with its urban/rural ambiguity and tension, birthing Sylvian and the rest of Japan, Hollis and the rest of Talk Talk, and Bush. And with respect to Bush, her perspective is profoundly and unavoidably that of an English *woman*. From the very start of her career, she struggled to, and before long succeeded in, embracing her femininity while avoiding being trapped in the subordinate role of singer-sex object to which the industry tended to assign women. The more she assumed control over her creative life, the freer she became to be herself – her female and feminist self. By laying 'direct claim to the spiritual and artistic powers traditionally denied to women', she refused 'to accept that spirit, creativity and womanhood must be opposed terms.'[468] *Aerial* is the apex of that journey, being, 'arguably, the most female album in the world, ever' (as one British reviewer, Kitty Empire, declared when it came out).[469]

One might go further and suggest that Bush is the most female artist ever. By that, I don't mean that she is uniquely talented for a woman or that she is a creative genius who happens to be a woman; I mean that she is a creative genius whose gender has been elemental to the unique world that she created and to which she has kept true. To add a tag like 'feminist' or 'female' to genre labels relevant to Bush's work – whatever the stop along her winding journey from pop to art pop, prog pop and post-pop – does not, therefore, qualify or limit the label. Rather, it recognises the complete nature of that genius and the significance of her creative output. As Empire noted, the problem with female genius for some men 'is that, very frequently, it is not like male genius.' So, inevitably, male critics made lazy, sexist jabs at Bush for singing a song about washing clothes ('Mrs. Bartolozzi'). But, as Caitlin Moran noted in a 2022 BBC interview with Bush, men have, for decades, written songs, including celebrated and classic ones, about things far more mundane.[470] Furthermore, those critics failed to grasp the ways in which the track is – in classic Bush style – both personal and proverbial, linking the little moments of daily life to larger existential themes. It manages to be a piano ballad about a washing machine that is (as one biographer put it) 'both erotic and disturbing.'[471] When Bush seems simple or silly, she's deceptively so, both musically and lyrically; to miss that is simply to be deceived.

Whether erotic or humorous, dark or disturbing, the properties of Bush's songs often have a spectral quality, and this is certainly true of *Aerial*. Creators of post-pop are all haunted by ghosts and all use the creative process to exorcise those ghosts. As argued earlier, post-pop is, by definition, hauntological. *Aerial* is, likewise, an exercise in exorcism. But for Bush, the ghosts are less emotional and psychological and more literally the memories of the departed.

Bush was devastated by the death of her mother, taken by cancer in 1992, having always been extremely close to her. The material on *Aerial* was composed during the dozen years before its release, when Bush was slowly processing that loss. Her father was still alive when the album came out, but he was 85, and no child of an 85-year-old is not conscious every day of that parent's mortality (indeed, Bush's father died three years later). Meanwhile, her 15-year romantic relationship with Del Palmer ended soon after her mother's passing; while Palmer remained her close friend, bassist and sound engineer (he played bass on and engineered *Aerial*, for example), Bush soon formed a new partnership (the above-mentioned Danny McIntosh, who plays the guitars on *Aerial*), with whom she had a son in 1998 (he, too, appears on the album).[472]

Even before her pregnancy, Bush revealed (in rare interviews) that she was conscious of the visceral connection between becoming a mother and losing a mother.[473] *Aerial* is heavily imbued with that awareness, whether she is singing about her mother ('A Coral Room') or her son ('Bertie') or in numerous, less obvious moments throughout the album. In other words, this is far from an angst-ridden exorcism whose goal is to be rid of ghosts. On the contrary, the album celebrates the conviction that Bush's mother's ghost lives on in her and through her own motherhood. It may not go too far to imagine that Bush also anticipates a similarly joyful haunting by her father, and perhaps, too, the ghost of her relationship with Palmer, made manifest in his crucial contributions to the album. Call it art pop, prog pop or a pop/post-pop hybrid, the album's hauntology helps make it beautiful and stirring, soothing and surprising, poignant and provocative, endlessly rewarding, an extraordinary achievement.

Six years after *Aerial*, Bush released another concept album. *50 Words For Snow* comprised a single CD, but it was 80% as long as its predecessor. Its seven long-form tracks explore snow as both a mundane, quotidian occurrence (in some English winters, anyway) and as a vehicle for fantastic fables and existential explorations.[474] It is late-period, prog pop Bush, a mixture of art pop and post-pop, with the title track, in particular, representing a characteristically eccentric manifestation of that mix.

Snow compliments *Aerial* in the way that winter compliments summer, and it is more quietly contemplative and less exuberant than *Aerial*, befitting the seasonal contrast. Although there are no conceptual suites like 'The Ninth Wave' and 'A Sky Of Honey', the whole album is tied closely to its core concept of snow, and without any verse-chorus pop songs at all, this is arguably a further step into post-pop. As with *Aerial*, Bush used a scenius of session players on *Snow*, but again not as a band laying down whole tracks; each of them contributed to 'sections' or puzzle pieces (as drummer Steve Gadd put it), unaware of the whole puzzle that only Bush could see. She alone was 'looking at the whole thing', exploring a vision of how the sections and songs were 'all connected', said Gadd, 'a more symphonic thing.' She only gave the musicians a sense of 'what she was trying to create dynamically and emotionally', leaving them to play 'just colours and sounds' – to roam pop music's frontiers 'until you can arrive at someplace where you can get your feet on the ground. Like the journeys on songs like 'Snowflake'.'[475] Bush has spent decades exploring pop's outer edges, tinkering imaginatively with its boundaries without leaping completely over them; as sad as the prospect is, if *50 Words For Snow* marks the end of her journey, this album serves as a fitting culmination of that exploration.

I was unsure what to make of *50 Words For Snow* when it came out. I think I expected to be able to make the same emotional connection to the album that *Aerial* brought. But Bush had made that album as she turned 40 and moved through her early 40s, and as I was 41 when it came out, its vision of family resonated with me. In contrast, the dilemma of having sex with a melting snowman (the 13-minute 'Misty'), weirdly intriguing as it is, did not offer a metaphor to which I could easily relate (and, as Bush repeatedly clarified in interviews at the time, before the snowman melts away, 'obviously there is a sexual encounter going on').[476] In fact, 'Misty' is one of four stunningly beautiful compositions on *Snow*. As much as I appreciate and am amused by the guest turns from Andy Fairweather Low (backing vocals on 'Wild Man'), Elton John (co-lead vocals on 'Snowed In At Wheeler Street') and Stephen Fry (intoning the mostly made-up words for snow on the title track), I only really grew to love this album after I created a four-song 41-minute edit of it – a poignant tear-inducing post-pop ballad album that I wish was on vinyl, with 'Snowflake' and 'Lake Tahoe' on one side, and 'Misty' and 'Among Angels' on the other. (I'm not suggesting that makes the album better; the better the album, the more ways there are to approach and enjoy it.)

My initial uncertainty also stemmed, I think, from being spoilt by the fact that Bush, Sylvian and Hollis made albums that channelled the angst of middle age's onset, timed just right for my own ageing – and I wanted more of it. Maybe that's okay; after all, as one scholar of *Hounds Of Love* concluded, 'music is a slippery beast' that 'seduces us into thinking that the sounds themselves are what is being scrutinised, whereas, to an extent, it is ourselves that we study.' Nonetheless, by putting my self-regard aside and opening my mind to the fundamental weirdness of the album's core concept, I was able to appreciate the humour and poignancy of *50 Words For Snow*. I was also able to see how very Bush it was, an album only she could make, one that represented her musical and lyrical evolution from her imaginative teenage years through *The Dreaming* and *Hounds Of Love* to *Aerial* and then to this – 'an album filled with some of the most haunting – and haunted – characters she'd ever created.' In 'Lake Tahoe', for example, the frozen ghost of a Victorian woman who drowned in that lake evokes the characters that populated Bush's early albums, and as a 'gothic set piece of a tale', it even calls 'Wuthering Heights' to mind – let alone 'The Ninth Wave', whose floating girl is seemingly spared the fate of the ghost that rises from the waters of Tahoe, only to sink back again into its freezing depths. Under ice, indeed. Musically, of course, 'Lake Tahoe' is far from 'Under Ice', closer to the moody poignancy of Japan's 'Ghosts'.[477]

Reflecting post-pop's hauntological nature, the album is often ghostly in its skeletal spareness, reminiscent of the minimalism that Hollis brought to his final album. Even the most pop moment of *Snow*, the John duet that is 'Snowed In At Wheeler Street', is too dark and brooding to be much of a celebration of her musical meeting with the idol whose picture was on her bedroom wall 40 years earlier. The theme of lovers crossing paths in different lives and incarnations is rendered as agonising, with the closest the song comes to a chorus being the repeated refrain, 'I don't want to lose you again' (which John laudably delivers with restrained passion befitting a Bush album, rather than a John duets album).

That tone of dark nostalgia is evident throughout *50 Words For Snow*, manifest in multiple ways – from the vocal appearance of Bush's son Bertie (Albert McIntosh) at the very start (reminiscent of *Aerial*) to that Victorian ghost story of 'Tahoe' (echoing those 1978-85 Bush antecedents). There are places where Bush seems to be on the verge of developing a pop song of the kind she had composed in previous decades, but she never does. Instead, it turns out, we are being led through a series of post-pop and art pop stories towards the exquisite closing track – what is, to date, Bush's final post-pop masterpiece, 'Among Angels'.

An unadorned structure of piano, strings and voice, 'Among Angels' forsakes pop's conventional features. It feels brief yet runs close to seven minutes. It seems spare yet conveys so much. It is spiritual yet secular, light yet deep. It is 'a beautiful expression of transcendence.' And it is an antidote to Japan's 'Ghosts', in which self-doubt is replaced by reassurance: Bush sees that whomever she is addressing drifts 'in and out of doubt', but she comforts them with her vision of 'angels standing around you'. The youthful angst and uncertainty of 'Ghosts' here meet a mature, gentle assertion that there are angels to 'carry you over the walls'. Bush offers us an alternative to silence – the post-pop terminus offered by Sylvian and Hollis. In her own words: 'In a lot of ways, this record has moved away from a pop song format; it's not an album of pop songs, it's a more grown-up world of music.'[478]

Is post-pop, then, just a 'more grown-up' kind of pop? If so, and if 'Among Angels' is the sound of that destination, reached at last by Bush and other remaining purveyors of post-pop, then long may it last.

19: Playground Martyrs

'**Playground Martyrs**' Steve Jansen (2007, 3:02/3:05)

In this century's post-genre world, then, the story must break up; we are now all at sea.

In a way, that means the journey into post-pop is over. Yet, it also means that the journeys have multiplied and that numerous other voyagers have and can be seen as part of the story. My focus on Sylvian, Hollis and Bush, in that order of attention, is partly an argumentative choice – I have been making a case for their primacy in the narrative. But it is also a literary choice; you might have picked others or given more attention to those who have made appearances as supporting acts in the chapters above. What, for example, have been the contributions in the past three decades of other former members of Talk Talk and Japan?

Paul Webb and Lee Harris had been friends since childhood and they were still teenagers when Ed Hollis found them and delivered them to his brother. They have thus been an inseparable rhythm section for their entire lives, driven only temporarily apart in the years surrounding the making of *Laughing Stock*, reuniting musically soon after that to form their own band. It is ironic – considering Hollis's reputation for a commitment to uncompromising anti-commercialism – that Hollis had given his band the very marketable name of Talk Talk, while Webb and Harris chose the impossible name of .O.rang (sometimes written 'O'rang, which doesn't help much).

Furthermore, they then proceeded to make two albums – *Herd Of Instinct* (1994) and *Fields And Waves* (1996) – that picked up Talk Talk's fledgling post-rock legacy and ran with it. They recruited musicians and others from the Talk Talk family, such as keyboardist Phil Ramocon (who had almost been a Talk Talk member in the early 1980s), as well as Mark Feltham and Mark Ditcham. Phill Brown came in to mix and co-produce with Harris. Aspden was the band's manager. There were other guests who had not been involved in Talk Talk, such as Portishead's Beth Gibbons, but – significantly – guitar was played by Graham Sutton, whose own band, Bark Psychosis, were in the process of making *Hex* (1994), the first album that Simon Reynolds described as 'post-rock'. The results were the opposite of Hollis's calm, slow journey towards silence; as Rob Young put it, .O.rang's albums were 'an exhilarating and frequently claustrophobic jumble of parts', prevented from flying off in different directions only by the 'lock-tight rhythm section' of Harris and Webb. In Chuter's words, '.O.rang probably had *more* to do with the imminent incarnation of post-rock than Talk Talk did.' [479]

One suspects that .O.rang's lean into formative post-rock territory was fuelled more by Lee Harris than by Paul Webb, not just because Harris stuck it out longer with Talk Talk – drumming to the bitter end – but because Webb's subsequent solo output has sat more firmly in psychedelic folk territory, tinged with moody art rock ('baleful folk' is the term one reviewer used). Reviews of his three albums, released under the name Rustin Man (the first as Beth Gibbons and Rustin Man), tended to mention Talk Talk and Gibbons' band Portishead. But while there are hints of Portishead, especially on the first, it requires imagination to hear echoes of Talk Talk, even on the tracks where Harris drums (the two remain close musical partners, 'a rhythm section for decades', as Webb recently said, 'everything I try is rooted down in Lee assisting me'). Still, there was inevitably some Hollis influence, and it is impossible not to sense his spectral presence in the occasional Rustin Man track.[480]

Likewise, the Held By Trees project, whose 2022 instrumental release, *Solace*, was created mostly by musicians who had played on later Talk Talk albums, is only reminiscent of Hollis's work because the connection is set in the listener's head by the album's presentation (from the listing of musicians to the cover art).[481] I played *Solace* dozens of times while writing this book – I love the album – but it only picks up on the Hollis legacy in certain ways, capturing the careful placing of notes but choosing never to disturb or unsettle. Even when it borrows the technique of a discordant one-note guitar solo (long ago made a hallmark of post-rock), the album remains too beautiful to be disquieting. By contrast, I listened to *Spirit Of Eden* and *Laughing Stock* countless times in order to write this book, but I could not play them *while* writing.

As we have seen, one crucial element of the relationship between pop and post-pop is that the former funds the latter. Post-pop artists emerge from pop for creative reasons but also because they can thereby afford to explore the non-commercial territories of post-pop's nexus of overlapping experimental genres. But that was only possible in the cases of Sylvian and Hollis because their bands' managers favoured them, helping them to exclude their bandmates from almost all of Japan and Talk Talk songwriting royalties. Conversely, that meant that those excluded band members struggled in their subsequent careers, obliged to take session work to pay their bills, finding their options for making their own experimental albums highly limited. The exception that proves the rule is Richard Barbieri's role in Porcupine Tree, whom he joined in 1994 (having played on the previous year's album), gradually acquiring some songwriting and even production credit as the band eventually became more commercially successful than Japan had been. Under the circumstances – no other Japan or Talk Talk member finding equivalent sales success – it is astonishing how many albums, especially how many experimental albums, ex-Japan and ex-Talk Talk musicians made from the 1980s into the 2020s.

Considering Japan's former members alone, in the four decades since that band dissolved, its three core members other than Sylvian released close to 70 albums; if we include all of Sylvian's output, the total is well over 80. Two aspects of all that creative product are worth noting. One is the high degree of collaboration between ex-Japan artists. They have constantly worked together, each one rarely producing an album on which another did not play or enjoy equal billing. It is almost as if Japan never broke up but instead evolved into multiple manifestations of itself. One is reminded of the prog rock phenomenon called the Canterbury scene (but centred mostly in London) in the late 1960s and early 1970s; membership in bands was highly fluid, groups rapidly formed and disbanded and reformed with slightly different players, band names frequently changed, solo albums were never really that and the result was an exceptionally dynamic creative scene – a scenius.[482] Ex-Japan has been an evolving scenius for almost 40 years.

Describing the musical genre of that scenius is not easy, as not one ex-Japan artist has stayed within the flow of a single genre, let alone all of them. Mick Karn recounted a story in his memoir of two brothers who played in a covers band in Cyprus, and who were hired to do some work on the house where Karn was living. Excited to discover Karn was a fellow musician, they asked what he played. 'Actually, the music's hard to describe', Karn told them, as he struggled to avoid 'admitting that it wasn't pop or rock or any other easily acceptable genre.' When he confessed that 'I write my own music', the drummer 'looked aghast.' His advice to the veteran bassist was, 'Don't play your own music, people won't like it. It'll be hard to find work anywhere that way.' Sighed Karn: 'How very, very true.'

'How very generous that Dave gave me half of one track' on *Tin Drum*, Karn sarcastically remarked in his memoir, 'and to bestow the same generosity upon his younger brother Steve, with two halves' of writing credit from the same album. As he moved into his third post-Japan decade, Karn was increasingly aware that, among his former bandmates, his career had faltered the most. Lacking income either from Japan's back catalogue (almost all of it going 'straight into David's pocket full of dirty change') or his subsequent solo and collaborative projects (they didn't sell enough), he moved to the island of his birth, Cyprus, where the living was cheaper. Despite raving over how the place was also 'much simpler and a lot safer', he admitted that he'd move back to London 'tomorrow ... if I could afford to.' In a cruel twist of irony, he was only able to relocate to London in 2010 after former collaborators, such as Midge Ure, Masami Tsuchiya and Porcupine Tree, played concerts to raise funds to pay for Karn's cancer treatment; he died later that year, aged 52.

Bitterness and self-pity bubble beneath the surface of Karn's 2009 memoir, but he labours affectingly to suppress them. Those efforts often fail with respect to Sylvian, but he generously wishes Barbieri well in his career with Porcupine Tree. 'It seems only fair, having had less session work than the rest of us to keep him afloat, that it should be he who is constantly working and building a career for himself', wrote Karn, wryly noting that Porcupine Tree's 'music is quite close to the progressive rock collection of albums Rich tried so hard to impress us with over games of Cludo [sic] in Catford.'[483]

Debating Porcupine Tree's genre would be as much fun as debating the genre of each Talk Talk album (in all muso seriousness). I would argue that their experimental musicality and inventive use of song structure make the band central to the revival of progressive rock in the 1990s, perhaps better articulated as post-progressive rock. But there are elements in their catalogue of post-rock and even post-pop. As at least one critic has observed, Barbieri's influence on the Porcupine Tree sound was significant, giving the subsequent albums his 'electronic signature' and, on certain tracks (like the title track to 1993's *Up The Downstair*), a 'dreamy pop ambience' that was very much of the post-prog genesis. Barbieri himself places particular emphasis on the Japan and Porcupine Tree albums that stand out as unlike any others and that defy genre labelling. For him, that means *Tin Drum* ('selected on the basis of its uniqueness'), *Rain Tree Crow* ('something completely different') and two Porcupine classics (2002's *In Absentia* and 2007's *Fear Of A Blank Planet* – 'the album that I'm really proud of').[484]

Barbieri, meanwhile, made albums with the other Batt brother, Steve Jansen. I mentioned earlier their 1980s projects – their underrated pop album as The Dolphin Brothers and their first ambient instrumental album – and it was the latter genre that they pursued in the next decade.

Stories Across Borders (1991) is today classified by Apple Music as 'pop', while its 1995 sequel, *Stone To Flesh* (1995), is deemed 'rock', but neither category makes much sense. The first is an instrumental album, more like a film soundtrack that flows between modern classical and jazz-rock fusion; the second is more jazz-rock fusion but with some pop elements. The streaming service's difficulties with labelling such albums are hardly surprising. As we've seen repeatedly, popular music genres are a moving target – increasingly so as we move through the 1990s and through the early decades of this century.

Barbieri has remained central to the ex-Japan scenius, his trajectory from Japan to Porcupine Tree to a solo artist of Eno-esque experimental electronic and ambient albums taking one arc of the post-pop story back full circle to its origins in the late 1960s and 1970s. His 2021 album, *Under A Spell*, is aptly named; it has a bewitching quality to it, full of subtle echoes of those two great bands in which Barbieri played. Although, to my ears, it sounds more like a Sakamoto album than anything else, a reminder that the Japanese connection had a lasting influence on all the ex-Japan members and not just Sylvian – who himself never made an instrumental album as Sakamoto-esque as *Under A Spell*. A darker sequel to his lighter, jazz-inflected *Planets + Persona* (2017), *Under A Spell* shows Barbieri on a solo roll, but one that is centred on 'working closely with other musicians' to generate 'a more expansive sound', one with 'more flavours.' That includes Jansen, with whom – as of the early 2020s – he is back to collaborating with again.[485]

Barbieri is not the only ex-Japan member with whom Jansen has stayed close in creative terms. Indeed, Karn could not help but envy the brotherly bond that permitted the relationship between the Batts, David and Steve, to weather the storms of Japan and the four subsequent decades. 'Steve is now back to working with his big brother as if they'd never left Hither Green,' Karn observed in the 2000s, 'and hopefully earning an equal share for co-writing. A testimony to his immense power for forgiveness and understanding.' (A shot is then fired: Jansen was 'the most musically knowledgeable' of anyone in Japan, said Karn, and for that, he was 'the one person Dave was ultimately out to get').[486]

For Jansen, the journey away from pop had begun all the way back with the final Japan album. *Tin Drum*, whose sound was forged by him as much as the others, was 'so odd, and to my ear awkward', he later insisted. Making an interesting comment on genre, he added that the album 'was essentially created by a pop band and attained the success of a pop album, yet [it] isn't remotely pop music – a real one-off.' Jeremy Lascelles, who worked at the time for the band's label, Virgin, put it similarly: the album was 'truly innovative' and the band 'were, particularly for the era, truly ground-breaking by not just sticking with the standard pop format.'[487] That legacy was largely ignored by Jansen in the 1980s, but, as we saw earlier, a seed was planted in 1985 in the form of an ambient, instrumental album made with Barbieri. The duo then brought in Karn, and as a threesome, they made four albums in the mid-to-late 1990s. Not pop albums, they do rather sound like albums that are three-quarters Japan/Rain Tree Crow, waiting for Sylvian to bring vocals and his pop sensibilities – although some might see that as overly privileging Sylvian's role in the entire scenius.

Most of Jansen's 21 albums made outside Japan/Rain Tree Crow have been collaborations with fellow members of that band, although not until 2007 did he release a solo album. As of 2022, he has made four such albums, all various shades of ambient electronic. That said, some tracks featured guest vocalists, including on the first – *Slope* – his brother. When Karn commented in his memoir that the Batt brothers were working together again, he was thinking of the Nine Horses project, which had yielded an album in 2005 and a remix follow-up two years later. That rapport also led to Sylvian contributing to Jansen's debut: he appears as co-writer, singer or guitarist on three of the tracks; he was responsible for the cover artwork; and it was released on his label, Samadhi Sound. Jansen moved his family to New Hampshire for a year to help his brother set up his new home studio and work on some of the material that would be released on the new label.[488] What ended up as *Slope* sounds a lot like a Sylvian album; Sylvian's voice is missing from ten of the 12 tracks, but then his voice is missing from numerous of his own tracks – even entire albums. *Slope* is as rich and compelling as any 20th-century project by his brother.

And yet, it is very different. The better comparison would be with his brother's 21st-century albums, as *Slope* captures something of the studied beauty and delicacy of Sylvian's pre-*Blemish* work, lacking the unsettling rawness of *Blemish* and *Manafon*. In other words, *Slope* isn't post-pop at all; it is low-key art pop at its best, 'a mixture of exquisite, groove-based soundscapes and introspective torch songs' (as praised in *The Guardian*).[489] What is most fascinating about *Slope* for our story here is how it reveals what Sylvian brings to these ingredients and how his absence or muted presence changes their final impact. Take away his control over the improvisational elements, over the final mix, over the vocals – take away his voice – and the music rights itself, no longer tilting with pleasure/pain angst towards post-pop's unsettling territory. That is not to say that tracks like 'Sleepyard' (sung by Tim Elsenburg of the English folk/art rock band Sweet Billy Pilgrim) or 'Cancelled Pieces' (sung by Norwegian singer-songwriter Anja Garbarek – with whom Hollis fleetingly collaborated in 2001) are any less for being Sylvian-less. Nor that 'Ballad Of A Deadman', co-written by Sylvian and Jansen and sung by Sylvian with Joan Wasser (who records as Joan As Police Woman), is any less for not being more Sylvian-like. Not less, just not the same.

The track that makes the point most starkly is 'Playground Martyrs', also co-written by the Batt brothers. It is sequenced at the centre of the album, with a reprise at the end, and is, in a way, the centrepiece. The lyrics seem to hint at the schoolboy experience as one of a cycle of abuse and shaming, with phrases such as, 'you suffer alone, in the skin and bone', 'it's for your own good' and 'trade you my unhappily everafters'. It disturbingly evokes an image of the Batt brothers and Mick before he was Karn suffering through childhood at the Catford Boys' School. When Sylvian sings it, as he does on the first version, it comes close to realising that grim potential. But this is Jansen's album, not Sylvian's, and the piece doesn't quite get to the darkest place it could – to the listener's relief. On the reprise version, sung beautifully by Swedish folk/pop singer Nina Kinert, the song goes from dark to poignant. With Jansen playing piano and arranging a gentle touch of strings on both versions, the song is a masterful three-minute pop gem.

What are we to make of all this ex-Japan creative activity? I see three possible analytical conclusions. The first is that this is all evidence of Sylvian's influence; that he is at the forefront of the creation of post-pop, with his former bandmates sometimes following him on that path, often not, along with an increasing number of other artists. The second way to see it is that Japan never really broke up: the group continued in all but name for 40 years (and counting) after its official split, with the four band members regularly collaborating on each other's solo projects, forming temporary bands and so on. Sylvian's hand may be prominent on most of this material, but the journey into post-pop – and the resultant decades-long exploration of the territory where pop, art-rock and ambient music meet – is *their* journey, not Sylvian's. A third perspective is to conclude that the story is less about Sylvian's genius, or even the scenius of ex-Japan, but about the larger scenius; all four ex-Japan members play central roles in that scenius, but by the 1990s – after Rain Tree Crow – the scene became too diverse and populated with too many creative minds to be attributable to any handful of them.

This book is not about all those other voyagers, but it is worth taking a moment to mention just four of them. One, Scott Walker (1943-2019), has been briefly discussed earlier as an artist often paired or categorised with Sylvian as a former pop star who journeyed into avant-garde pop music that seemed to defy genre. His trilogy of *Tilt*, *Drift* and *Bish Bosh*, spread out between 1995 and 2012, lie at the horror-movie end of the post-pop/rock spectrum, where the prettiness of pop has given way to the dark, disturbing beauty of the apocalypse.

Hollis was rather stymied by Walker's journey, not seeing it as parallel to his: 'What can I say? He's obviously someone with a mission, for which I wish him well.' But as noted by Jeanette Leech, who grouped Walker together with Hollis and Sylvian in her study of 'the making of post-rock', Sylvian admired Walker. The Englishman approached the American with a song and they met and discussed making an album together, but neither 'of us believed for one second that anything was going to happen, and it didn't' (said Sylvian). Walker saw Sylvian as 'more of an ethereal merchant than I am. I'm a man who struggles with spirituality, whereas he's given in to it.' Walker viewed his own albums as battles through nightmares, 'a real fight for me in every line.' It shows. Leech described *Tilt* as 'a record rotted in on itself, buried in the ground and left to decompose into a black mesh of sounds.' Its sequels fester just as much in their grizzly subject matter and deliberately jarring musical arrangements. There is a strong case for Walker being a post-rock pioneer, but for me, his 'mission' took him so far from his pop origins that – unlike Hollis and Sylvian, and especially unlike Bush – there is no hint of pop left; it has completely rotted away. But Walker should have the final word on that: 'I've been writing the same stuff since 1969,' he said after *Tilt*, 'just paring it down.'[490]

Another example of a voyager through genres, who seemed at various points across the decades to be on the brink of moving into post-pop, is John Foxx. Earlier, we left him quitting the music business in 1985, leaving a varied and significant legacy of synthpop and pop/rock albums. He chose the option that Hollis would later claim, and Sylvian and Bush would, in their own ways, choose, too: he disappeared from public view to live a normal life. Resuming his birth name of Dennis Leigh, he worked as a graphic artist (his original vocation), designing book covers, and for a while, taught at Leeds Metropolitan University. When he resurfaced as Foxx in the late 1990s, it was to create a stunning series of ambient electronic albums, often collaborative projects – including one with Jansen and another with the avant-garde/minimalist Californian composer Harold Budd (1936-2020). Asked to cite a favourite artist and album – of any genre – Foxx recently named Budd and the classic 1984 ambient album he made with Eno, *The Pearl*. The double album that Foxx made with Budd, 2003's *Translucence/Drift Music*, cannot match *The Pearl*, but it comes surprisingly close. Listening to the Foxx/Budd albums, 'you can feel your nervous system slowing to a reptile placidity', wrote Fisher. He meant it as a compliment.[491]

Ever the traveller, and always surprising, Foxx resumed his winding road in the 2010s (he has 'invented, reinvented and repurposed himself across many frontiers'). With a new band called John Foxx and the Maths, he has so far released half a dozen rock albums, a far cry from his ambient work, with some echoes of his early 1980s solo albums, as well as of the last album he made with Ultravox (1978's *Systems Of Romance*). The Maths' albums aren't post-rock, but there is something 'post' about Foxx's self-referencing, and it is hard to imagine them sounding as they do without post-rock having happened in the decades in between.[492]

A third example of a band often discussed in the post-rock context is Radiohead. There is a long literature on Radiohead's importance in the history of modern pop, to which I cannot possibly do justice here. So, suffice to quote Leech again, who persuasively argues that two of Radiohead's albums – *Kid A* and its sibling sequel, *Amnesiac* – not only featured 'every one of post-rock's primary attributes' but served as 'a culmination of sorts' to post-rock's 1990s development. They were released in 2000 and 2001, respectively, and almost immediately shifted the new century's rock soundscape. Those attributes, as described by Leech in a deft updating of Reynolds' original 1994 articulation of the genre, are worth quoting in full, as they reveal how post-rock is both distinct from post-pop while also paralleling and dovetailing with it:

> Guitars as texture, lack of group hierarchy, spaciousness, deconstruction, incorporating disparate influences, distorted or abstracted vocals, dizzying flexibility, anti-nostalgia, using the studio's outer limits, colourful timbre, incorporation of sampling and electronic technology, an obsessive focus on packaging and tactility.[493]

If Radiohead thereby re-set post-rock with the *Kid A/Amnesiac* pair – commemorated in the *Kid A Mnesia* reissue of 2021 – their journey over the subsequent two decades took them closer to Talk Talk and, arguably, a little closer as well to that vast body of ex-Japan work. Indeed, reviews and impressions of Radiohead albums today often echo comments made about the later Talk Talk records. 'It feels like an alien communique, music from another planet' is an example from Embrace's Danny McNamara (referring to 2017's *A Moon Shaped Pool* – for him, Radiohead's best). When he says that the music 'can initially seem quite prohibitive', but that highlights 'how much soul and otherworldliness there is in Thom Yorke's delivery', he's not far from how some Hollis and Sylvian vocals struck listeners.[494] In time, it may be that Radiohead's journey is seen as one into a kind of post-pop.

The fourth and final fellow voyager worth a mention here is the northern Englishman, Paddy McAloon. With his band Prefab Sprout and with Thomas Dolby behind the producer's desk, McAloon 'created some of the most beautiful and intelligent records of their era' – a run of pop gems that stretched from 1984's *Swoon* to the 1992 compilation *A Life Of Surprises*.[495] Over the decades since, there have been a handful of Prefab Sprout 'comeback' albums, sufficiently in the vein of their imperial phase to satisfy loyal fans. One album was the exception.

Finding himself temporarily blind for much of 1999 due to detached retinas, McAloon immersed himself in shortwave radio chat shows and phone-in programs, soon creating a library of recorded spoken-word samples. These he added to music composed on his computer and then recorded by a chamber orchestra. The result, *I Trawl The Megahertz*, was released in 2003 as a McAloon solo album – for the same truth-in-advertising reasons that Hollis released the final Talk Talk album as a solo project – but reissued in 2019 under the Prefab Sprout name. It was, in McAloon's own words, a 'personal vision, something unusual', a record that was 'so important to me.' It was also completely ignored. *I Trawl The Megahertz* is a beautiful and affecting album, but it is not pop in any sense, not even post-pop. It is 'hard to explain easily', an album that is almost entirely instrumental, yet it doesn't even occupy that liminal place where ambient and minimalist classical music meet. In a way, it is simply classical music in the style of composers working almost a century earlier, most notably Claude Debussy and Maurice Ravel – the very impressionists, that is, who had inspired Hollis, Sylvian and Bush. The one track on which McAloon sang only served as the exception that proved the genre.[496]

Where *I Trawl The Megahertz* differed most from its influences was the use of spoken-word samples, especially those that run all through the

22-minute title track, all fragments of autobiographical snippets spoken by an American woman named Yvonne Connors, who happened to be working in London as a stockbroker. The track seemed to anticipate Sylvian's *There's A Light That Enters Houses With No Other House In Sight* (2014), albeit with differing contrasts between music and speaker. In Sylvian's project, the music was the most unconventional element, bordering on background computer noises that are experimental electronic in genre; his speaker, Franz Wright, was a Pulitzer Prize-winning poet reading one of his latest poems.[497] By contrast, McAloon's project creates music that is original but not experimental, whereas his speaker is a kind of everywoman, not a professional wordsmith, and her words are sampled fragments of personal confessions and mundane thoughts. No wonder Apple Music's algorithm despairingly classified *I Trawl The Megahertz* as 'pop'. It is, in fact, so far beyond pop that it has passed beyond post-pop, too, existing in a world outside our genre categories, as myriad as they are. Perhaps it is enough to classify it simply as a wonderfully original and powerfully poignant work of art.

As I came close to finishing the writing of this book, I took the opportunity to see Jon Anderson perform in my local downtown theatre. As *Aerial* had inspired me to revisit the nature-themed concept albums of Yes, especially *Close To The Edge*, the *Close To The Edge 50th Anniversary Tour* proved irresistible. As it turned out, I was fortunate to catch the penultimate of just 13 concerts, all performed with students from the Paul Green School of Rock Music. I wasn't sure what to expect: a bunch of high school kids playing classic rock with Grandpa?

My apprehension could not have been more misplaced. It is difficult to describe how deeply thrilling and moving the experience was. The root of my reaction was less the music itself – yes, the setlist of Yes classics, including a complete rendition of *Close To The Edge*, preceded by and mixed with covers of songs by artists ranging from Heart and Led Zeppelin to Lenny Kravitz and Radiohead, was riveting. But really, what caused my thrilled response was the students. There were two dozen of them, seemingly in their late teens, half on the stage at any one time, all stunningly multi-talented. They were all brimming with sheer elation and unbridled joy, embracing the music with such energy and skill, performing it with the man who had created much of it and sharing it with an enraptured audience ranging in age from their peers to couples older than Anderson himself. They sang from their souls, they shredded solos with glee, they jumped and laughed and threw their arms around each other, and every time they caught Anderson's eye, he seemed to get younger and younger.

The music was all rock and prog rock, all from the last four decades of the 20th century. Nothing about it was post-pop. But the School of Rock students were all born in *this* century, and the entire performance had a postmodern, 2020s feel to it in a dizzyingly positive way. The collapse of cultural time, it turned out, was constructive, not destructive. The future was not cancelled after all. It was right here, filled with the ecstasy of access to all songs, all generations, all genres, all at once.

20: Approaching Silence/Do You Know Me Now?

'**Approaching Silence**' David Sylvian (1994/1999, 38:17)
'**Do You Know Me Now?**' David Sylvian (2013, 4:21)

If you were in the German city of Cologne in 2013 and happened into the Museum Ludwig, you might have heard David Sylvian. A new song of his, written for an installation in one of the galleries, played repeatedly. It revealed the 55-year-old Sylvian still battling those old ghosts of celebrity and identity: 'And if you think you knew me then/You don't know me now'. We didn't, of course, and we still don't. And that is surely the point. Our desire to know, and Sylvian's anxious ambivalence over us knowing, is a cornerstone of his enduring appeal. Appropriately, then, the song is musically straightforward, gentle art pop, its lack of a parent album helping to give it an anchor-less position in the Sylvian catalogue. He could reveal that it was left over from almost any of the solo albums between the late 1980s and 2000s, and we would believe him.

'Do You Know Me Now?' was also released as a standalone single on 10' white vinyl. Despite being easily accessible as a digital file and then being added to the 2022 reissue of the *Sleepwalkers* compilation CD, over the decade following its original release, used copies of the 10' were selling for between $100 and $220. Prices of the 10' only fell a little in 2023 upon the release of the ten-CD box set of all Sylvian material released on his own Samadhi Sound label (2003-2014), also titled *Do You Know Me Know?*. People, it is clear, still want to know Sylvian; he has a fierce following. But his attitude towards that – or at least his response to it, his apparent attitude – remains ambiguous. He has come close to his goal of being a minor Left Bank poet, largely invisible.

And yet his celebrity is a dormant beast, fierce when aroused. In 2022, Sylvian broke silence for the first time since *Manafon*. The BBC promotion for the interview trumpeted it as more than that, as 'his first public dialogue for around 15 years' (and by his own admission, his first radio contact since 2005). In fact, it was not really a dialogue or interview but something over which Sylvian could exercise total control: an 'audio diary' recorded by him at his home in the US, mostly a 12-minute monologue (interspersed with song excerpts) telling the ten-year story of his Samadhi Sound record label. He revealed little in the monologue beyond technical details of his home studio, describing in positive terms the experience of working with others during that decade, calling his time running Samadhi as highly 'productive' and 'enjoyable'; nothing, in short, that might help his fans to 'know me now'. Those fans, however, heard his voice – the smoky mid-Atlantic accent that he now has – and they no doubt savoured phrases that seemed to offer glimpses inside. As the BBC host noted, 'So many people are just freaking out at the idea that we actually have David on the show for the first time in 14 years, and social media is simply melting down.'[498]

In slight contrast, Kate Bush has taken a more measured approach, disappearing à la Sylvian (and Hollis) for long periods, then emerging with an album or giving an interview before going silent again. Her catalogue of recordings and her lifetime list of concerts given are both far smaller than Sylvian's. But when she does surface (as in her response to 2022's 'Running Up That Hill' revival or to 2023's Rock & Roll Hall of Fame induction), she is less guarded than he is. She has never avoided all radio and television contact for a decade and a half, as Sylvian did (although she chose not to attend the Hall of Fame ceremony, instead sending a thank-you message that downplayed her induction as a result of the 'RUTH' revival and focused more on congratulating new inductee Bernie Taupin). Fanbase differences aside, one cannot imagine there ever being dozens of books in print on Sylvian as there now are on Bush. Whether that is a career being driven forward or 'a career in reverse' (in Alan Wilder's phrase), it is, nonetheless, one being driven – by her.[499]

In stronger contrast, Hollis's commitment to a career in reverse constituted an unambiguous, deafening silence. No teaser tracks, no brief comebacks, no nostalgia gigs for charity. A career that went, like his life, from cradle to grave. As he moved from his late 40s into his early 60s, he continued to play and even write music – it is hard to imagine him not doing that at all – but overwhelmingly as a private affair. His collaborations were so slight as to make the point that he no longer collaborated in making music; the last was a brief appearance on Anja Garbarek's *Smiling & Waving*, released 18 years before his death. His solo work was even more ephemeral, making a similar point with what I can only imagine was a touch of Hollis humour: a 30-second instrumental titled 'ARB Section 1' that appeared on the 2012 soundtrack to the television series *Boss*.[500]

A half-minute of piano on a TV episode is, in a way, an extreme – and very Hollis – version of the art gallery installations that Sylvian has composed on and off for four decades (such as 'Approaching Silence', the working subtitle to this book). Such compositions reflect both the influence of ambient music on post-pop, as well as the desire by post-pop artists to efface themselves: the listener sees not the musical artists, but art created by someone else. The older notion of music as creating a space in which the listener can enter is rendered more literal in a gallery installation, either enhancing that experience or limiting its imaginative possibilities (depending on one's perspective). For the listener, who must travel somewhere and physically enter a specially designed space, the experience is a step closer to a live show – and yet the music is recorded, with the composer neither present nor visible. The experience is also temporary: you can leave and return, but eventually, the installation will be taken down. For the musical artist, that is an invisibility that approaches silence. Hollis simply went silent; Bush keeps us on tenterhooks with the prospect of, eventually, more music, but Sylvian, with his installation compositions, prepares us for the silence that must inevitably arrive.

Gallery installation compositions of the 20th century anticipated a further step that emerged in the 2010s: the use of immersive technologies, drawing musical artists from various points along the post-pop spectrum – from Brian Eno to Thom Yorke. As Eno said in 2018, talking about an art and music installation in Amsterdam titled *Bloom* (based on a smartphone app he had co-created a decade earlier): 'I want to be able to be inside the music, to walk around and examine it from different places.' Whereas the likes of Eno, Yorke, Sylvian and Hollis have constructed such spaces for us with 20th-century technology, Eno anticipates, with a mix of trepidation and optimism, 21-century technologies – from virtual reality goggles to inventions yet to come – further enabling listeners to step inside.[501]

That is the brave new world against which Jimmy Webb protested and from which Hollis shrank: one in which songs are all code, generated by computer programs, imitating the pop elements that Webb loves and the analogue instruments that Hollis collected.[502] Even Sylvian and Bush, with their less ambiguous embrace of technological possibilities, have retained an attachment to 'found sounds' made from analogue sources like shortwave radios and the birds in the garden outside. If algorithms can digitise the pop formula, can they do the same for post-pop, codifying the pleasure/pain paradox, mimicking the hauntological thread that runs through the artistic work of those on that post-pop journey? Or would even the most sophisticated algorithm fail to grasp the elusive shimmer of post-pop's relationship to pop, that crucial connection that prevents the slide into mere 'post' – and beyond it, into silence?

'In a profound way, music imitates life', philosophised Kraftwerk's Karl Bartos when he turned 70. 'It's born in silence, unfolds in space and time, then fades away and dies in silence. That's what people do, too.' That is a perspective that Mark Hollis would have appreciated, a poignant thought considering the permanence of his posthumous silence. As a musician, he embraced, even embodied, the minimalist notion that we should not simply await that fading away but actively pursue it. 'Before you play two notes, learn how to play one note', he once quipped, now an oft-quoted comment, 'and don't play one note unless you've got a reason to play it.'[503]

As just noted, Hollis did play the occasional note in the early years of this century, but a mere handful were recorded and none were performed. Publicly, he was silent. 'If you're going to break into it' – into silence, of course – 'just try and have a reason for doing it.' After all, silence is not mere absence of sound but also a tool. As Hollis also said, 'Silence is the most powerful instrument I have.' And on another occasion: 'I like sound. And I also like silence. And in some ways, I like silence more.'[504] Similarly, by the end of the 2010s, David Sylvian's journey through genres was over. He 'had reached the borders of music' and could only now strive for 'the goal of no sound.' Those are the words of Arena (the Sylvian-fan philosopher), for whom there is postmodern logic to Sylvian's trajectory, leading him inevitably to a kind of meaningful nihilism, 'dispensing music that would like to fade away' that 'can be found at the borders of silence.'[505]

At the borders, not inside. For, as John Biguenet notes (at the start of a whole book on the topic), 'our imagination misleads us if we conceive of silence as a destination at which we might arrive.' Silence is a term for what is inaudible to us, and it is, thus, 'a measure of human limitation.'[506] As something imperceptible and inaccessible, we have no choice but to merely believe in it – the way we might believe in, say, ghosts.

In the four decades since 'Ghosts', Sylvian searched restlessly for new collaborators, new inspirations and ways to blend new ideas with old and new places to settle. But while the ghosts of his life may not have grown wilder than the wind, they never seemed to dissipate completely, eventually luring him into isolation. 'I do enjoy solitude', he said recently. 'It is a very necessary component of my daily life that supports mental well-being.' Solitude, but not silence, for 'silence remains forever beyond our reach', a goal invaluable in 'a clamorous world', even more so for being unattainable.[507]

The irony of musicians, once pop stars no less, striving for such a goal was not lost on Hollis, who contemplated it askance with wry humour.

Nor is it lost either on Bush, who has, for decades, managed to move in and out of a kind of public silence, or on Sylvian, who seems to have suffered for it more. Like Hollis, Sylvian came to accept that the ultimate destination would be silence. But unlike Hollis, he cannot find that place and stay there, sensing that such a destination can only be imagined. In fact – and isn't this the ultimate definition of post-pop? – he never quite arrives, condemned to exist in a perpetual state of approaching silence.

Discography

Japan released five albums, with a sixth album released under the name **Rain Tree Crow**: *Adolescent Sex* (1978), *Obscure Alternatives* (1978), *Quiet Life* (1979), *Gentlemen Take Polaroids* (1980), *Tin Drum* (1981), *Rain Tree Crow* (1991). As with the Talk Talk half-dozen, these are best appreciated when played in sequence (with the 1979-81 trio as the band's crowning achievement). The peak chart position of these six albums, in order, was as follows: the first two did not chart in the UK (but reached 20 and 21 in Japan); the other four peaked at 72, 51, 12 and 24 in the UK; at 24, 51, 38 and 49 in Japan. (But *Quiet Life* reached number 53 upon reissue in 1982, and then number 13 upon reissue in the very different chart world of 2021). No Japan album charted in the US (a US-only compilation released on Epic in 1982 reached number 204).[508]

Of Japan's ancillary releases, there is likewise a single live album, *Oil On Canvas* (1983) (reached number five in the UK, number 11 in Japan), and a long list of compilations: nine of them released between 1981 and 2009, with only *Assemblage* (1981) and *Exorcising Ghosts* (1984) charting (at 26 and 45, respectively, in the UK); an additional US-only compilation (1982) (mentioned above) and seven compilations released only in the country of Japan bring the grand total to 17. None of these covers all five 1978-81 albums, partly due to copyright issues stemming from the band's move from Hansa to Virgin in 1980 and partly due to the disparaging attitude towards the 1978 albums by Sylvian and, to a lesser extent, his bandmates. Tracks from *Quiet Life* and its sessions tend to be the overlap point between compilations either focusing on the Hansa period (such as *Assemblage*) or the Virgin period (such as *Exorcising Ghosts* and 2006's *The Very Best Of Japan*). *Quiet Life* received a beautifully packaged vinyl plus three-CD re-release in 2021.[509]

David Sylvian has released 17 post-Japan albums, half of them under his name only, half of them as collaborations with ex-Japan bandmates and other artists. The solo nine are *Brilliant Trees* (1984), *Alchemy: An Index Of Possibilities* (1985), *Gone To Earth* (1986), *Secrets Of The Beehive* (1987), *Dead Bees On A Cake* (1999), *Blemish* (2003), *When Loud Weather Buffeted Naoshima* (2007), *Manafon* (2009), *There's A Light That Enters Houses With No Other House In Sight* (2014). The collaborative eight, released under the names in parentheses, are *Plight And Premonition*

(1988, with Holger Czukay), *Flux + Mutability* (1989, with Holger Czukay), *Ember Glance: The Permanence Of Memory* (1991, with Russell Mills), *The First Day* (1993, with Robert Fripp), *Snow Borne Sorrow* (2005, as Nine Horses), *Uncommon Deities* (2012, with Jan Bang, Erik Honoré, Arve Henriksen and Sidsel Endresen), *Wandermüde* (2013, with Stephan Mathieu, a remix of the instrumental elements of *Blemish*), *There Is No Love* (2017, with Rhodri Davies and Mark Wastell).

Sylvian's solo and collaborative release history is complex, with various overlaps, re-releases and limited-edition bonus discs. He also appears on numerous albums by other artists, most notably his former Japan bandmates. This is thus a simplification rather than an exhaustive list. He has released four excellent compilations offering overviews of his post-Japan work: *Everything And Nothing* (2000) and *A Victim Of Stars (1982-2012)* (2012) are both nicely representative two-CD compilations; *Camphor* (2002) is a single disc of instrumentals, and *Sleepwalkers* (2010 and 2022) collects collaborative tracks, many remixed by Sylvian, and many appearing originally on other artists' albums.[510] Sylvian's collaboration with Fripp also produced a live album, *Damage: Live* (1994). The solo release *Approaching Silence* (1999) comprises 1991's *Ember Glance* and the title track, a collaboration with Fripp originally accompanying the Tokyo art gallery installation 'Redemption' and released in 1994 on cassette. Nine Horses released a remix album with three new tracks, *Money For All* (2007). Finally, Sylvian released a reworked version of *Blemish* as *The Good Son Vs. The Only Daughter* (2005), and a similar reworking of his subsequent solo album, *Died In The Wool – Manafon Variations* (2011). All 2003-2014 releases (from *Blemish* through to *There's A Light*) were reissued in 2023 in the *Do You Know Me Now?* ten-CD box set.

The other core members of Japan have been too prolific to permit a comprehensive listing of all the albums they have released under their own names or to which they have contributed. But the following comes very close to including all albums to which they were given credit as an artist or full-band member (I've surely overlooked some, but I hope not many). Sylvian's brother **Steve Jansen** has released 22 albums outside Japan and Rain Tree Crow, 16 of which were partial or full collaborations with ex-Japan bandmates. They include four solo albums, all in this century and all very loosely in the genre of ambient electronic, featuring various vocalists (including, on the first, his brother): *Slope*

(2007), *Tender Extinction* (2016), *The Extinct Suite* (2017) and *Corridor* (2018) (almost all tracks on the latter two were also released as an all-instrumental double LP in 2020). With the exception of his work with Yukihiro Takahashi (a pair of albums in 1997-98), his collaboration with John Foxx and Steve D'Agostino (2009's ambient *A Secret Life*) and his work as a founding member of Exit North since 2018, Jansen's other 12 albums are collaborations with former members of Japan: between 1985 and 2015, he and Richard Barbieri released six albums together, five as Jansen/Barbieri, one as The Dolphin Brothers (1987's *Catch The Fall*); the duo also released four albums with Mick Karn, as Jansen/Barbieri/Karn, between 1993 and 2001 and one album in 1997 with Japanese electronic musician Nobukazu Takemura as Jansen/Barbieri/Takemura; and in 2005, the Batt brothers Jansen and Sylvian released *Snow Borne Sorrow*, an album made with German electronic composer Burnt Friedman under the name Nine Horses. Outside Japan and Rain Tree Crow, **Richard Barbieri** has made 31 albums, including the ten already mentioned with Jansen and Karn. He also made five albums between 1996 and 2014 with various (non-ex-Japan) collaborators (such as No-Man's Tim Bowness and Marillion's Steve Hogarth); released six solo albums between 2005 and 2021 (one of which, 2017-18's *Variants*, was a set of five albums); and – his best-known role – has also been a member of Porcupine Tree since 1993, playing on their ten studio albums from *Up The Downstair* to 2022's *Closure/ Continuation*. **Mick Karn** (1958-2011) made 15 albums outside Japan and Rain Tree Crow (not counting his session work). Those comprised eight solo albums, from *Titles* (1982) to *The Concrete Twin* (2009); one album made with Peter Murphy of Bauhaus, 1984's *The Waking Hour*, released under Dalis (or Dali's) Car; one album released under David Torn/Mick Karn/Terry Bozzio (1994's *Polytown*); one under Yoshihiro Hanno Meets Mick Karn (1998's *Liquid Glass*); and the four collaborations with Jansen and Barbieri mentioned above.

Talk Talk released five studio albums, with a sixth album released as a solo album under the name **Mark Hollis**: *Talk Talk* (1982), *It's My Life* (1984), *The Colour Of Spring* (1986), *Spirit Of Eden* (1988), *Laughing Stock* (1991), *Mark Hollis* (1998). The peak chart position of the five Talk Talk albums, in order, was 21, 35, eight, 19 and 26 in the UK; and in the US, it was 132, 42 and 58, with the last two not charting. The Hollis solo album did not chart anywhere. Their extraordinary creative arc is best understood if they are enjoyed in sequence.

Of Talk Talk's ancillary releases, the live offering is very sparse – a recording of their final performance in the UK was put out in Europe only in 1999, titled *London 1986*. Bootlegs are few, too; the most recent is 2023's *The German Broadcast Live 1984*. However (as discussed in Chapters 2, 8 and 12), there are an excessive number of compilations: eight released between 1990 and 2013 (starting with *Natural History: The Very Best Of Talk Talk*); there were also four remix compilation albums released between 1985 and 1999. The only compilation with Hollis's full endorsement – in fact, created by him – was 2012's *Natural Order*. Also unique in its inclusion of the Polydor/Verve material as well as the EMI years, the ten-track CD privileged the post-pop albums (1988-91) over their more pop predecessors (1982-86); it is the sole compilation to come close to the coherence of Talk Talk's albums. As of 2022, it had never been released outside Europe (and used copies were difficult to find).

The other two core members of Talk Talk, **Lee Harris** and **Paul Webb**, have been gently active. In Talk Talk's wake, they formed their own band in 1992 (Webb had left Talk Talk in 1988 after *Spirit Of Eden*; Harris left in 1991 after *Laughing Stock*). Called .O.rang (or 'O'rang), they released two albums, *Herd Of Instinct* (1994) and *Fields And Waves* (1996). In 2002, Webb adopted the stage name Rustin Man and released an album with Portishead's Beth Gibbons, *Out Of Season*, on which Harris played drums. Webb then retired from recording and performing for a while until resurfacing to release two psychedelic folk-rock solo albums as Rustin Man: *Drift Code* (2019) and *Clockdust* (2020). Harris has occasionally contributed to albums as a session drummer, one example being *Codename: Dustsucker* (2004) by east London post-rock band Bark Psychosis.[511]

Kate Bush has so far released nine studio albums of original material: *The Kick Inside* (1978), *Lionheart* (1978), *Never For Ever* (1980), *The Dreaming* (1982), *Hounds Of Love* (1985), *The Sensual World* (1989), *The Red Shoes* (1993), *Aerial* (2005) and *50 Words For Snow* (2011). The peak chart position of these nine was, in order, three, six, one, three, one, two, two, three, five in the UK (where her fan base is fiercely strong); in the US, the first three albums did not chart, and subsequent peaks were (starting with *The Dreaming*) 157, 12, 43, 28, 48, 83.[512]

Bush's ancillary releases are thin in all categories: one compilation of hits, *The Whole Story* (1986); one re-recording of selected tracks from her 1989 and 1993 albums, *Director's Cut* (2011); and two live albums – a 1994 CD re-release of recordings from her 1979 tour, originally released on home video in 1981, and the three-CD *Before The Dawn* (2016). A compilation of B-sides and other rarities, titled *The Other Sides*, was released in 2019 – but it had been included in the double box set *Remastered* (2018), which included all the studio albums listed above.

Bibliography

Abbreviations
CP   *Classic Pop* magazine
NME   *New Musical Express* newspaper
NYT   *The New York Times* newspaper
NYTM   *The New York Times Magazine*
RC   *Record Collector* magazine
RS   *Rolling Stone* magazine
TNY   *The New Yorker* magazine

Cited Books, Articles, Essays, Blogs And Interviews

Arena, L. V., *David Sylvian As A Philosopher: A Foray Into Postmodern Rock* (Milan: Mimesis International, 2016)

Attali, J., *Noise: The Political Economy Of Music* (Minneapolis: University of Minnesota Press, 2009)

Barnes, M., *A New Day Yesterday: UK Progressive Rock & The '70s* (London: Omnibus Press, 2020)

Barnes, M., and J. Kendall, 'I Trust My Feet When They Go Walking', in *RC* #538 (December 2022), 56-64

Barry, R., *Compact Disc*. Object Lessons series (New York & London: Bloomsbury, 2020)

Beaumont, M., 'Super Shy Guy', in *NME* (14 February 1998), accessed at *web.archive.org/web/20101222125924/http://users.cybercity.dk/~bcc11425/IntNME140298.html*.

Beaumont, M., 'Talk Talk's Mark Hollis: 2019 is full of the notes he isn't playing', in *NME* (26 February 2019), accessed at *nme.com/features/talk-talks-mark-hollis-1955-2019-nme-obituary-2454143*

Berlin, K. C., 'Abba singer says fame drove her to become a recluse' (21 May 2005), in *Independent.ie*, *independent.ie/world-news/ 25986069*

Biguenet, J., *Silence*. Object Lessons series (New York & London: Bloomsbury, 2015)

Blabey, A., *Thelma The Unicorn* (New York: Scholastic, 2018)

Bourdieu, P., *Distinction: A Social Critique Of The Judgment Of Taste*. Richard Nice, trans. (Cambridge: Harvard University Press, 1984)

Bradley, A., *The Poetry Of Pop* (New Haven: Yale University Press, 2017)

Bromley, T., 'Back In The Day', in *CP* (Nov/Dev 2012), 94-99

Brooker, W., *Why Bowie Matters* (London: William Collins, 2019)

Brown, P., *Are We Still Rolling? Studios, Drugs And Rock 'n' Roll: One Man's Journey Recording Classic Albums* (Portland, OR: Tape Op Books, 2010)

Browning, K., and K. Hill, 'The Price Of Online Fame', in *NYT* (31 July 2022), *Sunday Business*, 1, 6-7

Burke, D., 'Japan And David Sylvian', in *CP* (May 2019), 48-51

Cage, J., *Silence* (Middletown, CT: Wesleyan University Press, 1973)

Cárdenas, P., 'Orchestral Manoeuvres in the Dark Pioneered Millennium Pop Music', in *Miami New Times* (27 August 2019), *miaminewtimes.com/music/things-to-do-miami-orchestral-manoeuvres-in-the-dark-at-broward-center*

Cavanagh, J., *The Piper At The Gates Of Dawn*. 33 1/3 series #6 (New York & London: Bloomsbury, 2003)

Chow, L., *You're History: The Twelve Strangest Women In Music* (London: Repeater, 2021)

Chuter, J., *Storm Static Sleep: A Pathway Through Post-Rock* (London: Function Books, 2015)

Classic Rock Presents Prog, *Classic Rock* magazine issue 22 (London: Future Publishing, December 2011)

Coronil, F., 'Latin American Postcolonial Studies and Global Decolonization', in P. K. Nayar, ed., *Postcolonial Studies: An Anthology* (Chichester: Wiley, 2016), 175-92.

Coscarelli, J., 'Raw and Ready for the Mainstream', in *NYT* (29 November 2020), *Arts & Entertainment*, 13

Cowley, J., 'The journey from Talk Talk to listen listen', in *The Times* (13 February 1998), *Arts*, 37

Crawford, B., 'A Man for This Season', in *NYTM* (Fall 2006), 122-24

Crosby, A. W., *The Measure Of Reality: Quantification And Western Society, 1250-1600* (Cambridge: Cambridge University Press, 1997)

Crossley, N., 'The Colour of Spring', in *CP* (September/October 2020), 30-34

Dafoe, C., 'Inside the Sleeve Pop: Plight and Premonition', in *Globe & Mail* (2 June 1988)

Dayal, G., *Another Green World*. 33 1/3 series #67 (New York & London: Bloomsbury, 2009)

Dean, C., and D. Leibsohn, 'Hybridity and Its Discontents: Considering Visual Culture in Colonial Spanish America', in *Colonial Latin American Review* 12:1 (2003), 5-35

Delve, B., *On Track ... Electric Light Orchestra: Every Album, Every Song* (Tewkesbury, UK: Sonicbond, 2021)

Derrida, J., *Specters Of Marx: The State Of The Debt, The Work Of Mourning, & The New International* (New York: Routledge, 1994 [1993])

Doggett, P., *Electric Shock: From The Gramophone To The iPhone – 125 Years Of Pop Music* (London: The Bodley Head, 2015)

Doyle, T., *Running Up That Hill: 50 Visions Of Kate Bush* (London: Nine Eight Books, 2022)

Doyle, W., 'Conform to Deform', in *RC* #519 (June 2021), 72-77

Earls, J., 'Being Human', in *CP* (July/August 2022), 22-29

Earls, J., 'Light in the Darkness', in *CP*, *Classic Pop Presents Synthpop*, Volume II (Special Edition 2020), 86-91

Earls, J., 'Stockhausen or ABBA? Can't We Be Both?' in *CP* (November 2019), 24-31

Edwards, T., *One Step Beyond...* 33 1/3 series #66 (New York & London: Bloomsbury, 2009)

Empire, K., 'Admit it, guys, she's a genius,' in *The Guardian* (29 October 2005), at *theguardian.com/music/2005/oct/30/popandrock.shopping1*

Fezco, M. A., 'Talk Talk Single is Hot Hot', in *Billboard* (21 April 1984), 49

Fisher, M., *Ghosts Of My Life: Writings On Depression, Hauntology, And Lost Futures* (Winchester, UK: Zero Books, 2014)

Fitzmaurice, L., 'Hating Fame', in *NYTM* (13 March 2022), 38-39

Flanders, J., *A Place For Everything: The Curious History Of Alphabetical Order* (New York: Basic Books, 2020)

Frere-Jones, S., 'Ambient Genius: The working life of Brian Eno', in *TNY* (7 July 2014), accessed at *newyorker.com/magazine*

Gaar, G. G., *She's A Rebel: The History Of Women In Rock & Roll* (New York: Seal Press, 2002 [1992])

Gann, K., *No Such Thing As Silence: John Cage's 4'33"* (New Haven: Yale University Press, 2010)

Garbarini, V., 'Robert Fripp', in *Musician* (1 February 1987), 88

Gehr, R., 'Brian Eno/Various Artists', in *Spin* (1 July 1994), 71-72

Gett, S., 'David Sylvian Talks 'Secrets'', in *Billboard* (12 December 1987), 17

Goia, T., *Music: A Subversive History* (New York: Basic Books, 2019)

Gordon, J., 'Growing Older', in *NYTM* (13 March 2022), 16-17

Grella Jr., G., *Bitches Brew*. 33 1/3 series #110 (New York & London: Bloomsbury, 2015)

Hegarty, P., and M. Halliwell, *Beyond The Before: Progressive Rock Across Time And Genre*. Expanded edition (New York & London: Bloomsbury Academic, 2022)

Henderson, B., 'Talk Talk', in *The Orlando Sentinel* (20 November 1988), 6

Hensey, G., 'The Strange World of … John Foxx', in *The Quietus* (28 July 2020)

The History Of Rock: 1978, issue 14, published by *Uncut* (London: Time Inc., 2016)

Hochman, S., 'Brian Eno, R&D Entrepreneur of New Music', in *Los Angeles Times* (17 August 1988), *Calendar*, 4

Hsu, H., 'Machine Yearning: Holly Herndon's search for a new art form for our tech obsessions', in *TNY* (20 May 2019), 83-84

Hsu, H., 'Whims: Paul McCartney's surprisingly playful pandemic album', in *TNY* (21 December 2020), 80-81

Hughes, R., 'Would You Believe?' in *RC* #531 (May 2022), 80-91

Humphries, P., and S. Blacknell, *Top Of The Pops: 50th Anniversary* (London: McNidder & Grace, 2014)

Hutlock, T., 'David Sylvian and Japan' (9 April 2015), daily. redbullmusicacademy.com

Hyden, S., *This Isn't Happening: Radiohead's Kid A And The Beginning Of The 21st Century* (New York Hachette, 2020)

Hyland, V., 'Kacey Musgraves Is In Her Feelings', in *Elle* (June/July 2021), accessed at *elle.com/culture/a36398996/kacey-musgraves-2021-album-interview/*

Jameson, F., 'Reification and Utopia in Mass Culture', in *Social Text* 1 (Winter 1979), 137-38

[n.a.] 'Japan: Occidents Will Happen', in *RS* (23 July 1981), 28-29

Jeffrey, A., *Once Upon A Time*. 33 1/3 series #157 (New York & London: Bloomsbury, 2021)

Jones, A., 'Howling into the void', in *CP* (July/August 2020), 38-45

Jones, D., *Sweet Dreams: The Story Of The New Romantics*. London: Faber & Faber, 2020

Jones, D., *The Wichita Lineman: Searching In The Sun For The World's Greatest Unfinished Song* (London: Faber & Faber, 2019)

Kardos, L., *Blackstar Theory: The Last Works Of David Bowie* (New York & London: Bloomsbury Academic, 2022)

Karn, M., *Japan And Self Existence*. Self-published by MK Music (available via Lulu Books, 2011)

Kate Bush Essentials: The Collectors' Series, published by *Mojo* (Peterborough: H. Bauer, 2023)

Keaveney, C. T., *Western Rock Artists, Madame Butterfly, And The Allure Of Japan: Dancing In An Eastern Dream* (Lanham, MD: Lexington Books, 2020)

Kernfeld, B., *What To Listen For In Jazz* (New Haven: Yale University Press, 1997)

Kheshti, R., *Switched-On Bach*. 33 1/3 series #141 (New York & London: Bloomsbury, 2019)

Kleeman, A., 'Music Not Made for This World', in *NYTM* (10 March 2019), 40

Knopper, S., *Appetite For Self-Destruction: The Spectacular Crash Of The Record Industry In The Digital Age* (Createspace, 2017; 1st edition, New York: Free Press, 2009)

Kreps, D., 'Talk Talk's Mark Hollis Dead at 64', in *RS* (26 February 2019), accessed at rollingstone.com/music/music-news/talk-talk-mark-hollis-dead-800033

Kulikowski, M., *On Track ... Roxy Music: Every Album, Every Song* (Tewkesbury, UK: Sonicbond, 2024)

Leech, J., *Fearless: The Making Of Post-Rock* (London: Jawbone, 2017)

Lester, P., 'Words of the Shaman', in *Melody Maker* (16 September 1989), 40-41

Lester, P., 'Paddy McAloon: 'I'll do without an audience to make the music I want'', in *The Guardian* (5 September 2013), *theguardian.com/music/2013/sep/05/paddy-mcaloon-prefab-sprout-make-music*

Light, A., *The Holy Or The Broken: Leonard Cohen, Jeff Buckley, And The Unlikely Ascent Of 'Hallelujah'* (New York: Atria Books, 2012)

Lindgren, H., 'Fresh Tunes Follow a Long Wait', in *NYT* (26 September 2021), *Arts & Entertainment*, 8

Lindsay, M., 'The Dreaming', in *CP*, *Classic Pop Presents 1982* (Special edition, 2021), 76-79

Lindsay, M., '30 Years On: The Dreaming by Kate Bush', in *The Quietus* (11 September 2012), accessed at *thequietus.com/articles/09945-kate-bush-the-dreaming*

Lindsay, M., 'New Music Night and Day', in *CP*, *Classic Pop Presents Synthpop*, Volume II (Special Edition 2020), 9-17

Lindsay, M., 'Strange Fascination: The New Romantics', in *CP*, *The New Romantics* (Special Edition, 2019), 6-19

Lindsay, M., 'Thursday Night Fever', in *CP* (January 2020, *classicpopmag.com/2020/01*)

Lindsay, M., 'Together in Electric Dreams?' in *CP*, *Classic Pop Present Synthpop*, Volume I (Special Edition, 2019), 50-59

Margolick, D., *Strange Fruit: The Biography Of A Song* (New York: Ecco, 2001)

Marsh, J., C. Roberts, and T. Benjamin, *Spirit Of Talk Talk* (London: Rocket 88, 2019; 1st edition, 2012)

Mask, D., 'From A to Z', in *NYT* (6 December 2020), *Book Review*, 63

Matos, M., 'Mapping the Vast Influence of Holger Czukay, Alchemist of Krautrock Legends Can', in *The Record* (6 September 2017), npr.org/sections/therecord/2017/09/06/548955213

McGorray, M., 'Gaps in music: the neuroscience of pauses', in *Medical News Today* online newsletter (9 August 2021), *medicalnewstoday.com/articles/gaps-in-music*

Mednicov, M. L., *Pop Art And Popular Music: Jukebox Modernism* (New York: Routledge, 2018)

Meyer, B., 'Techno Musician: the time may be right for Holger Czukay, master of sound collages, to be heard', in *Chicago Tribune* (5 January 1997), *Arts & Entertainment*, 7

Milano, B., *Vinyl Junkies: Adventures In Record Collecting* (New York: St. Martin's Griffin, 2003)

Moorefield, V., *The Producer As Composer: Shaping The Sounds Of Popular Music* (Cambridge, MA: MIT Press, 2005)

Morrison, S., *Avalon*. 33 1/3 series #155 (New York & London: Bloomsbury, 2021)

Morton, T., *Spacecraft*. Object Lessons series (New York & London: Bloomsbury, 2022)

Moy, R., *Kate Bush And Hounds Of Love* (Aldershot, UK: Ashgate, 2007)

MTV News Staff, 'No Doubt to Tell Fans 'It's My Life'' (15 September 2003), mtv.com/news/1478221

Napier-Bell, S., *I'm Coming To Take You To Lunch* (New York: Wenner Books, 2005)

Napier-Bell, S., *Ta-Ra-Ra-Boom-De-Ay: The Dodgy Business Of Popular Music* (London: Unbound, 2014)

Nelson, S., *Court And Spark*. 33 1/3 series #40 (New York & London: Bloomsbury, 2007)

Niester, A., 'Robert Fripp', in *Globe & Mail* (17 January 1998), *C*, 9

O'Brien, L., 'Aerial', in *Kate Bush Essentials: The Collectors' Series* (*Mojo*, 2023), 72-77

O'Brien, S., 'Tin Drum', in *CP, Classic Pop Presents 1981* (Special Edition, 2021), 114-17

Padgett, R., *I'm Your Fan: The Songs Of Leonard Cohen*. 33 1/3 series #147 (New York & London: Bloomsbury, 2020)

Pareles, J., 'Sophie, 34, Whose Music Burst with Energy, Dies', in *NYT* (31 January 2021), *National*, 25

Pegg, N., *The Complete David Bowie* (London: Titan Books, 2000; revised and updated, 2016)

Petrusich, A., 'Domestic Arts: Bill Callahan on home and its comforts', in *TNY* (10 & 17 June 2019), 88-89

Petrusich, A., 'Merging Lanes: The notion of genre is disappearing', in *TNY* (15 March 2021), 68-72

Petrusich, A., *Pink Moon*. 33 1/3 series #51 (New York & London: Bloomsbury, 2007)

Petrusich, A., 'What's That Noise?' in *TNY* (16 November 2020), 72-73

Power, M., *David Sylvian: The Last Romantic* (London: Omnibus, 1998; revised and updated in 2004 and 2012)

Prasad, A., 'Chasing the Muse', in *Guitar Player* (July 2005), 48-49, 146-52

Price, S., 'Hounds Of Love', in *Record Collector Presents Kate Bush: A Deeper Understanding* (London: Diamond, 2020), 55

Prochnik, G., *In Pursuit Of Silence: Listening For Meaning In A World Of Noise* (New York: Doubleday, 2010)

Quantick, D., 'Aerial', in *Record Collector Presents Kate Bush: A Deeper Understanding* (London: Diamond, 2020), 87

Questlove Thompson, A., 'Collecting Things is an Act of Devotion', in TNY (27 March 2022), *Arts & Entertainment*, 10

Ratliff, B., 'Precise Electronic Mix from a German Pioneer', in *NYT* (6 January 1997), *C*, 12

Record Collector Presents Kate Bush: A Deeper Understanding, published by *RC* (London: Diamond, 2020)

Reesman, B., 'Pop Provocateur: David Sylvian', in *Keyboard* (May 2001), 52

Restall, M., *Blue Moves*. 33 1/3 series #146 (New York & London: Bloomsbury, 2020)

Restall, M., *On Elton John*. Opinionated Guides series (New York: Oxford University Press, [2025])

Reynolds, A., *Cries And Whispers: Sylvian/Karn/Jansen/Barbieri/Dean, 1983-1991* (Norwich, UK: Burning Shed, 2018)

Reynolds, A., 'Dr in the House', in *CP* (May/June 2021), 58-61.

Reynolds, A., 'European Sons Rising'. Liner notes for deluxe (3CD+vinyl) reissue of *Quiet Life* (BMG/Sony, 2021)

Reynolds, A., 'Gentlemen Take Polaroids', in *CP*, *The New Romantics* (Special Edition, 2019), 108-12

Reynolds, A., *The Impossible Dream: The Story Of Scott Walker And The Walker Brothers* (London: Jawbone, 2009)

Reynolds, A., *Japan: A Foreign Place. The Biography (1974-1984)* (Norwich, UK: Burning Shed, 2015)

Reynolds, S., *Blissed Out: The Raptures Of Rock* (London: Serpent's Tail, 1990)

Reynolds, S., *Bring The Noise: 20 Years Of Writing About Hip Rock And Hip-Hop* (Berkeley: Soft Skull, 2011; London, 2009)

Reynolds, S., 'Kate Bush, the queen of art pop who defied her critics', in *The Guardian* (21 August 2014), accessed at *theguardian.com/music/2014/aug/21/kate-bush-queen-of-art-pop-defied-critics-london-concerts*

Reynolds, S., *Retromania: Pop Culture's Addiction To Its Own Past* (London: Faber & Faber, 2011)

Reynolds, S., *Shock And Awe: Glam Rock And Its Legacy, From The Seventies To The Twenty-First Century* (London: Dey Street Books, 2016)

Roberts, C., 'A Quiet Storm', in *RC* #517 (April 2021), 72-76

Ross, A., *Listen To This* (New York: Farrar, Straus and Giroux, 2010)

Said, E., *Orientalism* (New York: Vintage, 1979)

Sandall, R., 'Unmasking of the man from Japan', in *The Sunday Times* (UK) (17 September 1989), *Review*, C9

Schwartz, R. J., 'David Sylvian: The Sound of Things Falling Apart', in *Musician* (1 August 1987), 11

Scoppa, B., 'David Bowie: Low', in *Phonograph Record* (December 1977), reproduced in the boxset booklet to *A New Career In A New Town (1977-1982)* (Parlophone, 2017), 16

Seabrook, T. J., *Bowie In Berlin: A New Career In A New Town* (London: Jawbone, 2008)

Sheffield, R., 'Dim All the Lights for Donna Summer', in *RS* (17 May 2012), accessed at *rollingstone.com/music/music-news/dim-all-the-lights-for-donna-summer-242108/*

Sheffield, R., *Talking To Girls About Duran Duran: One Young Man's Quest For True Love And A Cooler Haircut* (New York and London: Plume, 2011 [2010])

Shenton, L., *Kate Bush: The Dreaming* (Bedford: Wymer, 2021)

Shepherd, F., 'He was made in Japan, but David Sylvian had a beautiful reason to go west', in *The Scotsman* (14 May 1999), 22

Sheppard, D., *On Some Faraway Beach: The Life And Times Of Brian Eno* (London: Orion, 2008)

Siegal, N., 'Going 'Inside the Music' With Brian Eno', in *NYT* (20 March 2018), *C*, 6

Silverman, H., and M. Restall, 'Hello Earth: A Discographic Journey into Kate Bush', on *Picking Up Rocks* (11 July 2022), at *pickinguprocks.com/2022/07/11/hello-earth-a-discographic-journey-into-kate-bush/*

Simon, P., 'Isn't It Rich?' in *NYT* (27 October 2010), accessed at *nytimes.com/2010/10/31/books/review/Simon-t.html*

Simonert, S., 'Return of the Snow Queen', in *Classic Rock* issue 22 (December 2011), 34-36

Sloan, N., and C. Harding, 'The Culture Warped Pop, For Good', in *NYT* (14 March 2021), *Opinion*, accessed at nytimes.com/interactive/2021/03/14/opinion/pop-music-songwriting.html

Smith, J., 'The Album Changed My Life', in *The Irish Times* (24 March 2018), E20

Solanas, J., 'The Barmy Dreamer', in *NME* (1982?), accessed at gaffa.org/reaching/i83 nme1.html

Soloski, A., 'Debbie Gibson Wants Vinyl', in *NYT* (23 January 2022), *Sunday Styles*, 6-7

'Sounds of the Scene – 40 Essential Tracks', in *CP, The New Romantics* (Special Edition, 2019), 96-105

Spelman, N., *Popular Music And The Myths Of Madness* (Farnham, UK: Ashgate, 2012)

Spence, S., *Just Can't Get Enough: The Making Of Depeche Mode* (London: Jawbone, 2011)

Spitz, B., *Led Zeppelin: The Biography* (New York: Penguin, 2021)

Spitzer, M., *The Musical Human: A History Of Life On Earth* (London and New York: Bloomsbury, 2021)

Steel, G., *On Track ... Talk Talk: Every Album, Every Song* (Tewkesbury, UK: Sonicbond, 2023)

Stone, A., 'Feminism, Gender and Popular Music', in C. Partridge and M. Moberg, eds., *The Bloomsbury Handbook Of Religion And Popular Music* (London: Bloomsbury Academic, 2017), 54-64

Stubbs, D., 'Talking Liberties: Mark Hollis', in *Vox* (February 1998), 38-41

Stubbs, D., 'Mark Hollis, 1955-2019', in *RC* #489 (February 2019), 49

Suárez, J., *Pop Modernism: Noise And The Reinvention Of The Everyday* (Chicago: University of Illinois Press, 2007)

Sullivan, J., 'Robert Fripp unfixes rock', in *Boston Globe* (19 November 1998), *Calendar*, 9

Tennent, S., *Spiderland*. 33 1/3 series #75 (New York & London: Bloomsbury, 2011)

Thomas, B., *On Track ... Kate Bush: Every Album, Every Song* (Tewkesbury, UK: Sonicbond, 2021)

Thompson, D., *I Feel Love: Donna Summer, Giorgio Moroder, And How They Reinvented Music* (Lanham, MD: Backbeat Books, 2021)

Thomson, G., *Under The Ivy: The Life And Music Of Kate Bush* (London: Omnibus, 2010)

Tipp, G., 'Spellbound', in *CP* (March/April 2021), 28-31

Toop, D., 'David Sylvian, Blemish', in *The Wire* (6 June 2005), accessed at *samadhisound.com/reviews*

The Ultimate Music Guide: Kate Bush, 'Deluxe Remastered Edition', published by *Uncut* (London: Time Inc., 2018)

Ultimate Record Collection ('The 1970s, Part 2: 1975-1979'), published by *Uncut* (London: BandLab, 2019)

Van der Kiste, J., *Kate Bush: Song By Song* (Stroud: Fonthill, 2021)

Van Matre, L., 'Recordings: Brian Eno', in *Chicago Tribune* (17 September 1992), 57

Walker, C. J., 'The Artsy Rocker Looks Back with Two Projects: David Sylvian', in *Mix* (November 2002), 159, 170-72

Wallace, W., 'Five Decades of Duran Duran', in *CP* (November/December 2012), 52-59

Wallace, W., 'Hit ... Or Myth? The Legends of Mark Hollis', in *CP* (May/June 2022), 38-43

Wallace, W., 'Spirit of Eden', in *CP* (April 2019), 32-36

Walters, J. L., 'Music: Notes from a quiet life', in *The Independent* (26 March 1999), 11

Wardle, B., *Mark Hollis: A Perfect Silence* (London: Rocket 88, 2022)

Washburn, M., *Southern Accents*. 33 1/3 series #139 (New York & London: Bloomsbury, 2019)

Weaver, C., 'Keke Palmer Will Take You There', in *NYT* (30 August 2020), *Sunday Styles*, 1, 4

Weigel, D., *The Show That Never Ends: The Rise And Fall Of Prog Rock* (New York: Norton, 2017)

Wilson, S., *Scott Walker And The Song Of The One-All-Alone* (New York & London: Bloomsbury Academic, 2020)

Wolin, A., *Golden Hits Of The Shangri-Las*. 33 1/3 series #138 (New York & London: Bloomsbury, 2019)

Wong, T., A. Jones, and Y. Kato, 'David Bowie's love affair with Japanese style', in *BBC News* (12 January 2016), accessed at *bbc.com/news/world-asia-35278488*

Wright, S., 'Too Much, Too Soon: Ed Hollis and Speedball Records', originally posted 15 March 2017, on *onlyrockandroll.london*

Young, C., *On The Periphery: David Sylvian: A Biography* (Holywell, Wales: Malin Publishing, 2013)

Young, R., *Electric Eden: Unearthing Britain's Visionary Music* (London: Faber and Faber, 2010)

Zaleski, A., *Rio.* 33 1/3 series #156 (New York & London: Bloomsbury, 2021)

Zoladz, L., 'Designing Music to Create a Mood', in *NYT* (8 November 2020), *Arts & Entertainment*, 9-10

Websites And Films

Anthonyreynolds.net

BBC Radio 6, *Sounds*, 'Spirit of Sylvian', M. A. Hobbs and D. Sylvian, initially posted 27 October 2022, temporarily available at *www.bbc.co.uk/programmes/m001d5w7*

Brëes, G., dir., *In A Silent Way* (La Rochelle: Dérives Productions, 2020)

Davidsylvian.com (official website)

Duranduran.com (official website)

Kijak, S., dir. *Scott Walker: 30th Century Man* (London: Missing in Action Films, 2006)

Katebushnews.com

Kulturekiosk.com/david-sylvian-the-sound-atlas (fan website)

Nightporter.co.uk (fan website created and run by P. Rymer)

Samadhisound.com (official website of Sylvian's own record label)

Snowinberlin.com (fan website subtitled 'A Mark Hollis and Talk Talk Resource')

Sylvianvista.com (fan website)

Endnotes

1. Dayal, *Another Green World*, xix; Frere-Jones, 'Ambient Genius'. Also see Sheppard, *On Some Faraway Beach*.

2. Singer-songwriter Duncan Sheik has argued that the complexity of Talk Talk's later albums ranks them among 'the best 20th-century composers' (Marsh et al., *Spirit Of Talk Talk*, 154); can the category of 'modern composer' be meaningfully extended to include Hollis, Sylvian and Bush?

3. Bradley, *The Poetry Of Pop*, 4-5; Jameson, 'Reification And Utopia In Mass Culture', 137-38; both quoted by Mednicov, *Pop Art And Popular Music*, 5, 7.

4. Useful here were Suárez, *Pop Modernism*, 3, cited by Mednicov, *Pop Art And Popular Music*, 8; Attali, *Noise*; Bourdieu, *Distinction*; and Arena, *Sylvian As A Philosopher*.

5. Moorefield, *The Producer As Composer*; Young, *Electric Eden*, 5-7; Leech, *Fearless*, 18. As Hegarty and Halliwell, *Beyond And Before*, 281, point out, attaching 'post' to a genre of music is 'not a synonym for 'postmodern'', but I argue below that there is something functionally postmodern to the relationship between, for example, pop and post-pop.

6. Reynolds, *Bring The Noise*, 186; Chuter, *Storm, Static, Sleep*, 4-5; Tennent, *Spiderland*, 139-41.

7. Hegarty and Halliwell, *Beyond And Before*, 280-83; Reynolds, *Bring The Noise*, 186-93; Wolin, *Golden Hits*, 13-20; Leech, *Fearless*; Chuter, *Storm, Static, Sleep*, 5 ('muscle' and 'innovation').

8. I return later to define what I call the Album/Singles Era. As an example of the numerous threads that connect this book's protagonists, the producer and sound engineer on the Tight Fit single were Tim Friese-Greene and Phill Brown; stemming from this first experience working together, they would go on to help create the final two Talk Talk albums, and Brown would engineer Hollis's swansong record (Brown, *Are We Still Rolling?*, 277).

9. CP (May 2019), 51; as of 2020, there were at least three different postings of this *TOTP* performance on YouTube. Japan biographer Reynolds calls the appearance 'a classic of the era', noting that the band were immediately followed by the more upbeat and popular Gary Numan – who had followed Japan to the country Japan the previous year, a bizarre stalking affair that nonetheless led to Karn playing on Numan's next album (*A Foreign Place*, 112-16, 178; Karn, *Japan And Self*, 344).

10. Lindsay, 'Thursday Night Fever'; also see Humphries and Blacknell, *Top Of The Pops*; Bromley, 'Back In The Day.'

11. Hutlock, 'David Sylvian And Japan'; Power, *David Sylvian*, 66; CP (April 2020), 63.

12. UK (BBC) charts accessible at www.officialcharts.com/charts/singles. 'Ghosts' subsequently slid from number seven to number 14 to number 25 to number 54 – where it slipped past Talk Talk's 'Talk Talk', which had dropped to number 53 following its peak at number 52 – before exiting the charts in mid-May.

13 Frequently quoted, e.g. *CP* (May 2019), 50; *CP* (April 2020), 63; Steve O'Brien, 'Tin Drum', 115.

14 Fisher, *Ghosts Of My Life*, 35.

15 I was very wrong about the words to 'Sat In Your Lap', but perhaps not completely wrong in my interpretation of the song; at least one biographer of Bush argues that it suggests sex is a means to enlightenment (Thomson, *Under The Ivy*, 23). For reasons mentioned in Chapter 7, men discussing Bush and sex is always problematic. Bush slightly remixed 'Sat' for *The Dreaming*, released 15 months later (Thomas, *Kate Bush*, 40-42); see also Shenton, *Kate Bush*.

16 Arena, *Sylvian As A Philosopher*, 15.

17 I did not see the *Old Grey Whistle Test* performance until many years later: it was included on a DVD release of excerpts from the show (which ran from 1971 to 1988) and is now accessible on YouTube, but best seen via *sylvianvista.com/2020/07/31/ghosts-live/*.

18 Ryuichi Sakamoto (1952-2023) died as I was writing this book; he haunts its pages.

19 Reynolds, *A Foreign Place*, 176; Karn, *Japan And Self*, 340; *sylvianvista.com/2020/07/31/ghosts-live/*.

20 Sylvian's comment in 2003; *sylvianvista.com/2020/07/31/ghosts-live/*.

21 Wallace, 'Hit ... Or Myth?' 41; Marsh et al., *Spirit Of Talk Talk*, 139.

22 Quotes, in sequence, from obituaries in *Record Collector*, *NME* and *Rolling Stone*: Stubbs, 'Mark Hollis', 49; Beaumont, 'Talk Talk's Mark Hollis'; Kreps, 'Talk Talk's Mark Hollis Dead at 64'.

23 Setlist.fm/stats/covers/no-doubt-3bd6b81c.html. For Tom Dumont on how the key change in 'It's My Life' makes it 'a really fascinating song to learn and cover', see Marsh et al., *Spirit Of Talk Talk*, 125-26.

24 MTV News Staff, 'No Doubt'; also quoted on various Wikipedia pages. Dumont has said that the tritone key change from verse to pre-chorus 'is theoretically the most dissonant and difficult key change to make', but Talk Talk 'make it sound exciting and musical' (Steel, *Talk Talk*, 27).

25 As *CP* writer Steve O'Brien recently put it, while nonetheless rating it as one of the best five 'reboots of 80s classics', No Doubt's version 'misses the sulky melancholy of the original' (*CP*, January 2020, 73).

26 Alphaville lead singer and co-writer Marian Gold has said that the yearning is by 'a couple of lovers trying to get off heroin' (see, e.g., the song's entry in *storyofsong.com*).

27 The videos can be found online; also see Wardle, *A Perfect Silence*, 126-28; Steel, *Talk Talk*, 26.

28 There are, apparently, some promotional CDs out there, thus labelled; this part of the album's story is told in Brown, *Are We Still Rolling?*, 345-49, and briefly revisited in Chapter 19.

29 As far as I can tell, *Mark Hollis* has never been released in the US on CD;

a Polydor album, it was licensed to Ba Da Bing! for the 2011 US vinyl release (*discogs.com/Mark-Hollis-Mark-Hollis/master/80116*), with Hollis's enthusiastic approval (Wardle, *A Perfect Silence*, 321).

30 Beaumont, 'Super Shy Guy'.

31 Beaumont, 'Super Shy Guy'. Less funny but far more astute is Steel's verdict that the song is Hollis's closest to 'a prog masterpiece', rivalling Kate Bush's "Ninth Wave' suite for its ability to transport the listener' (*Talk Talk*, 93).

32 Beaumont, 'Super Shy Guy'.

33 *CP* (April 2019), 9.

34 *CP* (April 2019), 9; see links to court records in 'Contract dispute with EMI' section of the Wikipedia entry for *Spirit Of Eden*.

35 John Earls in *CP* (February 2019), 28.

36 Kleeman, 'Music Not Made For This World'.

37 Here I quote Hegarty and Halliwell, *Beyond And Before*, 280, discussing Simon Reynolds' 1994 definition of 'post-rock' (see Reynolds, *Bring The Noise*, 186-93). A line of Reynolds' ('counter-culture [sic] is a home from home'; *Blissed Out*, 9) inspired my 'home from home' line.

38 Hollis lived from 4 January 1955 to 25 February 2019; Sylvian was born 23 February 1958; Bush was born 30 June 1958.

39 Fisher, *Ghosts Of My Life*, 8-9 (this para), 6-16 (next).

40 The comment, frequently cited (e.g., Reynolds, *A Foreign Place*, 6; Pegg, *Complete David Bowie*, chap. 3), was from an interview in September, when Bowie's first hit single, 'Space Oddity', peaked at number five in the UK charts, giving him a chance to promote the Arts Lab that he had co-founded in the Three Tuns Pub in Beckenham. On his origins, see Brooker, *Why Bowie Matters*, 18-74.

41 Weigel, *The Show That Never Ends*, 10.

42 Weigel, *The Show That Never Ends*; Barnes, *A New Day Yesterday*; Hegarty and Halliwell, *Beyond And Before*. For a parallel (and largely compatible) argument that art schools, mostly in London, were the incubators of prog rock, see Spitz, *Led Zeppelin*, 49-51, 69.

43 Spence, *Just Can't Get Enough*, 24-161.

44 Listening to band interviews from the 1980s, available on YouTube (e.g., a typically awkward exchange from 1986 at *youtube.com/watch?v=g3bvBu5m6Y4 from 1986*), Hollis's speech is arguably an Essex/East London cockney mix, where Harris and Webb are more Essex, but the distinction is slight. On Hollis's childhood: Wardle, *A Perfect Silence*, 14-42.

45 Doyle, *Running Up That Hill*, 36.

46 Power, *David Sylvian*, 13-14. In the early 2020s, the average house price in Lewisham and Catford was over half a million pounds (just under two-thirds of a million US dollars).

47 Reynolds, *A Foreign Place*, 5-11; Karn, *Japan And Self*, 16-21, 25.

48 Reynolds, *A Foreign Place*, 13, 21, 35 ('worse' and 'reaction' quotes by Nick Huckle).
49 Reynolds, *A Foreign Place*, 38; Doyle, *Running Up That Hill*, 59-64.
50 Reynolds, *A Foreign Place*, 20, 25; Karn, *Japan And Self*, 49-50.
51 Karn, *Japan And Self*, 28.
52 Hughes, 'Would You Believe?' 88; Reynolds, *A Foreign Place*, 8, 10 ('pecking' and 'heroes' quotes by their childhood friend Nick Huckle); Kulikowski, *Roxy Music*, 17-26. The two albums were released on 16 June (1972), the Croydon show was on 25 June and the 'Starman' performance on 6 July.
53 Doyle, *Running Up That Hill*, 41; Simonert, 'Snow Queen', 36 (Bush quote); Restall, *On Elton John*, chapters 2-3.
54 The Finsbury Park concerts were at the Rainbow Theatre, starting on 19 August (1972), and Roxy were on *Top Of The Pops* on 24 August; Hughes, 'Would You Believe?'
55 Karn, *Japan And Self*, 35.
56 The two albums were released in March and April (1973), and the Earl's Court concert was on 12 May; Reynolds, *A Foreign Place*, 8, 10; Hughes, 'Would You Believe?' See also Kulikowski, *Roxy Music*, 32-41.
57 Karn, *Japan And Self*, 33-35; Power, *David Sylvian*, 18.
58 Reynolds, *A Foreign Place*, 10; Karn, *Japan And Self*, 35. Two months after that Earl's Court concert, on the tour's final night at the Hammersmith Odeon, Bowie famously announced Ziggy Stardust's demise; Bush was there, and wept, then wrote a song, 'Oh, Davy', that would evolve into 'Humming' but remain unreleased until after Bowie's death (Doyle, *Running Up That Hill*, 42-44, 47-48; Thomas, *Kate Bush*, 19).
59 Reynolds, *A Foreign Place*, 24; Karn, *Japan And Self*, 53-55.
60 According to Napier-Bell, Hansa were unhappy with the name changes and threatened to void the band's contract. Reynolds, *A Foreign Place*, 27; Power, *David Sylvian*, 23.
61 His verbal emphasis; Sandall, 'Unmasking of the man from Japan'. Karn's later verdict was milder but still dismissive, remarking that he had 'not much' to say about the two albums: 'I don't find them very interesting and the last thing I'm going to do is listen to them in order to jog my memory' (*Japan And Self*, 125).
62 Sylvian claimed not long ago that 'I haven't heard them since 1982 or whatever. I have no interest' (Roberts, 'A Quiet Storm', 73); breaking a 15-year radio silence in 2022, he again insisted, 'I've not heard a note of that material since the band broke up' (*www.bbc.co.uk/programmes/m001d5w7*).
63 Reynolds, *A Foreign Place*, 28.
64 Reynolds, *A Foreign Place*, 31 ('overboard' quote by Sylvian).
65 Reynolds, *A Foreign Place*, 32 ('monsoon' and 'weird'); Thompson, *I Feel Love*, 7 ('art-punk'; exclamation point his); Power, *David Sylvian*, 25-32. On that adolescent-lust trilogy: Thomas, *Kate Bush*, 16-17; Moy, *Kate Bush*, 16-17.

66 Was it inevitable that the band's name would garner positive attention in Japan the country? Karn had a point when he noted that if a Japanese band had called themselves Scotland, they would have been 'ridiculed out of existence' in the UK, whereas the Japanese 'were flattered and curious at our choice of name' (*Japan And Self*, 124). We return to the band's name, its origin and significance, in the next chapter.

67 Reynolds, *A Foreign Place*, 33, 46; Power, *David Sylvian*, 26; *Ultimate Record Collection*, 61.

68 Sylvian's denials regarding influences and parallels to other artists are numerous, and not always convincing, but this rings true (from 1978): 'There is no comparison. The only thing that's similar between the Dolls and ourselves is that we are both self-indulgent; we are totally into ourselves' (Reynolds, *A Foreign Place*, 28).

69 Sandall, 'Unmasking Of The Man From Japan'.

70 Coronil, 'Latin American Postcolonial Studies', 186; I thank Fernando Quiñones Valdivia for leading me to this source.

71 Morrison, *Avalon*, 3, 7, 9, 14.

72 Morrison, *Avalon*, 14; 2014 interview by Taylor Parkes in *The Quietus* (thequietus.com/articles/16665-bryan-ferry-interview); on *Avalon*, see also Kulikowski, *Roxy Music*, 106-13.

73 Hughes, 'Would You Believe?' 84. According to Arena, *Sylvian As A Philosopher*, 7, Sylvian is on a postmodern philosophical 'path' (he 'aims for perfection, though he does not look for it').

74 Scoppa, 'David Bowie: Low'.

75 Seabrook, *Bowie In Berlin*, 172.

76 Seabrook, *Bowie In Berlin*, 172-73; Wilcken, *Low*.

77 If the tracks with non-verbal vocals are counted as instrumentals, then *Low* has five pop-rock songs and six instrumentals, whereas *'Heroes'* comprises six rock songs and four instrumentals; the numerical difference may seem trivial, but the contrast in coherence and overall impression is significant.

78 Pegg, *Complete David Bowie*, 260; Seabrook, *Bowie In Berlin*, 132.

79 Seabrook, *Bowie In Berlin*, 161-62, 169; Dayal, *Another Green World*; Van Matre, 'Recordings'.

80 Seabrook, *Bowie In Berlin*, 163; Frere-Jones, 'Ambient Genius'; Leech, *Fearless*, 20-24; Sheppard, *On Some Faraway Beach*. Eno first created the 'Oblique Strategies' cards with painter and old art school friend Peter Schmidt.

81 Seabrook, *Bowie In Berlin*, 166; Reynolds, *A Foreign Place*, 39 (the source, boyhood friend of the band Nick Huckle, suspected the manager never contacted Fripp).

82 Dayal, *Another Green World*, 98.

83 Reynolds, *A Foreign Place*, 42; Power, *David Sylvian*, 31.

84 F. Quiñones Valdivia's personal communication, 11 November 2021

('postcolonialism is its own walking ghost'); *Blackstar* (ISO/Columbia/Sony, 2016); Kardos, *Blackstar Theory*.

85 Napier-Bell, *Lunch*, 77 (also quoted in Jones, *Sweet Dreams*, 419-20). Another version of the story names tour manager Jake Duncan as the culprit, for which the band gave him 'a right bollocking' (Reynolds, *A Foreign Place*, 193).

86 Reynolds, *A Foreign Place*, 12. It seems characteristic of Sylvian to later condemn the name: 'I hated it then. I still do' (Power, *David Sylvian*, 18).

87 Reynolds, *A Foreign Place*, 12; Karn, *Japan And Self*, 36. I vaguely remember a silly 'like some Catford from Japan' joke from my early 1980s Tokyo days, made up by me or my sister or Shoe/Xu.

88 Wong et al., 'David Bowie's love affair'; Keaveney, *Western Rock Artists*, 50, 83-84; Reynolds, *Shock And Awe*; Restall, *On Elton John*, chapter 4.

89 Reynolds, *A Foreign Place*, 36, 44; Doyle, *Running Up That Hill*, 53-58.

90 Napier-Bell, *Lunch*, 9.

91 Napier-Bell, *Lunch*, 10. The same motivation would result in Napier-Bell's groundbreaking success at arranging for Wham! (whom he managed after Japan) to play in China in 1984 (the core topic of his memoir, *I'm Coming To Take You To Lunch*).

92 Napier-Bell, *Lunch*, 62.

93 Reynolds, *A Foreign Place*, 47 (the journalist was a Los Angeles freelancer, Sylvie Simmons, who would go on to write acclaimed books on Serge Gainsbourg, Leonard Cohen and others). Karn remembered only four US concerts in 1978, noting that Japan never again returned there because 'David decided he didn't like American audiences' (*Japan And Self*, 128); as we shall see, Sylvian would much later settle and raise a family in the United States.

94 Doyle, *Running Up That Hill*, 77-78 (Bush In Tokyo). Oscar, the star of Riyoko Ikeda's *La Rose De Versailles* (in Japanese, despite its title), posed 'as a man whilst endeavouring to save Marie Antionette during the French Revolution' (Reynolds, *A Foreign Place*, 44).

95 Karn, *Japan And Self*, 95-97 (for Karn's story of a young Japanese fan wanting to be his 'pie', and he not realising until later that she had understood 'groupies' to mean the group's pies); Reynolds, *A Foreign Place*, 44, 54-59; Power, *David Sylvian*, 35-36; setlist.fm/ search?artist=73d6ba91&query =tour:%281979+Japanese+Tour%29.

96 To quote the subtitle to Thompson, *I Feel Love*.

97 Although hasn't it turned out to be 45 years – and counting? Reynolds, *A Foreign Place*, 59; Thompson, *I Feel Love*, 3; Sheffield, 'Dim All the Lights'.

98 Thompson, *I Feel Love*, 179-80.

99 Jones, *Sweet Dreams*; Spence, *Just Can't Get Enough*, 209; *CP, Classic Pop Presents Depeche Mode* (2019).

100 Reynolds, *A Foreign Place*, 59-60. Burke, 'Japan And David Sylvian', 50

('trademark' quote). Faltermeyer would win Grammy Awards in the 1980s for his synth-pop compositions for the *Beverly Hills Cop* and *Top Gun* film scores.

101 *Billboard* (23 June 1979), 69. Re-released in 1981, following the success of Japan's fourth album, 'Life In Tokyo' flopped again; Hansa tried a third time in the autumn of 1982, and this time the song hit number 28 in the UK (and number 26 in Ireland), riding the wave of popularity created by *Tin Drum* and 'Ghosts'.

102 Power, *David Sylvian*, 37.

103 Burke, 'Japan And David Sylvian', 50; Lindsay, 'New Music Night And Day', 12; Reynolds, *A Foreign Place,* 60, 62; 'Sounds Of The Scene', 100.

104 Reynolds, 'Dr In The House', 60.

105 Ian Penman was the offender; Reynolds, 'A Life Less Ordinary', 25. That kind of overt bigotry is mercifully gone from record reviews, and even at the time, there were some critics willing to listen without prejudice; for example, Derek Jewell's response to the new album was to call Japan 'one of our most talented and unfairly neglected young groups', long 'abused, mocked and under-regarded in Britain' despite being 'the most original sound to emerge in rock in the last two or three years' – a hyperbole that appeared in *The Sunday Times* of all venues (Reynolds, *A Foreign Place*, 90). Jewell's view is more in line with opinion on *Quiet Life* today, although it still gets mixed comments; for example, *Uncut*'s recent verdict was that the album showed Japan 'not yet refined and poised', while conceding the back-handed compliment that its 'disco-fied synthpop' is 'still miles away from the New York Dolls poses of their debut' (*Ultimate Record Collection*, 61).

106 In Napier-Bell's telling, Hansa's reaction was even more damaging to Japan; two of the label's directors (married to each other) disagreed over the verbal agreement whereby Japan had been released from their contract, and in the resulting lawsuit and settlement with the band, Hansa effectively were given 'the advance from Virgin' (Power, *David Sylvian*, 43-44).

107 Power, *David Sylvian*, 38-39.

108 Reynolds, 'A Life Less Ordinary', 22.

109 Power, *David Sylvian*, 23.

110 Reynolds, 'European Sons Rising'; *A Foreign Place*, 65; 'A Life Less Ordinary', 23.

111 During the recording of 'Despair', Kate Bush, working on her third album, *Never For Ever*, in the adjacent studio at AIR, dropped in to listen (having already crossed paths a few times with the Japan boys). She sat cross-legged on the floor while Punter played back the track. Her response was 'Oh, wow!' – her signature exclamation, and the title of a recent hit single of hers – 'It's so *big*, isn't it?' (Reynolds, *A Foreign Place*, 69; *RC* #517 [April 2021], 75).

112 Quotes by photographer, journalist, and late 1960s 'Swinging London' figure John 'Hoppy' Hopkins (1937-2015) in Cavanagh, *The Piper At The Gates Of Dawn*, 11.

113 Gann, *No Such Thing As Silence*, 1-22, quotes on 8, 15, 120; Biguenet, *Silence*, 49-51; also see Barry, *Compact Disc*, 36-37, 63-65; Prochnik, *In Pursuit Of Silence*; and Cage's own *Silence*. I have listened to recordings of *4'33'* several times, hearing above all the rush of my own tinnitus, that scourge of middle-aged music lovers from which Cage himself seems to have eventually suffered (Gann, op. cit., 164; Prochnik, op. cit., 182).

114 McGorray, 'Gaps In Music'.

115 Simon, 'Isn't It Rich?'; also quoted by Biguenet, *Silence*, 66.

116 From a 2005 *Sound On Sound* interview quoted in Dayal, *Another Green World*, 103; also see Zoladz, 'Designing Music'; Van Matre, 'Recordings'.

117 In *CP*, (September/October 2021), 33.

118 Reynolds, 'A Life Less Ordinary', 25; *A Foreign Place*, 65; Tipp, 'Spellbound', 29 ('synth-wizard'). A beautiful piano-and-synth instrumental written by Barbieri and Sylvian, titled 'A Foreign Place', full of breathing space and even tiny moments of silence, was intended as the closing track to *Quiet Life* (but ended up as a later B-side). It arguably doesn't fit the album's mood, but it does fascinatingly anticipate where Japan and solo Sylvian would go, and, eventually, Barbieri, too.

119 Reynolds, *A Foreign Place*, 69-70; 'European Sons Rising'; Power, *David Sylvian*, 39-40; Karn, *Japan And Self*, 158-59.

120 Reynolds, *A Foreign Place*, 69; Power, *David Sylvian*, 40-41; Kulikowski, *Roxy Music*, 59-60.

121 Burke, 'Japan And David Sylvian', 49.

122 Spence, *Just Can't Get Enough*, 135; Doyle, 'Conform To Deform'.

123 A number 18 hit in the UK, spawning a pair of modest hits singles ('Underpass' and 'No One Driving' peaked in the low 30s), *Metamatic* was largely ignored elsewhere, and its mixed reception persists (e.g., it 'has not worn well' in *RC* #343 [November 2007], but appreciation for 'Underpass' as 'iconic' in *CP*, *Synthpop*, Volume I, 96); however, it is to my mind an important and undervalued achievement.

124 Spence, *Just Can't Get Enough*, 55, 117.

125 Doyle, *Running Up That Hill*, 113, 121 ('startling'); Thomas, *Kate Bush*, 29-49; Spence, *Just Can't Get Enough*, 209 (the 1983 Depeche Mode *TOTP* performance is available on YouTube, although this joke synth label is not visible to me).

126 E.g., Earls, 'Stockhausen Or ABBA?'; Earls, 'Light In The Darkness', 91; wikipedia.org/wiki/Orchestral_Manoeuvres_in_the_Dark; also see *CP* (February 2020), 40.

127 Earls, 'Stockhausen Or ABBA?' 30

128 Karn, *Japan And Self*, 191; Reynolds, *A Foreign Place*, 95.

129 Karn, *Japan And Self*, 192; Reynolds, 'Gentlemen Take Polaroids', 109.

130 Reynolds, 'Gentlemen Take Polaroids', 109 (Dean), 112 (Reynolds); Karn, *Japan And Self*, 191 (Karn); Zaleski, *Rio*, 35 ('seminal').

131 Chris Roberts in *RC* #517 (April 2021), 74.

132 Reynolds, 'Gentlemen Take Polaroids', 110; Power, *David Sylvian*, 45, 47.

133 Reynolds, 'Gentlemen Take Polaroids', 109; Kulikowski, *Roxy Music*.

134 'Torch song' verdict by Reynolds; all quotes from 'Gentlemen Take Polaroids', 110; also see his *A Foreign Place*, 95, 97.

135 Power, *David Sylvian*, 45.

136 In March 1980, flying home from another hit tour of Japan, the bandmembers circulated a cassette copy of YMO's *Solid State Survivor*, playing it on their brand-new Sony Walkmen (purchased for them in Tokyo by Napier-Bell); they all loved it, feeling that it 'somehow captured the very spirit of Japan' (Karn's words, meaning the musical spirit of the country). That autumn, Sakamoto and the rest of YMO came to London on tour, and after a Hammersmith Odeon gig in October, all members of both bands met; friendships and collaborations would long outlast both bands. Reynolds, *A Foreign Place*, 89, 98, 107.

137 Reynolds, *A Foreign Place*, 98 (Sylvian); Roberts, 'A Quiet Storm', 73 (Barbieri); Karn, *Japan And Self*, 191, 192 (Karn's 'boring': Jansen later admitted that this 'momentary lapse' happened 'just the once though'; Reynolds, *A Foreign Place*, 118), 193 (Karn's 'focus').

138 The EP took the format of two 7' records, rounded out with a Sylvian mix (different from the album mix) of 'Burning Bridges' – which was used as the B-side to 'Gentlemen' in Japan. 'Swimming' and 'Room' were included on EMI's 2003 CD re-issue of *Gentlemen Take Polaroids*.

139 www.anthonyreynolds.net/pages/Classic_Album_GTP_Japan.htm; Reynolds, *A Foreign Place*, 97.

140 A Bogarde fan, Sylvian had named a track on *Quiet Life* 'Despair' after a 1978 film of the same name starring the English actor (1921-1999).

141 Reynolds, *A Foreign Place*, 102 (Sylvian's 'muzak'); Karn, *Japan And Self*, 189 ('too poppy'; Barbieri confirmed this story, adding 'we didn't really like the tape at the time', although 'Duran Duran were very pleasant the few times we met them'; Reynolds, *A Foreign Place*, 100); Reynolds, 'Gentlemen Take Polaroids', 111 ('bigger').

142 Reynolds, *A Foreign Place*, 49; Wallace, 'Five Decades Of Duran Duran', 54.

143 Zaleski, *Rio*, 47, 142.

144 The idea was borrowed, but the sound wasn't sampled: one band used an arpeggiator, the other an LFO; Wyndham Wallace review of *Quiet Life* 2021 reissue in *CP* (March/April 2021), 90.

145 Zaleski, *Rio*, 7-8, 138.

146 Power, *David Sylvian*, 50 ('fashion'). I here borrowed the title phrase of Dean and Leibsohn's 'Hybridity And Its Discontents', but the phrase goes back to at least 2000.

147 Lindsay, 'Strange Fascination', 12.

148 'Stand And Deliver' was the lead single from Adam and the Ants' third

album, *Prince Charming* (CBS, November 1981); it was number one for five weeks in May and June in the UK (in the US, where the Second British Invasion had yet to land, it peaked at number 38 on *Billboard*'s Dance chart). In 2009, No Doubt covered the song and released it as a promotional single.

149 As Rob Sheffield put it, 'No other genre would have wanted them, but new wave had to take them in because it was the island of misfit toys, with funny-looking people who decided to be gorgeous and boring-looking people who decided to be funny-looking' (*Talking To Girls*, 81).

150 Visage released two top 20 albums in the UK, in 1980 and early 1982, before a third flopped and the band dissolved in 1985 (to re-form repeatedly in this century); it thus peaked before the Second British Invasion of the US began in the summer of 1982. 'Fade To Grey' was number eight in the UK, and number one in Germany and Switzerland.

151 Lindsay, 'Strange Fascination', 9.

152 Zaleski, *Rio*, 105.

153 The cover can be found on numerous websites and as the final image in the colour gallery to Jones, *Sweet Dreams*. Tellingly, the cover designers were more likely referencing 'England Swings (Like A Pendulum Do)', the 1965 country music hit (in both the UK and US) by Oklahoman singer-songwriter Roger Miller, than they were Japan's 'Swing'.

154 Zaleski, *Rio*, 137.

155 Karn, *Japan And Self*, 189.

156 Karn, *Japan And Self*, 189, 222; Roberts, 'A Quiet Storm', 76.

157 'Japan: Occidents Will Happen'; also quoted in Jones, *Sweet Dreams*, 417.

158 Zaleski, *Rio*, 10.

159 Jones, *Sweet Dreams*, 418, 419 (Napier-Bell; on the band's hairstyle development, see Reynolds, *A Foreign Place*, 106); Zaleski, *Rio*, 56; Power, *David Sylvian*, 54.

160 John Earls in *CP* (February 2019), 26.

161 Lindgren, 'Fresh Tunes'.

162 Berlin, 'Abba singer' ('weight' quote is Faltskog herself).

163 Jason Anderson in *Ultimate Music Guide*, 114 ('proponent'); Doyle, *Running Up That Hill*, 100-7, 293; Napier-Bell, *Lunch*, x.

164 Roberts, 'A Quiet Storm', 73-74.

165 Napier-Bell, *Lunch*, 176, 214, 265, 290; Thomson, *Under The Ivy*, 107-231; Doyle, *Running Up That Hill*, 7, 74.

166 Blabey, *Thelma The Unicorn*. 'Fatal fame' is from 'Frankly, Mr. Shankly' on The Smiths' *The Queen Is Dead* (1986); the hilarious little song is apparently a barb aimed at Geoff Travis, then the head of Rough Trade, the label which the band left after conflict over this album.

167 Browning and Hill, 'The Price Of Online Fame', 6 ('parasocial'); Fitzmaurice,

'Hating Fame', 39 ('perils'). Mitchell's immortal phrase, 'the starmaker machinery behind the popular song' is in 'Free Man In Paris' on *Court And Spark* [Asylum, 1974]; the remaining quote by Mitchel is in Nelson, *Court And Spark*, 51-58, 111.

168 Jeffery, *Once Upon A Time*, 63. I am not suggesting that popular music's gender problem is a thing of the past: for example, of the 700 songs that topped the US charts in 2012-18, 21.7% were by female artists and 2.1% were produced by women (Padgett, *I'm Your Fan*, 51-52). In the 2000s, 23% of those in music promotion and management, and only 5% of producers and engineers, were women. Furthermore, while women in that decade sang in numbers almost equal to men, band musicians were 2-10% female (depending on the instrument) – an increase from the 1980s, when one study suggested musicians in pop/rock bands were a mere 3% female (Stone, 'Feminism', 54).

169 Petrusich, *Pink Moon*, 114.

170 Cavanagh, *The Piper At The Gates Of Dawn*, 51; Napier-Bell, *Lunch*, 176.

171 Coscarelli, 'Raw And Ready', 13; Weaver, 'Keke Palmer', 4.

172 Roberts, 'A Quiet Storm', 74-76.

173 Napier-Bell, *Lunch*, 63; Reynolds, *Cries And Whispers*, 25.

174 Paul Morley, quoted in *CP* (May 2019), 49, and in O'Brien, 'Tin Drum', 115; John Earls in *CP* (February 2019), 28; also see Reynolds, *A Foreign Place*, 159.

175 Roberts, 'A Quiet Storm', 73; O'Brien, 'Tin Drum', 117; Power, *David Sylvian*, 60-61.

176 Power, *David Sylvian*, 48, 62; O'Brien, 'Tin Drum', 115.

177 Roberts, 'A Quiet Storm', 73-74.

178 Quote is borrowed from description of *Tin Drum* track and fourth single, 'Visions Of China', in *CP, Classic Pop Presents 1981* (Special Edition, 2021), 74. Note that *Tin Drum* producer Steve Nye, protégé and former sound engineer to Japan's previous producer, John Punter, had, in 1980, produced Sakamoto's debut solo album, *B-2 Unit*.

179 Reynolds, *A Foreign Place*, 140, 159.

180 I am drawing here upon Edward Said's iconic *Orientalism*; also see Keaveney, *Western Rock Artists*, 5.

181 Reynolds, *A Foreign Place*, 139.

182 Karn, *Japan And Self*, 327-32; Reynolds, *A Foreign Place*, 123, 133.

183 Reynolds, *A Foreign Place*, 134-35, 141.

184 O'Brien, 'Tin Drum', 117; Reynolds, *A Foreign Place*, 143.

185 Reynolds, *A Foreign Place*, 191. Even Japan's Bowie influences had been worked through to the point where they were no longer transparent, as symbolised perhaps by the lack of any mention of Bowie's cover of 'Wild Is The Wind' as an inspiration for 'Ghosts' – despite the fact that the 1976 *Station To Station* album track was released as a single in November 1981

to promote the *Changestwobowie* compilation, reaching number 24 just four months before 'Ghosts' was a hit. I might be wrong – Arena thinks the 'Ghosts' chorus line, 'blew wilder than the wind', is a Dylan reference (*Sylvian As A Philosopher*, 14-15) – but I suspect Sylvian was inspired by the *Station To Station* track, and critics failed to pick up on the coincidence of it being released as a single the month *Tin Drum* came out.

186 Silverman and Restall, 'Hello Earth' (which includes mention of those first videos, which spawned, what is today, a global phenomenon; see Wikipedia and other online coverage of 'The Most Wuthering Heights Day Ever'); Thomson, *Under The Ivy*, 56-175; Hegarty and Halliwell, *Beyond And Before*, 259-65; Gaar, *She's A Rebel*, 222-24; Young, *Electric Eden*, 568-71; *Ultimate Music Guide*, 18-21, 114; *Record Collector Presents*, 32, 56. Bush's debut album failed to crack the top 200 in the US, and her next two albums (1978's *Lionheart* and 1980's *Never For Ever*) were consequently not even released there until 1984 – when they, too, failed to chart. This was a self-fulfilling prophecy by EMI; veteran music manager Gail Colson: 'If we believe the A&R men, Kate Bush will never make it in America. Because her voice 'isn't right for American radio'. Which is a terrible thing. What does that mean...?' (Gaar, *She's A Rebel*, 316-17).

187 Reynolds, 'Kate Bush'; also next paragraph ('middlebrow'); *Melody Maker* interview reprinted in *Ultimate Music Guide*, 6-9; Thomas, *Kate Bush*, 13-14 (I borrow 'jaw-dropping' from him).

188 1982 *NME* interview quoted in Gaar, *She's A Rebel*, 223; *History Of Rock*, 38-43 (1978 *Melody Maker* interviews); Doyle, *Running Up That Hill*, 105 ('scary', 2005); Shenton, *Kate Bush*, 88 ('sweet' and 'cuddly').

189 Doyle, *Running Up That Hill*, 74; Solanas, 'The Barmy Dreamer'.

190 Doyle, *Running Up That Hill*, 70, 79; Sara-Jane Power in *Record Collector Presents*, 53 ('unprecedented').

191 Hegarty and Halliwell, *Beyond And Before*, 264-68; Silverman and Restall, 'Hello Earth'. Bush has said that her trip to the US to sit 'in a hotel room with a cup of tea talking to some journalists' did little to help sales, but the popularity of the 12' version of 'Running Up That Hill' did (Doyle, *Running Up That Hill*, 293).

192 Hegarty and Halliwell, *Beyond And Before*, 259.

193 Alun Hamnett in *Record Collector Presents*, 45 ('one writer').

194 Despite its Australian connection, 'The Dreaming' single peaked at number 91 in that country; Thomas, *Kate Bush*, 45-46. The quotes above are on the album's Wikipedia page, but also see Lindsay, '30 Years On'; Lindsay, 'The Dreaming'; Silverman and Restall, 'Hello Earth'; Thomson, *Under The Ivy*, 176-96; also, music press and Bush quotes in Shenton, *Kate Bush*, 29 ('oddball'), 81 ('cornerstone'), 103 ('seems mad'); the fan is David Brown in *Record Collector Presents*, 57.

195 Previous two paragraphs: Hegarty and Halliwell, *Beyond And Before*, 260-61; Bush quote in *NME* interview quoted on genius.com/albums/Kate-bush/The-dreaming; Thomas, *Kate Bush*, 43-44; Van Der Kiste, *Kate Bush*, 49;

Alun Hamnett in *Record Collector Presents*, 45; Chow, *You're History*, 43-49.

196 1985 Canadian TV interview quoted in Shenton, *Kate Bush*, 85 ('picture').

197 Music press reviews quoted in Shenton, *Kate Bush*, 29 ('oddball'), 81 ('cornerstone'); *Kate Bush Essentials*, 35.

198 Gaar, *She's A Rebel*, 224.

199 Doyle, *Running Up That Hill*, 179.

200 *History Of Rock*, 43 ('a man'); *Record Collector Presents*, 53 ('anger').

201 I am here paraphrasing Washburn's use of 'Rashomon slippage' in his *Southern Accents*, 46; Roberts, 'A Quiet Storm', 76 (Sylvian).

202 Fujii also sang backing vocals on 'Talking Drum', according to Karn; Karn, *Japan And Self*, 327-32.

203 Reynolds, *A Foreign Place*, 162-63, 167, 171-72.

204 Karn, *Japan And Self*, 335-36.

205 Power, *David Sylvian*, 64-65.

206 Napier-Bell, *Lunch*, 48.

207 The Bush brothers come up well over a hundred times in Thomson's biography, *Under The Ivy*, and frequently in Doyle, *Running Up That Hill* (20-36, 68, 81, etc.). The Batt brothers' bond is similarly apparent in Reynolds' *A Foreign Place* and *Cries And Whispers*.

208 *RC* #537 (November 2022), 99; *NME*, 21 February 1976, 31; *NME*, 28 February 1976, 'Thrills' column.

209 Credited simply to Rods, the song peaked at number nine in August; *NME* critics voted it the ninth-best song of 1977. Ed Hollis also produced the track. The band's sound – 'what could have passed as pub rock, but it was harder and faster' (Barnes, *A New Day Yesterday*, Ch. 41 [Loc 10902]) – influenced the development of UK punk more than is often recognised. Eddie and the Hot Rods reformed, split and reformed repeatedly from 1984 into the 2020s, with various personnel changes and the return of old members; as recently as 2022, they were on tour in the UK. After their 1981 split, however, Ed Hollis moved on to work with The Damned, Stiff Little Fingers and Elvis Costello before his heroin addiction ended in tragedy in 1989.

210 *RC*, March 2022, 40; Wardle, *A Perfect Silence*, 33.

211 These kinds of details were sketchy, or wrongly recorded, prior to Wardle's fine work: *A Perfect Silence*, 14-18, 21; next paragraph: 19-20.

212 Wardle, *A Perfect Silence*, 22-34; Leech, *Fearless*, 88-89; Chuter, *Storm, Static, Sleep*, 10.

213 Wardle, *A Perfect Silence*, 35-39, 47; Marsh et al., *Spirit Of Talk Talk*, 24-25; Wright, 'Too Much, Too Soon'.

214 Previous two paragraphs draw on Wardle, *A Perfect Silence*, 37-42 and 43-54 respectively; see also Steel, *Talk Talk*, 11-13.

215 Previous three paragraphs draw on Wardle, *A Perfect Silence*, 56-58, 58-61,

and 63-65 respectively; also see Brenner's own short narrative in Marsh et al., *Spirit Of Talk Talk*, 13-17.

216 Wardle, *A Perfect Silence*, 66-68. The three Miller demos were released in the UK only on a 7' record that came as a bonus with the 1984 release of 'Such A Shame'.

217 Wardle, *A Perfect Silence*, 69.

218 Zaleski, *Rio*, 21; Wardle, *A Perfect Silence*, 69-71. Black remembered Aspden's managerial offer thus: Hollis came into the Island rehearsal room 'and he said, 'Keith just came in and he said he wants to leave and manage us.' I asked Mark what he was going to do, and he said, '*What do you mean?!* I said *yes*, of course – he's given up his [company] car! He's given up his Volvo Estate, you cunt!" (op. cit., 74).

219 Wardle, *A Perfect Silence*, 72-81 ('poacher' on 75); Zaleski, *Rio*.

220 Wardle, *A Perfect Silence*, 81-84.

221 *En.wikipedia.org/wiki/The_Party%27s_Over_(Talk_Talk_album)* likewise ignores Robinson. Wardle, *A Perfect Silence*, 84. The reputation of *The Party's Over* in this century is very different from its original reception, no doubt a result of the band's subsequent critical acclaim; in 2020, *Classic Pop* rated the album in the top 40 finest debut albums of the 1980s (at number 20; David Sylvian's *Brilliant Trees* was number 16); *CP* (February 2020), 38-43.

222 Wardle, *A Perfect Silence*, 86. Fun Boy Three, a new wave pop act founded by Golding and two other former members of the ska band The Specials, were active between 1981-83, enjoying seven UK top 20 hits.

223 *CP, Classic Pop Presents 1982* (Special Edition, 2021), 84; Wardle, *A Perfect Silence*, 87-89.

224 Wardle, *A Perfect Silence*, 88. A recent review in *Classic Pop* suggested that the debut album's 'title track arguably is a takedown of the new romantic movement itself' (*CP*, February 2020, 41); the pre-New Rom roots of the song undermine that argument somewhat, although it does appeal to me, and the timing doesn't mean Hollis didn't think of it that way, especially when singing it to Duran Duran fans.

225 Doyle, *Running Up That Hill*, 7, 13, 74.

226 Wardle, *A Perfect Silence*, 93-95, 98; Steel, *Talk Talk*, 15-20. *The Party's Over*, meanwhile, peaked at number 21 and would spend almost half a year on the album charts.

227 On the possibility that Japan influenced Hollis: there is no evidence of a direct link, but, as critics have observed for decades, while Japan released a trio of increasingly original albums in 1980-81, the budding 'Talk Talk were surely listening.' Specific tracks have been fancied as sources of inspiration – the 'epic piece' that was *Tin Drum*'s 'Sons Of Pioneers', for example, is 'one that I could imagine might have influenced Talk Talk's Mark Hollis' (Roberts, 'A Quiet Storm', 73; O'Brien, 'Tin Drum', 115).

228 Wardle, *A Perfect Silence*, 102, 105, 113; Marsh et al., *Spirit Of Talk Talk*, 37-

44.

229 Previous three paragraphs draw on Wardle, *A Perfect Silence*, 113, 149-50; 114-17; and 119, 121, respectively; see also the interview with Curnow in Marsh et al., *Spirit Of Talk Talk*, 61-63.

230 Wardle, *A Perfect Silence*, 121; Marsh et al., *Spirit Of Talk Talk*, 54; Steel, *Talk Talk*, 26-27.

231 Mednicov, *Pop Art And Popular Music*, 16-114.

232 The live Rotterdam version was so good that EMI released it as a single in the Netherlands, where the other three singles from *It's My Life* had been hits (peaking between number nine and number 31); the full 6:42 of the Rotterdam version is posted variously online, e.g., www.youtube.com/watch?v=uUU0Z4hnAiQ. Also see Marsh et al., *Spirit Of Talk Talk*, 53; Wardle, *A Perfect Silence*, 121, 148-49.

233 Dayal, *Another Green World*, xix; Frere-Jones, 'Ambient Genius'.

234 Catanzarite, *Achtung Baby*, 92.

235 'Loner genius': as Wardle told Wallace, 'Hit … Or Myth?' 40. *Bravo*: Wardle, *A Perfect Silence*, 134-35.

236 Previous two paragraphs draw on Wardle, *A Perfect Silence*, 134, 136; and 82, 122, 144, 149, respectively.

237 Note the contrast between Hollis's unchanging cockney/Essex accent and Bush's unchanging middle-class home-counties accent, with the ever-evolving inflections of Sylvian, the Bowie-like chameleon: Sylvian's working-class London burr as a young Batt softened steadily during the 1980s so that, by 1986, you could 'detect just a trace of cockney running underneath the absence of accent' (interviewer Chris Roberts; Reynolds, *Cries And Whispers*, 86), and in 1989, 'only the faintest trace of South London remains in his voice' (Lester, 'Words Of The Shaman', 40). Soon after that, Sylvian moved to the United States, and by 1999, a British journalist noted that 'his accent has an Anglo-American burr, but his manner seems wholly British' (Walters, 'Notes From A Quiet Life'). By the time of his 2022 BBC interview – his first in 14 years – he had acquired a hybrid accent of region-less Received-Pronunciation English and region-less American. South London was completely gone. 'I apologise for what I'm sure is my mid-Atlantic accent. I've lived in America for 29 years, my children were born here, it's inevitable, but it would annoy the fuck out of me if I had to listen to it', said Sylvian (2022 BBC Radio 6 audio monologue at www.bbc.co.uk/programmes/m001d5w7).

238 Wardle, *A Perfect Silence*, 68-69.

239 Wallace, 'Hit … Or Myth?' 42.

240 For example, the keyboard hook on Neneh Cherry's 1988 worldwide hit, 'Buffalo Stance', which Ramocon co-wrote, is his. Ramocon has suggested it was EMI who blocked him from becoming a formal band member (Wardle, *A Perfect Silence*, 112).

241 Wardle, *A Perfect Silence*, 122-23; Marsh et al., *Spirit Of Talk Talk*, 67-68.

242 Wardle, *A Perfect Silence*, 41.
243 Wardle, *A Perfect Silence*, 106, 108, 140; Wallace, 'Hit ... Or Myth?', 43.
244 Wallace, 'Hit ... Or Myth?' 43; Wardle, *A Perfect Silence*, 151-52, 313-14.
245 Karn, *Japan And Self*, 109; Napier-Bell, *Lunch*, 29-30.
246 Wardle, *A Perfect Silence*, 124-27.
247 Marsh et al., *Spirit Of Talk Talk*, 162-209 (these pages are a richly illustrated summary, with text by Marsh himself, of his work with the band) (Tow quote on 180); Wardle, *A Perfect Silence*, 90-91; Hegarty and Halliwell, *Beyond And Before*, 288. Note that my count of 14 Talk Talk singles omits re-issues and the occasional one-country release.
248 Four paragraphs above, beginning with 'As 1984 dawned', draw upon Wardle, *A Perfect Silence*, 130-32, 135, 137, 139, 143, 147-49.
249 Wardle, *A Perfect Silence*, 145.
250 Fezco, 'Talk Talk Single Is Hot Hot'. After the lazy negativity of their earlier treatment of Talk Talk, full of dismissive sarcasm and knee-jerk Duran Duran references, Hollis simply did not trust journalists and music critics, especially British ones. As a result, he deployed a variety of defensive mechanisms – sullen or cryptic comments, sarcasm and silliness, a flat refusal to discuss his private life and frequent mentions of obscure musical influences (the sincerity of which eluded, confused or irritated interviewers). Wardle found the line in a 1986 interview that deftly sums up the press reaction: 'Talk Talk are a remarkable example of the thin borderline between genius and sheer cretinism' (*A Perfect Silence*, 184; also quoted in Wallace, 'Hit ... Or Myth?' 41).
251 The album's success – it spent 13 weeks in the UK charts – may have been helped by the inclusion of three new studio tracks, albeit all instrumentals, and the re-recording of so much of it that the listener felt as if they'd been invited to an intimate, exclusive performance rather than a noisy Hammersmith Odeon concert. (That was certainly how it felt to me at the time.) Power, *David Sylvian*, 74; Reynolds, *Cries And Whispers*, 22.
252 Bowie allegedly objected to Sylvian's version being played during the movie, and so only the instrumental version (with the same title as the film) is heard prior to the end credits. Bowie remained miffed by Sylvian, for some unknown reason – perhaps a misunderstanding over 'Forbidden Colours' or something back as far as the circumstances of Bowie's introduction to Sylvian by his then-estranged wife Angie in 1977, or perhaps the refusal to let Bowie into Japan's final London gig. Either way, as late as 1992, he feigned ignorance and implied disdain of Sylvian, describing him to fellow Tin Machine member Reeves Gabrels – apparently without intended irony – as 'a peroxide singer who likes to wear make-up and dress like a woman. He was in a strange group called Japan.' Arena, *Sylvian As A Philosopher*, 17; Power, *David Sylvian*, 76-77; Reynolds, *Cries And Whispers*, 15-16 ('peroxide'), 34.
253 The 'Bamboo' double-A single peaked at number 30 in the UK. In addition to working with Sakamoto himself before 'Forbidden Colours', Sylvian had

also contributed to the new album by Akiko Yano, whose second husband was Sakamoto; Karn and Jansen also played on Yano's album. Karn, *Japan And Self*, 340; *CP* (April 2020), 58-61; Reynolds, *Cries And Whispers*, 13-16; Keaveney, *Western Rock Artists*, 179. By the time of his death in 2023, Sakamoto had written almost 50 film soundtracks and made 24 solo studio albums – in addition to recordings with the Yellow Magic Orchestra and numerous other collaborations and projects. Examples are nicely described in *RC* #528 (February 2022), 146; also see *RC* #526 (Christmas 2021), 120.

254 Sandall, 'Unmasking Of The Man From Japan'.

255 *CP* (February 2020), 42 ('as much'); Reynolds, *Cries And Whispers*, 17 ('guest musicians').

256 Reynolds, *Cries And Whispers*, 23.

257 Power, *David Sylvian*, 85; Reynolds, *Cries And Whispers*, 17, 20; Karn, *Japan And Self*, 152-54; sylvianvista.com/2021/02/05/pulling-punches/.

258 Power, *David Sylvian*, 85, 88. In the year he played on *Brilliant Trees*, Isham began contributing to film and television soundtracks, playing on some 150 from 1983 to 2022.

259 Power, *David Sylvian*, 86-87; Matos, 'Mapping The Vast Influence Of Holger Czukay'; Meyer, 'Techno Musician'; Leech, *Fearless*, 17-20.

260 Power, *David Sylvian*, 87-88; Reynolds, *Cries And Whispers*, 17, 20-21.

261 Reesman, 'Pop Provocateur'; Power, *David Sylvian*, 87; Reynolds, *Cries And Whispers*, 21; Matos, 'Mapping The Vast Influence Of Holger Czukay.'

262 Power, *David Sylvian*, 81-82.

263 Napier-Bell, *Lunch*, 61-62; Reynolds, *Cries And Whispers*, 25.

264 Batt brothers' quotes in Reynolds, *Cries And Whispers*, 19; 'device' is Reynolds himself (37).

265 Rocksbackpages.com/Library/Artist/david-sylvian; Reynolds, *Cries And Whispers*, 42. The album was also a modest hit in Ireland, where its singles did well ('Guitar' and 'Ink' charting higher than in the UK).

266 Zoladz, 'Designing Music', 9 (Eno); Power, *David Sylvian*, 83. 'My whole life': For Hegarty and Halliwell, *Beyond And Before*, 284, the next phrase is crucial – 'reaching up like a flower, leading my life back to the soil' – as it underscores how the album is 'a meditation on locatedness', emphasising rootedness in the land and an awareness of death as a means to authenticity, in line with the thought of Martin Heidegger.

267 Arena, *Sylvian As A Philosopher*, 50; *Times* quote in Reynolds, *Cries And Whispers*, 42.

268 Hegarty and Halliwell, *Beyond And Before*, 283, for whom *Brilliant Trees* 'established a marker for post-progressive and, to some extent, post-rock.'

269 Derrida, *Specters Of Marx*; Barry, *Compact Disc*, 116-17; Fisher, *Ghosts Of My Life*; and Reynolds, *Retromania*.

270 As Petrusich put it in her brilliant book on the album: *Pink Moon*, 16-17, 60 ('mind'). In a 2009 interview, Sylvian mentioned Nick Drake, along with

Robert Wyatt and Tim Buckley; he primarily had in mind their vocal styles, intimate rather than virtuoso, but the three are also famously tragic figures (Wyatt was partially paralyzed by a fall from a building, the other two died young of overdoses), all underappreciated when their albums were first made. Jazz Magazine/Jazzman #607 (28 October 2009), accessed via *davidsylvian.com/texts/interviews*; Arena, *Sylvian As A Philosopher*, 32-34.

271 Thomson, *Under The Ivy*, 199-204 (on Bush). I have taken license here with Napier-Bell's quote, originally 'I think he has angst in his soul' and in reference to Michael (*Lunch*, 214), but – based on his comments on Sylvian in this book and elsewhere – equably applicable to the Japan singer.

272 'Secrets Of The Beehive' on *musicaficionado.blog/2018/11/07*; Lester, 'Words Of The Shaman', 40.

273 Power, *David Sylvian*, 58, 61, 108; Reynolds, *Cries And Whispers*, 135; *theartsdesk.com/new-music/reissue-cds-weekly-japan*. Also see Reynolds, *Impossible Dream*; and Kijak, *Scott Walker* (under Websites and Films). In his *Scott Walker*, Wilson does not frame his analysis of selected songs in terms of post-rock and genre history, but his book could be read as an argument for Walker's development of a certain kind of dark, disassembled avant-garde rock or post-rock.

274 Power, *David Sylvian*, 9; Reynolds, *Blissed Out*, 22-23; Reynolds, *Bring The Noise*, 42-46. Sylvian once remarked that 'Morrissey and I share a sensibility, but we are also quite different, I think' (Reynolds, *Cries And Whispers*, 136).

275 Previous two paragraphs draw on Power, *David Sylvian*, 39, 46; and 80, 114, respectively.

276 Oasis: Very widely quoted, e.g., *irishtimes.com/culture/the-self-importance-of-being-a-coke-addled-rock-n-roll-star-1.1209567*. 'Agreeable': Power, *David Sylvian*, 82. 'Piece' and 'pruned': Young, *Electric Eden*, 574.

277 Power, *David Sylvian*, 82-83.

278 Young, *On the Periphery*, 16-52.

279 Reynolds, *Blissed Out*, 28.

280 Power, *David Sylvian*, 85, judges *Brilliant Trees* to be 'a deeply personal and, some would say, even courageous record'; Young, *Electric Eden*, 574 ('pressure').

281 Power, *David Sylvian*, 99-100; Young, *On The Periphery*, 53-66. *Melody Maker* dismissed *Alchemy* as 'music for Japanese airports.' Sylvian later explained that the cassette-only release was a reluctant reaction to the tape hiss on the masters acquired from the Japanese studio (Reynolds, *Cries And Whispers*, 78).

282 Power, *David Sylvian*, 145-48; Dafoe, 'Inside The Sleeve Pop'; Reynolds, *Cries And Whispers*, 181-84; *wikipedia.org/wiki/Flux_%2B_Mutability*. The two albums were re-released together, as a double LP and double CD, in 2018 (using the version of *Plight & Premonition* remastered by Sylvian in 2002).

283 Weigel, *The Show That Never Ends*, 266.

284 Young, *Electric Eden*, 575-76; the *Gone To Earth* entry on *davidsylvian.com* (also quoted by Hegarty and Halliwell, *Beyond And Before*, 283).

285 Schwartz, 'The Sound Of Things Falling Apart'. Reynolds rightly draws attention to the 'imperial' drumming performance by Jansen throughout the album (*CP* [Nov/Dec 2021], 49).

286 Young, *Electric Eden*, 576; Power, *David Sylvian*, 104; Young, *On The Periphery*, 67-93. Also see Reynolds, *Cries and Whispers*, 81-99.

287 *Gone To Earth* has always divided critics and fans more than *Trees* and *Secrets* have. In contrast to my view, for example, at the time of its release, Chris Roberts in *Sounds* called it 'an '80s masterpiece ... almost as breathtaking as it is life-giving' (Reynolds, *Cries And Whispers*, 97), and Leech, *Fearless*, 94, recently called the album 'Sylvian's most notable achievement since *Brilliant Trees*.'

288 Power, *David Sylvian*, 130-31; Young, *On The Periphery*, 94-116. 'Melancholic' phrase from *musicaficionado.blog/2018/11/07*.

289 Power, *David Sylvian*, 130, 137-38.

290 Power, *David Sylvian*, 130. Also see Reynolds, *Cries And Whispers*, 123-37. Those who heard only misery in the album would not be surprised that when Sakamoto selected his funeral playlist – anticipating his passing in March 2023 – amidst the Satie, Debussy, Bach and film score selections was one Sylvian track: *Secrets Of The Beehive*'s 'Orpheus'.

291 Power, *David Sylvian*, 126. Pondering the pathos of Sylvian's vocal style, I am reminded of Arena's amusing observation: 'Sylvian is not suitable for karaoke, which is a strong point' (*Sylvian As Philosopher*, 42).

292 Power, *David Sylvian*, 127.

293 Spelman, *Popular Music And The Myths Of Madness*.

294 Power, *David Sylvian*, 133.

295 Wardle, *A Perfect Silence*, 131, 133.

296 Crossley, 'The Colour Of Spring' ('ethereal' and 'poignant'; the guitar solo, attributed here to McIntosh, was actually Curnow on a synthesizer, as detailed below; Wardle, *A Perfect Silence*, 159); op. cit., 181 (*NME*); *snowinberlin.com/colourofspring.html*; Steel, *Talk Talk*, 31-42. Gloomy or not, there was nothing depressing about the sales figures for *The Colour Of Spring*, which marked the peak of Talk Talk's imperial phase in Europe and that success spread to their home country, too: soon after its February 1986 release, the album reached number eight in the UK (their only top 20 album), while proving a huge hit all across continental Europe, climbing to number one in the Netherlands and number three in Switzerland.

297 Wardle, *A Perfect Silence*, 165-67. The memorable guitar riff on 'Life's What You Make It' was played by David Rhodes, best known for playing on most Peter Gabriel solo albums and tours, but who also contributed to three tracks on *The Colour Of Spring*, and who had also played on one version of Japan's 'The Art Of Parties'.

298 Wardle, *A Perfect Silence*, 167 (McIntosh quote). Hollis did not much enjoy having to make a video to promote the single; Tim Pope directed it, and although the two had worked together on previous videos and were friends, Hollis was 'a character. He was very difficult, and the most extreme person I've ever met', Pope noted decades later: 'He was a tricky character to work with, but not with me because, for some reason, we got on' (*CP*, October 2019, 70; a Steve O'Brien interview with Pope). Of the album's four singles, two were international hits: global hit 'Life's What You Make It' reached number 16 in the UK, even charting in the elusive US (at number 90); 'Living In Another World' was a modest hit, going top 40 in half a dozen countries (peaking at number 48 in the UK).

299 Wardle, *A Perfect Silence*, 136.

300 Power, *David Sylvian*, 54.

301 Reynolds, *Cries And Whispers*, 139-79; Power, *David Sylvian*, 134-44; Gett, 'David Sylvian Talks 'Secrets'.' At the time of the tour, *Brilliant Trees* had yet to be released in the US, while neither *Gone To Earth* nor *Secrets Of The Beehive* (both released in the US in 1987) charted there.

302 Power, *David Sylvian*, 142-44.

303 There are various postings of the concert footage: e.g., *youtube.com/watch?v=SNdgw73wTIA*.

304 An example of the footage (accessed September 2022) is *youtube.com/watch?v=IehQA_Mpsso*.

305 Wardle, *A Perfect Silence*, 195-96.

306 Power, *David Sylvian*, 127.

307 Wardle, *A Perfect Silence*, 154, 157, 162. The friend of Sylvian's who introduced him to *The Colour Of Spring* later claimed Sylvian 'loved it' (Reynolds, *Cries And Whispers*, 98).

308 Matos, 'Mapping The Vast Influence Of Holger Czukay'.

309 Wardle, *A Perfect Silence*, 156. Graham Sutton of Bark Psychosis, a band later recognised as central to 1990s post-rock (Leech, *Fearless*, 120-36, 159-64), commented on how taken he was as a teenager by the 'strange and unfamiliar' sonic tones of what 'would end up being a defining Talk Talk sound.' He also cited a third track in this vein, 'It's Getting Late In The Evening', recorded for *The Colour Of Spring* but left off and used as a B-side to 'Life's What You Make It' (Marsh et al., *Spirit Of Talk Talk*, 129-32). As Wardle notes (*A Perfect Silence*, 155), the 'stark, minimal and chorus-free' B-side would signpost Talk Talk's 'way forward.'

310 Henderson, 'Talk Talk'.

311 Previous three paragraphs: Petrusich, 'Merging Lanes' (quotes by her on 70, 72); *musicgenrelist.com*; Fisher, *Ghosts Of My Life*, 8-9.

312 Crosby, *The Measure Of Reality*; Flanders, *A Place For Everything*; Questlove Thompson, 'Collecting Things'; Hornby, *High Fidelity*, 54-55; Milano, *Vinyl Junkies*, 14 (Moore); 'we think': Flanders, also quoted in Mask, 'From A To Z', 63.

313 Hornby, *High Fidelity*, 55; Barnes, *A New Day Yesterday*, Ch. 9 (Loc 3413).

314 Wardle, *A Perfect Silence*, 306.

315 Kernfeld, *What To Listen For In Jazz*.

316 Among many sweeping histories of popular music, I found enjoyable and useful Doggett, *Electric Shock*; and Napier-Bell, *Ta-Ra-Ra-Boom-De-Ay*. A very different but no less engaging history is Spitzer, *The Musical Human*. On jazz/classical categories, Grella, *Bitches Brew*, 30. On pop/classical, see Ross, *Listen To This*, 3-21.

317 Hailed in *Rolling Stone* as 'the ultimate rock & roll call to arms, declaring a new era' when listed in 2004 as number 97 of 'The 500 Greatest Songs of All Time', 'Roll Over Beethoven' is one of the most covered songs in the history of recorded music. The ELO version was on *ELO2* when the band were still making prog rock records; a half-length edited version, which nonetheless makes the same statement about genre, was a hit single (the band's second) in half a dozen countries, the UK and US included. See Delve, *Electric Light Orchestra*, 24-26.

318 As Jeffrey (*Once Upon A Time*, 25) put it, 'Beethoven perhaps would have preferred his deafness to Walter Murphy's chart-topping 'A Fifth Of Beethoven', but the funky clavinet comping that answers the 'ta-ta-taaaaaa' fate motif is a brilliantly pithy musical joke.' A top 30 hit worldwide, the Walter Murphy and the Big Apple Band instrumental topped the US and Canadian charts in 1976.

319 In the words of Robert John Godfrey, self-confessed 'toff' composer and pianist, discussing his work with working-class northern UK band Barclay James Harvest (Barnes, *A New Day Yesterday*, Ch. 15 [Loc 5163]).

320 Edwards, *One Step Beyond*, 113-15; wikipedia.org/wiki/Hooked_on_Classics_(series); *CP* (March/April 2021), 76-79.

321 Kheshti, *Switched-On Bach*, 8, 16.

322 Weigel, *The Show That Never Ends*, 5-6.

323 Weigel, *The Show That Never Ends*, 284; Cavanagh, *The Piper At The Gates Of Dawn*, 123. The music historian is Weigel and the BBC producer is Stewart Cruickshank.

324 *Q* magazine (April 2019), 43, 52, 54; *CP*, *Synthpop*, Volume I, 16-19.

325 'Loops' quote in *CP* (January 2019), 89, which also notes the 'sublime, beatific' quality of the tape-loop compositions that comprised 1978's *Ambient 1: Music For Airports*. 'Proud' quote made in 1988 to Hochman, 'Brian Eno'.

326 Gehr, 'Brian Eno/Various Artists', 72.

327 Weigel, *The Show That Never Ends*, 265 ('as ever'); Hegarty and Halliwell, *Beyond And Before*, 83-86, 210-15, 280-84; Barnes and Kendall, 'I Trust My Feet'.

328 Power, *David Sylvian*, 145-48; Young, *Electric Eden*, 575-76; Barnes and Kendall, 'I Trust My Feet'; Garbarini, 'Robert Fripp'.

329 Reynolds, *Cries And Whispers*, 158; Ian Peel in *CP* (March 2019), 21. Both Wikipedia and Apple Music tags are as of October 2022, liable to have changed by the time you are reading the above, although my point surely still stands. The sub-genre of 'sophisti-pop' is defined as a distinctly mid-1980s British phenomenon (although Talk Talk are not mentioned) in *CP* (July/August 2022), 66-67.

330 Wardle, *A Perfect Silence*, 10; also quoted in Wallace, 'Hit ... Or Myth?' 41.

331 Chuter, *Storm, Static, Sleep*, 11.

332 Wallace, 'Hit ... Or Myth?' 42; Wardle, *A Perfect Silence*, 157-58.

333 Wardle, *A Perfect Silence*, 159; *wikipedia.org/wiki/Ambrosian_Singers*.

334 The previous three paragraphs draw on Wardle, *A Perfect Silence*, 159; 161; and 179-82, respectively; and *snowinberlin.com/colourofspring.html* (note that either Wardle inserts 'lad' after 'well good', or the *Snow In Berlin* website transcription omits it).

335 *Snowinberlin.com/colourofspring.html*. The site includes reviews in their original languages with translations (although those above are mine); note that some positive reviews by British writers are also posted.

336 Wallace, 'Hit ... Or Myth?' 40; Wardle, *A Perfect Silence*, 255.

337 1998 interview accessed at youtu.be/8mTlYPEH3jI.

338 Same 1998 interview accessed at *youtube/8mTlYPEH3jI*. I leave it to the reader to imagine (or hear via YouTube) the dropped 'h', initial 'th' as 'f', internal 'th' as 'v', glottalised 't' and so on, of Hollis's accent. See notes 44 and 257 above on accent.

339 Reynolds, *Blissed Out*, 131-32 ('ethereal'); Steel, *Talk Talk*, 46-63. 'It's Getting Late In The Evening', the above-mentioned B-side (bumped from *Colour* to make way for 'Life's What You Make It'), also heralded *Spirit Of Eden*, as noted by Bark Psychosis's Graham Sutton; Wardle, *A Perfect Silence*, 155; and Leech, *Fearless*, 91-92, 96.

340 'Army' is Brown's phrase: Wardle, *A Perfect Silence*, 212. Also see Marsh et al., *Spirit Of Talk Talk*, 78-79.

341 Brown, *Are We Still Rolling?*, 279-88; Wallace, 'Hit ... Or Myth?', 42; Wardle, *A Perfect Silence*, 200-3; Wallace, 'Spirit Of Eden'. Hollis and Friese-Greene had not invented such a method; it was used by Eno during the making of *Another Green World* in 1975 (Dayal, *Another Green World*, 27, 32, 51, 55, 59), for example. Although Hollis never cited Eno in this context, Eno was very open about his studio method, telling *NME* in 1976 that he had 'tried all kinds of experiments, like seeing how few instructions you could give to the people in order to get something interesting to happen' (ibid., 51).

342 Previous two paragraphs draw on Wardle, *A Perfect Silence*, 205, 207, and 199, 202, 206, respectively.

343 Petrusich, 'What's That Noise?'

344 Previous two paragraphs draw on Wardle, *A Perfect Silence*, 218-20, 23, and 214, 216-17, respectively.

345 Wardle, *A Perfect Silence*, 215-18; Brown, *Are We Still Rolling?*, 285; Leech, *Fearless*, 92.

346 Henderson, 'Talk Talk'; Wardle, *A Perfect Silence*, 229-30; Wallace, 'Spirit Of Eden', 35-36; Marsh et al., *Spirit Of Talk Talk*, 82, 153. Also see Chuter, *Storm, Static, Sleep*, 12-15.

347 CP, *Classic Pop Presents Depeche Mode* (2019), 127; *Q* Magazine (April 2019), 80.

348 Chuter, *Storm, Static, Sleep*, 13.

349 Wallace, 'Hit ... Or Myth?' 42 ('always popular'); Wardle, *A Perfect Silence*, 221-25; Brown, *Are We Still Rolling?*, 288-89; Leech, *Fearless*, 86-97 (nicely contextualising the Talk Talk legend).

350 Wardle, *A Perfect Silence*, 222-35.

351 Wardle, *A Perfect Silence*, 232-34, 237; Wallace, 'Spirit Of Eden', 34 ('elegance'); Young, *Electric Eden*, 578 ('wicked'); Marsh et al., *Spirit Of Talk Talk*, 80-81; Chuter, *Storm, Static, Sleep*, 14-15.

352 Wardle, *A Perfect Silence*, 243-44, 253-54, 267-68; Leech, *Fearless*, 87 (the deft 'bodge' verdict is hers). The court case over *History Revisited* concluded in the summer of 1992.

353 Wardle, *A Perfect Silence*, 257-59.

354 Knopper, *Appetite For Self-Destruction*, 49, 52, 62, 157; Napier-Bell, *Ta-Ra-Ra-Boom-De-Ay*, 282.

355 Wardle, *A Perfect Silence*, 302-3, 318. 'It's My Life' was Hollis's 'Running Up That Hill', which reputedly earned Bush $2.3m in 2022 alone (Doyle, *Running Up That Hill*, 348).

356 Albums by the Jimi Hendrix Experience (1968), Roxy Music (1974), The Pixies (1988) and Happy Mondays (1988).

357 German artist Beuys (1921-1986) was a key inspiration for the work of 23 Envelope, the design agency that created the *Beehive* cover, as well as album covers for bands on the 4AD label (such as Cocteau Twins, Dead Can Dance and This Mortal Coil). 'Pop Song' would not be the only Sylvian cover with a black-and-white photograph of a bare-breasted woman: his compilation album *Sleepwalkers* (2010; 2022) is likewise adorned.

358 Sandall, 'Unmasking Of The Man From Japan'; Lester, 'Words Of The Shaman', 40.

359 Reynolds, *Cries And Whispers*, 184-89.

360 Lester, 'Words Of The Shaman', 41.

361 Sandall, 'Unmasking Of The Man From Japan'.

362 Roberts, 'A Quiet Storm', 73.

363 As articulated by Sean Nelson in *Court And Spark*, 33.

364 Morton, *Spacecraft*, 78; Nelson, *Court And Spark*, 3.

365 Jones, *The Wichita Lineman*, 252.

366 Soloski, 'Debbie Gibson Wants Vinyl', 6-7.

367 Zaleski, *Rio*, 3, 131-32 (Gibson); Sheffield, *Talking To Girls About Duran Duran*, 256; Zaleski, *Rio*, 3 (bracketed aside is mine); Stone, 'Feminism', 56-59.

368 Kelefa Sanneh defined rockism in an October 31, 2004, *NYT* article, cited in Knopper, *Appetite For Self-Destruction*, 101, as 'idolising the authentic old legend (or underground hero) while mocking the latest pop star; lionising punk while barely tolerating disco; loving the live show and hating the music video; extolling the growling performer while hating the lip-syncher.' Also see Wolin, *Golden Hits*, 13-20.

369 Jones, *Sweet Dreams*, 419.

370 Lindsay, '30 Years On'; Lindsay, 'The Dreaming'; Thomas, *Kate Bush*, 40-49.

371 Thomson, *Under The Ivy*, 199 ('doom'); Doyle, *Running Up That Hill*, 146 ('mental').

372 Thomas, *Kate Bush*, 51 ('talent'); Price, 'Hounds Of Love' ('eternity').

373 Price, 'Hounds Of Love' ('masterpiece'); Thomson, *Under The Ivy*, 217, 260.

374 Thomson, *Under The Ivy*, 223, 266; Graeme Thomson in *The Ultimate Music Guide*, 66-75; *Kate Bush Essentials*, 36-49. Youth is Martin Glover (born 1960), founder and bassist in Killing Joke.

375 *Classic Rock Presents Prog*, 47; *Kate Bush Essentials*, 107.

376 Thomson, *Under The Ivy*, 209, 262; Van Der Kiste, *Kate Bush*, 63; *Kate Bush Essentials*, 48; and I thank Dominic Sanderson for prompting some of this analysis.

377 Silverman and Restall, 'Hello Earth'; Cawood, 'Don't let me go!' 44 (rightly calling *Hounds Of Love* 'one of the finest popular music works of the modern era'); Young, *Electric Eden*, 571-73; *CP, Classic Pop Presents Kate Bush* (2022 edition), 54-55.

378 Doyle, *Running Up That Hill*, 346-53 ('weird pop'); Price, 'Hounds Of Love'; Mat Snow in *Kate Bush Essentials*, 40.

379 Barnes, *A New Day Yesterday*, Ch. 42 (Loc 11698).

380 Lindsay, 'Together In Electric Dreams?' 51. Bob Stanley's personal memory of this moment was that Dazzle Ships, 'now-acclaimed' but 'a total misfire at the time', was an album 'I adored and held close as the conservative forces regrouped' (*RC #537* [November 2022], 42).

381 Critic quotes from *Record Mirror*, *Time Out* and the *Sun Times*, all cited in wikipedia.org/wiki/Dazzle_Ships; McCluskey quote in wikipedia.org/wiki/Junk_Culture; and Cárdenas, 'Millennial Pop Music'. Also see classicpopmag.com/2022/09/classic-album-architecture-morality; *CP* (February 2020), 40; Earls, 'Stockhausen or ABBA?'; and Earls, 'Light In The Darkness'.

382 For a view of where the Cocteau Twins fit into the post-rock story (but not as a post-rock artist), see Leech, *Fearless*, 67-72. Although never a synth-pop artist, it is worth mentioning Bowie's 1980s evolution, as his Berlin trilogy played such an influential role in this story: having shifted into mainstream pop in the early 1980s, he then burnt out his imperial pop phase, re-

booting his image and sound by creating the alt-rock Tin Machine; he then re-emerged as an alternative rock artist in the 1990s, an increasingly avant-garde position to take as hip-hop and EDM took over the global music scene. ZTT Records was a London-based label founded in 1983 by Trevor Horn, Paul Morley and Jill Sinclair.

383   Reynolds, *Cries And Whispers*, 70, 76. Amidst the bewildering variety of different versions and editions of *A Secret Wish*, released between 1985 and 2010, one can find some of Sylvian's demo ideas.

384   Spence, *Just Can't Get Enough*, 111 ('blew'), 206-8 (Garden). Rocket 88 will publish a book on 'the visual art of John Foxx' in 2024.

385   Note that Jansen also played on various albums as a session drummer and/or drum programmer (one stand-out example is Annie Lennox's acclaimed 1992 solo debut *Diva* (*CP*, July/August 2022, 31). *Catch The Fall* is a great deal better than its sales record and reputation suggest; Reynolds, *Cries And Whispers*, 108-21.

386   *Worlds In A Small Room* was recorded in 1984 in Tokyo for an unsuccessful home 'Back Ground Videos' series (Reynolds, *Cries And Whispers*, 73-76). Barbieri also joined Jansen in the early 1980s in strengthening musical ties with two Japanese artists, Masami Tsuchiya's band Ippu Do (Tsuchiya had played with Japan) and YMO's Yukihiro Takahashi (Power, *David Sylvian*, 70-71) – whose vocals on his early 1980s solo records have intriguingly been described as a 'Sylvian-like croon' (*RC* [June 2020], 106).

387   Taylor's remarks were made upon Karn's death in January 2011 (*duranduran.com/2011/john-remembers-mick-karn*); Karn's characteristically honest recollection of his *Titles* is in *Japan And Self*, 305-7.

388   Karn, *Japan And Self*, 316, 285, 333, 343-44.

389   Karn, *Japan And Self*, 316-20; Power, *David Sylvian*, 94-95; Reynolds, *Cries And Whispers*, 53-61. Karn and Murphy reconciled and had begun work on a second Dali's Car album when Karn died in January 2011.

390   Karn, *Japan And Self*, 311; Power, *David Sylvian*, 120-22; Len Brown's review in *NME* (21 February 1987) accessed at *rocksbackpages.com*.

391   Karn, *Japan And Self*, 284, 287-88, 323-24, 363; Power, *David Sylvian*, 70, 155; Reynolds, *Cries And Whispers*, 103.

392   Power, *David Sylvian*, 154-56; Reynolds, *Cries And Whispers*, 195-99.

393   Karn, *Japan And Self*, 199, 202-3; Power, *David Sylvian*, 156-57; Reynolds, *Cries And Whispers*, 200-8, 215-19.

394   Music writer Steve O'Brien recently called *Rain Tree Crow* 'incredibly Japan-like ... as if it was simply the next album in line' (*CP* [July/August 2020], 75).

395   Power, *David Sylvian*, 158-59, 161 ('Lanois'); Leech, *Fearless*, 95 ('rockishness'); *CP* (July/August 2020), 75 ('beguiling' is by O'Brien); Burke, 'Japan And David Sylvian', 49; Reynolds, *Cries And Whispers*, 220.

396   Bonus tracks so often ruin the intended impact of closing songs, and in this case, the 2003 addition of the 1:46 instrumental 'I Drink To Forget'

detracts from the sequenced effect of 'Cries And Whispers'. The decision by Reynolds to title his biography of the ex-Japan members during the 1983-91 years *Cries And Whispers* was very apt.

397 Karn, *Japan And Self*, 362, 372; Power, *David Sylvian*, 159-61; Burke, 'Japan And David Sylvian', 49.

398 Burke, 'Japan And David Sylvian', 49; Karn, *Japan And Self*, 362-72; Power, *David Sylvian*, 161. Also see Young, *On The Periphery*, 118-52; *CP* (July/August 2020), 75.

399 On collecting: Milano, *Vinyl Junkies*; Restall, *On Elton John*, chapter 9. Hollis's reputation for winding up journalists, combined with the growing legend of his alleged one-man war with the industry, contributed to the story that the album's title was a deliberate jab at the press and the label, perhaps even at consumers; in fact, Hollis borrowed it from a 1968 B-side by one his favourite bands, Love, a band introduced to him by his brother Ed, and one he mentioned several times in talking about *Laughing Stock* (although not its title). Another Love song title, 'The Daily Planet', would be borrowed to title a track on the *Mark Hollis* solo album (Wardle, *A Perfect Silence*, 255). A balanced, insightful critique of *Laughing Stock* is Steel, *Talk Talk*, 55-63. After Phill Brown had finished with *Laughing Stock*, a job that had lasted a couple of years and almost broken up his marriage, he sat his wife and children down, 'turned out all the lights' and played them the album; afterwards, 'nobody said a word', his wife turned the lights back on and the album was never played in the house again (Brown, *Are We Still Rolling?*, 302).

400 Wardle, *A Perfect Silence*, 245-49; Young, *Electric Eden*, 581; Chuter, *Storm, Static, Sleep*, 16. The extreme loud/quiet contrast is also characteristic of Slint's *Spiderland*, a parallel foundation post-rock album released in the same year as *Laughing Stock* (Tennent, *Spiderland*, 92-93, 138-42).

401 Marsh et al., *Spirit Of Talk Talk*, 144; Brown, *Are We Still Rolling?*, 290, 298, 302-3. The promotional cassette of *Laughing Stock* came with an hour of Hollis talking about the making of the album, including the toll the recording sessions took on everyone; as Chuter, *Storm, Static, Sleep*, 16, notes, Hollis's monologue is 'a fantastic listen', most of which can be found online, albeit in segments (e.g., *youtube.com/watch?v=rARC2TU7VjI*).

402 Wardle, *A Perfect Silence*, 259; Wallace, 'Spirit Of Eden'; Washburn, *Southern Accents*, 40; Morrison, *Avalon*, 19; Pareles, 'Sophie'. Also see Moorefield, *The Producer As Composer*.

403 Young, *Electric Eden*, 582; Wardle, *A Perfect Silence*, 251.

404 Young, *Electric Eden*, 582 (from whom I borrowed the adjective 'purging'); Wardle, *A Perfect Silence*, 247, 251-52, 263; Brown, *Are We Still Rolling?*, 296, 300.

405 Young, *Electric Eden*, 579, 581; Leech, *Fearless*, 97 ('no notes'); Garvey quote found in many places, but e.g., Crossley, 'The Colour Of Spring'.

406 Napier-Bell, *Lunch*, 265.

407 Gordon, 'Growing Older', 17.

408 Cavanagh, *The Piper At The Gates Of Dawn*, 121.
409 Thomson, *Under The Ivy*, 256; Silverman and Restall, 'Hello Earth'; Power, *David Sylvian*, 176. Derek 'Del' Palmer (1952-2024) died shortly before this book went to press.
410 Power, *David Sylvian*, 163.
411 Power, *David Sylvian*, 165 ('murmur'), 88 (Czukay); Reynolds, *Cries And Whispers*, 21, 124; *CP* (November/December 2021), 49.
412 Power, *David Sylvian*, 163; Reynolds, *Cries And Whispers*, 126.
413 Arena, *Sylvian As A Philosopher*, 44; Power, *David Sylvian*, 167-69.
414 Power, *David Sylvian*, 171, 173; Young, *On The Periphery*, 153-73.
415 Power, *David Sylvian*, 175-83. The 1994 *Damage* release was mixed by Fripp; Sylvian remixed and re-released it in 2002 (Walker, 'The Artsy Rocker').
416 *Ember Glance* is actually two pieces, consisting mostly of 'The Beekeeper's Apprentice' followed by the brief 'Epiphany'.
417 Power, *David Sylvian*, 173.
418 Sullivan, 'Robert Fripp Unfixes Rock'.
419 Barry, *Compact Disc*, 5, 40-57 (quotes on 5, 55, 56, 57); Knopper, *Appetite For Self-Destruction*, 37-38. Philips engineer Kees Immink remembers the negotiations slightly differently (*wikipedia.org/wiki/Kees_Schouhamer_Immink*).
420 Or, if the CD versions of *Secrets Of The Beehive* are counted, 40 minutes. The double 80-minute LP *Gone To Earth* is counted as two LPs of 40 minutes each. Obviously, all minute counts are rounded out.
421 Doyle, *Running Up That Hill*, 226 ('pee'); Thomas, *Kate Bush*, 91 ('breathing space').
422 Both quotes by Barry, *Compact Disc*, 5; also see 131.
423 Barry, *Compact Disc*, 102; Padgett, *I'm Your Fan*, 132; Knopper, *Appetite For Self-Destruction*, 208, 210, 243.
424 Barry, *Compact Disc*, 112-13; also see Fisher, *Ghosts Of My Life*.
425 Wardle, *A Perfect Silence*, 270-75. Wimbledon is an upscale corner of the great southern swathe of the Green Belt that birthed the Batts and Bush.
426 Wardle, *A Perfect Silence*, 277-81; Brown, *Are We Still Rolling?*, 336-50. The album briefly charted in the UK, reaching number 53.
427 Wardle, *A Perfect Silence*, 286-87; Wyndham Wallace in *CP* (December 2019), 88 ('fragile'); Smith, 'This Album Changed My Life'; Stubbs, 'Talking Liberties'.
428 Young, *Electric Eden*, 582-84; Wardle, *A Perfect Silence*, 295; Cowley, 'The Journey From Talk Talk.'
429 Reynolds, *Blissed Out*, 132, also quoted by Hegarty and Halliwell, *Beyond And Before*, 288. As American Music Club's Mark Eitzel remarked in *Melody Maker* – referring to 'New Grass' but he might have been talking about the

whole album: 'By the end, it's almost like he's had a religious revelation. I'm not saying he did. Maybe he just would have liked to have had one. But that's enough' (Marsh et al., *Spirit Of Talk Talk*, 87).

430   Young, *Electric Eden*, 583; Wardle, *A Perfect Silence*, 291; Hegarty and Halliwell, *Beyond And Before*, 286.
431   Wardle, *A Perfect Silence*, 265, 298-99.
432   Marsh et al., *Spirit Of Talk Talk*, 226; Wardle, *A Perfect Silence*, 314-17.
433   Brëes, *In A Silent Way*; Wardle, *A Perfect Silence*, 293; Marsh et al., *Spirit Of Talk Talk*, 9; Cowley, 'The Journey From Talk Talk'. Because Brëes neither gained access to Hollis nor won permission to use his original recordings, *In A Silent Way* has a meta-narrative quality to it that I think Hollis – ironically – would have appreciated.
434   Wyndham Wallace in *CP* (December 2019), 88.
435   Shepherd, 'He Was Made In Japan'.
436   Shepherd, 'He Was Made In Japan'; Power, *David Sylvian*, (2012 edition) Loc. 2849.
437   *CP* (February 2019), 88.
438   *CP* (May 2019), 49; Walters, 'Notes From A Quiet Life.'
439   Walters, 'Notes From A Quiet Life'; I agree with Reynolds that the longer re-issue is 'more cohesive': *CP* (November/December 2021), 50.
440   Power, *David Sylvian*, (2012 edition) Loc. 2794. On the album and the years surrounding it, also see Young, *On The Periphery*, 185-235.
441   Petrusich, 'Domestic Arts', 88.
442   Arena, *Sylvian As A Philosopher*, 35.
443   Reesman, 'Pop Provocateur'.
444   Hyland, 'Kacey Musgraves Is In Her Feelings'.
445   Partial enough to write a book on it: Restall, *Blue Moves*.
446   Indeed, the track was created by Sylvian laying down sounds on synths and guitar that he then edited using samplers, after which it was played five times to British jazz pianist John Taylor (1942-2015) (a founder of acclaimed British jazz trio Azimuth with another Sylvian collaborator, Kenny Wheeler [mentioned in chapter 9], Taylor taught numerous classical and jazz musicians and taught jazz piano at the Cologne College of Music and the University of York). Taylor then laid down the piano track in one take, although Sylvian and Nye further manipulated it. Reynolds, *Cries And Whispers*, 186-87.
447   As the closing track to the instrumental album, *Camphor*, and added to the 2003 reissue of *Alchemy*. The timing of these releases (1989 and 2002/2003) with breakup crises in Sylvian's personal life is approximate.
448   Both quotes in Burke (who is the 'critic'), 'Japan And David Sylvian', 49.
449   Toop, 'David Sylvian'.
450   *CP* (November/December 2021), 50; Prasad, 'Chasing The Muse', 146; *CP*

(September/October 2022), 91. In the 2022 BBC audio monologue (styled as a Radio 6 'interview'), Sylvian talked of the recording of *Blemish* entirely in technical terms, as motivated by a desire to do something 'improvisational', 'new', 'radical', with no mention of the emotional content or context (*www.bbc.co.uk/programmes/m001d5w7*).

451 Toop, 'David Sylvian'. In 2022, Sylvian himself called the guitar work and orchestration by Christian Fennesz, credited with co-writing the song, 'gorgeous' and 'really beautiful' (*www.bbc.co.uk/programmes/m001d5w7*).

452 Prasad, 'Chasing The Muse', 146.

453 'Deep' quote in Chris Roberts' eloquent review of the 2022 vinyl re-release in *RC* #537 (November 2022), 104. Also see Young, *On The Periphery*, 238-64.

454 Walker, 'The Artsy Rocker'. The compilations were a two-CD compilation, *Everything And Nothing* (2000), and the all-instrumental compilation *Camphor* (2002).

455 Crawford, 'A Man For This Season', 124. Also see Young, *On The Periphery*, 285-99.

456 Posted online and quoted by Young, *On The Periphery*, 341 (also see 300-36). Sylvian's comment on Thomas in *CP* (November/December 2021), 51.

457 As of 2022, still posted at wikipedia.org/wiki/David_Sylvian (but not on the *Manafon* page), citing 'David Sylvian By Keith Rowe', in *Bomb Magazine* (1 April 2010; retrieved for Wikipedia on 12 January 2015; accessed by me at bombmagazine.org/articles/david-sylvian/). For those wanting a dive into the darkest deep end of Sylvian's work, courtesy of fresh vinyl, *Blemish* and *Manafon* were given 180g re-issues by his own label, Samadhi Sound, in 2022. The review in *CP* (September/October 2022), 91, found *Manafon* the 'more approachable' of the two, lacking the 'unrelentingly grim' moments of *Blemish*.

458 I refer to Simon Reynolds and Mark Fisher; Fisher, *Ghosts Of My Life*, 6, 16.

459 Hegarty and Halliwell, *Beyond And Before*, 259-67, 275-77. Also see *CP, Classic Pop Presents Kate Bush* (2022 edition), 78-79. According to Doyle, *Running Up That Hill*, 269, Bush conceived of *Aerial* 'very much as an extended *Hounds Of Love*.'

460 Young, *Electric Eden*, 7; 'meditation' quote by Hegarty and Halliwell, *Beyond And Before*, 277. On *Close To The Edge*, also see Weigel, *The Show That Never Ends*, 104-10.

461 Cawood, 'Don't Let Me Go!', 48.

462 Hegarty and Halliwell, *Beyond And Before*, 275-77; on 'recluse', Doyle, *Running Up That Hill*, 3.

463 Doyle in *Kate Bush Essentials*, 105; Thomas, *Kate Bush*, 118-22. Also see Silverman and Restall, 'Hello Earth'.

464 Michael Bonner in *The Ultimate Music Guide*, 96; Quantick, 'Aerial'.

465 Erskine in 'An Architect's Dream', *Uncut* issue 316 (December 2023), 99; O'Brien, 'Aerial', 75.

466 Thomas, *Kate Bush*, 100 (I've pluralised his 'masterclass' line); Van der Kiste, *Kate Bush*, 105.
467 Young, *Electric Eden*, 567.
468 Stone, 'Feminism', 63; Hegarty and Halliwell, *Beyond And Before*, 267.
469 Empire, 'Admit It, Guys, She's A Genius'.
470 Silverman and Restall, 'Hello Earth'. The BBC Radio 4 *Woman's Hour* interview of Bush and Moran by Emma Barnett on 22 June 2022 can easily be found on bbc.co.uk, youtube.com and various podcast sites.
471 Thomson, *Under The Ivy*, 299; Silverman and Restall, 'Hello Earth'.
472 Thomson, *Under The Ivy*, 253-54, 256, 294, 306.
473 Thomson, *Under The Ivy*, 287.
474 Or, as Hegarty and Halliwell put it, the album 'explores a natural phenomenon that is equally quotidian, universal and mythical' (*Beyond And Before*, 264).
475 *Uncut* issue 316 (December 2023), 100.
476 Bush interviewed in *The Quietus*, quoted in *The Ultimate Music Guide*, 104; see also Simonert, 'Snow Queen'.
477 Moy, *Kate Bush*, 133 ('beast'); Doyle, *Running Up That Hill*, 299 ('haunting'); see also Kevin Harley in *Record Collector Presents*, 99.
478 Doyle, *Running Up That Hill*, 299; Thomas, *Kate Bush*, 116. Also see Silverman and Restall, 'Hello Earth'.
479 Young, *Electric Eden*, 584-85; rocksbackpages.com/Library/Article/bark-psychosis-ihexi/; Chuter, *Storm, Static, Sleep*, 20-23.
480 One review of *Drift Code* called Webb's voice 'Robert Wyatt mimicking Mark Hollis': *CP* (February 2019), 82; *CP* (April 2019), 19 (Webb's quotes); *CP* (September 2019), 10; *CP* (November 2019), 88; *CP* (March 2020), 83.
481 *CP* (May/June 2022), 14-15, 93. Talk Talk album cover artist James Marsh is credited with the 'Logo' and the cover painting by Nicola Stockley is a tribute to Marsh's work with the band. The project's scenius of 25 musicians included Martin Ditcham, Robbie McIntosh and Laurence Pendrous, all mentioned in this book, and five of the eight tracks were mixed by Phill Brown. The project's creator, David Joseph, emphasised that 'we're not Talk Talk' and the album was assembled with 'utmost care and reverence' for the Hollis legacy.
482 Barnes, *A New Day Yesterday*.
483 Karn quotes in previous three paragraphs: Karn, *Japan And Self*, 172-73; 109, 381; 380.
484 Weigel, *The Show That Never Ends*, 258; Tipp, 'Spellbound', 31; also see Hegarty and Halliwell, *Beyond And Before*.
485 Tipp, 'Spellbound'; *CP* (March/April 2021), 86.
486 Karn, *Japan And Self*, 380.
487 Reynolds, *A Foreign Place*, 159, 173.

488 See *sylvianvista.com/2018/09/07/playground-martyrs/*.

489 Accessed at *theguardian.com/music/2007/dec/07/jazz.shopping3*. Note that a triple-CD version of *Slope*, including a 2008 live recording made in Tokyo, as well as additional ambient tracks, was released in 2013.

490 Leech, *Fearless*, 98-101. On the early history of Walker, through to the final dissolution of the 'brothers' band, see *The Impossible Dream* by the always-worth-reading Anthony Reynolds; Wilson, *Scott Walker*, focuses more on the later solo albums. On Sylvian and Walker: Reynolds, *Cries And Whispers*, 126.

491 Fisher, *Ghosts Of My Life*, 156.

492 The John Foxx and the Maths album that sounds most like *Systems Of Romance* is *Howl* (2020), not coincidentally made after Robin Simon – who was also in Ultravox when *Systems* was made – had joined the Maths. Jones, 'Howling Into The Void'; *factmag.com/2010/05/26/john-foxx-systems-of-romance/*; Hensey, 'The Strange World' ('frontiers').

493 Leech, *Fearless*, 346. Also see Reynolds, *Bring The Noise*, 186-93. On *Kid A*, see Hyden, *This Isn't Happening*. Hegarty and Halliwell, *Beyond And Before*, 293-99, argue that, on *OK Computer* (1997), Radiohead used a kind of progressive rock to 'blow apart the genre of 'alternative rock", so as to then 'dismantle [their] own sound' on *Kid A*; that album in turn gave 'mainstream listeners the chance to engage with experimental and difficult music' (298), which, it seems to me, could be said of *Spirit Of Eden*.

494 *RC* (August 2022), 137.

495 Lester, 'Paddy McAloon'. Also see the album-by-album overview in *CP* (July/August 2021), 48-51; and *CP* (December 2019), 87.

496 McAloon quotes in Lester, 'Paddy McAloon'; 'easily' quote by John Earls in *CP* (July/August 2021), 51.

497 The album is introduced in Chapter 1; also see *CP* (November/December 2021), 51.

498 Initially posted on 27 October 2022 on BBC Radio 6, the interview was temporarily available at *www.bbc.co.uk/programmes/m001d5w7*. His comments on Samadhi and his albums on the label are a shorter version of the two-page essay in the book accompanying the *Do You Know Me Now?* box set. Following his summary of his label's history, Sylvian spent about ten more minutes (similarly interspersed with excerpts of music) responding to questions unheard by us, perhaps written by the BBC's Mary Anne Hobbs, including one on Japan: 'I can honestly say that I've not heard a note of that material since the band broke up.'

499 For Bush books, see the detailed list in *CP*, *Classic Pop Presents Kate Bush* (2022 edition), 122-23 (which did not yet include Doyle, *Running Up That Hill*). The 'career in reverse' quote by Depeche Mode's Wilder is cited in Chapter 2 (Wallace, 'Hit ... Or Myth?' 41; Marsh et al., *Spirit Of Talk Talk*, 139).

500 The length of 'ARB Section 1' is variously described (e.g., 'less than a minute long'; Wallace, 'Hit ... Or Myth?' 39), but it is given 1:32 on the soundtrack

album and that appears to be a triple loop of the single 30-second composition that was included on the TV episode.

501 Siegel, 'Going 'Inside The Music".

502 Hsu, 'Machine Yearning'; Jones, *Wichita Lineman*, 251-52. Also see Sloan and Harding, 'The Culture Warped Pop'.

503 Earls, 'Being Human' 24; *CP* (September/October 2021), 36.

504 Wardle, *A Perfect Silence*, 245, 290.

505 *CP* (September/October 2021), 36; Wallace, 'Hit ... Or Myth?' 40; Arena, *Sylvian As A Philosopher*, 8, 19, 29, 46.

506 Biguenet, *Silence*, 3.

507 Sylvian quote from a 2007 interview with Arena, in *Sylvian As A Philosopher*, 24; Biguenet, *Silence*, 4 ('world').

508 As mentioned in Chapter 5, *Quiet Life* was technically released on 17 November 1979, but only Canadians could find it in record shops that month (and they cleared the shelves, as the band played in Toronto the following weeks); the Japanese had it on 20 December, but distribution problems meant that it was not available in the UK (and many other countries) until 18 January 1980.

509 The 1984 CD release of *Exorcising Ghosts* contained only 11 of the 16 tracks on the 1984 double vinyl release; the latter is thus by far the superior version, and it was re-issued as a half-speed mastered 2LP in 2022. A fuller discography of Japan and Sylvian, at least through 1998 in the book's first edition, is in Power, *David Sylvian*, 191-208; also see the discographies on the official and fan websites listed below.

510 Note that the two editions of *Sleepwalkers* vary by two tracks: the 2022 version omits two of Sylvian's collaborations with his brother (originally on Jansen's *Slope*), substituting a 2011 collaboration with Jan Bang and Sylvian's 2013 single 'Do You Know Me Know?' The double LP 2022 edition was also the first issue of the compilation on vinyl.

511 A comprehensive evaluation of the discography of Talk Talk and former band members – including Tim Friese-Greene, whom I omitted – is Steel, *Talk Talk*.

512 As mentioned in chapter 7, as *The Kick Inside* did not chart in the US, the second and third Bush albums were not released there until after *The Dreaming*, when they then failed to chart (*Lionheart* reached number 201 in 1984). I have not included chart re-appearances, such as *Hounds Of Love*'s 2022 resurgence. For a chronological evaluation of the Bush catalogue, see Silverman and Restall, 'Hello Earth'; and Thomas, *Kate Bush*.

Also available from Sonicbond

On Track Series
AC/DC – Chris Sutton 978-1-78952-307-2
Allman Brothers Band – Andrew Wild 978-1-78952-252-5
Tori Amos – Lisa Torem 978-1-78952-142-9
Aphex Twin – Beau Waddell 978-1-78952-267-9
Asia – Peter Braidis 978-1-78952-099-6
Badfinger – Robert Day-Webb 978-1-878952-176-4
Barclay James Harvest – Keith and Monica Domone 978-1-78952-067-5
Beck – Arthur Lizie 978-1-78952-258-7
The Beat, General Public, Fine Young Cannibals –
Steve Parry 978-1-78952-274-7
The Beatles – Andrew Wild 978-1-78952-009-5
The Beatles Solo 1969-1980 – Andrew Wild 978-1-78952-030-9
Blue Oyster Cult – Jacob Holm-Lupo 978-1-78952-007-1
Blur – Matt Bishop 978-178952-164-1
Marc Bolan and T.Rex – Peter Gallagher 978-1-78952-124-5
Kate Bush – Bill Thomas 978-1-78952-097-2
The Byrds – Andy McArthur 978-1-78952-280-8
Camel – Hamish Kuzminski 978-1-78952-040-8
Captain Beefheart – Opher Goodwin 978-1-78952-235-8
Caravan – Andy Boot 978-1-78952-127-6
Cardiacs – Eric Benac 978-1-78952-131-3
Wendy Carlos – Mark Marrington 978-1-78952-331-7
The Carpenters – Paul Tornbohm 978-1-78952-301-0
Nick Cave and The Bad Seeds – Dominic Sanderson 978-1-78952-240-2
Eric Clapton Solo – Andrew Wild 978-1-78952-141-2
The Clash – Nick Assirati 978-1-78952-077-4
Elvis Costello and The Attractions – Georg Purvis 978-1-78952-129-0
Crosby, Stills and Nash – Andrew Wild 978-1-78952-039-2
Creedence Clearwater Revival – Tony Thompson 978-178952-237-2
The Damned – Morgan Brown 978-1-78952-136-8
David Bowie 1964 to 1982 – Carl Ewens 978-1-78952-324-9
Deep Purple and Rainbow 1968-79 – Steve Pilkington 978-1-78952-002-6
Depeche Mode – Brian J. Robb 978-1-78952-277-8
Dire Straits – Andrew Wild 978-1-78952-044-6
The Divine Comedy – Alan Draper 978-1-78952-308-9
The Doors – Tony Thompson 978-1-78952-137-5
Dream Theater – Jordan Blum 978-1-78952-050-7
Bob Dylan 1962-1970 – Opher Goodwin 978-1-78952-275-2
Eagles – John Van der Kiste 978-1-78952-260-0
Earth, Wind and Fire – Bud Wilkins 978-1-78952-272-3
Electric Light Orchestra – Barry Delve 978-1-78952-152-8
Emerson Lake and Palmer – Mike Goode 978-1-78952-000-2
Fairport Convention – Kevan Furbank 978-1-78952-051-4
Peter Gabriel – Graeme Scarfe 978-1-78952-138-2

Also available from Sonicbond

Genesis – Stuart MacFarlane 978-1-78952-005-7
Gentle Giant – Gary Steel 978-1-78952-058-3
Gong – Kevan Furbank 978-1-78952-082-8
Green Day – William E. Spevack 978-1-78952-261-7
Steve Hackett – Geoffrey Feakes 978-1-78952-098-9
Hall and Oates – Ian Abrahams 978-1-78952-167-2
Peter Hammill – Richard Rees Jones 978-1-78952-163-4
Roy Harper – Opher Goodwin 978-1-78952-130-6
Hawkwind (new edition) – Duncan Harris 978-1-78952-290-7
Jimi Hendrix – Emma Stott 978-1-78952-175-7
The Hollies – Andrew Darlington 978-1-78952-159-7
Horslips – Richard James 978-1-78952-263-1
The Human League and The Sheffield Scene –
Andrew Darlington 978-1-78952-186-3
Humble Pie –Robert Day-Webb 978-1-78952-2761
Ian Hunter – G. Mick Smith 978-1-78952-304-1
The Incredible String Band – Tim Moon 978-1-78952-107-8
INXS – Manny Grillo 978-1-78952-302-7
Iron Maiden – Steve Pilkington 978-1-78952-061-3
Joe Jackson – Richard James 978-1-78952-189-4
The Jam – Stan Jeffries 978-1-78952-299-0
Jefferson Airplane – Richard Butterworth 978-1-78952-143-6
Jethro Tull – Jordan Blum 978-1-78952-016-3
Elton John in the 1970s – Peter Kearns 978-1-78952-034-7
Billy Joel – Lisa Torem 978-1-78952-183-2
Judas Priest – John Tucker 978-1-78952-018-7
Kansas – Kevin Cummings 978-1-78952-057-6
Killing Joke – Nic Ransome 978-1-78952-273-0
The Kinks – Martin Hutchinson 978-1-78952-172-6
Korn – Matt Karpe 978-1-78952-153-5
Led Zeppelin – Steve Pilkington 978-1-78952-151-1
Level 42 – Matt Philips 978-1-78952-102-3
Little Feat – Georg Purvis – 978-1-78952-168-9
Magnum – Matthew Taylor – 978-1-78952-286-0
Aimee Mann – Jez Rowden 978-1-78952-036-1
Ralph McTell – Paul O. Jenkins 978-1-78952-294-5
Metallica – Barry Wood 978-1-78952-269-3
Joni Mitchell – Peter Kearns 978-1-78952-081-1
The Moody Blues – Geoffrey Feakes 978-1-78952-042-2
Motorhead – Duncan Harris 978-1-78952-173-3
Nektar – Scott Meze – 978-1-78952-257-0
New Order – Dennis Remmer – 978-1-78952-249-5
Nightwish – Simon McMurdo – 978-1-78952-270-9
Nirvana – William E. Spevack 978-1-78952-318-8
Laura Nyro – Philip Ward 978-1-78952-182-5

Also available from Sonicbond

Oasis – 978-1-78952-300-3
Mike Oldfield – Ryan Yard 978-1-78952-060-6
Opeth – Jordan Blum 978-1-78-952-166-5
Pearl Jam – Ben L. Connor 978-1-78952-188-7
Tom Petty – Richard James 978-1-78952-128-3
Pink Floyd – Richard Butterworth 978-1-78952-242-6
The Police – Pete Braidis 978-1-78952-158-0
Porcupine Tree – Nick Holmes 978-1-78952-144-3
Procol Harum – Scott Meze 978-1-78952-315-7
Queen – Andrew Wild 978-1-78952-003-3
Radiohead – William Allen 978-1-78952-149-8
Rancid – Paul Matts 978-1-78952-187-0
Lou Reed 1972-1986 – Ethan Roy 978-1-78952-283-9
Renaissance – David Detmer 978-1-78952-062-0
REO Speedwagon – Jim Romag 978-1-78952-262-4
The Rolling Stones 1963-80 – Steve Pilkington 978-1-78952-017-0
Linda Ronstadt 1969-1989 – Daryl O. Lawrence 987-1-78952-293-8
Sensational Alex Harvey Band – Peter Gallagher 978-1-7952-289-1
The Small Faces and The Faces – Andrew Darlington 978-1-78952-316-4
The Smashing Pumpkins – Matt Karpe 978-1-7952-291-4
The Smiths and Morrissey – Tommy Gunnarsson 978-1-78952-140-5
Spirit – Rev. Keith A. Gordon – 978-1-78952- 248-8
Soft Machine – Scott Meze 978-1078952-271-6
Stackridge – Alan Draper 978-1-78952-232-7
Status Quo the Frantic Four Years – Richard James 978-1-78952-160-3
Steely Dan – Jez Rowden 978-1-78952-043-9
The Stranglers – Martin Hutchinson 978-1-78952-323-2
Talk Talk – Gary Steel 978-1-78952-284-6
Tears For Fears – Paul Clark – 978-178952-238-9
Thin Lizzy – Graeme Stroud 978-1-78952-064-4
Tool – Matt Karpe 978-1-78952-234-1
Toto – Jacob Holm-Lupo 978-1-78952-019-4
U2 – Eoghan Lyng 978-1-78952-078-1
UFO – Richard James 978-1-78952-073-6
Ultravox – Brian J. Robb 978-1-78952-330-0
Van Der Graaf Generator – Dan Coffey 978-1-78952-031-6
Van Halen – Morgan Brown – 9781-78952-256-3
Suzanne Vega – Lisa Torem 978-1-78952-281-5
Jack White And The White Stripes – Ben L. Connor 978-1-78952-303-4
The Who – Geoffrey Feakes 978-1-78952-076-7
Roy Wood and the Move – James R Turner 978-1-78952-008-8
Yes (new edition) – Stephen Lambe 978-1-78952-282-2
Neil Young 1963 to 1970 – Oper Goodwin 978-1-78952-298-3
Frank Zappa 1966 to 1979 – Eric Benac 978-1-78952-033-0
Warren Zevon – Peter Gallagher 978-1-78952-170-2

Also available from Sonicbond

The Zombies – Emma Stott 978-1-78952-297-6
10CC – Peter Kearns 978-1-78952-054-5

Decades Series
The Bee Gees in the 1960s – Andrew Mon Hughes et al 978-1-78952-148-1
The Bee Gees in the 1970s – Andrew Mon Hughes et al 978-1-78952-179-5
Black Sabbath in the 1970s – Chris Sutton 978-1-78952-171-9
Britpop – Peter Richard Adams and Matt Pooler 978-1-78952-169-6
Phil Collins in the 1980s – Andrew Wild 978-1-78952-185-6
Alice Cooper in the 1970s – Chris Sutton 978-1-78952-104-7
Alice Cooper in the 1980s – Chris Sutton 978-1-78952-259-4
Curved Air in the 1970s – Laura Shenton 978-1-78952-069-9
Donovan in the 1960s – Jeff Fitzgerald 978-1-78952-233-4
Bob Dylan in the 1980s – Don Klees 978-1-78952-157-3
Brian Eno in the 1970s – Gary Parsons 978-1-78952-239-6
Faith No More in the 1990s – Matt Karpe 978-1-78952-250-1
Fleetwood Mac in the 1970s – Andrew Wild 978-1-78952-105-4
Fleetwood Mac in the 1980s – Don Klees 978-178952-254-9
Focus in the 1970s – Stephen Lambe 978-1-78952-079-8
Free and Bad Company in the 1970s – John Van der Kiste 978-1-78952-178-8
Genesis in the 1970s – Bill Thomas 978178952-146-7
George Harrison in the 1970s – Eoghan Lyng 978-1-78952-174-0
Kiss in the 1970s – Peter Gallagher 978-1-78952-246-4
Manfred Mann's Earth Band in the 1970s – John Van der Kiste 978178952-243-3
Marillion in the 1980s – Nathaniel Webb 978-1-78952-065-1
Van Morrison in the 1970s – Peter Childs – 978-1-78952-241-9
Mott the Hoople & Ian Hunter in the 1970s –
John Van der Kiste 978-1-78-952-162-7
Pink Floyd In The 1970s – Georg Purvis 978-1-78952-072-9
Suzi Quatro in the 1970s – Darren Johnson 978-1-78952-236-5
Queen in the 1970s – James Griffiths 978-1-78952-265-5
Roxy Music in the 1970s – Dave Thompson 978-1-78952-180-1
Slade in the 1970s – Darren Johnson 978-1-78952-268-6
Status Quo in the 1980s – Greg Harper 978-1-78952-244-0
Tangerine Dream in the 1970s – Stephen Palmer 978-1-78952-161-0
The Sweet in the 1970s – Darren Johnson 978-1-78952-139-9
Uriah Heep in the 1970s – Steve Pilkington 978-1-78952-103-0
Van der Graaf Generator in the 1970s – Steve Pilkington 978-1-78952-245-7
Rick Wakeman in the 1970s – Geoffrey Feakes 978-1-78952-264-8
Yes in the 1980s – Stephen Lambe with David Watkinson 978-1-78952-125-2

Rock Classics Series
90125 by Yes – Stephen Lambe 978-1-78952-329-4
Bat Out Of Hell by Meatloaf – Geoffrey Feakes 978-1-78952-320-1
Bringing It All Back Home by Bob Dylan – Opher Goodwin 978-1-78952-314-0

Crime Of The Century by Supertramp – Steve Pilkington 978-1-78952-327-0
Let It Bleed by The Rolling Stones – John Van der Kiste 978-1-78952-309-6
Purple Rain by Prince – Matt Karpe 978-1-78952-322-5

On Screen Series
Carry On... – Stephen Lambe 978-1-78952-004-0
David Cronenberg – Patrick Chapman 978-1-78952-071-2
Doctor Who: The David Tennant Years – Jamie Hailstone 978-1-78952-066-8
James Bond – Andrew Wild 978-1-78952-010-1
Monty Python – Steve Pilkington 978-1-78952-047-7
Seinfeld Seasons 1 to 5 – Stephen Lambe 978-1-78952-012-5

Other Books
1967: A Year In Psychedelic Rock 978-1-78952-155-9
1970: A Year In Rock – John Van der Kiste 978-1-78952-147-4
1972: The Year Progressive Rock Ruled The World – Kevan Furbank 978-1-78952-288-4
1973: The Golden Year of Progressive Rock 978-1-78952-165-8
Babysitting A Band On The Rocks – G.D. Praetorius 978-1-78952-106-1
Eric Clapton Sessions – Andrew Wild 978-1-78952-177-1
Dark Horse Records – Aaron Badgley 978-1-78952-287-7
Derek Taylor: For Your Radioactive Children – Andrew Darlington 978-1-78952-038-5
The Golden Age of Easy Listening – Derek Taylor 978-1-78952-285-3
The Golden Road: The Recording History of The Grateful Dead – John Kilbride 978-1-78952-156-6
Iggy and The Stooges On Stage 1967-1974 – Per Nilsen 978-1-78952-101-6
Jon Anderson and the Warriors – the road to Yes – David Watkinson 978-1-78952-059-0
Magic: The David Paton Story – David Paton 978-1-78952-266-2
Misty: The Music of Johnny Mathis – Jakob Baekgaard 978-1-78952-247-1
Nu Metal: A Definitive Guide – Matt Karpe 978-1-78952-063-7
Remembering Live Aid – Andrew Wild 978-1-78952-328-7
Tommy Bolin: In and Out of Deep Purple – Laura Shenton 978-1-78952-070-5
Maximum Darkness – Deke Leonard 978-1-78952-048-4
The Twang Dynasty – Deke Leonard 978-1-78952-049-1

And Many More To Come!

Would you like to write for Sonicbond Publishing?

We are mainly a music publisher, but we also occasionally publish in other genres including film and television. At Sonicbond Publishing we are always on the look-out for authors, particularly for our two main series, On Track and Decades.

Mixing fact with in depth analysis, the On Track series examines the entire recorded work of a particular musical artist or group. All genres are considered from easy listening and jazz to 60s soul to 90s pop, via rock and metal.

The Decades series singles out a particular decade in an artist or group's history and focuses on that decade in more detail than may be allowed in the On Track series.

While professional writing experience would, of course, be an advantage, the most important qualification is to have real enthusiasm and knowledge of your subject. First-time authors are welcomed, but the ability to write well in English is essential.

Sonicbond Publishing has distribution throughout Europe and North America, and all our books are also published in E-book form. Authors will be paid a royalty based on sales of their book.

Further details about our books are available from www.sonicbondpublishing.com. To contact us, complete the contact form there or email info@sonicbondpublishing.co.uk